THE INVESTIGATIVE JOURNALIST
Folk Heroes of a New Era

James H. Dygert

PRENTICE-HALL, INC., Englewood Cliffs, New Jersey

We acknowledge with thanks permission to use the following material:

Excerpts from "The Toughest Reporter in America" by Joe Eszterhas.
From *Rolling Stone*, © 1975 by Rolling Stone.
All Rights Reserved. Reprinted by Permission.

Excerpts from *My Lai 4*, by Seymour M. Hersh, © 1970 by Seymour M. Hersh,
reprinted by permission of Random House, Inc.

Excerpts from *The Mafia Is Not an Equal Rights Employer*, by Nicholas Gage,
© 1971 by Nicholas Gage, used with permission of Mc-Graw Hill Book Company.

Excerpts from *The Anderson Papers*, by Jack Anderson, © 1973
by Jack Anderson, reprinted by permission of Random House, Inc.

Excerpts from *Inside Story*, by Brit Hume, © 1974 by Brit Hume;
and from *Invitation to a Lynching*, by Gene Miller, © 1975 by Gene Miller.
Both reprinted by permission of Doubleday & Company, Inc.

Excerpts from the following articles by Spotlight Team, courtesy of the Boston *Globe:*
"Somerville Corruption series" published Feb. 11-20, 1971
"Mass. Turnpike Authority series" published May 9-12, 1971
"Central Towing Company series" published Mar. 27-29, 1972
"Career School series" published Mar. 25-April 3, 1974

Excerpts from *Exclusive*, by Marilyn Baker, published by Macmillan Publishing Co., Inc.

Excerpts from "Rush to Judgment in New Orleans,"
by James R. Phelan, published by *The Saturday Evening Post*.

Permission from Tad Szulc for material appearing in *Esquire*.

Prentice-Hall International, Inc., London
Prentice-Hall of Australia, Pty. Ltd., Sydney
Prentice-Hall of Canada, Ltd., Toronto
Prentice-Hall of India Private Ltd., New Delhi
Prentice-Hall of Japan, Inc., Tokyo
Prentice-Hall of Southeast Asia Pte. Ltd., Singapore
10 9 8 7 6 5 4 3 2 1

Library of Congress Cataloging in Publication Data

Dygert, James H.
    The investigative journalist.

    Includes index.
    1. Reporters and reporting.   I. Title.
PN4781.D87   070.4'3   76-13042
ISBN 0-13-502310-6

To Mabel Ann: editor, critic, helpmate, love of my life.

FOREWORD

RICHARD NIXON'S resignation as President of the United States in 1974 marked the first time in American history that a president had fallen from power in mid-term. Two of the chief figures behind this momentous event were unlikely agents of cataclysm. No powerful manipulators or shadowy conspirators, Robert Woodward and Carl Bernstein. They were newspaper reporters, just doing their job.

They had been assigned to investigate a break-in of the Democratic Party's national headquarters in the Watergate office-hotel complex in Washington, D.C., and subsequent attempts by government officials to prevent discovery of the truth. Though ridiculed by colleagues for their tenacity through long, often frustrating weeks, Woodward and Bernstein uncovered the facts that compelled the nation to take the Watergate case seriously. The pressures they originated eventually built into the scandal that toppled Nixon. Woodstein, as they were called by then, became famous.

Their success gave America a new kind of knight in shining armor. Senator Lowell Weicker of Connecticut said every major scandal in the past twenty years had been uncovered by the press. Journalism schools were swamped with applications and soon thousands of would-be Woodwards and Bernsteins swarmed out across the nation in search of opportunities to expose corruption, their fervor undampened by the hard reality that newspaper jobs were scarce. The investigative journalist was the new American hero.

Woodward and Bernstein felt embarrassed by their glamor-boy celebrity. Other journalists disdained it as unbecoming to their profession. Many feared it would distort the public's image of the journalist. But most investigative reporters were pleased. They had been working long, tedious hours only to be tolerated as practitioners of a second-class, slightly tawdry brand of journalism. This sense of being not quite respectable was alleviated only once a year by a Pulitzer Prize for investigative reporting. Now they welcomed the recognition as long overdue.

Many had been soldiering in the trenches for years. Modern-day investigative journalism took root slowly in the years after World War II. It blossomed in the late 1960s and early 1970s into a widely scattered force for informing the public about misconduct in government and prodding authorities to act against crime and corruption. Some reached the public eye on the pages of magazines like *Life* and *Look,* but most investigative reporting received little public attention outside each newspaper's circulation area. An organization called the Fund for Investigative Journalism was formed in Washington in 1969 to finance investigative endeavors, but few Americans have ever heard of it.

More important than the recognition, to many journalists, was Watergate's uplifting of their image. If there was any distortion, it was in the right direction. No longer did the public see the reporter as a flamboyant, hard-drinking bully who never let the facts get in the way of a sensational story, or the venal, grubbing, amoral lout often portrayed in the movies. Now he could be perceived more clearly as he really was, a serious, persevering searcher for truth in the public service, a person in pursuit of facts, not a juicy angle. At least that's the way investigative reporters see themselves.

They constantly fret over the quality and perfection of their work, though beneath the cool exterior they're actually fervent idealists teetering on the brink of righteousness. They've begun to form associations to promote professional standards and further common interests, such as The Reporters Committee for Freedom of the Press in Washington and the Investigative Reporters and Editors Group in Indianapolis, Indiana.

They've revived the tradition of the first great American muckrakers, the small band of writers who exposed government corruption, corporate villainy, and wretched conditions in industry shortly after the turn of the century. *The New York Times* unhorsed Boss Tweed, Joseph Pulitzer's New York *World* crusaded against crooked politicians, and reporter Jacob Riis exposed New York City housing scandals in the nineteenth century, but the first golden era of investigative journalism flourished from 1902 to 1912, mostly in magazines and books. Lincoln Steffens revealed corruption in the big cities. Ida Tarbell exposed the ruthless manipulations behind John D. Rockefeller's creation of the Standard Oil empire. Upton Sinclair shocked America with his writings about filth in Chicago's meat packing plants. David Graham Phillips disclosed corrupt machinations in the United States Senate. When President Theodore Roosevelt coined the word, "muckraker," in a 1906 speech, taking it from the Man with the Muckrake in *Pilgrim's Progress*, he meant it as a derogation. But the journalists to whom he referred took it as a badge of honor.

The new muckrakers, however, view themselves as more impartial, more sophisticated. Over the years, the term was unable to shed Roosevelt's unflattering connotation. It suggested raking around in surface muck rather than digging up new ground. The muckrakers of old were crusaders, activists, zealots in pursuit of a particular brand of reform. The new muckrakers are dispassionate professionals who probe soberly beneath the surface of events and conditions to uncover the whole truth about the causes and motivations behind them, thereby to alert the public to take appropriate action.

The Founding Fathers did not draft the First Amendment to benefit publishers and writers, but to provide for the preservation of democracy. An informed populace is necessary to the intelligent exercise of democratic rights and duties. Ignorance threatens the life of a democratic body politic just as unsuspected disease endangers the human body. The press must be free to expose tyrants, scoundrels, and charlatans before their intrigues subvert democracy. This is the purpose that motivates the investigative journalist. Fame, yes, but only for genuine achievement in the public interest.

Woodward and Bernstein, and perhaps Seymour Hersh and Jack Anderson, may be the visible heroes, but dozens of other investigative journalists have been probing and exposing wrongdoing and abuse of power across the United States with equal skill and perseverance. Their only recognition and reward so far has been the admiration of fellow journalists and pride of achievement. This book tells about many of them, and the contributions they have made. Some have undoubtedly been missed. Apologies to them if they deserve to be listed with these who have given America a new golden age of investigative journalism.

CONTENTS

The only security of all is in a free press

Thomas Jefferson

The Best in the Big City

FORT BENNING, GEORGIA, is a huge, sprawling Army base. No one in his right mind tries to find a soldier there without an address or the number of his unit. But that's exactly what Seymour M. Hersh intended to do on the morning of November 11, 1969. He had flown in from Washington to track down Lt. William L. Calley, Jr. and ask him about charges that he had murdered South Vietnamese civilians. And that's what Hersh would do.

The question was, where to look next?

Calley hadn't been listed in the phone book, nor with the information operator. He wasn't on the roster for the Bachelor Officers' quarters or the Senior Officers' quarters. The personnel office had never heard of him. Hersh had found Calley's Army lawyer, Major Kenneth A. Raby, teaching a military law class, but Raby wouldn't talk to him.

If Calley is charged with murder, Hersh reasoned, he must be in the post stockade. Driving over in his rented car, Hersh walked in with his briefcase, hoping to look like a lawyer.

"Sergeant," he said crisply, "looking for Bill Calley."

"Who?"

"Bill Calley."

The sergeant checked his records. No Calley. He consulted his boss. Nope.

Hersh drove around the base checking guardhouses. No luck.

He'd been searching for three hours. He'd covered all the obvious places. Now where?

Hersh went unhappily to the Judge Advocate General's office, which he had hoped to avoid. A sergeant wanted him to wait for the colonel. Hersh left.

After lunch, he hit upon the idea that Calley's name might be in an old phone book. He called the information operator again. It was. Calley had been listed as attached to a company in the main training unit for recruits, where Hersh found a captain whose smile disappeared when Hersh announced his purpose.

"I'm not authorized to talk about Calley." The captain picked up his phone. "In fact, I'm supposed to refer all calls to the colonel."

"Look, I don't want any hassle," said Hersh. He turned and walked out.

The captain hung up the phone and followed Hersh outside the barracks. "Give me a break," he said. "I'm just a captain trying to mind my own business. I want to make major and you're going to ruin my career if you do this. Please go. I'm sorry. I'm just trying to ask you like a man."

"Captain, don't worry about it, if you've got nothing to give me. Calley's not in there?"

"No," said the captain. "I give you my word."

A few moments after the captain went inside, Hersh slipped back in, too, stealing past the captain's office and up the stairs to the second-floor sleeping area. The recruits were out training and the barracks were empty except for a lone soldier asleep in a corner.

This, Hersh thought triumphantly, was his man.

He kicked the side of the bunk. "Get up, Calley!"

The sleeping soldier was a twenty-year-old National Guardsman from Iowa whose records had been lost. "This no-good fucking Army," he said. "All I do is sleep." He had heard of Calley, but had no idea where he was. He had a friend named Smitty who sorted mail at battalion headquarters, though, and he might be able to help. Smitty had just been busted from sergeant to private.

"Would you take me over there?" Hersh asked.

"No way."

"Take me over there."

"No way!"

"Look, it's three thirty-five. Synchronize our watches. I'm driving a blue Ford. In exactly five minutes I'll drive around the back and pick you up. You dash out, hop in the car, show me where to go. No one will see you."

Hersh figured a bored twenty-year-old wouldn't pass up action of any kind. When he wheeled the car around, the young Iowan jumped in and directed him to an old wooden barracks across the base.

After taking his young guide back, Hersh returned to the old wooden barracks. A grizzled old sergeant was lounging on the porch. Jumping out of his car with his briefcase, Hersh barked, "Tell Smitty I want him right away." The sergeant went in and brought out Smitty.

Hersh put Smitty in the car. "I've been hunting this goddamned Calley all day and I know Calley's mail is in there. Where is he?"

Smitty was relieved that Hersh was only a reporter. "Mister, I'd like to help you," he said. "But no one around here knows where he is. We used to get his mail and forward it somewhere, but I don't see it anymore. The only thing I know is that we've got his personnel file in there. I'd have to steal it out of there."

After a pause, Hersh said, "Well?"

"I don't know," said Smitty.

"C'mon," said Hersh. "I'll just look at it for a minute."

"I don't know."

"C'mon."

"Well," said Smitty. "Wait here."

When Smitty came back, he took a file folder from under his shirt. In the file was a street address for Calley in Columbus, the city outside the base.

The street was lined with modest ranch-type houses. As Hersh began to turn into the driveway of one, another car pulled into it ahead of him. Three young second lieutenants emerged. Hersh stopped behind them, jumped out, and said, "Hey, I'm looking for Bill Calley."

One of the trio said, "He doesn't live here anymore."

"Who are you guys?" Hersh inquired.

They invited him in for a drink and told him Calley had lived there with them for a while, but the Army had ordered him back on the post. They said the charges against Calley were all wrong. It was a real battle he had been in.

Hersh asked where he could find Calley now.

"I don't think we should tell you."

They chatted some more. Hersh was careful to be friendly, sympathetic. They obviously liked Calley and were convinced he was being treated unfairly. They said he had a girl friend.

"Where is he?" Hersh asked again.

"He's staying at the Senior Officers' quarters. Near the tennis courts."

"Which room?"

"I don't think we should tell you that. You can find him. He's around."

It was almost six o'clock. Rushing back to the base, Hersh found the Senior Officers' quarters to be three large buildings, each with about eighty rooms. He started knocking on doors. "Hello, Bill." "Bill, are you in?" Hersh went from door to door, knocking, for two hours. More than 200 rooms. Half were empty. Some had occupants who replied, "Wrong door." None of the rooms contained Calley.

It was late, about nine, and Hersh was exhausted. Maybe he should get some sleep and try again in the morning. Getting this far had been tough enough, but now it was a real baffler.

Learning Calley's name had used up several days after Hersh got the original tip in a telephone call from Geoff Cowan, a lawyer he knew only slightly. Hersh had been working on a book about the Pentagon in his rented house in northwest Washington on the afternoon of October 22, 1969. Cowan said, "I heard the Army is trying to court-martial some guy in secret down at Fort Benning for killing seventy-five Vietnamese civilians."

Hersh was then a brash, frenetic, thirty-one-year-old maverick journalist who had started his newspapering as a police reporter in Chicago. He had quit the Associated Press and its new investigative team in 1967 after his 10,000-word exposé on America's chemical and biological warfare program had been cut to 1,700 words (he later wrote a book on it). While covering the Pentagon for AP and later working as press secretary in Senator Eugene McCarthy's 1968 peace campaign for the presidency, Hersh had become bothered about the Vietnam War. A good reporter never ignores a tip, but now Cowan's struck him as a rumbling of something big and awful. Besides, he was bored with the Pentagon book.

After Cowan's call, Hersh got on the phone and began to poke around. Friends and sources in the government, the military, Congress. Newspaper morgues, clerks in Pentagon records offices. After three days and dozens of calls, he got a few sketchy details from a Congressional source who asked him not to pursue the story because it would hurt the Army. Hersh decided to call Fort Benning's public information office and ask for the names of soldiers facing court-martial for murder. The only one they had was Calley. A news release had been issued back on September 5. In fact, the story had been in *The New York Times* on September 7, page fourteen.

"What did the release say?" Hersh inquired.

It said Calley was being retained on active duty past his normal release date because he was under investigation to determine if he would be court-martialed on a charge of murder against civilians while serving in Vietnam in March, 1968. It did not say how many civilians had been killed. No one in the information office knew.

Several reporters, Hersh learned later, had started out to follow up the story, but had been diverted by other assignments, lost interest, or failed to see it as significant. An NBC network news show mentioned in a brief item that Calley had been accused of murdering "a number of South Vietnamese civilians." But that was all.

Hersh went to see an Army colonel he knew. "What's this all about?" he asked.

"This Calley is just a madman, Sy," said the colonel. "Just a madman. He went around killing all those people. Little babies! There's no story in that. He's just pathetic and should be locked up in an institution."

A source who worked for Congressman Mendel Rivers of South Carolina, chairman of the House Armed Services Committee, told Hersh, "Don't write about this one, Sy. It would do nobody any good. The kid was crazy. You know, I heard he took a machine gun and shot them all himself."

Hersh was beginning to suspect a massacre of massive proportions, a story much bigger than Calley. Everyone was too anxious to discourage a story, to toss all the blame on the poor, demented lieutenant. But before he could write a story, he had to find Calley and his lawyer.

He contacted Cowan, who called back in a couple of days with the name, Latimer, as Calley's lawyer. Hersh called lawyers named Latimer out of the phone book until one said, "You must mean Judge Latimer." This was Judge George Latimer, formerly of the Military Court of Appeals, now retired and practicing law in Salt Lake City, Utah.

Hersh put in a call to Salt Lake City.

"What a tragedy," said Latimer. "The government's making a grave mistake."

"I happen to be coming to Salt Lake City," said Hersh. "How about if I see you in your office about nine o'clock tomorrow morning?"

"Boy, if you want to come out here, that's fine."

Hersh had no money, but he did have an American Express card. He got a commitment for a $1,000 grant from the Fund for Investigative Journalism in Washington and bought a plane ticket.

Latimer would talk only if Hersh agreed to hold his story until Latimer exhausted all chances of getting the charges dropped. Hersh said okay.

"Look, I have an awful lot," Hersh told the lawyer. "Calley did a lot of killing that day and the Army's telling bad stories about him."

"That's just not true," Latimer replied. "The boy was under command. Can you imagine them charging him with a hundred and nine deaths?"

"No," said Hersh matter-of-factly, "I thought it was a hundred and twenty-seven."

Latimer showed him the charge sheet. "It's right here. One hundred and nine."

"Let me talk to him," said Hersh.

"No, I don't think so."

"Can you reach him?"

"Oh, yeah. I talked to him yesterday, but I don't think I'll tell you where he is. I don't think that's right."

Okay, Hersh thought. He could find Calley.

Now, in the dark outside the Senior Officers' quarters thirteen days later, Hersh, for a brief painful moment, almost suffered doubt. But there was one more thing he could try before heading back to the motel.

He went to the parking lot entrance and for half an hour flagged down cars as they pulled in. "Hey, I'm looking for Bill Calley. Have you seen him?"

When that didn't work, Hersh started off toward his Ford two blocks away. He passed two men working over a car with its hood up. It occurred to Hersh it would be stupid not to ask them, too. He had asked everyone else. He walked over and said, "Hey, you guys seen Bill? Bill Calley?"

One of the men answered, "Yeah, he's over there. Two twenty-one."

Hersh hesitated. "Excuse me, which building?"

The other turned around. He was an officer of about forty-five. "What do you want with Calley?"

Hersh told him. "I just want to get his side of the story."

The officer wiped his hands on a rag. "Come in. I'll give you a drink. Calley's not here. He'll be back later. He lives right above me."

Hersh asked if he was sure Calley wasn't in. They knocked on Calley's door and got no answer.

The reporter and the officer drank and talked until almost midnight, the officer relating a good deal of Calley's story.

They were standing by the door. "I gotta go," said Hersh, tired.

"Hey, wait a second. Hey, Rusty," the officer called to someone down the hall. "I want you to meet this guy."

"No, I've got to go," Hersh insisted.

"No, no. Hey, Rusty!" To Hersh he said, "That's Calley."

A small, pale man who looked boyish and nervous came over.

"Are you Calley?" Hersh asked.

"Yeah."

"My name is Hersh."

"He's a good guy," said the officer.

"Let's go talk," said Hersh. "I know the story."

"Yeah," said Calley. "I know." Latimer had told him.

They went to Calley's room. The lieutenant told him about the search-and-destroy operation at My Lai, his version of what had happened, how he had just been following orders, how many civilians he had been accused of killing. "Look," he said, "I gotta go over to my girl's house. Want to come along?" They left the girl friend's house at 3 A.M. and went to a party. Then Calley wanted to go bowling. But Hersh had learned enough. He crept back to his motel, groggy with fatigue and excited with the knowledge that he was going to win a Pulitzer.

However, there were more obstacles yet to overcome. Before he'd gone to Fort Benning, Hersh had tried in vain to interest *Life* magazine in the story. *Look* magazine hadn't nibbled either. Hersh discovered later that Ronald Ridenhour, the Vietnam veteran whose persistent letters to the Pentagon and Congress had instigated the Army's investigation of the My Lai massacre, had also failed to sell *Life* the story. A third magazine was interested, but wanted a political slant. A twenty-four-year-old neighbor, David Obst, said he could sell it through his fledgling feature syndicate called Dispatch News Service. Obst sold it to thirty-six newspapers.

Though an instant sensation, the story's full impact took time to gather momentum. Many papers and broadcasters handled it gingerly, with skepticism. *The New York Times* ran a front-page report from a correspondent in Saigon, but the Washington *Post* countered with the Pentagon's reply that the *Times* story was exaggerated.

A story out of Phoenix, Arizona, revealed Ridenhour's role and Hersh flew to California to interview him. Ridenhour told him about Michael Terry and Michael Bernhardt, two soldiers who had witnessed some of the carnage, and gave him their addresses.

Hersh found Terry in a rickety old house in Orem, Utah. "I want to hear about the shooting," said Hersh.

"You want me to tell you the same thing," asked Terry, "that I told the colonel?"

Hersh said, "Yeah."

"It was a Nazi-type thing," said Terry, who had been a squad leader. He had seen Calley and others shoot women and children in a ditch. Later Terry and his men found some of the victims still breathing. "They were pretty badly shot up. They weren't going to get any medical help, and so we shot them. Shot maybe five of them."

Hersh tracked down Bernhardt outside a barracks at Fort Dix, New Jersey.

Bernhardt had been in the thick of that day's grisly events, and talked about it freely. He had seen Captain Ernest Medina's men "doing strange things. They were setting fire to the hootches and huts and waiting for people to come out and shooting them. They were going into the hootches and shooting them up. They were gathering people in groups and shooting them. The whole thing was so deliberate. It was point-blank murder and I was standing there watching it."

Bernhardt described Medina's shooting of a Vietnamese woman 100 meters away. "Then he walked up. He got up real close, about three or six feet, and shot at her a couple of times and finished her off. . . . I could see her clothing move when the bullets hit. . . . I could see her twitch."

Hersh wrote the story on the plane back to Washington. It made a bigger splash than the first.

Hersh kept traveling the country on his American Express card, writing more stories, getting more names and interviewing more ex-soldiers who gave him more eyewitness material about the murder of Vietnamese women, children, and elderly men. Paul Meadlo of New Goshen, Indiana, told him how Calley had ordered him to kill civilians.

"We went into this village," said Meadlo, "and I was guarding all these people and Calley said, 'Waste 'em.' I said, 'What do you mean?' and he said, 'Waste 'em,' so I just fired on them."

"How many did you kill?" Hersh asked.

"Oh, maybe seventy."

A soldier who had taken pictures of the slaughter showed them to the Cleveland *Plain Dealer*, which published some of them along with a story on his observations. That, plus Meadlo's public confession in a national TV appearance arranged by Hersh and Obst, produced a crescendo of national shock and revulsion.

Hersh wrote two books about the massacre and the Army's attempts to cover it up. He also won a Pulitzer Prize and became famous.

Hersh next became famous for his December, 1974, exposé of illegal spying inside the United States by the CIA. By then an investigative reporter for *The New York Times*, Hersh wrote, "The Central Intelligence Agency, directly violating its charter, conducted a massive, illegal domestic intelligence operation during the Nixon Administration against the antiwar movement and other dissident groups in the United States, according to well-placed Government sources.

"An extensive investigation by *The New York Times* has established that intelligence files on at least 10,000 American citizens were maintained by a special unit of the CIA that was reporting directly to Richard Helms, then the Director of Central Intelligence and now the Ambassador to Iran.

"In addition, the sources said, a check of the CIA's domestic files ordered last year by Mr. Helms's successor, James R. Schlesinger, produced evidence of dozens of other illegal activities by members of the CIA inside the United States, beginning in the nineteen-fifties, including break-ins, wiretapping and the surreptitious inspection of mail."

This was the story that, despite a flurry of denials, touched off two Congressional committee investigations. Gradual admissions by CIA officials began to surface. Former CIA agents spoke up in corroboration of Hersh's disclosures. The Rockefeller Commission, appointed to probe all aspects of American intelligence activities, discovered the CIA had participated in assassination plots against foreign political leaders that the CIA considered dangerous or unpalatable. In the case of one, Cuban Premier Fidel Castro, the CIA enlisted the aid of American gangsters. These revelations made the CIA the biggest scandal of 1975, almost rivaling the historic proportions of the Watergate catastrophe of 1973 and 1974.

Hersh had worked the CIA story off and on ever since he first got a hint of it late in 1973. He attacked it full time in the fall of 1974. Some Washington journalists are convinced that he got his hands on a copy of the internal report on CIA activities prepared for Schlesinger in 1973. Hersh denies he ever had possession of a secret document describing CIA operations, though he had heard about Schlesinger's report. He says the story was pieced together pains-takingly from sources inside the CIA who looked askance at the agency's illegal domestic spying. He got unexpected confirmation and guidance on many points from Schlesinger's successor as CIA director, William E. Colby, during a phone call in which Colby said several times, "If you write that, you're wrong. This is what happened."

Hersh followed up his CIA blockbuster with disclosures of CIA meddling in Chile against the late Premier Salvador Allende. For that he won the 1976 Drew Pearson Investigative Reporting Award from the National Press Club in Washington, D.C.

Though superb at developing sources and all the other skills of investigative journalism, Hersh has one aptitude that dwarfs the others. He has a phenomenal ability to get people to tell him things they shouldn't. He's been said to be utterly ruthless, to argue, badger, flatter, cajole, bluff, charm, insult, bully, threaten, wheedle, terrorize, come on strong and hostile or sweet and friendly, use whatever trick will work. "I can be awfully difficult," Hersh conceded in a lengthy 1975 interview with *Rolling Stone*. But, he adds, "Do you think you could do that with high-level government officials who've been around a while? With generals and admirals? That's not the way you do it. You hustle and you work. You know what's the way to do it? You work your ass off."

Sources, says Hersh, never walk in and lay a story on a reporter all ready for the print shop. It's a matter of fitting a piece from one source with pieces from three others. When someone shrugs off one of his scoops as having been leaked to him, Hersh said in the *Rolling Stone* interview, "That's usually a story you put three hundred man hours in on. Yes, somebody did come in and tell me something. Yes, I did learn something, but it wasn't publishable. You have to do an immense amount of work to make it publishable."

One reporter who knows Hersh credits his success to his tenacity in pursuing the obvious. Working in the *Times'* Washington bureau shortly after joining the paper in 1972, Hersh heard rumors of something unsavory behind the demotion of Air Force General John D. Lavelle from four stars to three stars as he was retired. That was an extraordinary thing. Lavelle had been relieved from his post as commander of U.S. Air Force units in Southeast Asia. To Hersh it was clear who knew best what had happened and why. Lavelle.

Hersh checked around to get the name of Lavelle's aide in Saigon. Several phone calls located him. "I'm looking for the general," said Hersh. "Do you have his number?"

"Yeah," said the aide. "Hold on."

"I'm writing the story, anyway," Hersh told Lavelle on the phone, "but I want your side of it, too. People are saying bad things about you, saying you broke all kinds of laws, but I hear there's another side to it." Lavelle was noncommittal, had little to say. "I'm coming out this afternoon to see you," said Hersh.

Lavelle was playing golf that afternoon, so Hersh met him on the course and hit a few iron shots himself. Then they went to a bar for a few beers. After an hour or so, Lavelle opened up with the story of his sacking for having ordered bombing attacks in North Vietnam without authorization from higher headquarters and falsely reporting them as authorized "protective reaction" raids. Lavelle believed he had acted properly in his interpretation of the bomb raid rules, but Pentagon officials disagreed.

"Why the hell weren't you court-martialed?" Hersh asked.

Lavelle replied, "When was the last time you heard of a four-star general court-martialed?"

Hersh was rushed into the Watergate breach in the fall of 1972 to resurrect the *Times'* reputation from the drubbing administered by the Washington *Post*. Hersh zeroed in on one of the Watergate defendants, Frank Sturgis. He found out about an outline of Sturgis' story submitted to publishers by freelance writer Andrew St. George. Arranging to meet St. George, Hersh led him to believe he had a copy of the outline. St. George later insisted that Hersh had it in his hand and quoted from it. St. George was cooperative. He set up a meeting between Hersh and Sturgis in Miami. The result was one of the *Times'* best Watergate exclusives, Hersh's January 14, 1973, story that four Watergate defendants were receiving $400 or more every month from a secret source. It was one of the first revelations that a Watergate cover-up was still going on.

Over the next few months Hersh produced several more Watergate scoops, derived mostly from sources developed among the Watergate prosecutors, defense lawyers, and Congressional committee staff members. Among them were disclosures that Attorney General Richard Kleindienst had disqualified himself from the Watergate investigation because he expected several of his friends in the Nixon Administration to be indicted, that the White House had set up a secret group in 1972 to spy on radicals and antiwar activists, and that the White House had put pressure on the FBI in 1970 to start a spying, wiretapping, and burglary campaign against antiwar groups and black militants. Sources that Hersh cultivated in Washington during this time led to his breaking the story in July, 1973, of America's secret bombing in Cambodia in 1970.

Beliefs that Hersh will stop at nothing to get a story apparently stem from his superhuman success record. Ordinary mortals don't see how it can be done without mirrors, magic, or unethical practice. Hersh says he's never lied, never broken a law. He doesn't have to. He works ethically, honestly, he says, and still gets the stories.

Hersh is disdainful—or so he says—of hero mythology about himself or other investigative reporters that may have blossomed in the wake of My Lai, Watergate, and the CIA scandal. It's a lot of crap, he says, a passing phase. A reporter's everyday job is to reveal as much truth as he can about events, not parrot what he's told by government or business. If anything, the My Lai story, Watergate, and the CIA's depravity were bungled by the news media. Someone should have caught on to them a lot sooner.

Nicholas Gage was ready for the last crucial step in his investigation, the climactic confrontation interview with the suspect. Gage had learned most of the story from art dealers and scholars in Geneva and Rome. Even without the interview, he could write a passable story on how the New York Metropolitan Museum of Art's mysterious, million-dollar, 2,500-year-old Greek vase by the master painter, Euphronios, had been purchased from bootleg excavators and smuggled illegally out of Italy. But the story would have so much more substance, so much more class, if the suspect would fill in the details, perhaps even confess.

The suspect was Robert E. Hecht, Jr., a fifty-three-year-old American art dealer who had lived in Rome for twenty-five years. The heir of a prominent department store family in Baltimore, Hecht had once operated a coin shop in New York and was known as an expert on Greek and Roman coins. He had run afoul of Italian and Turkish authorities twelve years earlier when they charged him with illegal purchases of excavated art treasures. He had recently been acquitted in Italy. The charges in Turkey had been dropped, but Hecht had been declared persona non grata.

Gage, a top investigative reporter for *The New York Times* since 1970, had developed sources in all parts of the world. He had put some to work on Hecht's background as soon as he arrived in Rome. Then he took a plane to Geneva with a list of Swiss art dealers given him by the *Times'* art critic, John Canaday, who had suggested the investigation after the Museum announced the vase's acquisition with great fanfare in November, 1972. Museum Director Thomas P. F. Hoving had said it was "one of two or three finest works of art ever gained by the Metropolitan," but refused to give the purchase price, identify the seller, or say anything about the vase's history except that a European collector had bought it in London before World War I.

The most promising name on Canaday's list appeared to be Nicholas Koutoulakis, a Greek dealer in antiquities. Koutoulakis knew all there was to know about the Euphronios vase, Canaday had said, and would surely tell it to Gage, a fellow Greek who had been born Nicholas Ngagoyeanes and emigrated to the United States at the age of ten. Koutoulakis and Gage drank wine and discussed philosophy and women for six convivial hours, during which it became clear that, on the subject of the Euphronios vase, the Greek art dealer would tell the Greek reporter exactly nothing.

Others on the list were more helpful, especially a dealer in Basel who spoke several languages and viewed the purchase and resale of smuggled art treasures as a service to the art world. Greeks, Italians, and Turks were ignorant about proper care and restoration, he said. He and dealers like him were "saving art for posterity."

Gage learned that European art dealers believed the Euphronios vase had been dug up illegally at night by bootleg excavators, or grave robbers, from an archeological digging site twenty-five miles northwest of Rome in 1971. The bootleg diggers reportedly had taken the vase to a middleman, who in turn arranged to sell it to Hecht for $100,000. One Swiss dealer said he knew the middleman's name, but would not disclose it because he had dealings with the man himself.

Now, back in Rome, on February 17, 1973, a Saturday, it was time to put a few questions to Hecht. Gage phoned him and requested an interview.

Hecht invited him to dinner.

Gage said he'd rather keep it just an interview.

The only interview time he had available, Hecht replied, would be at dinner.

Okay, said Gage.

Phoning across the Atlantic to *Times* Metropolitan Editor Arthur Gelb, Gage said he would file a story as soon as they finished dinner. Reporters Dave Shirey and John Hess, who had been working the New York end of the investigation, were summoned to get the reaction of Museum officials to Gage's article as soon as it arrived.

Hecht's name had never been mentioned by Museum Director Hoving, nor by Greek and Roman Art Curator Dietrich von Bothmer. Gage had dug it out of customs records at Kennedy International Airport after Shirey learned from a museum source that the vase had entered the United States at Kennedy airport on August 31, 1972. Though 16,000 items had come through customs that day, Gage prodded a source in the customs office to sort through them. It took three weeks to find the customs declaration for the vase, which listed its value as one million dollars and said the "supplier" was "Robert E. Hecht, Zurich, Switzerland." Hecht, the papers disclosed, had personally accompanied the vase on its journey from Zurich to New York.

At dinner with Hecht and his wife, Gage found the atmosphere cordial. Mrs. Hecht's hometown of Worcester, Massachusetts, was the same as Gage's, they discovered, and that kindled a certain heartiness. Hecht asked the reporter what had brought him to Rome.

"The Euphronios vase," said Gage. "Have you seen it?"

Hecht said he had seen it when he was in New York three weeks earlier.

"Was that the only time you saw it?" Gage asked.

"No," said Hecht, beginning to look uncomfortable. "I've seen it before." He changed the subject.

Later, as they sipped wine, Gage inquired if Hecht had delivered the vase to the Metropolitan the previous August 31 after landing at Kennedy International Airport aboard Trans World Airlines Flight Number 831.

Momentarily startled, Hecht poured more wine in his glass and said, "Have you seen my tax returns, too?"

Hecht explained he had delivered the vase for a friend in another country, a "very nice man" he could not identify because it would cause him tax problems in his country. The vase, he said, had been in the man's family for more than fifty years.

Gage outlined what the Swiss art dealers had told him.

"They're liars," Hecht said.

Gage asked if anyone at the museum had ever met the man he said he represented.

"No," said Hecht. "I acted for him." He acknowledged he had conducted all negotiations with museum officials and the money (later determined to be $1,024,000) had been paid to him. "What difference does it make whether the museum pays the owner and he compensates me for my efforts, or it pays me and I pass it on to him?" he said.

Hecht asked Gage not to publish a story because it might precipitate his expulsion from Italy. Mrs. Hecht called Gage at his hotel the next day to promise a better story if he would wait, but it was too late. Gage had filed his story, and it appeared on the *Times'* February 19 front page.

Von Bothmer disputed that the vase could have come recently from the archeological site near Rome. He told reporter Shirey in New York he didn't care where it had come from, anyway, as long as it was a genuine art object. He confirmed, however, that the vase had been purchased from Hecht.

Shirey then learned from a museum official the identity of the man whom Hecht had claimed to represent. Gage hopped a plane to Beirut, and met an elderly Lebanese coin dealer named Dikran Sarrafian in the bar of Beirut's most luxurious hotel, the St. Georges. Sarrafian did not object to discussing the vase.

A modest, self-effacing old gentleman, whose father had been a major Middle East dealer in ancient art objects, Sarrafian said the vase had lain in pieces in a hatbox for fifty years until one day he consigned them to Hecht to be sold. He didn't remember much about the pieces except that they contained paintings of "old Greeks and a lot of inscriptions." He said some of the pieces had been missing. Only a small part of the $1 million paid by the museum had reached him, he said. Hecht had kept most of it.

Museum officials acknowledged that the vase had been in fragments, but said no pieces had been missing. They conceded they had paid more than a million dollars for the vase. They said the restoration had been done by a Swiss cabinetmaker and vase specialist named Fritz Buerki, who was never available for an interview.

Italian police, meanwhile, announced they had identified the grave robber who had "handed the vase to Mr. Hecht." They said six thieves had unearthed the vase and other art objects at the Etruscan tomb near Cerveteri, a town north of Rome. The vase had been taken from Italy illegally, they said, and belonged to the Italian government.

Returning to Rome, Gage drove with Gene DiMaria of the *Times'* Rome bureau to Cerveteri to look for a man mentioned by a source as the suspect identified by police. His name was Armando Cenere, and Gage found him in a two-room stone house where Cenere lived with his invalid mother. A part-time farmhand, Cenere described the pieces of vase that he and five colleagues had dug up illegally at the Etruscan tomb.

Four months later, the Italian authorities issued a warrant for Hecht's arrest, charging him with illegally purchasing and exporting the vase. They said they would try to recover the vase from the United States. Hecht had disappeared, but a *Times* reporter reached him by telephone at the Zurich Airport. He stuck to his story, but said he would stay out of Italy.

Museum president Douglas Dillon said later that an investigation by museum officials concluded the Euphronios vase had not been smuggled out of Italy. The vase's true source was never conclusively established. It was announced, however, that the Museum would henceforth be more open and candid about new acquisitions.

A dapper, handsome journalist with a precise and slightly wary manner, Gage usually works alone. The Euphronios vase case, besides involving several reporters, was unusual in that it had originated on the newspaper's own initiative. Most of Gage's investigations are activated by a tip from a source.

Gage was about to return to New York from covering Watergate in Washington in August, 1973, when he stopped off to visit a source connected with the investigation of Vice President Spiro Agnew. It was a week after the *Wall Street Journal* had broken the story of the investigation. Gage's visit led him to one of the stories for which he's best known among journalists, his report revealing the specific charges against Agnew. Gage's story said that more than twenty Maryland businessmen had told prosecutors about having paid cash to Agnew associates to get state and federal contracts, and that three of Agnew's associates had admitted turning over some of the money to Agnew. Agnew had Gage subpoenaed in an unsuccessful attempt to smoke out his source.

A short time later, Gage plucked another scoop out of Washington through a source in the Justice Department. Gage wrote, "Former Attorney General Richard G. Kleindienst has told the Watergate prosecution that President Nixon had personally ordered him not to press a series of antitrust actions against the International Telephone and Telegraph Corporation, according to sources close to the case.

"The sources said that the President telephoned Mr. Kleindienst in 1971, when he was Deputy Attorney General and the top man in the Justice Department on the case, and directed him not to appeal an ITT ruling to the Supreme Court.

"The appeal in the case was held up and the Government agreed to an out-of-court settlement generally considered favorable to the corporation. The settlement followed ITT's agreement to help finance the 1972 Republican National Convention with a gift from one of its corporations reported variously at $100,000 to $400,000."

It was the first story that tied Nixon directly to the ITT scandal, which had made headlines the previous year after columnist Jack Anderson published the contents of an internal ITT memo on a deal with the Justice Department.

Earlier that year, Gage got a tip that New York State Representative Mario Biaggi, a leading contender for election as New York City's mayor, had lied about his testimony before a federal grand jury investigating his personal finances. Biaggi was claiming to have answered all questions, according to the tip, but in fact had refused to answer several, citing his Fifth Amendment right against self-incrimination. Gage didn't believe it, but decided to investigate.

It was a tricky case. Revealing grand jury testimony is illegal, and Gage says it's never necessary to break a law to get a story. Though he declines to say exactly how he nailed down the Biaggi story, he told a January, 1975, meeting of the Overseas Press Club that he had on occasion followed prosecutors around and sat at tables near them in restaurants to eavesdrop on their conversations, because he didn't feel right about asking anyone to violate grand jury secrecy.

Gage's April 18, 1973, story, which attributed his facts to "authoritative sources," said Biaggi had taken the Fifth Amendment more than thirty times. Biaggi acknowledged that he had been called to testify, but maintained that he had answered all questions. He said Gage's story was "part of a conspiracy to destroy" him with smears. Biaggi dared Gage to produce his sources and accused him of "moral cowardice."

It took Biaggi about three weeks to admit the truth, which he did on television just prior to the release of his testimony on the order of a federal judge in a proceeding begun by Biaggi. When Biaggi's testimony was released, it showed that Gage had been wrong. Biaggi had taken the Fifth Amendment only sixteen times. Biaggi did not become mayor.

Sources are important to Gage. He wines them and dines them and goes to their children's weddings. Seventy percent of his social life is spent with sources. "Sources won't trust you," Gage says, "unless you're close to them." The telephone is not close enough. He often takes law enforcement sources to breakfast. He may have a hundred breakfasts with a source just to build rapport. When the time comes that he needs the source, he doesn't pick up the phone; he takes him to breakfast again. The *Times* won't pay for information, but it does pay for breakfasts. If a source says he can't discuss the matter, Gage asks who else knows about it. If he gets a piece of the story, he's confident he can bluff his way to the rest. Sources, he wrote in his 1971 book, *The Mafia Is Not an Equal Opportunity Employer*, are more important to an investigative reporter than his editor, his wife, and even his children. They are to be protected above all else. He can always find another job, but if he betrays a source, he's through.

Sources might be law enforcement officials, disgruntled employes, angry ex-wives, conscience-stricken public servants, political or business rivals, or ordinary citizens. His job, says Gage, it not to determine the source's motive or fret over his imperfect reputation, but to check the accuracy of the information. Gage cultivates new sources constantly. He gets letters from all over the world seeking his help in exposing some terrible wrong. Never failing to reply, Gage says he can't do anything at the moment, but perhaps later. Then, when he has occasion to go to a city where he's sent such a reply, he contacts the individual and uses his help. Sources not only provide information, they supply the names of more sources.

Gage is known as a Mafia expert. Though only a tenth of his stories concern organized crime, his articles and books on the inner workings of the Mafia are more widely known than his other stories, or the two novels he's written, *Bones of Contention* and *The Bourlotas Fortune*.

Shortly after joining the *Times* in September, 1970, Gage described in a front-page story how organized crime bled millions of dollars from the New York slums every year through narcotics, loan sharking, and the numbers rackets. The following May, he wrote one of the first stories about the new style of Mafia leader exemplified by Joseph Colombo, the urbane, publicity-conscious head of the Italian-American Civil Rights League who infiltrated his men into legitimate businesses and advocated college educations. Days before Colombo was gunned down at the League's second annual rally in June, 1971, Gage disclosed that a special task force of federal prosecutors had singled out Meyer Lansky as the guiding genius behind organized crime. Gage later revealed the story behind the murder of Joseph (Crazy Joe) Gallo in retaliation for the shooting of Colombo.

While a reporter for the *Wall Street Journal* from 1967 to 1970, Gage obtained a copy of a 1962 Justice Department report on the gangster associations of singer Frank Sinatra. It said Sinatra had been in contact with ten top mob leaders in the previous few years and he had done favors for some of them. Robert Kennedy, when he was attorney general, used this report to persuade his brother, the President, to drop his friendship with Sinatra. Sinatra was backing Hubert Humphrey in 1968, but after Gage's story broke, Humphrey cut him off, too.

Gage wrote a series for the *Wall Street Journal* on the infiltration of organized crime into England's gambling industry. Though only in his late twenties, he went on a gambling junket to London posing as a rich Greek shipowner. He believes newspapers in cities where organized crime exists should assign a reporter to cover it—and the corruption it causes—full time.

Reporting on the Mafia is not usually dangerous if the reporter doesn't enter into personal relationships or dealings with gangsters, Gage says. Most underworld figures realize that harming a reporter brings on the very heat they want to avoid. Besides, mobsters, like other people, are delighted to see their names in the paper. One phoned him once to complain that Gage had misspelled his name.

Gage also digs stories out of public records. He once waded for two months through Securities and Exchange Commission documents and House Banking and Currency Committee files to get the story of a complicated $4-million swindle of the Penn Central Railroad by two Washington lawyers. Gage says an investigative reporter spends far more time ''shuffling through file drawers full of dusty legal papers, or cooling his heels in the waiting rooms of men who do not want to talk to him'' than ''seducing beautiful secretaries.'' Despite occasional gratification from sparking reform, an investigative reporter's life is neither glamorous nor enviable.

Gage has assumed false identities to get a story, though the *Times* won't let him do it, on the ground that it's entrapment. Gage considers trickery acceptable, and often necessary, in the absence of subpoena power and search warrants. While at the Boston *Herald-Traveler* for a few months in 1967, he took a job as an attendant in a state institution for the mentally retarded. His articles led to reforms.

Gage was one of three reporters on the Boston paper's crack team of investigators. The others were Hank Messick, later to achieve fame as an author of books on organized crime, and James Savage, now a prize-winning investigative reporter for the Miami *Herald*. All three left after the paper refused to publish their discovery of underworld ties to a prominent citizen who, they learned later, was a stockholder in the newspaper.

Investigative reporting's new popularity has drawbacks, Gage believes. The image of a hero or ''glamor boy of journalism'' entices young people into the profession for such wrong reasons as money, power, and prestige. The proper motive, he says, is a low level of tolerance for fraud, corruption, and misuse of power, combined with a faith in the power of exposure to achieve correction. The press can't save society, but it can provoke others to take action.

It looked like the end of their hopes, Selwyn Raab had to admit. All attempts in state and federal appellate courts to get another trial for young George Whitmore had come to naught. Now Whitmore's appeal bail had been revoked and he was on his way to Green Haven State Prison in upstate New York to complete a term of five to ten years for the attempted rape of a twenty-year-old Puerto Rican nurse. There seemed nothing for Raab to do except learn to live with bitter defeat.

Raab's frustration affected him acutely because he knew Whitmore was innocent. A thirty-eight-year-old reporter-producer for New York City's public television station, Channel 13, Raab had been investigating Whitmore's case for eight years, ever since a few months after Whitmore confessed in 1964 to three crimes he hadn't committed—the attempted rape, the stabbing murder of another woman, and the grisly slayings of two well-to-do young career women, Janice Wylie and Emily Hoffert, in their fashionable Manhattan apartment. Whitmore maintained that police had beaten him until he confessed.

During those eight years, Raab had dug up evidence that exonerated Whitmore in the Wylie-Hoffert murders, the other murder charge had been dropped, and two convictions on the attempted rape charge had been overturned on appeal. But Whitmore had been convicted of the attempted rape a third time in 1967. Now, five years later, with appeals exhausted, Raab still was convinced that Whitmore had not committed the rape attempt, either.

A slender, dark-haired man whose relentlessness lies concealed beneath a mild, slightly disheveled exterior, Raab turned to Myron Beldock, the eleventh in a succession of lawyers who had tried to help Whitmore. "I'm not going to let it happen," Raab said. "I know this guy is innocent."

"Let's get together one more time," Beldock replied, "and see if we can figure out something."

Raab and Beldock went over the case again. The main witness against Whitmore was the victim, Mrs. Ella Borrero, who first identified Whitmore as her attacker at the police station where the nineteen-year-old Whitmore had been brought for questioning as a witness.

Whitmore apparently had seen Mrs. Borrero's attacker as he fled from the policeman who had happened upon the incident in a slum section of Brooklyn shortly after midnight in April, 1964. A poor, uneducated black youth from Wildwood, New Jersey, 120 miles away, Whitmore had been sleeping in stairwells or staying with a cousin in Brooklyn while looking for work. Later that morning, Whitmore saw the policeman, Frank Isola, again. He told Isola the man Isola had chased had come up to Whitmore, asked for help, and run off again. A police detective, Richard Aidala, came and asked Whitmore to go with him to the precinct station, where Aidala told him in a sharp voice to take off his coat and hat and empty his pockets. Informed later that he had been identified by the victim as her assailant, Whitmore insisted he had nothing to do with it. Aidala and a young policeman beat him in the stomach, back, chest, and neck—never in the face—until finally, Whitmore, sobbing, almost unconscious, his muscles quivering out of control, hardly able to know what he was doing, heard himself admit he had wanted to rape the woman.

There were at least two things wrong with Mrs. Borrero's identification of Whitmore. First, the procedure was improper. Suspects are supposed to be placed in a lineup with three or four others of similar height and build to avoid leading an eyewitness or victim to an identification he believes the police desire. Whitmore had been alone in the detective squad room while Mrs.

Borrero viewed him through a peephole in a door. Secondly, Whitmore did not match the description that Mrs. Borrero had given to Patrolman Isola a few minutes after Isola had chased off her attacker.

But these discrepancies had already been debated before a jury. They could be of no further help.

The same was true of the "button discrepancy." In Whitmore's first trial, the prosecutor made a big point of the fact that a button had been missing from Whitmore's coat when he was arrested. Mrs. Borrero had pulled a button from her assailant's coat. The prosecutor implied the button had come from young Whitmore's coat. Raab got a tip that the button evidence was phony. Surmising that the police would have asked the FBI for lab tests, he got a copy of the lab report through a friend who had a connection in the FBI. The report said the strands of thread on the button did not match those of Whitmore's coat.

The only other lead was an obscure reference that Beldock had spotted during a meticulous review of the case record, a notation in a detective's notebook that a sister-in-law of Mrs. Borrero had seen the attacker. Isola's notebook contained the sister-in-law's description of the man, and it did not fit Whitmore. The existence of this witness had not been known to defense lawyers during any of Whitmore's trials. However, no one had been able to locate the sister-in-law, who had left Brooklyn in 1966, and the appellate courts had rejected arguments that she might have important new evidence.

The situation was clearly hopeless.

"The only thing we've got left," said Raab, "is to try and find that sister-in-law, even though it looks impossible."

"Let's try it anyway," said Beldock.

Beldock had a private detective working for him named Richard Tracy. Raab and the detective tried tracing the woman through the telephone company and mail drops, but got only dead ends. They began calling everyone in the New York vicinity with the same last name as the sister-in-law, identified in Isola's notebook as "Mrs. Viruet."

Shortly after they started the telephoning, Tracy died, but not before he found a Viruet in the Bronx who remembered that a woman named Celeste Viruet and her husband had run a grocery store and had moved to Puerto Rico in 1965 or 1966. He was not related to them, but thought they had bought a bar in Puerto Rico with the word, "orange," in its name. There was also something about a "green island."

They knew the sister-in-law had run a grocery and suddenly Raab and Beldock were excited. "Green island" in Spanish was "Isla Verde," and Raab recognized that as a section near the airport in San Juan, Puerto Rico's capital.

But they could find no Viruet or a bar containing "orange" in its name in the Puerto Rico phone directory. Channel 13 declined to pay for a trip to Puerto Rico. The clue was too tenuous.

Talking to a Puerto Rican named Maria Mena who worked at Channel 13, Raab learned that she had a friend in Puerto Rico. He asked her to see if her friend would drive out by the airport and look for a bar with "orange" in its name. Two months later, the friend phoned from Puerto Rico to report he had seen a bar called El Narangal, which was Spanish for The Orange Grove.

"Please," said Raab, "one more thing. Go in the bar and find out if there's a Viruet there."

A week later, Maria Mena's friend called again. At the bar he'd found a Viruet family that had moved to Puerto Rico from Brooklyn.

The clue was no longer tenuous.

Raab, Beldock, and Mena went to Puerto Rico in December, 1972, and interviewed Mrs. Viruet. What they learned exceeded their wildest dreams. Mrs. Viruet, who had lived in the same building as Mrs. Borrero, had been waiting up for her the night of the attack and had seen the man from her third floor window. She had not seen his face, but could describe his height, weight, and build. She had told police all this, but had never been asked to identify Whitmore or testify in court. She also said Mrs. Borrero had given her a description of her assailant that contradicted her courtroom testimony.

Raab put the story on TV while Beldock turned over the new evidence to Brooklyn District Attorney D. A. Gold. Gold went to Puerto Rico to interview Mrs. Viruet himself and came back with even more startling information about evidence that police had concealed. Before Whitmore had been brought to the station, Mrs. Borrero had selected from a rogues' gallery file a photograph of a convicted sex offender whom she identified as the man who had assaulted her.

One day in April, 1973, nine years after his volunteering of information to a policeman had plunged him into a tangled multiple crime case as a battered, innocent defendant, Whitmore, now twenty-eight, walked out of prison a free man at last. His life lay in ruins, but at least he was no longer a convicted felon.

Raab, the man most responsible for Whitmore's exoneration, first became interested in the case somewhat by accident. A reporter for the New York *World-Telegram* in the summer of 1964, he was combing the newspaper's files for material on police brutality. He noticed a reference to Whitmore's claim of having been beaten at his arraignment in the Wylie-Hoffert murders. When he checked the status of the case, Raab found that Whitmore had been in Bellevue Hospital for a psychiatric exam much longer than the normal thirty days. That made him curious. Then he learned that the prosecutors hadn't decided which of the three cases against Whitmore they would bring to trial first. That seemed odd, since one would expect the Wylie-Hoffert murder case to be automatically first. That crime had been the first to occur and was the most sensational. Raab grew more curious. As a native New Yorker who grew up in a poor East Side neighborhood, he also knew what it felt like to be an underdog.

Whitmore's lawyer refused to talk to Raab. The reporter contacted the defendant's mother, who told him her son had been in Wildwood on August 28, 1963, the day of the Wylie-Hoffert killings. In fact, she said, he had been in Wildwood all that summer and had not gone to New York until later. Raab drove several times to Wildwood in search of witnesses who could corroborate the mother's story. He found two who remembered seeing him there that day, but much later than noon, the time of the murders.

The unlucky Whitmore had been charged with the Wylie-Hoffert killings because of a snapshot he carried in his wallet. After he confessed to the rape attempt, he was asked about an earlier rape-murder in the same neighborhood. Additional persuasion was applied and he confessed to that too. Meanwhile, detectives were drifting in and out of the squad room where the meager possessions taken from Whitmore's pockets lay on a desk. Among them was a photograph of two white girls. One of the detectives, Edward Bulger, had been working on the Wylie-Hoffert case. When a detective named Fazio picked up the snapshot and showed it to Bulger, Bulger said one of the girls, a blonde, looked like Janice Wylie. At first Whitmore said a girl had given him the photograph, then that he had found it in a junkyard in Wildwood. Detectives kept badgering him. Come on, George, why don't you admit you stole it from an apartment in Manhattan. Whitmore finally told them what they wanted to hear, just to get the pressure stopped. Soon he was confessing to the brutal, bloody murders of the two young women.

In Wildwood, Raab was told by a policeman named Parker Johnson that New York detectives had been there to inquire about the photograph. Johnson had identified the blonde woman as a Wildwood resident named Arlene Franco.

Whitmore was tried first on the rape attempt charge. His attorney refused to accept Raab's help or look at his evidence. Raab believes the prosecutor knew his evidence was weak in the murder case and hoped to bolster it with an attempted rape conviction. In November, Whitmore was found guilty.

Raab began writing stories about the discrepancies in the evidence, but no one paid much heed. Raab found three lawyers willing to take on an appeal. One of them, Arthur A. Miller, went to Wildwood to follow up Raab's leads. He interviewed Arlene Franco, who said she had identified the snapshot for New York police detectives. Miller learned that police had also talked to the witnesses found by Raab who had seen Whitmore in Wildwood the day of the Wylie-Hoffert murders.

This evidence got Raab's articles more attention. Other newspapers picked up the story. In January, 1965, Miller located a seventeen-year-old boy who remembered talking to Whitmore in Wildwood at noon or 1 P.M on the crucial day. Reporters pressed Manhattan District Attorney Frank Hogan for explanations. Whitmore's lawyers bombarded Hogan with demands that he bring Whitmore to trial or drop the charges.

On January 26, Hogan announced that a twenty-one-year-old narcotics addict, Richard Robles, had been arrested for the Wylie-Hoffert murders, and charges against Whitmore were to be dismissed. Robles had been a suspect almost from the beginning. Hogan said the case against Whitmore had always been weak and his office had uncovered evidence exonerating him. His investigators had been suspicious of Whitmore's confession and had doubted the girl in the snapshot was Janice Wylie. In October, before Whitmore's rape attempt trial, they had traced Mrs. Franco's companion in the photograph to Philadelphia and learned it had been discarded in the trash in Wildwood two years before the murders.

Why had Hogan waited so long to drop the charges? Until after the rape attempt trial, for instance? Hogan said he hadn't wanted to foul up his investigation of Robles by putting him on guard.

Raab wrote a book on the case, called *Justice in the Back Room*. That became the basis for a TV movie entitled *The Marcus-Nelson Murders,* in which a police detective named Kojak is the hero. That led to the CBS-TV series starring Telly Savalas. *Time* magazine once referred to Raab as "the original Kojak."

"In real life, no detective did anything to help Whitmore," Raab wrote in a 1973 article criticizing America's criminal justice system in *The Nation* magazine. "Their silence [of Hogan and his aides] helped to associate him falsely with the heavily publicized Wylie-Hoffert murders, and that in turn worked to bring about his first conviction for attempted rape and complicated his other two trials." No one, Raab complained, ever took any action against the policemen and prosecutors who suppressed evidence proving Whitmore's innocence.

Raab had gone to Channel 13 in 1971 after five years at the NBC station in New York, where he had set up a full-time "probe unit," one of TV's first. He found TV a difficult medium for investigative reporting, but feasible if a station commits enough time and money. He did an exposé on Port Authority profits that won a Sigma Delta Chi Award, and several reports on phony doctors and health care frauds. At the *World-Telegram*, he had won two local awards for investigative reporting before the paper folded in 1966.

At Channel 13, he investigated phony methadone clinics by sending in young reporters to get the heroin substitute without tests. Posing as a potential buyer of a clinic that was up for sale, Raab was told how it ripped off the federal government's Medicaid program through $4-a-dose reimbursements for the methadone it disbursed so freely. As a result of Raab's televised disclosures, two clinics were closed.

After Whitmore's final vindication in 1973, which won Raab a local Sigma Delta Chi Award, the reporter was deluged with letters from penitentiary inmates and their friends who wanted him to take up their causes, too. There was no way he could investigate them all, but one did intrigue him.

He was approached by friends and lawyers on behalf of Rubin "Hurricane" Carter, a thirty-seven-year-old middleweight boxer serving a life term for a June 17, 1966, triple murder in a Paterson, New Jersey, bar. Raab was impressed by the intensity of their belief in Carter's innocence. "A lot of this business has to do with gut feelings," he says. "And this one felt right."

Carter and an acquaintance, John Artis, both black, had been convicted in the shooting deaths of two men and a woman, all white, on the testimony of two witnesses who said they had seen Carter and Artis leaving the Lafayette Grill with guns. The witnesses were Arthur D. Bradley, a twenty-three-year-old holdup man, and Alfred P. Bello, also twenty-three, a parolee from a robbery and burglary conviction. They had been breaking into a nearby factory the night of the killings. Carter and Artis had been picked up half an hour after the incident because they were driving a white car similar to one seen leaving the tavern. They were released after an injured survivor of the shooting incident failed to identify them as the gunmen. But Carter and Artis were arrested four months later.

Raab agreed to read the trial record, which led him to inspect the scene of the crime. There he became convinced that Bradley had lied. He could not possibly have seen anyone coming out of the Lafayette Grill with a shotgun from the factory he was burglarizing. The factory was two blocks away. When he asked what had happened to Bradley and Bello, he found they had received no prison sentence for the burglary, and Bradley had gotten off with only three years for a string of armed robberies. No one knew where either could be found.

Raab and Fred W. Hogan, an investigator for the New Jersey Public Defender's Office, began tracking down Bradley and Bello. Hogan found Bello in November, 1973, but Bello was noncommittal. Raab tried to reach him by phone and left messages that he was doing a TV show on the case. Bello called Raab, but remained evasive. "Someday I'll tell the whole story," Bello said. "What was said on the witness stand was not the way it happened. But I'm not ready."

Raab was appointed executive editor of Channel 13's news program in January and turned the case over to reporter Hal Levison. In May, Hogan and Levison found Bradley, who admitted having lied but gave a vague statement that, according to Raab, was "wishy-washy" and not strong enough to get Carter a new trial.

When Channel 13's news budget was cut in June, 1974, Raab looked for another job and found one on *The New York Times*. He returned full time to investigating the Carter case.

Raab visited Bradley several times and finally got him to sign a long statement admitting he had lied in a deal with police for lighter treatment. Then Raab finally prevailed on Bello to admit he had lied, too. He had seen two men outside the Lafayette Grill, but not Carter and Artis. Raab's story ran on the front page of the *Times* on September 27, 1974. Levison, now with Channel 5, had broken it on his 10 P.M. news show the previous evening. Raab won the 1974 Heywood Broun Award for public interest reporting.

A motion for a new trial based on the recantations and other new evidence was turned down, however. The judge said the recantations "lacked the ring of truth." Pending an appeal to the state supreme court, Governor Brendan Byrne appointed a state legislator to investigate. Several prominent New Yorkers and national celebrities, including World Heavyweight Boxing Champion Muhammad Ali, actress Ellen Burstyn, and singers Bob Dylan and Joan Baez, joined a campaign to sell Byrne on granting a pardon. The state supreme court in March, 1976, overturned the conviction and ordered a new trial for Carter and Artis. The court ruled the prosecution's failure to disclose promises of leniency to Bradley amounted to withholding material evidence and denial of due process.

Meanwhile, Raab went back to his typewriter, covering criminal justice for the *Times*, writing about plea bargaining statistics and the latest crisis in New York City's "wide open" drug trade. For all this doggedness and zeal, he remains the cool professional. He's not out to show anyone up, he says, just to "unravel the truth."

Twenty-five welfare patients were waiting for treatment in the Park Community Medical Building in Queens when William Sherman walked in.

A woman dressed in white took Sherman's Medicaid card, made several Xerox copies, and asked his name, birth date, and phone number. "Why are you here?" she asked.

"I have a cold, I think," said Sherman. "I'd like to see a doctor."

"Well, the medical doctor is busy right now. First you should see the podiatrist, to have your feet checked. He's not busy."

"Why? I just have a cold."

"You should have your feet checked."

"Okay," said Sherman. He permitted himself to be ushered into the podiatrist's office where he was instructed to lie on a couch and relax.

The podiatrist removed Sherman's shoes and socks, squeezed Sherman's feet, and said, "Ever have any trouble with these?"

"Nope. I have a cold. How come I'm seeing a foot doctor?"

"Well, here we examine everybody from the ground up and we're starting with your feet. We'll get to the rest of you later." He spotted a light rash on the left foot. "How long have you had this?"

"A couple of days," said Sherman.

"I'll write you out some prescriptions," said the foot specialist. "You get them filled upstairs. Rub the cream on and it will be all better."

"Why should I get them filled upstairs? I have a drugstore in my neighborhood."

"The pharmacist here knows what the doctors write for, and they stock accordingly."

Sherman was whisked to a small examination room where an internist inquired, "What's your trouble?"

"A cold."

"How long have you had it?"

"A couple of days. Since I caught it I haven't been sleeping so good."

The internist examined Sherman's throat, thumped his forehead with a finger, listened to his chest with a stethoscope, took a blood pressure reading, and asked Sherman if he had a fever.

Sherman said he didn't know.

"You have the London flu," the doctor announced. "I'm going to give you a shot of penicillin."

Sherman protested, refusing the shot. "I don't want it, I don't need it. Needles make me nervous."

"All right," said the doctor, making a notation of the refusal. "I'm writing you a prescription for penicillin, a cough medicine, and some pills to take twice a day that will relax you." He wrote on a sheet of paper that the patient should have an electrocardiogram, blood tests, X-rays, and a urine test.

Sherman objected to the urine test.

"The tests will determine if there is anything more seriously wrong," the doctor explained. Sherman relented.

The receptionist returned and escorted Sherman to another examination room. "Another doctor wants to see you," she said.

A man in a beige sports jacket came in and introduced himself as a doctor. "How do you feel?"

"I have this cold," said Sherman, "and I'm not sleeping so good."

"You look depressed. Are you always this depressed?"

"No."

"Do you have a girl friend?"

"Do you?"

The doctor ignored that and asked Sherman about his family background and job history. He leaned forward, looked into Sherman's eyes, and said, "You seem afraid."

"I'm not."

"Well, you shouldn't worry about injections," said the doctor. "I'm going to write you a prescription for some pills that will let you sleep better. You'll feel more relaxed. Come in Monday. I'd like to see you one day a week to work out your problems." The doctor had taken no notes and made no entries on the patient's chart.

On his way out, Sherman encountered the internist, who said, "Come back Wednesday, no matter how well you're feeling. I have to check you out again."

Upstairs at the pharmacy, Sherman got six prescriptions filled.

Returning two days later as directed, Sherman was given an electrocardiogram, two X-rays, a blood sugar test, a syphilis test, a blood count, and a second urine test, though the first urinalysis had come back from the lab as "okay."

Actually, Sherman did not have a cold. He was a New York *Daily News* reporter posing as a welfare patient to investigate frauds and abuses in New York City's $1.3-billion-a-year medical assistance program in cooperation with the city's Human Resources Administration and the Department of Health. A twenty-six-year-old mustachioed reporter with an air of being calm and serious, yet coiled to strike, Sherman was issued a temporary Medicaid card. He used it at several clinics and medical offices in Manhattan, the Bronx and Queens. Before he began his investigation, he was given a complete physical examination and found to be in sound health. The Health Department audited the treatment he received and analyzed the drugs he purchased with prescriptions.

The analysis of Sherman's experience at the Park Community Medical Building in Queens revealed several irregularities. He had been seen by a podiatrist without having complained of foot trouble. Penicillin is not effective against a cold or flu. There was no medical indication that blood tests or X-rays were needed, or a session with a psychiatrist. The electrocardiogram was contrary to a regulation that none be given to patients under forty without a specific reason. Medicaid rules required that patients have complete freedom in choosing a pharmacy to fill their prescriptions. One prescription called for four ounces of cough medicine, but Sherman received only three. Three of the drugs prescribed were dangerous when taken together.

Based on the city's Medicaid fee schedule, the city would be billed $63.80 for Sherman's first visit to the Park Community Medical Building—$5.20 for the podiatry exam, $15 for the internist, $20 for the psychiatrist, $2 for the urinalysis, and $21.60 for the prescriptions. The second visit cost $48.40—$4 for the blood count, $2 for the second urine test, $4 for the blood sugar test, $2.40 for the syphilis test, $12 for the internist, $12 for the electrocardiogram, and $12 for the X-rays. Total for the "cold": $112.20.

It was typical of Sherman's experiences.

At a lower East Side optical center, Sherman told the receptionist he wanted to have his eyes examined.

"Are you Medicaid?" she inquired.

Sherman, whose vision was 20-20, said, "Yes."

"Okay," said the receptionist. "Give me your card and go into that room and pick out the frames you want."

"I haven't had my eyes examined yet."

"Yes, I know, but it will save time."

She took him to a rack of eyeglass frames she said were "for Medicaid people only." After selecting a pair, Sherman was escorted to a waiting area. Presently an optometrist summoned him to a chair in an examining room.

"Ever wear glasses?" he asked.

"No."

"How are your eyes?"

"Perfect, I think."

"When was the last time you had them tested?"

"About four years ago."

The optometrist turned out the lights, shut the door and shined a light in Sherman's eyes. Then he opened the door and instructed him to read letters on a chart thirty feet away.

Sherman read three lines of letters.

The optometrist put a model frame on Sherman and started slipping lenses into it. "Can you see better with these?"

"No," said Sherman. "Things look fuzzy."

"How about these?"

"No, not really."

After three more sets, Sherman said he could see better. The optometrist handed him a piece of paper and said, "Give this to the people at the desk downstairs. Come back at four thirty, then you can pick up your glasses."

The five-minute examination was worth $8, the glasses $10, under the Medicaid fee schedule. A Health Department official said the optometrist had performed only six of the twenty-one tests required, and had not taken a proper case history. He also said Sherman didn't need glasses.

At the East Harlem office of a dentist named Fred Fisher, Sherman was met at the door by Fisher, himself, a fat man in a white smock. "Come inside, brother," said Fisher. "We'll take good care of you." The dentist took Sherman's Medicaid card and told him he would X-ray his mouth.

"Hold on a second," said Sherman. "You haven't looked at my teeth yet."

"I got to take X-rays, buddy."

"Look in my mouth first."

Sticking a finger in Sherman's mouth and looking inside without a mirror, the dentist said, "Seems okay to me but we've got to do a cleaning."

"Okay."

"But first I got to take X-rays."

"If all I need is a cleaning, why X-rays?"

"That's the way it's done, brother."

"Well, I don't want it done that way."

"All right, brother," growled the dentist. "Take a walk. Get out of here."

In a Health Department survey, forty-two of 173 sets of X-rays by Fisher were declared unnecessary. Fisher billed the city for $300,000 in Medicaid reimbursements in 1967, $500,000 in 1968. He was indicted in 1971 for double billing and billing for services and materials he had not furnished.

Sherman's investigation included long hours of inspecting records of doctors' billings and interviewing patients to determine if they had received the services for which the city had been billed. He worked full time for six and a half weeks on the project and wrote a fourteen-part series on his findings that started on January 23, 1973. Among his disclosures: One doctor billed the city for seeing 200 patients in an eight-hour period; psychiatrists routinely conducted ten-minute chats with patients and billed the city for hour sessions; fifty percent of all eyeglasses dispensed to Medicaid patients were unsatisfactory; doctors ran sick people through their examining rooms at the rate of one every three minutes, but made them sit through unneeded tests; one radiologist received $310,420 in Medicaid payments in six months; a hearing aid dealer got $6,000 for merchandise he never delivered.

Sherman's articles prompted government investigations that produced several indictments and recovered $1 million in fraudulent billings. They also won Sherman three big prizes—a Pulitzer for investigative reporting, a George Polk

Memorial Award for community service, and a New York Newspaper Guild Award for crusading journalism.

A native New Yorker who worked for the Boston *Globe* and the *Village Voice* in New York before joining the *Daily News*, Sherman hustled his way into investigative reporting by always looking for an angle that could turn an ordinary story into a gripping one. When George Wallace was shot down in a Maryland shopping center by Arthur Bremer of Milwaukee, Sherman didn't rush off to Maryland like most reporters. He went to Milwaukee. Delving into Bremer's background, he talked a clerk at the Juvenile court into letting him see confidential records about Bremer's troubles as a child. He got into Bremer's apartment by using an entrance the FBI forgot to guard, affecting an official air as he walked in, and helped himself to some of the young gunman's poetry.

When the nephew of America's top Mafia boss, Carlo Gambino, was kidnapped, all reporters but one stuck close to the police. Sherman hurried out to Gambino's house. There was only a maid at home, however, so Sherman tried next door, where the occupant turned out to be Gambino's bodyguard. He told the reporter the real story. The kidnappers just wanted the $60,000 they owed a loan shark. Gambino didn't like his nephew, anyway.

"If you push, you get results," says Sherman. "But you have to do it quietly. I don't believe in browbeating people. I'm just pleasantly persistent."

Someone mentioned to Stanley Penn of the *Wall Street Journal* in 1966 that he might find some hanky-panky behind a campaign in the Bahama Islands, the British colony off the southern tip of Florida, to promote tourism with gambling.

The New York Times had published a 1965 story about the Bahamas, their politics, and a new gambling casino. Native blacks comprising eighty percent of the population were trying to oust from power a small coterie of white merchants and professional men, several of whom were government ministers. The blacks were led by thirty-six-year-old Lynden Pindling, who accused the government of making a bad deal with an American investor named Wallace Groves for operation of the casino and development of 211 square miles of land on Grand Bahama Island. Pindling charged Sir Stafford Sands, Minister of Finance and Tourism and the most powerful figure in the government, with a conflict of interest because he had represented Groves and the casino as a lawyer at the same time he served in the government. In fact, Sands had sponsored the casino's successful request for a gambling license in the form of a ten-year exemption from the antigambling law.

Groves owned fifty percent of the Grand Bahama Port Authority, Ltd., a private firm set up by a group of American investors to develop the island. One of the firm's subsidiaries had built the luxurious Lucayan Beach hotel and casino. Under the agreement with the government, Groves and his companies were exempt from taxes until 1990, and partially exempt until 2054. Pindling complained that the arrangement gave the Groves organization too much control over too much land. He also criticized the casino's attractive tax deal, a flat annual levy of $280,000, plus $280 to $560 per slot machine, instead of a percentage of income. Groves could build as many gambling casinos as he wished on the 211 square miles. Sands defended the agreement as the catalyst needed to attract development to the Bahamas.

It struck Penn as a fascinating situation, pregnant with possibilities. Phone calls led him to a former executive of one of Groves' companies who said there had been under-the-table consultant fees for Sands and two other government officials, including Premier Sir Roland Symonette. All three were members of the Executive Council that had granted the gambling license. Sands was to get $50,000 a year from a Groves firm for ten years, or as long as the gambling license was good, in addition to legal fees. Symonette was to get $16,800 a year for five years.

It was explosive material, but Penn had only the word of a former executive who might have a motive to give him false or distorted information. Most good investigative stories originate from a tipster with an ax to grind, Penn says, and it's essential to check them out carefully. Contacting people who might corroborate the story, Penn located others who had been involved in the Bahamian venture with Groves but had grown disenchanted with it. One told Penn that Meyer Lansky, a top figure in the national crime syndicate, had helped set up the casino.

One contact led to another and Penn finally came to an investor who had an interest in the Bahamas, access to records of the Groves corporations, and a willingness to show the records to Penn. This was the decisive discovery. "I'm not sure we would have run the story if I hadn't seen those records," says Penn.

Not only did the documents confirm the consultant agreements, they revealed much more. Sands' attorney fees had exceeded $1 million. Another member of the Executive Council was leasing boats to a Groves company. Two other officials, including Premier Symonette's son, Bobby, were on the books as consultants.

A check of Groves' background showed he had been a Wall Street wheeler-dealer who was sentenced to two years in prison on a 1941 conviction for mail fraud.

Penn is quiet-spoken but talkative, a scholarly-looking journalism school graduate with the kind of precise mind that's needed to sort out the entanglements of business manipulations, which he's been doing for the *Wall Street Journal* since 1952. He doesn't like to bluff. He prefers to know as much as possible about his subject before confronting him in an interview. His style is to "wait till you have so much he can't wiggle out." In his investigation of gambling in the Bahamas, he now had enough to start interviewing.

Penn and another *Wall Street Journal* reporter, Monroe W. Karmin, went to the Bahamas. The Bahamian businessmen-officials, known as the "Bay Street Boys," denied the consultant agreements. All except one. Speaker of the

Assembly Bobby Symonette, the premier's son, acknowledged he had been under contract to give a Groves firm advice on marina construction for $14,000 a year. A sportsman and sailor, the forty-year-old politician defended it as a legitimate business deal based on his experience at sea.

Symonette's admission was just what Penn needed to firm up the story for publication.

The secret consultant deals, however, engendered less furor than the story's disclosure of the casino's ties with the underworld.

The Pulitzer Prize-winning article by Penn and Karmin began with the vivid detail that characterizes the *Journal*'s colorful style. "Scene: the gold-papered, crystal-chandeliered Monte Carlo room of the luxurious Lucayan Beach Hotel. Roulette wheels spin their reds and blacks. Crapshooters roll their sevens and elevens. Blackjack dealers turn their aces and kings. Slot machines whirl their lemons and plums.

"Surveying the quick play and quiet players is the affable but cold-eyed man in charge, a runaway New Yorker wanted by American authorities. He is balding, sixty-one-year-old Frank Ritter, alias "Red" Reed, whose natty appearance (mustard sports jacket with double vents, tapered beige slacks, brown suede shoes) fails to dispel the impression that he's familiar with the grime of the underworld.

"Ritter's presence and his suspected links with the U.S. crime syndicate cast a pall over this 'island in the sun' just seventy miles off the Florida coast."

Penn had discovered Ritter at the casino. He also found Pindling charging that the Bahamian people were being sold out to gangsterism. Ritter and two other casino employes, he learned, had run a nationwide bookie business in New York and had been indicted for tax evasion. Two known associates of Lansky had helped start the casino and had worked there until Bahamian authorities kicked them out. Law enforcement agencies in the United States suspected that some of the casino's profits went to Lansky.

Using the revelations to good effect in the 1967 elections, Pindling toppled the Bay Street Boys from power and took over as premier.

Penn, now forty-eight, considers the Bahamas story the highest achievement of his career. But he's kept trying to surpass it. As a full-time investigative reporter with the freedom to pick his own projects, he's come up with several more top-notch exposés, many by exploring through public records, especially lawsuits and bankruptcies.

Hearing talk that President Nixon's nominee to head the SEC, an electronics magnate named William Casey, had been in some controversial deals, Penn checked court records for lawsuits involving Casey. He found several. One had been settled and the records were stored in a Greenwich Village warehouse, where Penn promptly repaired for further searching. Exhibits in the case contained accusations by an investor in one of Casey's firms that Casey had duped him out of $10,000. Casey had settled the case for $8,000. Casey explained he hadn't been close to the company involved and he had paid the settlement to get rid of a nuisance suit. Penn's story led to a second look at Casey by the U.S. Senate before it confirmed his appointment.

Penn once happened upon a suit by an investment banking firm against Occidental Petroleum that piqued his interest. The investment firm accused the oil company of pirating oil rights in Libya and there was mention of a notorious French swindler. Every five or six months, Penn stopped by the courthouse to check the case's progress and look at new motions or depositions. The court file clerk got used to Penn's visits and began letting him thumb through the file on his own. One day he was surprised to find a lengthy deposition by a former Libyan oil minister that had been ordered sealed by the judge, but placed in the public file by mistake. It provided the breakthrough Penn needed to write about the complex dealings and the possibly questionable methods behind Occidental's acquisition of the oil concessions that had made it a major oil company. An intermediary paid $200,000 by Occidental had put up $100,000 for a documentary film about Libya. The former oil minister, who had been instrumental in getting the oil rights for Occidental, had written the script for the film, and his brother-in-law had shared in the profits.

Penn has written extensively about organized crime's infiltration of legitimate business, about complicated swindles by promoters, and once about a woman who claimed her stockbroker had sexually enslaved her and cheated her out of $600,000 in stock by "churning"—frequent buying and selling to generate commissions. Penn didn't take the woman's word for it, though. He insisted as usual on proof. "I don't feel comfortable with what people tell me," he says. "I want to see documents."

Flipping through mortgage records at the Middlesex County courthouse one day in 1969, Jonathan Kwitny never suspected that the discovery he was about to make would get him fired from his job at the *Evening News* in Perth Amboy, New Jersey.

Kwitny was looking for the name Wilentz. There had long been rumbles of corruption in the politically powerful Wilentz family, and the young reporter thought it was a good time to investigate.

David T. Wilentz, senior partner in the Perth Amboy law firm of Wilentz, Goldman & Spitzer, had been a prominent and influential Democrat in the state for forty years. He had once been attorney general for ten years and was credited with making Richard J. Hughes governor of New Jersey in 1960. At the age of seventy-four, he was one of two Democratic National Committeemen from the state. His son, Warren, had been Middlesex County prosecutor and the unsuccessful Democratic nominee for the U.S. Senate in 1966. Another son, Robert, was a state legislator. Attorney General Arthur J. Sills had been a member of the Wilentz law firm until he was appointed to his state post in 1961.

One of the mortgages in the records concerned a loan from the Edison Bank in Edison, New Jersey, to Warren Wilentz. The loan bore a lower-than-normal interest rate. Checking further, Kwitny learned that Warren Wilentz was a founder and director of the Edison bank, and its attorney. Though this by itself was not newsworthy, Kwitny's editor suggested he determine who else was getting loans from the Edison Bank. And check the records in neighboring Monmouth County, too, while he was at it.

Among Edison Bank mortgage loans recorded in Monmouth County, Kwitny found the name of Anthony Russo, better known among his friends as "Little Pussy" Russo, the county's gambling boss, a leading light in the New Jersey underworld, and a loyal member of the Vito Genovese Mafia family. There were several mortgages in the name of Russo and Donato-Russo Enterprises, Inc., a company in which Russo and Genovese's son, Philip, were officers. The law firm representing Russo in some of the transactions was Wilentz, Goldman & Spitzer.

This was something a reporter could sink his teeth into, and Kwitny did. He found that Russo had been making big profits in land with mortgage loans that were almost as large, and sometimes larger, than the purchase prices. Russo bought one parcel for $160,000 and got a mortgage loan from the Edison Bank for $165,000. He made a $270,000 profit when he sold most of the parcel to a realty firm and a small portion to the state for highway improvements. On the part sold to the state, the price was triple what Russo had paid. Russo and his companies also had obtained loans from the National State Bank in Perth Amboy, a bank which the elder Wilentz served as a director and legal co-counsel. Russo and his companies had borrowed more than $800,000 in mortgage loans from banks linked to Wilentz's law firm, and had defaulted on $400,000 of it.

Just before Kwitny's articles on Russo's land deals was scheduled to start, he was called into the editor's office. The series was not going to be published, the editor said.

"Why not?" Kwitny asked.

"We've decided it's not really news. It's not a story we can justify."

Kwitny was sure the story had been killed by the newspaper's general manager, who was business oriented and did not like to rock any boats in the community. Disappointed, but determined to get the story out even if it cost him his job, Kwitny tried to sell his articles to *Life* magazine, which wasn't interested. Neither was the *Saturday Evening Post*. *Look* magazine was busy with a Mafia exposé of its own. *The New York Times* offered to buy the material, but would have a staffer verify it and rewrite it. The *Times*, he was told, did not use articles by outsiders. Kwitny hit paydirt, however, at the New York *Post*, which bought the articles and published them under his byline in October, 1969.

Kwitny was summoned once more to the editor's office. "This is the saddest thing I've ever had to do," said the editor. "But we just can't permit that kind of thing."

While the New Jersey State Investigation Commission cranked up a probe into the land deals and the Internal Revenue Service began nosing into a couple of Russo's corporations, Kwitny was looking for a job. Nothing permanent turned up until fourteen months later when he joined the *Wall Street Journal*. A slightly built, earnest reporter with a frizzy beard, Kwitny does investigative work exclusively, like Penn, but is among those who maintain "investigative reporting" is a redundancy. "Every story is an investigation," he says.

Kwitny delved into the murky multimillion-dollar dealings of the International Brotherhood of Teamsters' largest pension fund—the Central States, Southwest and Southwest Areas Pension Fund headquartered in Chicago—in 1975. This happened because he had written a book called *The Fountain Pen Conspiracy* about Wall Street swindlers. It was read by Jim Drinkhall, editor of *Overdrive*, the West Coast trucking industry magazine that specializes in exposés of Teamster Union corruption. Drinkhall called to ask about someone mentioned in the book and they got to talking about the Teamsters and pension fund loans to Mafia-connected ventures. Kwitny was persuaded to investigate.

He went to Dallas, Texas, to examine the voluminous records in a 1972 lawsuit against the giant $1.4-billion pension fund by a disgruntled former Teamster official named Donald Vestal. Vestal had obtained the pension fund's loan records, until then the only copies ever pried out of the fund's tight secrecy. The court had sealed the records, but copies had leaked out to law enforcement agencies and Drinkhall. Kwitny got copies, too.

He interviewed retired truck drivers who had trouble getting their pensions. They had been put off with explanations that their employers had failed to forward payroll deductions to the fund, or that one of their jobs had been with a nonunion company.

Pension fund officials refused to talk with Kwitny and there were few records to work from. But he pieced together a three-part series that described with sharp contrast and careful detail how the pension fund refused $550-a-month pensions to retired Teamsters while it loaned millions of dollars to Las Vegas casinos and Mafia-controlled companies and country clubs. After his series appeared, the U.S. Department of Labor began plans for an investigation. A move originated for a U.S. Senate probe.

Early in Kwitny's reporting career at the Perth Amboy *Evening News*, he was asked to look into a tip that a lot of people were losing their homes to foreclosures on second mortgages. He studied mortgage records and talked to homeowners. He uncovered a loan racket by several fly-by-night firms that inflated the amounts of mortgage loans with phony charges. Homeowners who thought they had signed a $2,000 loan were shocked to discover later that they had agreed to pay $3,800, plus interest. Kwitny also found the state had no law to regulate second-mortgage lenders. His articles led to a state investigation, prosecutions, and a new regulation law.

Kwitny went off to Nigeria with the Peace Corps for two-and-a-half years. When he returned, he decided to see how the new law had improved the second-mortgage situation. He was flabbergasted to find it worse than ever. Not only had second-mortgage lenders conjured up new tricks for inflating loan totals, many of them didn't bother to comply with the requirement that they be licensed by the state. Enforcement by state authorities was nonexistent. The only bright spot was that borrowers could not be forced to repay loans made in violation of the law.

Kwitny got affidavits from thirty-six borrowers and wrote another series. This prompted another state investigation, which led to the closing of most of the companies he exposed. Another outcome was a court ruling that many of the loans were unenforceable. It taught him the importance of follow-up.

"The mortgage stories were the most gratifying I've ever done," says Kwitny, "because of the effect they had on thousands of families." A reporter on a local paper, he believes, can have a more telling effect on conditions and events. "Playing in the bigger league," he says, "seems to have less direct impact."

Jack Newfield of the *Village Voice* wanted to write an in-depth, down-to-earth account of a tough, honest white cop's work in a black ghetto. Once a week for six weeks in 1972 he rode around the seventy-ninth precinct in Brooklyn's Bedford-Stuyvesant section for eight hours with Sergeant Tom Santise.

One day Santise told him about a disturbing court experience by one of his undercover men. A heroin dealer arrested for possession of drugs had offered the policeman $1,000 to forget it, and the cop had charged him with attempted bribery, too. Though it was the dealer's eighteenth arrest, the judge let him go without bail and criticized the policeman.

"Which judge was it?" Newfield asked.

Dominic Rinaldi.

Over the next several weeks, Newfield investigated Rinaldi's record. He analyzed the Brooklyn judge's case dispositions, findings, and sentences. He interviewed prosecutors, defense attorneys, other judges.

He found that defendants connected with organized crime were permitted to plead to misdemeanors, favored with suspended sentences, and fined instead of jailed. Heroin dealers got inexplicably light sentences, even illegal conditional discharges. Certain lawyers always won. Blacks and Puerto Ricans, however, got high bail and stiff sentences.

Newfield wrote four articles about Rinaldi as an incompetent and possibly corrupt judge in the *Village Voice*, a onetime counterculture weekly in Greenwich Village now on the fringes of respectability. He also expanded his research to write a *New York* magazine piece naming the city's "Ten Worst Judges," including another who was lenient on Mafia figures, one who was severely biased toward the prosecution, and one with a nasty temper who insulted everyone.

Newfield did everything he could to keep public indignation aroused. He appeared on TV, and spoke before groups of lawyers. The *Voice* bought an ad in *The New York Times Book Review* to draw attention to his Rinaldi disclosures. "Writing an article is less than half the job," Newfield says. "The follow-up, creating a constituency for an idea by lobbying and writing repeated stories, is essential. The serious journalist must be an activist in order to affect events and institutions. Any personality, any bureaucracy, any institution can survive one or two embarrassing articles. It is only repeated exposure, with fact piled upon fact, that makes a difference. If you're going to have any lasting effect on public policy, the government has to know you're going to be relentless."

Though Newfield's articles detonated a blast of controversy, the institutions that could take corrective action reacted with indifference. The presiding judge of the court that could investigate and remove Rinaldi would not talk to Newfield. The Brooklyn Bar Association, which could investigate and censure a judge, attacked the articles as "malicious, unfounded and irresponsible." But Special Prosecutor Maurice Nadjari, appointed by the governor to investigate police and political corruption in New York City, did take an interest. On November 12, 1973, Rinaldi was indicted on three counts of perjury. Another judge was suspended and two resigned. Nadjari described Brooklyn courts as "a cesspool of corruption." A bar association committee at last bestirred itself to investigate. Two of the charges against Rinaldi were dropped and he was acquitted on the third. He filed a $5 million libel suit against Newfield, the *Village Voice*, and the publisher of a book based on the articles.

Two years later, the bespectacled, curly-haired, easygoing Newfield did an encore. He named "The Next 10 Worst Judges" in a *Village Voice* article based on more than 100 court transcripts, long hours of personal observation, reports by study committees, and interviews with trial lawyers, judges, bailiffs, court stenographers, prosecutors, policemen, and other reporters.

"Just a month inside the chaotic courtrooms," he wrote, "and you will see judges with unstable temperaments, judges with unmistakable biases, judges who are insulting and sarcastic, judges who open court at eleven A.M., take long lunches, and quit at three P.M., judges who are not intelligent enough to understand complex or subtle legal argument, judges who are incoherent from too many martinis at lunch, judges who bend the law to favor the clients of lawyers who are clubhouse cronies. . . . You will see judges coerce guilty pleas, improperly force settlements, malinger, manipulate the calendar, do anything to escape the mental labor of conducting a jury trial."

Newfield also took on nursing homes in 1974, exposing the hidden ownerships, political connections and organized crime ties of multimillionaire nursing home tycoon Bernard Bergman. He unearthed the fact that ten nursing homes "controlled by the Bergman cartel were forced to close by the city because of overcharges and subhuman conditions." In old health inspection reports Newfield found references to rodent poisons and urine-soaked sheets.

By talking to nurses, he learned about malnutrition, bed sores, and dehydration. In the files of the New Jersey Department of Health, the reporter discovered that federal Medicaid payments to a Bergman nursing home had been cut off because of fraud.

"He bills Medicaid for dead people," Newfield wrote. "His feeble patients must lie in their own urine all night because there is no staff on duty. Bergman's goons tried to evict the elderly residents of the Brewster Hotel, calling them 'old pieces of shit.' "

Newfield revealed the multimillion-dollar nursing home empire that Bergman had concealed behind a veil of dummy corporations and such devices as putting ownership in his wife's maiden name. He discovered that State Assemblyman Stanley Steingut had intervened to protect Bergman nursing homes from action by health authorities in return for insurance contracts on several nursing homes. Newfield disclosed that a Mafia hoodlum named Rocco Scarfone had been on the payroll at one Bergman nursing home and lived in the penthouse apartment at another.

Newfield first learned about Bergman in the 1974 book, *Tender Loving Greed*, a devastating compendium of corruption, fraud, patient abuse, and abysmal conditions in American nursing homes. Written by Mary Adelaide Mendelson, the book is based on a nationwide investigation that evolved from a statewide survey of nursing homes Mendelson had agreed to undertake as a part-time community planning consultant in Cleveland, Ohio.

The evidence was not hard to find, Newfield says. "It was all there, in the archives of the government itself"—the city and state health departments, the HEW regional office, the state welfare inspector general's office, a state legislative commission on cost of living.

Newfield attributes the success in provoking government action in the nursing home scandal—investigations, appointment of a special prosecutor, U.S. Senate hearings—to an unusual cooperation among newsmen from competing media. Newfield, John Hess of *The New York Times*, and Steve Bauman of WNEW-TV did not work together, but they exchanged ideas and their combined impact was greater. "Bergman could have outlasted any of us individually," Newfield says.

Such cooperation, he says, is not common enough. "Too often," he has written, "if one paper breaks a story, rival papers will purposefully ignore it, or even make an effort to knock it down." In the midst of New York City's near-bankruptcy crisis of 1975, Newfield exposed a plot to sell Madison Square Garden to the city-owned Off-Track Betting Corporation for $1 so the Garden Corporation could lease back the building and avoid paying $2.5 million per year in property taxes. *The New York Times* ignored the story until the state senate decided to investigate and the deal was called off.

Newfield, who had perceived himself as an advocacy journalist, began doing investigative articles for the *Voice* near the end of 1969. His first series revealed that 200 slum children died every year from lead poisoning contracted by eating paint flakes off tenement walls. A housing organizer tipped him to the story and doctors were willing to talk about it. "I never have any trouble finding sources," he says. However, no one informant hands over the whole story. "Investigative reporting," says Newfield, "is slow, piecemeal work."

Six years after he became investigative, Newfield, at the age of forty, was recognized as one of the premier investigative journalists in New York, a power to be reckoned with, even though his newspaper, while tamer and slicker, had yet to crash the inner circles of the New York newspaper establishment.

2

Washington's Master Watchdogs

IT WAS THE MIDDLE of August and the two-month-old Watergate story had bogged down again. Carl Bernstein and Bob Woodward of the Washington *Post* spent hours on the telephone every day, trying to turn up a fresh lead. All to little avail. Bits and pieces of information dribbled in, but not enough for a follow-up to their August 1 bombshell disclosing that $25,000 collected for President Nixon's reelection committee by Minneapolis businessman Kenneth H. Dahlberg had ended up in the Miami bank account of Watergate burglar Bernard L. Barker, the first public linking of the June 17, 1972, wiretapping incident with Nixon campaign funds.

Bernstein called employes of the Texas Committee for the Re-election of the President in search of new details about $89,000 that had reached Barker from Mexico City. He finally reached the head of the Texas committee, Robert H. Allen, but Allen wouldn't discuss the matter. Woodward pried some new tidbits out of a source in the Government Accounting Office, but they did not add up to a story. The most frustrating calls of all were those they made to officials and employes of the Committee for the Re-election of the President (CRP). A Washington *Post* researcher had obtained a copy of the campaign committee's telephone roster from a friend, and the reporters had deciphered the identities of such key people as division managers and secretaries from the extension numbers. But none of them would talk to Woodward or Bernstein on the telephone.

By now it was clear that CRP was deeply involved in the Watergate bugging incident. The best prospect for digging out more facts of its involvement was to find someone at CRP who had inside knowledge he could be persuaded to reveal. So Woodward and Bernstein, impelled by the determination that would eventually win them a Pulitzer Prize and contribute to the historic downfall of an American president, began to make personal calls at the homes of CRP members. They went at night, after regular working hours, knocking on their doors and using any means necessary: charm, cajolery, brashness or tricks, to get inside and erode their resistance. It was at this point that the two reporters' work on the Watergate story became true investigative reporting.

Until then, they had operated with persistence and resourcefulness, but not investigative originality. Most of their exclusives had been based on information obtained secondhand from government investigators, or extracted from other resources, with aggressive techniques that did not go beyond what most reporters and editors consider routine. Their efforts at times verged on the original unearthing of information, but did not really take on the characteristics of original investigation until that became the only way to make further progress.

Their first Watergate scoop had revealed that James W. McCord, Jr., one of the five men caught inside the Democratic National headquarters at the Watergate office-hotel complex, was a full-time salaried employe of CRP instead of a former contract consultant as described by U.S. Attorney General John Mitchell shortly before Mitchell resigned as head of CRP. This story, which ran two days after the Watergate arrests and which provided the first glimpse of a high-level cover-up, was obtained through resourceful telephoning.

From a cross-reference directory of addresses and phone numbers, Woodward and Bernstein got the names of tenants in the building where McCord had an office for his security consultant agency. Calling these tenants at home on a Sunday, they located an attorney who remembered that a former employe of his, or her father, knew McCord. Her name, he thought, was Westall. When the reporters could get nowhere with that name, they called people with similar last names, which led them to Harlan A. Westrell. Westrell not only told them a good deal about McCord, but also provided names of McCord associates and friends, who in turn gave them additional names as well as background information about McCord. Among the significant facts that emerged was that McCord was a full-time employe of CRP. This telephone tracking technique reflected considerable initiative and persistence on the reporters' part, but it's standard procedure in an aggressive newsroom.

So was the way they pieced together their next big Watergate exclusive, the story that linked Watergate to the White House through E. Howard Hunt's connections with both. A police reporter for the *Post* named Eugene Bachinski had learned from a police source that address books confiscated from two of the Watergate suspects contained Hunt's name and phone number, plus notations suggesting a White House connection. Woodward phoned the White House and asked for Hunt. The operator rang an extension, got no answer, then put the call through to the office of White House special counsel Charles W. Colson. A secretary there said Hunt wasn't in and gave Woodward the number of a public relations firm.

The reporter called the White House personnel office and learned that Hunt was on the payroll as a consultant to Colson. At the public relations firm, he got Hunt, himself, on the phone. Asked bluntly why his name and phone number were in the Watergate address books, Hunt was caught off guard. He betrayed astonishment before saying he wouldn't talk about it and hanging up. Woodward then phoned White House aide Ken W. Clawson, a former *Post* reporter, to ask about Hunt's White House duties. Clawson said Hunt had been a consultant on the Pentagon Papers and a narcotics project, but had not worked for the White House in almost three months. From the president of the public relations firm, Woodward learned that Hunt had been in the CIA. A CIA spokesman confirmed it. A friend in the government, who would later become the most celebrated of Woodward's and Bernstein's sources as "Deep Throat," told Woodward off-the-record that Hunt was a prime suspect in the case. It all added up to enough for a story saying a White House consultant was linked to the Watergate burglars.

Even the important Dahlberg disclosure, though perhaps the most decisive development in keeping Woodward and Bernstein on the Watergate story, was produced more by routine news-gathering methods, tenaciously applied, than by investigative journalism.

This part of the Watergate story began with a July 25, 1972, *New York Times* article on the discovery from "sources involved in" the FBI's Watergate investigation that several phone calls had been made to CRP headquarters from Barker's home and office in Miami prior to the June 17 break-in. Many of the calls had gone to an office used by G. Gordon Liddy, a campaign committee lawyer fired for refusing to answer the FBI's questions about Watergate. In the weeks preceding this article, there had been a long dry spell in new revelations. The *Post's* Watergate reporters had actually been taken off the story. Bernstein had been reassigned to Virginia politics and Woodward had gone on vacation. Now Bernstein was called back to work the phone call story. He confirmed the calls with a source in the telephone company, but, more significantly, also learned that some of Barker's phone records had been subpoenaed by a local district attorney in Florida.

Phone calls to Miami led to identification of Richard E. Gerstein, state attorney for Dade County, as the source of the subpoena. Gerstein referred Bernstein to his chief investigator, Martin Dardis, who invited the reporter to Miami to discuss subpoenaed phone records and bank records. Bernstein asked him about $89,000 that had been deposited and withdrawn from Barker's account, a matter explained by Barker's attorney as part of an aborted real estate deal not related to Watergate. Dardis said more than $89,000 was involved and it had come to Miami from a lawyer in Mexico City. When Dardis wouldn't discuss it further on the phone, Bernstein arranged an appointment in Miami for July 31.

On the plane to Miami, Bernstein discovered *The New York Times* had beaten him to the story of the $89,000's journey from Mexico City to Barker's account in the form of four cashier's checks bearing the name of Manuel Ogarrio Daguerre, a prominent Mexican lawyer who denied any knowledge of the checks or Barker. The *Times* story did not mention, however, a fifth cashier's check for $25,000 that Bernstein found in the records Dardis let him inspect.

The $25,000 check had been drawn on a bank in Boca Raton, Florida, and bore Dahlberg's name. Dardis, according to Woodward's and Bernstein's best-selling book on their Watergate exploits, *All the President's Men*, did not know who Dahlberg was. Dardis has said his office had already identified Dahlberg, but he has not said that he told Bernstein about it. In any case, Bernstein and Woodward, now back from vacation, set out to identify and locate Dahlberg. Their work now began to border on the investigative.

Up to then, most of what they knew about the case had come from sources who had information from government investigations, either by federal agencies or Gerstein's office. In a critique of the press' role in the Watergate scandal, Edward Jay Epstein, an author who has written extensively about the news media, wrote that "almost all the pertinent facts were in the hands of the FBI and federal prosecutors" within a week of the Watergate arrests, including the role of Dahlberg's $25,000. "It was thus governmental agencies that developed information about Watergate, not the press," Epstein said. "What the press did between the break-in in June and the trial in January was to leak the case developed by the federal and Florida prosecutors to the public." Though Epstein acknowledged that the "leaking" constituted a significant public service, he seemed to overlook the fact that reporters worked hard to pry the Watergate "leaks" out of their sources. No FBI agent or disgruntled CRP officer walked in unexpectedly with bundles of exclusive disclosures, as Daniel Ellsberg had done for *The New York Times* with the Pentagon Papers. Nor had many others volunteered "leaks." Woodward and Bernstein were among those who made their own leaks with tireless striving.

Yet, their reporting had not been truly investigative. Though investigative methods often are used to corroborate leaked information, follow up on tips, or get the additional material needed to construct a publishable story, Woodward and Bernstein had not done that, either, before they set out to identify Dahlberg. Now their fact-gathering, though again done by telephone, took on some investigative aspects.

Bernstein started with the bank in Boca Raton, getting a name and phone number of a bank officer from the police. The bank officer had never heard of Dahlberg, nor had two other bank officers, but the bank's president remembered him as the owner of a winter home there and a director of a Fort Lauderdale bank. Bernstein learned from that bank's president that Dahlberg had been a prominent Midwestern figure in Nixon's 1968 campaign. Bernstein promptly relayed that information to Woodward in Washington where his colleague had Dahlberg on the phone in Minneapolis. Woodward had located Dahlberg after a clipping of a photograph showing Dahlberg with Sen. Hubert H. Humphrey of Minnesota was found in the *Post's* files. Woodward got Dahlberg's phone number simply by calling information in Minnesota's largest city.

Under Woodward's questioning about the $25,000 check, Dahlberg said he had delivered funds only to the Nixon reelection committee. He was the committee's chief fund raiser for the Midwest, he explained. After a pause filled with silent tension, Dahlberg revealed he had given the $25,000 check either to Hugh W. Sloan, Jr., the campaign committee's treasurer, or to Maurice Stans, its finance chairman and Number One fund raiser.

The Dahlberg article put the *Post* in front of *The New York Times* for good in the Watergate story. It also revived the *Post's* enthusiasm for the story. After that, it seemed taken for granted that Woodward and Bernstein would stick with it, even when it stalled again a couple of weeks later. By this time, the two reporters also were taking for granted that they would keep working together.

In the beginning, when they had been assigned to cover the Watergate arrests because the incident appeared to be more than a routine burglary, though no one began to suspect its true dimensions, the two reporters had regarded each other warily. Woodward, a twenty-nine-year-old Yale graduate who dressed conservatively, had moved to the *Post* from a small Maryland newspaper by pestering a *Post* editor into hiring him. He was uneasy over Bernstein's reputation for moving in on another reporter's story and taking over, especially when he discovered Bernstein rewriting his Watergate stories to make them less awkward and more concise.

Bernstein is a totally different personality. While Woodward is conscientious and reserved, Bernstein is brash and freewheeling. A college dropout who started his newspaper career as a sixteen-year-old copy boy, Bernstein, at twenty-eight, had done a variety of reporting, including an investigative series on fraudulent practices in career schools. He feared Woodward might cramp his style.

By the time of the Dahlberg story, however, the two felt comfortable working together. They realized the project was too big for one reporter and each one's strong points complemented the other's. They made a good team. Colleagues at the *Post* had begun calling them "Woodstein."

Such was the situation when they embarked on the first full-fledged investigative endeavors of their Watergate coverage, their nightly calls on officials and employes of CRP in search of informed persons whose tongues might be loosened. They found it rough going. Most refused to talk with them. Many were openly frightened. But Woodward and Bernstein were not put off easily. They did everything they could think of to keep conversations going before doors were closed in their faces. Gradually they accumulated scraps of information indicating destruction of records after the Watergate arrests, instructions to CRP staffers not to volunteer information to the FBI, and a curiously limited scope to FBI interviews of CRP employes.

One night, after about a month, Bernstein visited the small suburban home of a CRP bookkeeper, a woman who told him to leave when she realized he was a reporter. In the foyer of the house where he had been admitted by the woman's sister, Bernstein noticed a pack of cigarettes on a table and asked for one. He started talking, then asked if he could sit down while he smoked the cigarette. The bookkeeper consented, but said she couldn't tell him anything. As they chatted, the woman began trying to guess the identities of the *Post's* sources, mentioning new names that Bernstein tried hard to impress on his memory. Finally she told him that many at CRP had lied to the grand jury, and that Sloan, who had left CRP, ostensibly for personal reasons, had quit because he wanted no part of what he suspected was going on. She said Jeb Stuart Magruder was involved, and another assistant to Mitchell at CRP. The bookkeeper told him that six men, including Magruder and Liddy, got money to finance political espionage activities from a $350,000 cash fund in Stans' safe. She said Sloan knew who the other four were, too. She wouldn't say their names, however, and couldn't say for sure that the Watergate bugging was one of the projects financed from the fund.

The interview was perhaps the most important that Bernstein ever conducted. It opened the floodgates. The two reporters and their editors at the *Post* were now convinced the scandal would reach at least to the top of CRP, and they had valuable new leads. Among the steps Woodstein took as a result was to put pressure on Sloan, who became one of their chief sources.

Another chief source, Deep Throat, the anonymous executive branch official who would meet Woodward in an underground garage at two o'clock in the morning after the reporter signaled him by moving a flower pot to the rear of the balcony on his sixth-floor apartment, served primarily to corroborate what Woodstein learned elsewhere. He rarely gave them fresh information, but helped them make sense out of new discoveries, and fit them into the growing tangle of facts, rumors, speculations, and clues. It was after the interview with the bookkeeper that Deep Throat's help became crucial.

Deep Throat confirmed that the $350,000 cash fund at CRP had paid for political espionage, and that top assistants of Mitchell were involved in disbursements. He corroborated the bookkeeper's naming of Magruder and Herbert L. Porter as two who got at least $50,000 from Stans' safe. Though Deep Throat was often the vital second source required by *Post* editors, he was the first to say definitely that the espionage fund had financed the Watergate bugging. The second source this time was Sloan, who reluctantly yielded to Bernstein's blandishments to reveal details when the reporter drove out to his home in the Virginia suburb of McLean.

Sloan also provided crucial confirmation for a story pieced together by Woodstein on the large-scale destruction of records at CRP after June 17 and other measures directed by Mitchell's top assistant to conceal information from the FBI and the grand jury. Sloan further gave Woodstein the basic information, later confirmed by a federal investigation source, for one of their biggest Watergate stories, that the authorization of Mitchell, himself, had been needed for expenditures from the fund.

Late in September, Bernstein got the telephone call that would lead to their next sensational revelation, the existence of a massive dirty-tricks campaign against Democratic presidential candidates in 1972 by a young attorney named Donald Segretti who had been recruited for the operation by White House appointments secretary Dwight Chapin. Investigative reporters often find that their reputations bring in useful tips and information and try to devise ways to get maximum benefit from this, but this was the only worthwhile tip Woodstein ever received unsolicited from a stranger. The call was from a government lawyer unconnected with the Watergate investigation who said his information might be related to the things the *Post* had been writing about.

The lawyer told Bernstein about a friend in Tennessee, an assistant state attorney general named Alex Shipley, who had been approached to take part in a program to disrupt the campaigns of Democratic candidates in the 1972 spring presidential primaries.

Shipley, contacted at his home by phone, gave Bernstein details, Segretti's name, the fact that he lived in California, possibly Los Angeles, and the names of three others he thought Segretti had approached in other states. These three confirmed Segretti's invitation into undercover campaign work of some kind, but declined to discuss details.

Through a contact in a credit-card company, Bernstein determined that Segretti had indeed traveled to many of the key primary states in 1971. During a telephone conversation with a Justice Department official, he threw out Segretti's name, and was told the matter was part of the investigation. The *Post's* West Coast stringer located Segretti's apartment in Marina del Rey, and learned that he had been a friend of Chapin, Porter, White House Press Secretary Ron Ziegler, and other White House aides at the University of Southern California. The Justice Department official acknowledged that Segretti was connected with political sabotage. Making more calls, Bernstein found a Justice Department attorney who was willing to tell him that Segretti's operation was part of basic campaign strategy that came right from "the top," higher than Mitchell. Deep Throat confirmed that sabotage activities by Segretti and others was part of a massive campaign masterminded from the White House, but that federal investigators had shelved that aspect of the case as unrelated to Watergate.

This story, the first alleging direct White House involvement in illicit campaign activities connected to Watergate, was acknowledged even by media critic Epstein as resulting from an instance "in which the press rather than government investigators uncovered evidence."

Woodstein added more exclusives later, most notably the involvement of Nixon's top aide, H. R. Haldeman, in control of the espionage fund. Their report that Sloan had told the grand jury of Haldeman's involvement was one of the few errors they committed during their Watergate reporting, which Epstein described as ninety-nine percent accurate. But the fact of Haldeman's involvement turned out to be true.

Woodstein made most of the important Watergate disclosures before McCord's March, 1973, letter to Judge John Sirica broke open the case, woke up the rest of the press to the full dimensions of the scandal, and confirmed much of what Woodward and Bernstein had written. Reporters for a few other publications—especially the Los Angeles *Times*, *Time* magazine, *Newsweek*, Jack Anderson's column, and, sporadically, *The New York Times*, the Washington *Star-News*, *Newsday*, and the Miami *Herald*—dabbled in pursuing parts of the Watergate story, but none with Woodstein's vigor or grasp of its potential until 1973. It was Woodward, Bernstein, and the Washington *Post* who did the most to keep the Watergate story alive despite savage attacks on their credibility by the White House and Republican leaders, and even criticism from some segments of the news media. They also gave the American people the first inklings of the complicity and cover-up at the very top level of their government, the story that later dwarfed all other aspects of Watergate.

Though Bernstein had done some previous investigative reporting, Watergate was his and Woodward's first investigative assignment of any magnitude. It's not surprising that investigative reporters who have been quietly plodding away at their tedious, painstaking, often frustrating work for twenty or twenty-five years without a major prize or other reward beyond the satisfaction of a job well done, might be a bit resentful toward the overnight celebrity attained by Woodward and Bernstein with their very first venture into investigative journalism. Woodward and Bernstein were not among the ten best investigative reporters in Washington named in an article by Washington *Star* writer Shirley Elder in the August, 1975, issue of *Washingtonian* magazine. "Were they one-shot wonders?" Elder asked.

Others are suspicious of the new public fascination with investigative reporting produced by Watergate, its myth-like popularity among young people who see it as a glamorous avenue to quick achievement and fame. They fear it will spawn a spate of hasty, over-zealous attempts to get in on the new fad, resulting in shoddy, superficial journalism, and possibly unjust harm to innocent targets.

However, most investigative journalists, even those who are critical of some Woodstein techniques or standards of proof, are pleased. They welcome the acceptance at last for what was long viewed as a slightly distasteful brand of journalism. They believe it will inspire journalists and news organizations to conduct more frequent serious probing beneath the surface of events.

As for Woodward and Bernstein, they have exhibited some discomfort with their celebrity status, long avoiding interviews, TV talk shows and other mainstays of the famous. They planned to resume their journalism careers and pursue investigative projects, but other demands intruded. There was the filming of the movie based on their first book, then the writing of a second book, *The Final Days,* about Nixon's last 100 days in the White House. Published in the spring of 1976 amidst new controversy, that book required another leave from the *Post* and was still being given final touches as 1976 began.

Woodward did return to reporting in the summer of 1975, and produced the only story either of them did since Watergate that attracted much attention. This was the article about Hunt's telling associates of a plan to assassinate Jack Anderson. (Hunt said the plot was only to drug Anderson to make the columnist sound bad on his radio show.)

Woodward and Bernstein reportedly discovered, while working on their books, that they couldn't work well together after all. But the question on most journalists' minds—and Woodstein's as well, whether they remained a team or not—was: What can they do for an encore? How can they possibly top their first big story?

After seventy-four-year-old Bernhard Rosee walked into his office one day in 1972 with a tale of illegal price manipulations in the Chicago Board of Trade, America's largest commodity exchange, Clark Mollenhoff tried to prod the federal Commodity Exchange Authority into an investigation.

When nothing happened, Mollenhoff, who perhaps has more investigative journalism under his belt than anyone else in Washington, turned to Congress for action. He told Congressman Neal Smith of Iowa about Rosee, who had won a $700,000 court judgment over his expulsion from the Chicago Board of Trade. Mollenhoff also informed Iowa's Senator-elect Dick Clark of the case, giving him copies of columns he had written about it, and making sure to stress "the importance of an honest and effective operation of commodity markets to the nation and especially to the Iowa farming communities."

When there was still no response by Congress or the CEA, Mollenhoff began preparing an investigation of his own, even though he was then confined to a hospital bed recovering from surgery for removal of a brain tumor the size of an orange. He wrote an outline for an in-depth probe of the commodity exchange by the Des Moines *Register and Tribune's* bureau in Washington. As bureau chief, Mollenhoff, a big, six-foot-four bear of a man with prodigious energy and a gruff manner, would direct a team effort, drawing on his knowledge of past grain scandals, and his familiarity with investigations by the Securities and Exchange Commission. The legwork would be done by two aggressive young reporters, George Anthan, thirty-six, and James Risser, thirty-four, who Mollenhoff considers among the best investigative journalists in the nation's capital.

Out of the hospital and back at work, Mollenhoff gave Anthan and Risser copies of a 1965 report on the CEA by the General Accounting Office, the watchdog fiscal agency set up by Congress to monitor spending by the executive branch. After saturating themselves with information about commodity markets and the CEA through intensive reading, the three reporters interviewed CEA administrator Alex Caldwell on whether changes recommended by the GAO in 1965 had been implemented and why the CEA had not acted in the Rosee case.

Mollenhoff also had information from a source in the U.S. Department of Agriculture that a more current report by the Agriculture Department's inspector general had repeated the 1965 findings and recommendations of the GAO. When Caldwell deprecated the GAO's understanding of commodity market operations and dismissed the recommendations as outdated, Mollenhoff asked if there had been any more recent investigations or reports. Unlike the tactic often used by investigative reporters of pretending to greater knowledge than one actually has, Mollenhoff's technique here was to appear less informed. This presented an apparent opportunity to get away with a lie. Caldwell fell into the trap, at first denying there had been a more recent investigation. But he gradually conceded its existence as it became clear that Mollenhoff, in pressing the question further, knew more than he had first let on. Caldwell finally admitted the recent report had raised some of the same questions as the earlier one because the improvements had not been made.

That interview, along with specifics on commodity market problems and operations gathered by Anthan and Risser in Chicago, Kansas City and New York, formed the basis for the team's first series of articles on irregularities and abuses in commodity trading, and weaknesses in the Agriculture Department's regulation system. Combined with follow-up work by Mollenhoff, who made sure key members of Congress saw the articles and were urged to do something about the wrongdoing they revealed, the articles prompted five congressional investigations. Mollenhoff also made sure his team continued to spew out stories about their discoveries, the Rosee case, the Congressional investigations, and proposed new legislation—all to keep the pressure for reform from faltering. In the end, Congress passed the Commodity Futures Trading Act of 1974, the first major reform of commodity market regulation in more than fifty years. It set up a new Commodity Futures Trading Commission to replace the ineffective CEA.

The investigations touched off by Rosee's visit to Mollenhoff's office also produced two more batches of articles on lawbreaking, conflicts of interest, and unethical practices in the food industry. The first was a seven-part series on meat packers and irregularities in the enforcement of the 1921 Packers and Stockyards Act. Much of the articles' impact was based on information pried out of government records through use of the federal Freedom of Information Act, an invaluable tool for investigative reporters, especially since it was amended in 1975. Senate and House probes followed, and bills to make sweeping changes in the law were introduced.

The second group of stories, which turned out to be the most sensational of all, were written by Risser, who, like Mollenhoff, is a lawyer as well as a journalist. Risser's investigation evolved from a trip by Mollenhoff to Mexico while working on the packers and stockyards articles. During a discussion at the U.S. Embassy on the way huge grain purchases and order cancellations by the Soviet Union and other foreign countries could disrupt American grain markets, an agricultural attaché mentioned that Japan had recently canceled a large contract to buy U.S. corn on the grounds that the quality was substandard.

Recalling scandals in the early 1950s about the mixing of rotten grain with good, Mollenhoff asked if America's grain inspection system was effective. He was told there were still so many problems that it was hard to tell if Japan's explanation was valid or just an excuse to get out of a bad contract. Ever alert to an area ripe for investigation, Mollenhoff verified the contract cancellation by Japan on his return to Washington and assigned Risser to investigate the Agriculture Department's grain inspection system.

Risser soon turned up a press release on the indictment of five grain inspectors who worked for a private firm rather than the government. It struck Mollenhoff that inspections by a private firm opened up a vast vulnerability to conflicts of interest. The indictment of five inspectors in New Orleans might be merely the tip of an iceberg of wrongdoing. Risser began making phone calls to New Orleans and Houston, where federal prosecutors appeared to be most active, and contacted helpful Washington sources. In April, Risser went to New Orleans and Houston to talk with investigators and federal officials, examine records, and conduct his own investigation.

What followed was a series of articles in May and June of 1975 exposing widespread corruption in the grading and shipping of export grain, including bribery and intimidation of inspectors to certify dirty ships as clean, and to overlook the false grading of grain. Risser's first story reported the activities of federal agents and prosecutors and the findings of his own probings, which, he wrote, "indicate that the government's system of grading export grain and inspecting ships is full of conflicts of interest and the potential for a variety of abuses." His article raised the question of whether indictments of inspectors would be enough, or a complete overhaul of the system would be necessary.

Subsequent articles revealed that Agriculture Department officials had been warned of possible bribery in New Orleans export elevators by foreign grain buyers as much as six years earlier; that the boards of trade and other private agencies for which the inspectors worked were controlled by grain and shipping interests; that several foreign countries had complained about receiving misgraded, low-quality, damaged, insect-infested, and short-weighted grain from the United States; and that an Agriculture Department official admitted there was no effective method in use to spot dishonesty in the weighing of grain.

The New York Times, jumping onto the story in the wake of Risser's first articles in the Des Moines *Register and Tribune,* reported that Agriculture Department employes charged with overseeing the inspection and grading of export grain had been harassed and threatened. Car tires had been slashed and one supervisor had been told his kneecaps would be broken.

Risser also used one of Mollenhoff's favorite ploys, getting government officials involved in the story by eliciting expressions of shock and demands for action to be quoted in follow-up articles—and by urging them to take action themselves. Senator Clark announced a probe by a Foreign Relations subcommittee on multinational corporations. Chairman Herman Talmadge of the Senate Agriculture Committee ordered an investigation by his committee. Iowa Congressman Edward Mezvinsky introduced a bill to put grain grading and ship inspections under direct control of the federal government. Agriculture Secretary Earl Butz was reported as favoring a government takeover of the grain inspection system. Senator Humphrey of Minnesota introduced a bill to give Butz emergency powers to revoke the licenses of private inspection agencies. Congressman Smith of Iowa and others were quoted on the need for changes in the system. Risser reported that Clark had learned of kickbacks to grain elevator operators to misweigh grain shipments. The reporter had grasped well how to make good use of a politician's eagerness to get his name in the paper in a favorable context.

Though much of the information in Risser's stories came from government investigations, the scandal might not have grown beyond a few little-noticed indictments if he hadn't exposed the inspection system's weaknesses. By the end of 1975, there had been fifty-seven indictments of individuals and firms on bribery, conspiracy, and other charges. Bunge Corporation, one of the world's largest grain companies, and several of its executives pleaded guilty or no contest to theft conspiracy counts. The investigation was spreading from New Orleans to other grain ports. All this might not have happened if Risser's articles had not exposed the scandal to public attention and generated pressure on authorities to pursue their prosecutions vigorously, and Congress might not have acted with alacrity to correct the system. Risser won three major journalism awards in 1976 for his stories—the Worth Bingham Memorial Award for investigative reporting, the Raymond Clapper Award for "exceptionally meritorious reporting," and a Pulitzer Prize for national reporting.

Mollenhoff does not believe that virtue triumphs without any help, or that corruption is excised merely by exposure. An investigative reporter who wants his work to produce reforms can't afford to just write his stories and go home. He must keep pounding away, applying constant pressure not only in print, but also by confronting those who have a responsibility or authority to act—a prosecutor or a congressional committee—and demanding to know what they will do about it. Mollenhoff goes further. He demands that they do something. "If you want to be effective in this business," he snorts, "you've got to follow through."

Much of Mollenhoff's success during thirty-five years as one of the nation's premier investigative journalists is due to his resourceful and tenacious follow-through. He never stops pushing. If no one pays much attention to his stories—which often happens since the Des Moines *Register and Tribune* circulates far from Washington—Mollenhoff doesn't let it go at that. He calls on congressmen, committee investigators, law enforcement agents, even other newsmen, to make sure they know about his revelations and are pressured to take action or give them wider exposure. Investigative disclosures, ironically, often have little impact unless they are picked up and expanded by other news media. Many an important story has vanished into the atmosphere with hardly a scratch in the course of events because it was ignored or overlooked by other media.

Though post-publication follow-up pressure is a common practice among many investigative journalists, some think Mollenhoff carries it too far. He gets even more disapproval for his habit of working closely with authorities before publication, and using them to get information for him or put it on the record so he can publish it without fear of libel judgment losses. Mollenhoff has practically perfected the tactic of feeding a senator or congressman facts that he hesitates to publish for lack of foolproof documentation, so that they can be used in a floor speech or put in the Congressional Record. Mollenhoff can then publish it as part of a privileged public record without danger of losing a libel suit. Other reporters also have employed this technique, but none with the verve and effectiveness of Mollenhoff, who also feeds information and questions to congressional committee investigators in return for a share in the fruits of their probings. Trading information and leads with government investigators and congressional committees that have the subpoena and immunity powers lacked by the press is also an accepted practice among most investigative reporters, but few can match Mollenhoff's adroitness at it.

In the Wolf Ladejinsky security case of 1954, which Mollenhoff says was "as much a one-man push as any I have seen in Washington," he persuaded a congressman to go on the record in Ladejinsky's defense. This not only gave the case official standing, it enabled Mollenhoff to break the story, which in turn brought in new leads. Mollenhoff had begun to dig after learning that Ladejinsky, a Russian-born employe of the Agriculture Department, had been fired for security reasons though cleared for security by the State Department. After several Mollenhoff stories, the Agriculture Department withdrew its charges against Ladejinsky. Besides rectifying what he perceived to be an injustice, Mollenhoff received several 1955 journalism awards, including the Sigma Delta Chi Award for Washington correspondence, a Heywood Broun Award, and the Raymond Clapper Award for Washington correspondence.

Years later, after five men were arrested inside the headquarters of the Democratic National Committee in the Watergate case, Mollenhoff almost succeeded in instigating a preelection investigation of the incident by Congress in the fall of 1972. As described in *Game Plan for Disaster*, one of several books Mollenhoff has found time to write, Mollenhoff was instrumental in an attempt by the House Banking and Currency Committee to launch a Watergate investigation.

He convinced the committee it had jurisdiction because an international flow of money between banks had been involved in the transfer of $89,000 from Mexico City to the Watergate burglars in Miami. Under the leadership of crusty, seventy-nine-year-old Congressman Wright Patman of Texas, the committee attempted to start hearings in October, 1972. President Nixon's aides, however, with help from Republican Congressman Garry Brown of Michigan, managed to thwart Patman's move by pressuring six Democrats on the committee to join with Republicans in voting down Patman's request for the necessary subpoena power.

Mollenhoff achieved his most spectacular success with his prodding of authorities in the area of labor union corruption. His investigations and relentless badgering of congressional committees over a period of years led to the famous McClellan Committee hearings on labor racketeering in the late 1950s, Robert F. Kennedy's crusade against Teamster Union president James R. Hoffa, and two of journalism's most prestigious awards in 1958, a Pulitzer Prize for national reporting and a Sigma Delta Chi Award for public service.

It all started in January, 1953. After six years of exposing corruption in Des Moines, Iowa, two years in the U.S. Navy, and a year at Harvard University on a Nieman Fellowship for distinguished journalists, Mollenhoff had been assigned in 1950 to the Des Moines *Register and Tribune's* Washington bureau, part of the Cowles Publications bureau, where he plunged uninhibitedly into exposés of the Truman Administration tax scandals, and later the Dixon-Yates and Sherman Adams scandals of the Eisenhower administration. In January, 1953, Mollenhoff went to Minneapolis at the request of Gideon Seymour, executive editor of the Minneapolis *Star and Tribune*, a Cowles newspaper, to investigate racketeering in the Teamsters Union. Mollenhoff had little experience in labor reporting, as he pointed out in his book, *Tentacles of Power*, but he went immediately to work.

Meeting with several rough-looking truck drivers in a tiny office in St. Paul, Mollenhoff was dumbfounded to hear tales of corruption, brutality, sweetheart contracts, and underworld infiltration. The meeting had been arranged after Mollenhoff began talking to a few Teamsters Union members and lawyers. Ironically, a prime influence behind their eagerness to reveal corruption was a certain up-and-coming force in the union who calculated that exposés would help him unhorse his Minneapolis rivals. This was an International Teamsters Union vice president named Jimmy Hoffa.

After hearing about misuse of union funds, intimidation by gun-toting business agents, looting of pension funds, and violations of federal and state labor laws, Mollenhoff inquired why local police and prosecutors had taken no action. The Teamsters laughed. The Minneapolis Teamsters had so much clout in state and local politics that a spot was reserved for them on every grand jury.

Editor Seymour wanted to start a series on Teamsters Union corruption at once, but Mollenhoff warned it would be better to publish only material that could be obtained from the records of a court or a congressional committee. He said the witnesses he had interviewed might not remain firm in their stories under oath or threats, and the paper could "be subject to losing a few million dollars in libel suits." Though eager to expose the misuse of union power, Mollenhoff was frankly frightened by the magnitude of that power. For the first time in his newspaper career, he found himself advising caution instead of "hitting fast and hard." He suggested an approach to Senator Charles Tobey of New Hampshire, head of a committee that was investigating labor racketeering in the International Longshoremen's Association along the New York-New Jersey waterfront. They agreed to get the story out carefully through a congressional committee and write only articles based on public records.

Tobey promised to investigate the Minneapolis Teamsters as soon as he was finished with the longshoremen, but died before he could. Senator John Bricker of Ohio, who took over chairmanship of the committee, showed little enthusiasm for a Teamster probe and later turned it over to the Senate Labor Committee. Mollenhoff looked about for another committee to undertake the task. Congressman Clare Hoffman of Michigan, head of the House Committee on Government Operations, was interested, but had too little support on the committee. It would be three years before a serious investigation of labor rackets by Congress would get underway. A subcommittee of the House Labor Committee held hearings on Teamsters Union affairs, but they were focused on Detroit and Chicago and took only meager testimony concerning Minneapolis. Little was accomplished. Mollenhoff, who had only scratched the surface of

Teamsters Union corruption in several cautiously worded articles, felt dejected. Fellow reporters needled him about his efforts to prod Congress into a big investigation, even calling him "reactionary." Most of the press ignored the union corruption story from 1953 to 1956.

In 1956, Mollenhoff began trying to talk Robert Kennedy, counsel for the Senate's Permanent Investigating Subcommittee, into a Teamsters investigation. He told Kennedy it was a great opportunity and needed to be done, but Kennedy showed faint interest. Mollenhoff kept hounding him, half-jokingly questioning his courage and insisting it would make him famous. Kennedy began to show flickers of interest.

In August, as the subcommittee wound up an inquiry into racketeering and fraud in the procurement of military clothing, Mollenhoff made another pitch to Kennedy. He insisted the Internal Revenue Service, the U.S. Labor Department, and other congressional committees had fallen down on the job, and there was no one else he could turn to. He maintained there was so much corruption to be exposed that an investigation could have more impact than the famous Kefauver hearings on organized crime a few years earlier. Mollenhoff gave Kennedy and the committee staff some of the information in his files, along with stories of similar corruption and underworld ties in Portland, Oregon, by reporters Wallace Turner and William Lambert of the Portland *Oregonian,* and in Seattle by Edwin Guthman of the Seattle *Times.* Mollenhoff arranged for some of the investigators who had participated in the earlier, limited congressional probes to talk to Kennedy.

Kennedy finally yielded. He got authority for an investigation from committee chairman John McClellan and it began September 12. Mollenhoff kept in close touch with Kennedy and his investigators, giving them leads, writing stories on their activities, and passing information to the committee from politicians who wanted to help, but not openly. Later, when a new special committee was formed to take over the investigation, Kennedy's brother, Senator John F. Kennedy from Massachusetts, became a member. Senator Kennedy backed the push for an all-out probe despite warnings from political friends that it would damage his presidential ambitions. Public hearings began February 26, 1957, with reporters Turner and Lambert as the first witnesses, and continued for four years, delving into the activities of Teamsters across the nation and to the highest leadership levels.

Teamster president Dave Beck and his successor, Hoffa, tried to thwart the committee at every turn, using all the political muscle they could muster. But in the end, Beck went to jail for failing to pay income tax on money taken from the union's treasury, Congress passed the Landrum-Griffin labor reform bill, Senator Kennedy became President, and Robert Kennedy, as Attorney General in his brother's administration, launched a concerted drive to prosecute Hoffa that eventually put him in prison for jury tampering and fraudulent handling of pension fund loans.

Mollenhoff, the catalyst who had made it all happen, went on to other stories and soon began displeasing his old friends, the Kennedys, with disclosures in the Billie Sol Estes and TFX fighter-plane scandals. Though he did not unearth those stories originally (the Estes story, for instance, was first exposed by a small Texas weekly called the Pecos *Independent & Enterprise*), Mollenhoff's aggressive follow-up digging turned up some of the more embarrassing revelations. The same was true later in the Bobby Baker case, which several reporters picked up after a lawsuit against Baker touched off the scandal.

Now fifty-five, Mollenhoff is as leading an expert on investigative journalism as one can find in America. He's won more awards than any other currently active reporter (including the 1973 Drew Pearson Foundation Award for sustained and significant contribution to investigative reporting), delivered more lectures on the topic, and played a larger role in the development of investigative reporting seminars for the American Press Institute over the past twenty years.

One of his permanent contributions to the API seminar program is a "Check List for Investigative Reporters" that outlines the places where misbehavior by public officials is most likely to be found. In local government, he includes the budget process; business interests of city councilmen and county commissioners; the system for purchasing and awarding contracts; licensing procedures, especially for liquor and beer interests; payroll padding, nepotism and patronage in hiring; travel expenditures; election procedures; the disposition of material seized by police; probate court records; the handling of criminal warrants by the prosecutor; civil suits, including divorces; real estate mortgage and tax records; school construction and purchasing contracts; highway department contracts; and health department records. Mollenhoff also is given credit for the phrase, "Follow the dollar," as the key to tracking down corruption.

Another critical place, says Mollenhoff, is the functioning of the courts and quasi-judicial agencies. "Lack of due process is often the root of corruption," he says. As a lawyer, Mollenhoff feels he understands due process better than the average journalist. "There's no question but that being a lawyer gives me an edge," he acknowledges, "in the business of analyzing evidence."

Mollenhoff's main weapon, however, is his incredible energy. Most investigative journalism is tedious, slogging work, a lot, as he says, of "routine crap," but that doesn't slow him any. He's the first in the office in the morning and the last to leave at night. He juggles several investigations at once; when one encounters a snag temporarily, he turns to another. "Too many people in this town just sit on their ass," he growls. Among the many books he's written are one on fraud and mismanagement in the Defense Department, and one on the influence of organized crime in government. His books aren't especially easy to read, but they're packed with facts. "I don't emphasize making it colorful," he explains. "I emphasize making it accurate."

Despite his unparalleled record, Mollenhoff is something of a pariah in the news media establishment. He's outspoken in his view that most Washington reporters don't do their jobs right, and many feel he's too rigid in other opinions as well. He was an investigative troublemaker long before it became fashionable, and much of his work has gone unappreciated even among journalists. He once lost an election for the presidency of the National Press Club because his ungentlemanly digging had irritated too many powerful members of the Washington press corps and their friends in government. Far from being bothered by any of this, Mollenhoff revels in his independence.

After he spent a year on the other side of the fence as a White House ombudsman in the Nixon administration in 1969–70, getting nothing but disillusionment for his belief that he could improve government ethics from within, fellow newsmen accorded him additional coolness. But he brushed it aside and went right back to booming tough questions at presidential news conferences and ferreting out unflattering facts about his former boss.

"Nixon made the mistake of thinking he could corral me in the White House and keep me under control," says Mollenhoff, who's a Republican. "But it doesn't make any difference to me if it's a conservative crook or a liberal crook, a Republican crook or a Democratic crook. A crook is a crook."

Mollenhoff views the new interest in investigative reporting as a "superficial faddist" one, but nevertheless welcome. Serious professional interest in investigative reporting has been on the rise steadily over the last twenty-five years, he believes, and Watergate provided a "sharp impetus" for further growth. The only problem, he says, is that there's "never enough time to do all the things we would like to do."

Jack Nelson always got along splendidly with the FBI when he was an investigative reporter for the Atlanta *Constitution*. Though newsmen seldom are able to cultivate a cooperative relationship with FBI agents, Nelson did so while covering the South's explosive civil rights scene in the early 1960s. He became close to Roy Moore, the FBI agent in charge of a special civil rights enforcement office in Jackson, Mississippi. When Nelson left the *Constitution* to set up an Atlanta bureau for the Los Angeles *Times* in 1965, he counted the federal agents among his friends as well as his sources. He even traded information with the FBI, giving agents access to what he learned in his investigations of Ku Klux Klan activities in Georgia and Mississippi. Everything was cozy. Some investigative reporters might say too cozy.

Six years later, on October 13, 1971, however, FBI Director J. Edgar Hoover called in David Kraslow, Nelson's boss as head of the Los Angeles *Times* Washington bureau, and tried to get Nelson fired.

Reading from papers on his desk, sometimes so rapidly as to be incoherent, Hoover accused Nelson of being "out to get" the FBI. He said Nelson had told an FBI informant that he was part of a nationwide movement to get rid of Hoover. Nelson, said Hoover, had boasted to other reporters that he was the only man in journalism with the courage to take on the FBI.

The famous G-man with the bulldog visage read to Kraslow from a memo he had sent to U.S. Attorney General John Mitchell describing a Los Angeles *Times* campaign against the FBI led by Nelson. He said Nelson had been heard at least four times, including by other newspapermen, to say he was "out to get" Hoover, and the reason he had been transferred from Atlanta to Washington in 1970 was to facilitate his pursuit of that nefarious goal.

Hoover ranted on. Nelson, he said, was well-known in Washington as an excessive drinker. He told Kraslow the FBI had learned from a publisher that Nelson, while drunk, had said Hoover was a homosexual. Agitated and tense, Hoover charged that inquiries by Nelson about the carpeting in Hoover's office proved a derogatory intent by Nelson.

Kraslow expressed incredulity that Nelson, whom he had known for years, could act that way, and defended him as a professional journalist of impeccable integrity. Hoover rejoined that Nelson was a Jekyll and Hyde personality who stayed on good behavior in Kraslow's presence, but was a different person otherwise. Hoover warned that Nelson would remain persona non grata at the FBI, but he would personally guarantee the FBI would cooperate with a "responsible member" of the *Times'* Washington bureau. Kraslow suggested that he discuss his complaints personally with Nelson, but Hoover recoiled at that idea, saying he had learned not to get in a pissing contest with a skunk.

A few days later Kraslow sent Hoover a letter stating that Nelson denied all the charges and he accepted Nelson's word. He enclosed a copy of a memo by Nelson replying specifically to each of Hoover's accusations. Kraslow also sent a letter of protest to Attorney General Mitchell. Nelson, a trim, square-faced man with a gracious manner and a soft Southern drawl who's been an investigative reporter ever since he exposed gambling payoffs as an eighteen-year-old reporter in Biloxi, Mississippi, in 1948, stayed on the job.

Since those cozy days in Atlanta, Nelson had written several things the FBI had found irritating. Hoover mentioned them all in his diatribe.

One was the Berrigan case fiasco, in which several antiwar activists —especially Philip Berrigan, a Catholic priest, and Elizabeth McAllister, a nun—were acquitted of plotting to kidnap Henry Kissinger, then President Nixon's national security adviser, and blow up the underground heating systems of government buildings in Washington.

Nelson and Washington bureau colleague Ronald J. Ostrow located lawyers who represented some of the witnesses in the case. Then they interviewed students and professors at Bucknell University while treating them to pizza and beer in a second-floor apartment. Their story revealed that the government's case rested almost entirely on a thirty-year-old convict at the Lewisburg federal penitentiary named Boyd Douglas. Douglas had become an FBI informer while smuggling letters between Father Berrigan, who was in prison, and Sister Elizabeth, on his trips to classes at Bucknell. Nelson and Ostrow also reported details about Douglas' criminal record and his bizarre behavior while posing as an antiwar activist on the Bucknell campus.

In the book they later wrote about the case, *The FBI and the Berrigans*, Nelson and Ostrow revealed how the FBI had not pressed the case until Hoover referred to it during his testimony on a budget request before a Senate committee. This, they wrote, made it clear to the agents in charge of the case that their boss considered it important, and they would be wise to adopt the same attitude, strong case or not. Hoover complained to Kraslow about alleged errors in Nelson's reporting of the Berrigan case, but offered no specifics.

Hoover accused Nelson and Charlotte (N.C.) *Observer* reporter Jack Bass of lying about the FBI in their book on the 1968 shooting of students at South Carolina State College in Orangeburg, South Carolina, during a protest demonstration against racial discrimination at a bowling alley. Nelson and Bass wrote in the book, *The Orangeburg Massacre*, that FBI agents were on the scene while state troopers gunned down unarmed students as they tried to flee or were lying on the ground. The information that FBI agents were there was based on trial testimony by three FBI agents. Nelson discovered the students were shot in the back and the bottoms of their feet by getting to the hospital and wangling a look at the medical records before authorities sealed them off from reporters. Nelson and Bass also disclosed that FBI agents had lied to Justice Department attorneys about the incident, but Hoover made no reference to that.

Nelson acknowledges he's been rough on the FBI. When he arrived in Washington, he says, he was appalled to find the FBI brushing aside questions of legitimate public interest with terse, arrogant ''No comment''s. He was also surprised that the capital press corps accepted this outrageous situation without question or challenge.

He began looking into the Bureau's affairs. He asked questions that FBI officials, unaccustomed to such impertinence, did not like. He discovered the FBI was not the pure, incorruptible agency of its image. FBI technicians, he learned, worked on Hoover's home and his personal TV set. The Bureau wasted money on eccentric purchases, manipulated the press, and violated its claim that it hired only attorneys and accountants as agents. Nelson soon felt a coolness toward him at FBI offices. His sources began to dry up. William C. Sullivan, who was kicked out as assistant director of the FBI in 1971 and who helped Nelson in his Berrigan case reporting, told Nelson he never could understand why Nelson had gone ''over to the other side.''

The only thing Nelson was ever out to get was the whole story, not just the surface, even if it meant losing friends or sources. That's the attitude that put him on the FBI's enemy list in the first place.

It began innocently, though sensationally, on June 30, 1968, when a twenty-six-year-old schoolteacher named Kathy Ainsworth was killed in a shoot-out with police as she and a fellow Ku Klux Klan member tried to bomb a Jewish businessman's home in Meridian, Mississippi. According to news reports at the time, including Nelson's, the police were lying in ambush for the Klan terrorists because they had been tipped to the bomb plans by an informant.

Later that year, while Nelson was chatting by telephone with Kenneth Dean, director of the Mississippi Council on Human Relations, Dean remarked there was "a lot more to the Meridian case." His curiosity aroused, Nelson checked with other sources. One of them was A. I. Botnick, director of the Anti-Defamation League's regional office in New Orleans, which had helped raise a reward fund for information on the bombings of synagogues and a rabbi's house in Jackson and Meridian in 1967 and early 1968. In April, 1969, almost a year after Kathy Ainsworth was killed, Botnick told Nelson in a long-distance telephone conversation that catching the two Klan members red-handed had cost "a lot of money." Botnick said it had been a trap, that he had helped plan it, and he would do it again because "we were dealing with animals." But he didn't want the Anti-Defamation League mentioned in any story about the case.

When Dean showed Nelson a copy of a memo that suggested there had been entrapment by Meridian police, the reporter was sure there were important facts still concealed. The whiff of something wrong wafted across the nostrils of his indignation, and he resolved to get to the bottom of it.

Nelson talked to Roy Gunn, the Meridian police chief, who said $36,500 had been paid from the reward fund to two Klansmen for the tip. Gunn referred him to detective L. L. Scarborough, who had participated in negotiations with the informants. Scarborough agreed to give Nelson the details, even show him the police files, but he wanted money. Nelson paid him $1,000. It's the only time in his twenty-eight years as a reporter, according to Nelson, that he ever purchased information. It was all right, he figured, because it wasn't just talk he was buying, but a look at records. Scarborough produced a stack of papers in which Nelson found the story.

Meridian police and FBI agents, frustrated by their failure to stop the bombing attacks, had met secretly several times with the two informants and an intermediary. Originally the informants were to tip the police to the next bombing. In return, they would get $69,000 in cash and immunity from prosecution in several church bombings. One memo in the files said Botnick agreed to fly in $25,000 in twenty-dollar bills to help raise the money. One of the informants was out of prison pending appeal of a ten-year sentence for a federal civil rights violation in the 1967 killing of three civil rights workers in Philadelphia, Mississippi.

But the situation became confused, and then gradually changed. Klansmen who had done the bombings now had other things on their minds. The informants feared there'd be no bombing for which they'd collect the $69,000 unless they instigated one themselves. The police became aware that their informants were now helping to set up a bombing by two other Klansmen who were suspects in previous bombings, but continued with the plan, anyway. At the last minute, Mrs. Ainsworth was substituted for one of the Klansmen. Police reduced the payoff to $36,000 but did not call off the deal, which by now had become a trap, even though they were prepared for a gun battle and did not expect to take anyone alive. They became so obsessed with catching some bombers, and were so spoiling for a fight, that good judgment was blotted out.

Though Nelson realized it was an explosive story, it apparently had not occurred to anyone else. Or no one thought that Nelson would publish it. No one had thrown up an obstacle or dodged a question. But when the police, the FBI, and others involved suddenly grasped what Nelson was about to do, the atmosphere grew frigid. Botnick denied having made his previous statements. Roy Moore, the FBI agent Nelson considered a friend, called him to "get it straightened out."

"You won't write a story like that," Moore said. "You'll yank the rug right out from under our informant system."

"I have to run it," Nelson replied. "It's an important story."

Gunn, Scarborough, and Jewish community leaders joined with the FBI and the ADL in trying to argue Nelson out of it. "It tied my stomach in knots," he recalls. He knew he would lose many good sources and friends.

The story ran on February 13, 1970, after Nelson had left for his new assignment in Washington. Moore would never speak to him again. Scarborough sent back the $1,000. "It was the first major thing on the FBI," says Nelson.

Soon afterwards an assistant director of the FBI, Tom Bishop, began telling people in Washington that Nelson often was drunk when he conducted interviews. Though Hoover later alleged to Nelson's boss that Nelson's Meridian story was false, the FBI did not challenge its accuracy at the time it was published.

Nelson, who has been on just about everyone's list of best investigative reporters, now has Kraslow's old job as chief of the Los Angeles *Times* Washington bureau. He likes that well enough, except that he's not able to do as much investigating as he'd prefer. He still keeps in touch with sources by phone, but finds himself relying more on inside sources and less on firsthand digging. It's also harder to maintain "that singlemindedness that investigative reporting needs." He says it a bit wistfully, since there's no scarcity of things to investigate in the nation's capital. It's just like Georgia when Nelson worked for the Atlanta *Constitution*.

That was from 1952 to 1965, when corruption enjoyed such a boom that Nelson couldn't be bothered with nickle-and-dime stories about public officials paving their private driveways with tax money. To get in the competition, a story had to be big. He did exposés on prostitution, gambling, purchasing scandals, a police lottery, junkets by state legislators, illegal highway contracts, and a trip by a temperance committee to study the treatment of drunks in New Orleans and Las Vegas. He became known as the "Affidavit Man" for his practice of persuading sources to back up their words with sworn affidavits. He posed as a mill worker to catch an official buying votes.

The mayor of Athens, Georgia, invited Nelson to investigate prostitution, slot machines, and organized crime in his city because he didn't trust his police department. Arriving in town, Nelson was told by police he was wasting his time because there was no prostitution or other crime in their spic-and-span city. But a cabbie showed him four brothels near the police station. Nelson and a photographer went to one called Effie's. Following the cabbie's instructions, they told the grandmotherly lady who answered the door they'd been sent by Number fifty-two. Inside, two girls glanced up briefly from TV, then got up and invited the men into bedrooms at the rear. Nelson began to haggle over price as one of the girls was taking off her dress. He said he wanted her to go out with him all night. Effie bustled in to say no dice. Nelson and his photographer departed, according to Nelson, without sampling the wares. Nelson later testified before a grand jury.

His biggest story in Atlanta was a 1959 investigation of the huge state mental hospital at Milledgeville after he got a tip that a nurse was performing major surgery while the surgeon was tending his practice at a private hospital. Nelson located an operating room technician who confirmed the story, but it took a while to get a second witness to talk on the record. In the process, he discovered a raft of shocking practices and conditions at the hospital. His stories led to an investigation by a special state commission, the implementation of reforms, and a Pulitzer Prize for Nelson.

Five years later when Nelson went back, things at the hospital were as bad as ever. He wrote another series, which led to a second investigating commission and another round of reforms. Nelson and the *Constitution*, realizing they had failed to sustain the pressure the first time, resolved to mount a crusade of stories and editorials until meaningful improvements were accomplished.

Despite his formidable record, Nelson does not come on strong. When interviewing people who refuse to tell him what he wants to know, he prefers gentle reasoning to bluff or bluster. "I sort of con them into cooperating," he says. "I tell them they're better off if they cooperate with me because they can get their side of the story across."

That's how Nelson got former FBI agent Alfred C. Baldwin III to hand him his biggest Watergate scoop in October, 1972. This was Baldwin's account of the break-in and his role as a lookout for the bugging team from a room in the Howard Johnson's Motor Lodge across the street. Nelson kept after Baldwin and his lawyers incessantly. "I told them he had to sit down with one guy and tell him the whole story. He'd be much better off." Nelson went back to the lawyers again and again, pleading, cajoling, pestering. Though Baldwin's lawyers were trying to sell an interview by their client—for as much as $5,000, according to one report—and Nelson refused to pay a penny, Nelson nevertheless got the interview. It almost got away when one lawyer said it was late and they had to leave for dinner. But Nelson picked up his tape recorder and went to dinner with them.

Nelson does not agree that all reporters should be investigative reporters. Special skills are needed, he believes, and a stomach for taking on difficult jobs and confronting difficult people. To be able to outmaneuver and overcome the obstacles thrown up by desperate people, investigative reporters need more than normal stamina and tough-mindedness. "It's a specialty," he says.

It's also more hard work than glamor, Nelson says, and until Woodward and Bernstein's Watergate success "gave us respectability," investigative reporters were looked down upon even by fellow journalists. What keeps them going is knowing that success can have an impact on the course of events. Success also breeds more success. Developing a reputation as a good investigative reporter attracts new leads to corruption, malfeasance and other wrongdoing. "People come to you," Nelson says. And it's truer today than ever.

Shortly after he joined *The New York Times* in 1967, David Burnham began to hear about "cooping," police slang for sleeping on duty during the night shift. Every night, all across New York City, policemen would pull their patrol cars off the streets and catch forty winks. It struck Burnham as a good subject for a story.

A patrolman who took Burnham out at night to see policemen napping in their cruisers was surprised by the reporter's interest. Cooping was nothing new. It was part of the system, a part of police life accepted by everyone on the force, even those who didn't approve. Sergeants and dispatchers were resigned to it, though some would occasionally grumble about the difficulty of raising a cop on the radio in the middle of the night.

Since the department was required by law to deploy its men in three equal shifts, and give them equal shift assignments, everyone drew night shift duty every third week. So, everyone was familiar with cooping, even if he did not indulge, himself.

When Burnham mentioned his cooping story to editors at the *Times*, it was his turn to be surprised. "Everybody knows about that," they shrugged. Burnham couldn't get authorization to take time off from regular daytime assignments to go out at night on the cooping story. "They thought it was a dumb idea," he recalls. So he did it on his own time. When he couldn't get a photographer to go along, he took a copy boy who knew how to use a camera.

"Most good stories," says Burnham, "are stories that everybody knows but nobody has written." To Burnham, however, this was more than a run-of-the-mill good story. Cooping was not just a petty misfeasance by a few sleepy cops, but a symptom of a grievous defect in the police department's ability to do its job.

Before Burnham joined the *Times*, he had served for two years on the President's Commission on Law Enforcement and Administration of Justice, an experience, he says, "like going to graduate school." Added to his prior work as a reporter for United Press International, *Newsweek* magazine and CBS, it gave him a broader perspective than most reporters. His beat was not just crime, but the criminal justice system. He had talked to several people about the handling of such a broad field of coverage. He had tried to think out what the main thrust should be. A systems analyst friend had told him, "What you ought to do is write about the things that prevent an agency from achieving its stated goals."

So, Burnham looked upon cooping as a practice that impeded the police department's performance, kept it from working the way it's supposed to. It was not just misbehavior by individuals, but a systematic breakdown of management and function. Burnham was excited about what he perceived as a revolutionary approach to this kind of story. His editors yawned.

The *Times* did, however, run the story on the front page of its December 16, 1968, issue, along with a photograph showing three cars of dozing policemen taken by copy boy Leland Schwartz. Burnham made a number of 2:00 A.M. excursions over several weeks to get eyewitness evidence. One night he found half a precinct's mobile force sleeping away the shift. He quoted a sergeant who said it was often impossible to find more than one car on duty in his precinct after 3:00 A.M. Some cops, Burnham revealed, took pillows and alarm clocks to work with them. In the uproar that followed, a crackdown against cooping was ordered by police officials, and state law was changed to eliminate the constricting requirement of equal assignment to three equal shifts.

Burnham regards it as perhaps the best story he's ever done.

The *Times'* interest in governmental performance receded again when Burnham turned his attention to judges. Using a stopwatch, he calculated how much time they worked each day. He also examined each judge's case load and disposition record. Disclosing indolence in the exalted realm of the judiciary, however, was not the same as blowing the whistle on lower-class types like cops. Burnham found this story much harder to get into the paper. It was published only after a long hassle, and then in a rewritten form. Instead of emphasizing the *Times'* investigation of judicial work habits, it dwelled first on criticism of short work days among judges and prosecutors by a judge. Burnham, whose own findings were not mentioned until the second half of the story, was so angry he almost quit.

But not quite. He stuck around to do the story that became the most famous he ever did, even though it made him not the least bit famous. It was a story that shocked the American people, then enthralled them from the movie screen, all without bringing much personal recognition to the intense, slightly-built reporter who brought it all to light. This was the story of policeman Frank Serpico and widespread corruption in the New York Police Department.

It's hard to say exactly when the story began. For Serpico, it took root gradually as he grew aware that police officials and Mayor John Lindsay's office were not going to do much about his allegations of an entrenched system of payoffs and bribes among detectives. For Burnham, it emerged bit by bit from rumors, scattered pieces of information, conversations with Serpico, a police sergeant named David Durk and other policemen, and his own efforts to dig out specific evidence.

Burnham viewed corruption the same as cooping. It was not a moral problem, but an institutional disease. His hope in exposing it was not to put crooked cops in jail, but to promote a lasting cure for the situation. It was a matter of practicality. "I'm not interested in headhunting," he says. "I'm interested in the institution and whether it's doing its job."

Convinced that widespread corruption was undermining the police department's effectiveness, the reporter went out and talked to bartenders, gamblers, contractors, and restaurant owners who gave money to policemen to overlook infractions of the law or give them special service. He spent hours in liquor stores because he knew "they had to pay off." He sought out honest cops who would tell him what they knew about the corruption, finding one valuable source in the narcotics division.

Though he gathered a lot of information, it was not jelling into a solid story. As in the case of the cooping story, in addition, Burnham noticed little enthusiasm for it at the *Times*. Metropolitan Editor Arthur Gelb seemed skeptical that a police department could be so corrupt.

The turning point came when Durk persuaded Serpico to go to a February 12, 1970, meeting arranged by Burnham with Gelb and two other *Times* staffers. Serpico and Durk brought along Police Inspector Paul Delise, who had tried to help Serpico stimulate internal action against corruption. Delise's presence was important, perhaps pivotal. He held high rank in the department and was taking a big risk by baring police secrets to outsiders. Since promotion to inspector was by politics, he was not protected by civil service rules, and could easily be demoted. "He took an extraordinary step," Burnham explains. "It was tremendously persuasive to Gelb."

After a fatiguing eight-hour session in which Serpico and Durk spilled out their story, Burnham wrote a three-part series. Gelb wanted him to concentrate on payoffs by heroin dealers, but Burnham insisted that petty graft—gifts and small amounts of money from businessmen—was more basic. It was the foundation on which all police corruption rested because it breaks the moral ice, makes graft "all right," and insinuates it into the system. Burnham also felt the story should hit hard on the inaction of police officials, because that also communicated to policemen that graft was "all right."

Once written, the three-part story took on similarities to the article on judges. It didn't get into the paper. There was nothing sinister behind this, Burnham is sure, but a vague uneasiness, which was expressed in an explanation that the *Times* was waiting for an event to make the story timely.

Serpico and Durk, meanwhile, developed second thoughts. Everyone in the police department could figure out where Burnham got the story. They nursed back to life old hopes that someone inside the department might yet clean up the mess out of public view. The more they thought about what their colleagues might do, the more frightened they grew. They asked Burnham to kill the story. Paranoia set in, engulfing Burnham, too. They were now convinced they were being followed and their phones were tapped. Burnham hid their notes and tapes in a locker.

Drained by the tension and impatient with his editors, Burnham cast about for a way to precipitate a resolution, something to force the story into the paper. The opportunity came unexpectedly, at a Saturday night cocktail party for a Yugoslavian diplomat given by Deputy Mayor Richard Aurelio, a close political adviser to Mayor Lindsay. Burnham rarely goes to such parties, but he and his wife were close friends of the diplomat. There he encountered Thomas B. Morgan, the mayor's press secretary. Calculating that Lindsay would hurry to protect his image in advance if he knew about the story, Burnham told Morgan he was preparing an explosive series on corruption. As Burnham had hoped, Lindsay and his advisers decided to head off the *Times* by announcing a committee to review procedures for investigating police corruption.

With this, Burnham persuaded Gelb it was time to publish. The three-part series was rewritten into one long article, however. It contained all that Burnham had dug up, along with Serpico's story of the graft he had personally witnessed and his futile attempts to prod his superiors to do anything. None of Burnham's sources were identified in the story, which began, "Narcotics dealers, gamblers and businessmen make illicit payments of millions of dollars a year to the policemen of New York, according to policemen, law enforcement experts and New Yorkers who make such payments themselves.

"Despite such widespread corruption, officials in both the Lindsay administration and the Police Department have failed to investigate a number of cases of corruption brought to their attention, sources within the department say.

"This picture has emerged from a six-month survey of police corruption by *The New York Times*. The survey included an examination of police and court records and interviews with scores of police commanders, policemen, former policemen, law enforcement experts and private citizens."

It created a sensation when it appeared on April 25, 1970, but took a while to build to its full impact. Lindsay said the city already had moved against police corruption, but the *Times'* allegations would also be investigated thoroughly. As other news media picked up the story in the days that followed, however, and as criticism of Lindsay's committee blossomed because it included Police Commissioner Howard R. Leary, whose department was the one under fire, Lindsay felt compelled to do more. He finally appointed a new citizens group chaired by sixty-one-year-old Wall Street lawyer Whitman A. Knapp. It was to become famous as the Knapp Commission.

Burnham kept writing, trying to get at least one story in the paper every day. He covered Knapp Commission proceedings and reported on developments rising from Serpico's earlier efforts. In June, Serpico testified at the trial of a patrolman charged with lying to a grand jury about his connections with gamblers. Serpico described systematic corruption in the police department, telling how gamblers paid $700 to $800 a month to patrolmen as he watched them take the money, and how policemen often had to share their bribe money with sergeants and lieutenants. Serpico's public testimony did much to build pressure for a cleanup and gave the case a hero. "The original story was important," says Burnham, "but it had limited impact. You have to keep at it over a period of time to get any results. You have to keep pounding."

The results—indictments, convictions, resignations, painful pressure on police officials—came from the Knapp Commission, Maurice H. Nadjari, a special prosecutor appointed by Governor Nelson Rockefeller at the Knapp Commission's recommendation, and the new police commissioner, Patrick V. Murphy. Nadjari brought corruption indictments against more than 290 persons, and convicted scores of police officers on graft charges. In its final report, the Knapp Commission said police corruption was "an extensive, department-wide phenomenon, indulged in to some degree by a sizable majority of those on the force." The report said high-level police officials had ignored information from federal law enforcement agencies that some of their men were suspected murderers, extortionists, and heroin dealers.

Serpico's emergence as the hero was due largely to a book by Peter Maas that focused on him, and a movie based on the book. Durk and Burnham, whose contributions were equally crucial to the outcome, received little acclaim. Burnham's role was so minimized in the movie that he insisted his name not be used, and it wasn't. Though the story was beyond a doubt one of the most significant and sensational of 1970, it won Burnham no prizes until 1973, after the Knapp Commission issued its final report, and then only a local award by the New York Newspaper Guild.

In the summer of 1974, the forty-one-year-old, prematurely balding reporter moved to the *Times'* Washington bureau to zero in on the federal regulatory agencies with his new ideas on the causes of governmental nonperformance. He was sure he'd find the same kind of corruption and malfunction that had sabotaged the fight against crime in New York City. No one had ever approached the Food and Drug Administration or the Atomic Energy Commission from that standpoint, and he was eager to try it. In Washington, he found more freedom and encouragement to pursue such stories. The *Times,* he discovered, was more free-swinging away from home, just like other newspapers and broadcast media across the country who find it easier to be aggressive in state capitals or Washington away from the pressures and sensitivities of hometown power structures and advertisers.

Burnham soon found the AEC absorbing his interest. Poking around in the commission's records, he began to suspect the AEC had been suppressing information about the hazards of nuclear power plants. He gained access to memos and letters by AEC members and industry officials in the hands of organizations that were critical of AEC policies. Some material had been obtained from AEC insiders who disagreed with the concealment. Other documents had been obtained through lawsuits under the federal Freedom of Information Act. Burnham also turned up salient details in the record of an obscure 1972 hearing by the AEC.

His front-page story of November 10, 1974, revealed that "for at least ten years the commission has repeatedly sought to suppress studies by its own scientists that found nuclear reactors were more dangerous than officially acknowledged or that raised questions about reactor safety devices.'' Burnham disclosed that the AEC had ignored urgings by its own scientists for more research on safety issues, and had decided not to publish a study that said a major reactor accident might shower disaster on an area as large as Pennsylvania.

Three days after his article appeared, Karen G. Silkwood, a twenty-eight-year-old laboratory technician at the Kerr-McGee Cimarron nuclear plant in Oklahoma, was killed when her car crashed into a culvert. This event became newsworthy when Anthony Mazziocchi, Washington representative for the Oil, Chemical and Atomic Workers Union, demanded a federal investigation. Mazziocchi said a fresh dent on the car's rear bumper showed that someone had forced Silkwood off the road.

Silkwood had been active in protests of unsafe conditions at the plant, which made uranium and plutonium fuel. She had herself been exposed to a large dose of radiation and this was under investigation by the AEC. She and two other employes had accused plant officials of endangering employes' lives, manufacturing faulty plutonium fuel rods, and falsifying inspection records. According to a report by Mazziocchi and a subsequent article by freelance writer Roger Rapoport in *New Times* magazine, Silkwood's exposure to radiation had resulted from someone's breaking into her apartment and contaminating food and several articles, including a toilet seat, with plutonium, a highly dangerous radioactive substance.

The Oklahoma State Highway Patrol said Silkwood had fallen asleep at the wheel and the dent on the bumper had been caused by hitting an abutment while the car was being towed away after the accident. But union officials remained convinced that it was no accident. At the time Silkwood went off the road, she was on her way to see Burnham in Oklahoma City, according to Mazziocchi, with documents to prove her allegations. The documents, said Mazziocchi, had disappeared.

Though investigations by Burnham and several agencies failed to back up Mazziocchi's suspicions of foul play, Silkwood's death may have been a factor in the closing of the Kerr-McGee nuclear plant a year later. A plant spokesman said it was due only to a decline in business, but officials and businessmen in the nearby town blamed it on bad publicity.

Burnham continued to write about nuclear safety problems and the AEC's tendency to worry more about the atomic energy industry's profits than the public's safety. One story told about the industry's decision to spend more money on improving its image among government officials, the news media, labor unions, and civic groups. Burnham managed to latch onto a copy of a memo in which the president of the industry's association, the Atomic Industrial Forum, spelled out the program.

In November, 1975, a year after Karen Silkwood died, Burnham wrote a front-page article that tied together the implications of what he had learned in more than a year of investigating; namely, "The long-held dream that nuclear power would give the United States and the world an endless stream of low-cost electric power has faded. . . . That nuclear dream is clouded by problems . . . a growing concern about the problems and costs of protecting reactors and their waste products from sabotage, the rising price of uranium, and a possible requirement of new and expensive safety devices."

Before going to Washington, Burnham also pioneered in the use of statistical methods and computers to analyze public records. His first venture into this vast, uncharted new territory of journalism was a study of police department performance by an exhaustive examination of crime records. The results, published in February, 1972, showed a great disparity in the incidence of crime in various New York City neighborhoods, and in the ability of police precincts to cope with it. Among the findings were wide differences in homicide, robbery, burglary, and car theft rates between one part of town and another, and in the proportion of arrests to reported crimes between one police precinct and another.

Another time he tracked down the disposition of 100 assault and robbery arrests to find out what happened to the average robber. He found it tough going just to get basic facts. Many records were handwritten, others were scattered in several locations. "The judges," says Burnham, "worked out a system so it's impossible to determine what happens." But he did learn that thirty percent of the cases had been dismissed, and the average sentence for the rest was only three months in jail, because in most cases the charges had been reduced.

Though this kind of story seldom generates excitement, recognition or discernible results, Burnham believes such "investigative sociology" is "just as important investigative work as the other kind."

Like many investigative journalists, Burnham believes there's a gold mine of information and stories in public records, waiting to be dug out. To tap this lode, one needs only a willingness to wade patiently through documents, a high tolerance for tedium, and an ability to perceive patterns or discrepancies when pulling together bits and pieces from dissimilar sources. Burnham looks closely at the point in a system where there's most freedom for the exercise of discretion. That, he says, is where most corruption occurs.

One such point in the criminal justice system is the prosecutor's office, where decisions are made on the sufficiency of evidence. Whether there's enough to prosecute is at the prosecutor's discretion. A failure to prosecute a particular case when evidence seems adequate may involve nothing more than a difference of opinion. But a pattern of such decisions over a period of time may reflect something more suspicious.

Burnham once wrote about a prosecutor's letting a police detective accused of selling four pounds of heroin plead guilty to a lesser charge and get off with a suspended sentence of one year in jail. The prosecutor claimed there was too little evidence to support the original charge because an undercover accomplice could not be produced in open court. But Burnham, through a criminal lawyer he knew, got a copy of a police report making it clear there was other evidence.

Burnham applies the same precept to the workings of federal agencies in Washington, that the most likely place to find the system shorting out is where someone has a lot of freedom to exercise discretion.

When Arthur Bremer shot presidential candidate George Wallace in 1972, Nicholas M. Horrock was the chief investigative reporter for *Newsweek* magazine. Things were happening so fast and there were so many bases to cover that *Newsweek* editors formed a team and put Horrock in charge. The ensuing exercise in hurry-up, deadline investigative journalism produced several exclusives, including the existence of Bremer's diary and his stalking of President Nixon before he turned his gun on Wallace.

Working from *Newsweek's* Washington bureau, Horrock sent Chicago bureau correspondent Berniece Buresh hurrying to Bremer's hometown, Milwaukee, where she was the first to locate Bremer's former girl friend. With other reporters working the scene of the shooting in suburban Silver Spring, Maryland, and covering the federal agencies investigating the case, Horrock did the coordinating. He had Buresh follow up in Milwaukee leads that the others uncovered in Washington, and vice versa.

The impromptu team approach worked so well that *Newsweek* kept it going to cover the Watergate story. With help primarily from Evert Clark and John Lindsay, Horrock put together what was up to the middle of September, 1972, perhaps the best account of events leading up to the capture of five men inside the Democratic National headquarters. Published in the September 18, 1972, issue, it included the formation of a White House "plumbers" unit to "plug leaks" to newsmen, the mounting of an anti-Democratic espionage campaign, the forming of a team of Cubans who E. Howard Hunt had known as a CIA agent, evidence of previous break-ins and wiretappings at Democratic party headquarters, and the existence of a $350,000 cash fund at the Committee for the Re-election of the President. Prophetically, the article said, "The Watergate affair has emerged as the most dramatic clear-cut disclosure of major political espionage in the history of U.S. Presidential elections."

Despite that, *Newsweek,* like most of the news media, still failed to perceive the story's true dimensions. As Horrock recalls, it was hard to see Watergate as the most important story to be covered during the election campaign. Though some Democratic candidates tried to make it a campaign issue, that, ironically, may have made newsmen more wary of the story than eager for it, for fear they'd be politically manipulated. *Newsweek* was the first magazine to run a cover story on Watergate, but that was not until March, 1973.

Once the *Newsweek* team got into gear on the Watergate story, however, it performed credibly, even to developing solid sources with colorful code names to match Woodstein's "Deep Throat." Horrock's band had a White House source called "Topless" because he had once taken off his shirt at a party, and others named "Moneybags" and "Diane's Friend." Horrock and company would meet them in a Georgetown bar or the corridor of an obscure government building.

In May, 1973, *Newsweek* was the first to report that thirty-four-year-old Presidential counsel John W. Dean III had spilled details of the White House cover-up to federal prosecutors. A federal investigator told Horrock that evidence had been obtained proving Nixon's involvement. In the search for corroboration, the team detected "real fear" among White House aides, indicating the tip was accurate. Now fired up, they contacted every imaginable source until they finally got confirmation that the evidence had come from Dean.

A soft-spoken, solid-looking man with a mustache—and an offhand manner to balance a somber demeanor—Horrock moved to *The New York Times* Washington bureau in January, 1975. His work there has been different from magazine journalism, which he deems harder because it requires all the elements of a story to be pulled together with accurate perspective.

At the *Times*, it is a day-to-day approach, investigating beneath the governmental surface as a regular beat instead of on a project basis. And he works alone rather than with a team.

But he still relies on well-placed sources in government agencies, law enforcement work, and congressional committees. He has no flashy tricks or magic methods. His style is steady, determined plodding to develop documentation for the leads he gets from sources.

His *Newsweek* story of January 24, 1972, with Evert Clark—and their 1973 book, *Contrabandista*—on the new Latin American connection for the smuggling of heroin into the United States was based mostly on records and dossiers made available to them by federal narcotics agents.

Horrock's *New York Times* story in September, 1975, of CIA plans to use shellfish poison for suicide pills and assassinations came from the Senate Select Committee on Intelligence.

His September 21, 1975, story on the FBI's failing to investigate CIA tape recordings of telephone conversations between Lee Harvey Oswald and the Cuban and Soviet embassies in Mexico City in 1963 came from government sources.

His October 26, 1975, revelation of wiretapping by the National Security Agency was extracted from law enforcement sources who told him a group of Justice Department lawyers was trying to determine if any laws had been broken.

Horrock calls them tips rather than leaks, and a lot of them don't come to him by themselves. He's out there looking. And he doesn't write stories until they're confirmed by records or independent sources.

Though he pursues his own investigations amidst regular coverage and believes all reporters should be investigators, Horrock sees great utility in a specialty approach. Many reporters are inhibited from aggressive digging or interrogating that might alienate valuable sources. This is labeled a sellout by some, who say sources should never be coddled, and winning their respect is more important—and more likely to keep them as sources—than pleasing them, anyway. Horrock suggests that one way to have one's cake and eat it, too, is to send in an investigative specialist, a "hired gun," to do the dirty work. This way a statehouse reporter, for instance, could turn over a suspected misuse of governmental power to another reporter for investigation without shattering his carefully cultivated source setup.

When the Washington *Post's* Ronald Kessler investigated the U.S. Postal Service in 1974, he was preceded on his travels to five of the nation's largest post offices by a memo from a high-ranking postal official in Washington.

The memo warned that Kessler had recently done an exposé on President Nixon's real estate in San Clemente, California, and was "apparently looking for trouble spots" in the postal system. It instructed local post office managers not to tell Kessler that he wouldn't be furnished any information, but to explain that a post office is a restricted area and he must go through the postmaster. The postmaster, according to the memo, should then "tactfully" suggest that Kessler take his inquiries to an assistant postmaster general in Washington.

An official of the Fort Worth, Texas, post office sent out a memo alerting employes to Kessler's imminent arrival "to criticize this office" and instructing that the building be cleaned thoroughly, that supervisors keep all employes busy, and that each employe be "prepared to answer any question."

Kessler was not hindered. As the *Post's* only full-time investigative reporter—also its best, according to many in the field—he had totally immersed himself in the project ever since he'd been given the assignment by Managing Editor Howard Simon, who wondered why his mail was always so late. Kessler usually takes on just one project at a time, and attacks it full blast, churning it over in his mind long after he gets home at night. To penetrate the deception of postal officials who blandly insisted everything was fine, Kessler had begun by "poking around the edges," as he puts it, developing sources among postal workers and other unofficial but knowledgeable contacts.

Not at all the ogre portrayed in the memo, Kessler is disarmingly mild and polite, almost deferential, as he patiently tracks down information from one interview to the next, asking each contact for the names of others. A big, boyish-looking man of thirty-two with thick glasses and an unhurried manner, he doesn't believe in coming on strong. "I try not to be in an adversary position," he says. "People involved in the things I write about are not necessarily evil people." If some firmness seems required, Kessler may go so far as to cite the Freedom of Information Act, appeal to a sense of public service, point out that he will get the information somewhere else anyway, or even throw a dash of indignation in his voice.

By the time he left Washington to delve into the postal situations of other cities, Kessler was well prepared. He knew what to look for and how to find it. Altogether, he spent four months on the investigation. He interviewed hundreds of postal officials and employes, former officials, technical experts, postal inspectors, and postal service users. He pored through hundreds of memos, reports, studies, letters, hearing transcripts, audits, and consultant reports.

His findings were chronicled in a six-part series published in June, 1974. Among those findings was evidence that the Postal Service had deliberately slowed down the delivery of first class mail by sorting it only during the day; that first class mail users were being overcharged $1 billion a year while commercial junk mail senders were undercharged; that $1 billion in new parcel sorting equipment didn't work; that a costly mechanized letter sorting system was slower than hand sorting; that millions of dollars in contracts were awarded without competitive bidding; that $140 million had been spent on contract cost overruns; that Postmaster General Elmer T. Klassen had given contracts to friends; that mail went through forty-seven processing steps, each capable of causing delay; that postal machines had an error rate as high as seventeen percent; and that the U.S. Postal Service, acclaimed as the path to a streamlined, efficient, self-sustaining, blissful future when Congress set it up in 1970 to succeed the rickety old Post Office Department, was actually giving slower, more erratic service, and losing more money, than the bureaucratic swamp it had replaced.

One thing about Kessler's post office disclosures that disappointed him was their lack of impact or results. No other news media hopped on the story. No Congressional investigations started up. Not even a promise from postal officials to shape up. One reason might have been Kessler's disdain for follow-up badgering and arm-twisting, a kind of purist attitude against helping a story make waves à la Clark Mollenhoff.

"I don't have any great personal vested interest in a story," says Kessler. "It's dangerous for a reporter to think of it as a personal campaign or crusade. I enjoy doing the work, enjoy doing a good job. But I'm pretty dispassionate. It's not my business what happens afterwards. What I enjoy is bringing out the truth. In the long run that will bring reform, though it might not happen right off. Most of my stories have had some kind of result, new laws or investigations by authorities."

The post office series might not have been a good test, he says. "It was not one of my best. It didn't reveal anything illegal or corrupt." A move to reform the postal service again, and make it more responsive to Congress, did get underway about a year later, after further disclosures by columnist Jack Anderson on contracts obtained by Klassen's friends and Klassen's eventual resignation. Kessler shrugs. "I don't really care that much."

By no means so casual about digging out the story in the first place, Kessler is also a purist in another sense, a practitioner of pure investigative journalism, in which the reporter starts from scratch, with not even a tip, and unearths all the information himself, not relying on unsolicited leaks or scavenging facts from police, FBI agents or other government investigators. Two such investigations from scratch in 1972 won Kessler the 1973 George Polk Memorial Award for outstanding community service.

The first was an exposé of illegal kickbacks behind the abnormally high closing costs for home purchases. Assigned to find out why settlement costs were so much higher in Washington than elsewhere, Kessler spent two months talking to lawyers, real estate brokers, developers, mortgage bankers, title insurance companies, and real estate experts. He found the practice of kickbacks by lawyers and title insurance companies to developers, brokers, builders and lenders so common, so routine, that many people were not aware it was illegal. It had "always been done that way."

Kessler's four-part series in January, 1972, explained how $200 charged a home buyer for title insurance might include $50 for the lawyer as a commission or discount for directing the business to the title insurance firm. Kessler also revealed that attorneys in suburban areas based their closing charges for services such as a title search and preparation of documents on a bar association fee schedule.

After the articles appeared, Congress enacted a law requiring full disclosure of settlement costs in all transactions involving federal banks, the Federal Housing Administration or another federal agency. A lawsuit was filed against attorney fee schedules that led to a U.S. Supreme Court decision outlawing bar association fee schedules as violations of laws against price fixing.

Kessler's other award-winning probe of 1972 concerned the finances of Washington area hospitals. It was prompted by a tip that the area's largest private nonprofit hospital, the Washington Hospital Center, was keeping huge sums of money in interest-free checking accounts at a bank where the hospital's treasurer served on the board of directors.

Starting out carefully by talking surreptitiously to hospital employes and doctors before asking to see records, Kessler discovered many conflicts of interest and other irregularities that contributed to fast-rising hospital bills. Administrators at Washington Hospital Center, for example, had formed a computer company that entered into a contract to provide the hospital's data processing services, good for $616,000 worth of business in 1971, without competitive bidding or board of director approval. Kessler documented similar conflicts of interest, nepotism, and lack of financial controls at other hospitals.

Kessler is perhaps best known, however, for the small piece of a story he picked up in the wake of an investigation by *Newsday*, the Long Island, New York, daily. Almost two years after *Newsday's* 1971 series on the Florida dealings and holdings of Nixon and his mysterious friend, Charles G. "Bebe" Rebozo, Kessler went to Miami during his investigation of Nixon's finances in the midst of the Watergate scandal. In a court file, he found a document that *Newsday* had missed, a deposition by an insurance investigator named George H. Riley, Jr.

Riley had sworn he told Rebozo in October, 1968, that certificates for 900 shares of IBM stock in Rebozo's possession had been stolen by Mafia figures from a New York City brokerage firm. Kessler's October 25, 1973, article reported that Rebozo, who had obtained the stock as collateral for a loan made by the bank he owned in Key Biscayne, sold 600 shares before Riley spoke to him, but the remaining 300 for $91,500 afterwards. The article included a statement by a lawyer for Rebozo denying that Riley had told Rebozo the stock was stolen.

Rebozo filed a $10-million libel suit against the Washington *Post*, claiming Riley could not have known at the time that the stock had been stolen. The *Post* replied that even if Riley's affidavit and its story had been wrong, the story had not been published "in reckless disregard for the truth" because it was based on a sworn deposition in a court record. A *Post* motion for dismissal of the suit was denied, and an appellate court upheld the denial in July, 1975.

Kessler's article on Nixon's finances, which appeared almost two months after the Rebozo piece, traced the mushrooming of the former President's net worth from $10,000 when he entered politics with his first election to Congress in 1947 to nearly $1 million in 1973. It detailed Nixon's income from government salaries, his partnership in a New York law firm from 1960 to 1968, real estate profits, speaking fees, and favors from private interests, including discounts on real estate purchases, loans, and noncampaign gifts from businessmen. Though an excellent summary of Nixon's finances based primarily on public records and Nixon's own disclosures, the article contained no startling revelations.

Kessler is very cautious and thorough. He double-checks and triple-checks. His special talent is getting people to tell him things they shouldn't, a talent he professes not to understand completely. For some reason, according to fellow reporters, people unburden all sorts of admissions when Kessler questions them in his quiet, sympathetic manner. Later they tell associates, "I don't know why I told him that. I must be crazy."

One factor, Kessler speculates, is that he tries to be open and sincere, while displaying a warm tolerance for human foible. It also helps, he says, to be from a powerful paper like the *Post*, which makes some people afraid to appear secretive. Kessler doesn't hesitate, however, to use deception or misdirection at times, such as giving the impression he is searching for something other than his true objective.

"I play it by ear," he says, "trying to get a feel for how a person reacts and what he responds to. People appreciate candor, but you also have to give the impression you know what you're talking about. They realize they might as well talk since you're going to find out anyway. It's a little more subtle than saying you're giving them a chance to give their side of it, though I'll use that as a last resort."

Early in 1975, Kessler got former FBI officials Cartha D. DeLoach and Louis B. Nichols to admit the FBI had compiled files on the sex lives and drinking problems of senators and congressmen. Assigned to look into the

CIA's domestic spying activities, Kessler came across a source who told him that old rumors of FBI spying on politicians were true. Columnist Jack Anderson had reported on such files at the FBI back in 1972, but their existence had never been acknowledged publicly by an FBI official.

Kessler contacted DeLoach and Nichols, both of whom had been close to the late J. Edgar Hoover, and confronted them with an allegation from his source that the files had been used for blackmail. In the course of denying any blackmail use, they confirmed the existence of the files, saying the information had been gathered only as by-products of legitimate investigations.

A month earlier, Kessler got a ballistics expert in California to admit there was no evidence to support his contention that two guns were fired in the killing of Robert Kennedy in 1968 because the bullet that killed him could not have been fired from the same gun as a bullet that injured a bystander.

With persistent questioning at the Pasadena home of seventy-one-year-old William Harper, Kessler elicited a concession that discrepancies between the characteristics of two bullets fired at the scene of the slaying were not sufficient to show they had been fired from different guns. Harper admitted the bullets were in too poor a condition to tell for sure.

He said he thought he had said, in a 1970 affidavit, only that no evidence existed to show the bullets came from the same gun. The affidavit, however, contained the words, "could not have been fired from the same gun." These words had become the chief support for a theory that Sirhan Sirhan was not Kennedy's assassin or was part of a conspiracy.

In a new examination of the bullets ordered by a California judge in 1975, a seven-man panel of forensic experts decided unequivocally that the bullets had been fired from the same gun, but couldn't say with certainty that it had been Sirhan's gun.

Kessler, who worked for the *Wall Street Journal* before going to the *Post* in 1970, has turned his investigative attention to business. "I prefer corporate corruption stories to government corruption stories," he said. "It's harder to get at and there are fewer people trying to do it. Corporations are more powerful and much less is known about the way they work."

Investigating corporate operations is more complicated and records aren't open to the public. It takes more determination, more tenacity, more hard work than ever. That doesn't seem to faze Kessler. "It takes a real gut desire to get at the truth," he says. "It goes beyond a professional interest in getting good stories. It takes a drive to find out what's really going on."

Ronald Ostrow noticed that grand jury members were going into Chief Judge John Sirica's office for private meetings. Sure that something unusual was in the Watergate wind, he and Robert Jackson, a colleague in the Los Angeles *Times* Washington bureau, began contacting people connected with the case. Surely one of their sources could tell them what was going on.

Most of Ostrow's sources were in the Justice Department. A forty-two-year-old reporter with an impish air and a background in business and financial reporting, including four years on the *Wall Street Journal*, Ostrow covered the Justice Department regularly. Now he phoned investigators, attorneys, and aides at home, and buttonholed them in the halls.

Jackson, a slender, easygoing forty-year-old who had exposed bribery among tax assessors in California before coming to Washington, had cultivated a stable of contacts among the Watergate conspirators and their lawyers. Now he contacted them again, even stopping them on the street.

Bit by bit it began to take shape that the mystery had something to do with Nixon. Then one of Ostrow's sources told him the grand jury had voted unanimously to name Nixon a coconspirator in the Watergate cover-up.

The two reporters got other sources to confirm it by using what Jackson calls "negative guidance," in which a source is told, "I understand you can't tell me anything about that, but let me tell you what I've got and you can steer me off it if it's wrong." An answer like, "I see no problem there," is perceived as confirmation. Woodward and Bernstein used the technique frequently in their Watergate stories. It's considered ethical by people in government, according to Jackson. It puts the burden on the reporter to phrase his questions in a way that enables the source to provide guidance without apparently telling them anything. If the source says, "If I were you, I'd be awful careful," that means it's wrong or he doesn't know. If he says, "Sorry, I can't help you," it means the reporter is on his own.

Ready to write the story, Ostrow and Jackson phoned the White House for a response. Two Nixon aides tried to talk them off the story, calling it old, shopworn speculation. When the aides became convinced there was going to be a story, a statement by Nixon's Watergate lawyer, James St. Clair, was read to the reporters. St. Clair's statement did not deny that the grand jury had so acted. It said only that any such action would be "totally unwarranted." Ostrow and Jackson interpreted this as additional confirmation.

Their June 6, 1974, story was the Los Angeles *Times'* biggest Watergate exclusive. Ostrow and Jackson covered most of the Watergate story for the bureau. Though they usually worked separately, some of their best stories were jointly produced. Their Watergate teamwork also revealed that Watergate burglar James W. McCord, Jr. had told Senate investigators about prior knowledge of the Watergate bugging on the part of Presidential Counsel John W. Dean III and CRP official Jeb Stuart Magruder; that Watergate conspirator G. Gordon Liddy had had access to a special fund of more than $100,000; and that Nixon's secretary, Rosemary Woods, was responsible for the eighteen-and-one-half minute erasure on one of the Nixon tapes.

Jackson says two heads often are an advantage in investigative reporting. "If one is down, the other picks up," he says. "Often an investigative reporter working alone gets discouraged because he's not getting anywhere. With two, you can talk about a story, make a new list of names to call, keep up each other's spirits, do something to keep it going."

One of the first stories that Ostrow and Jackson did together turned out to be a big one.

In 1969, when Ostrow was covering the U.S. Supreme Court for the Los Angeles *Times*, Jackson came down one Sunday afternoon to help him with stories about the disclosure to appear the next day in *Life* magazine concerning Supreme Court Justice Abe Fortas. The *Life* article said Fortas had received $20,000 from the family foundation of financier Louis E. Wolfson, then in prison for selling unregistered stock.

Fortas had been paid the money in 1966, a year after he had taken a seat on the U.S. Supreme Court, and a time when Wolfson was under investigation by the Securities and Exchange Commission. Fortas did not deny receipt of the $20,000 fee, but said he had returned it because it was for research and writing he had not had time to do.

While following up on the *Life* story, Jackson was told by someone familiar with Fortas that there was more to the story than *Life* was reporting. Pursuing that lead, Ostrow learned from a source in a federal law enforcement agency that Wolfson had told the FBI the $20,000 in 1966 was just one payment. The arrangement was for Fortas to get $20,000 every year for life.

The disclosures by *Life* magazine and the Los Angeles *Times* led to Fortas' resignation from the Supreme Court.

The Fortas story also led Ostrow and Jackson to a by-product that churned up repercussions in the lives of another Supreme Court justice and a future president of the United States. This was their story disclosing links between the Fortas case and the payment of $12,000 a year to Justice William O. Douglas by the Albert Parvin Foundation, a nonprofit organization set up by a Los Angeles businessman who dealt frequently with Las Vegas gambling casinos. Both Wolfson and Parvin, the two reporters discovered, had been named conspirators in a stock manipulation case by a federal grand jury in New York.

Ostrow had written the Douglas-Parvin story three years earlier, in October, 1966, after he'd been tipped to look at Parvin Foundation tax records that were open to the public. He discovered that Douglas was the only officer of the foundation to get regular compensation. Douglas said he received the money "largely as an expense account" for travel on behalf of the foundation, which funded fellowships for students from undeveloped nations at Princeton University and UCLA.

Much of the foundation's income, Ostrow found, came from a mortgage on the Flamingo hotel and casino in Las Vegas. The foundation also held stock in the Parvin-Dorhmann Company, a Los Angeles firm that sold restaurant fixtures to hotels on the Las Vegas gambling strip, and which owned the Fremont hotel and casino.

Ostrow's article raised the question of whether Douglas' acceptance of the money constituted a breach of judicial ethics, but raised no eyebrows that mattered. The story was widely ignored. Edwin Guthman, a onetime investigative reporter who uncovered Teamster Union corruption in Seattle, Washington, in the 1950s and later worked for Attorney General Robert Kennedy before becoming national editor of the Los Angeles *Times* in 1965, attributes the story's nonimpact to the fact that neither *The New York Times* nor the Washington *Post* deigned to pick it up. "I hate to sound like one of those right-wingers who blame everything on the liberal eastern press," says Guthman, "but it really gripes me that nothing happens after one of our stories unless it's carried by the *Post* or the *Times*, and they don't like to run a story that's not theirs."

Support for Guthman's complaint showed up in the Washington *Post*, itself, when Charles B. Seib, the *Post's* ombudsman, wrote a December, 1975, column on the story of President Kennedy's relationship with a woman who associated with Mafia figures. On the question of why the story took a month to become a big story after it was first mentioned on an inside page of the *Post*, Seib wrote, "That can be blamed in large part on the power of the Washington-New York news axis—meaning *The New York Times*, the Washington *Post*, the television networks, and the news magazines. A national news story, particularly one concerning official Washington, does not achieve full status until it gets recognition on the axis."

On the second time around for the Douglas disclosure, when it was linked to the Fortas story in 1969, it finally caused a stir. "The facts were the same," says Guthman, "but now it was a big deal." Gerald Ford, then a congressman from Michigan, started an ill-fated impeachment campaign against Douglas.

There was an additional element behind the excitement, however, that Ostrow hadn't had. Jean Heller of the Associated Press unearthed it; namely, the fact that the financial genius of organized crime, Meyer Lansky, had received a $200,000 fee for arranging Parvin's sale of the Flamingo, the proceeds of which had set up the foundation. It was Ostrow's and Jackson's article, however, that won that year's Sigma Delta Chi Award for national reporting.

Ostrow is another who believes a lot of good stories are waiting around in public records. He also considers it vital to cultivate sources who will point him toward a fertile record or fill him in on the things that don't get into any record.

An investigative reporter need not set himself single-mindedly on a target in order to be effective, in Ostrow's opinion. "You don't have to be convinced of someone's guilt," says Ostrow, who maintains he never had a "get Nixon" attitude. People who've been hurt by some of his exposés are still among his sources, he says, because they know it was nothing personal, he was just doing his job, and they respect him for it.

Unlike Ostrow, who's covered the Justice Department for several years, Jackson has been able to roam more freely with his penchant for digging because he's not been tied down to a beat. Like Clark Mollenhoff, he's not averse to trading information with congressional investigators or feeding them leads they can pursue with the subpoena power reporters don't have.

Among Jackson's 1975 exclusives were an IRS memo indicating Nixon had secret dealings with a Bahamian bank involved in tax evasion schemes with

Mafia figures, the existence of some 500 secret numbered accounts in four Florida banks, and the admission by a former CIA official that he had enlisted the Mafia in plots to assassinate Cuban Premier Fidel Castro.

The CIA admission came from Richard M. Bissell, former chief of clandestine services for the CIA. His admission that he personally had approved CIA cooperation with Mafia figures was the first public acknowledgment of the CIA-Mafia link by a high-level CIA official who had been directly involved.

The first time Jackson talked to Bissell, he didn't get much. But on the second try he persuaded Bissell to open up. Jackson pointed out that Robert A. Maheu, a former aide to eccentric billionaire recluse Howard Hughes, would probably discuss Bissell's involvement as well as his own in an upcoming press conference. Maheu told the Senate Intelligence Committee he had acted as an intermediary between the CIA and the Mafia. Jackson clinched the story by contending Bissell's role could not avoid exposure and he'd benefit by getting his version out first.

Earlier in 1975, Jackson tracked down a private detective who had been a party to the bugging of comedian Dan Rowan's Las Vegas hotel room by the CIA as a favor to Chicago Mafia chieftain Sam "Momo" Giancana in 1960. Giancana suspected Rowan of having an affair with Giancana's girl friend, singer Phyllis McGuire.

After the first report of the Rowan bugging appeared in the March 17, 1975, issue of *Time* magazine, Jackson was told by a Los Angeles reporter that a man named Arthur Villetti reportedly had done the bugging for the CIA. Jackson checked the name with congressional investigators, law enforcement agencies, and others who'd have reason to know about wiretap experts. No one had ever heard the name. Jackson called a man in security work he had met two years earlier in the Bahamas. The name meant nothing to him, either, but he phoned a friend of his in Miami and called Jackson back. The man Jackson wanted, he said, was a private detective named Arthur Balletti, not Villetti. Balletti had ties to Maheu and lived in Miami. He gave Jackson Balletti's address.

Jackson grabbed a plane to Miami and went out to Balletti's house. He pointed out to the detective that the Senate committee would soon be contacting him, and allowed how he'd be wise to get his story out fully and accurately from the beginning. Balletti talked freely, admitting he had conducted surveillance on Rowan at Maheu's request, but contending a coworker had done the bugging.

Jackson calls his tracking down of Balletti an example of "slogging," his word for the dogged, tedious work that's the essence of effective investigative journalism.

Shortly after President Nixon picked Spiro Agnew as his candidate for vice president on the 1968 Republican ticket, Jerry Landauer of the *Wall Street Journal's* Washington bureau began hearing talk of corruption by the little-known Maryland governor in the state's Baltimore County. Landauer began going to Baltimore as often as he could get away, to check out reports of payoffs and bribes by developers and contractors when Agnew was a zoning official and, later, the county executive. Such payoffs, he learned, had been a normal part of that area's politics for years. But he couldn't come up with enough specific evidence for a story implicating Agnew.

He got to know a lot of people who had dealt with Agnew, however—county officials, zoning board members, contractors, lawyers, developers, politicians, mortgage bankers. One lawyer he met became particularly helpful, but with a catch. Only after Landauer agreed to accept the information on an off-the-record basis, not to be used in a story, would the lawyer tell him about his own payoffs to Agnew for favorable zoning changes. He showed Landauer IOUs signed by Agnew for loans which, the parties involved understood, were never to be repaid. The IOUs were merely to serve as evidence, if needed, that the money was not a payoff.

Sure that he was on the right trail but still unable to publish the story, Landauer read through every zoning case that had come up while Agnew was in office. He found plenty of things that didn't look right, but still not enough evidence to support a story. A confrontation with Agnew eluded him. The Vice President refused to be interviewed, even though Landauer once followed him all the way to Jackson, Mississippi, while trying to provoke a response.

Knowing that federal agents had entered the case, Landauer checked periodically with the U.S. Attorney's office in Baltimore. One day in August, 1973, his seven years of inquiry paid off. He was told that Agnew had been formally notified of the Justice Department investigation. This enabled him to break the story, on which he was already well backgrounded. He reported that the probe included federal construction contracts awarded in Maryland after Agnew became vice president as well as state contracts during his two years as governor. Landauer won the 1973 Drew Pearson Prize for investigative reporting awarded by the National Press Club for his work on the scandal that led to Agnew's historic resignation.

In another case, Landauer's reporting led directly to the prosecution of a public figure. This was his 1971 exposé of Brooklyn Congressman Bertram L. Podell's attempts to help an airline client of his Manhattan law firm get approval from the Civil Aeronautics Board for a Florida-Bahamas route. Podell admitted to Landauer that he was guilty of an indiscretion. Federal prosecutors were more interested, however, in the fact that it was a crime for a congressman to accept compensation for services in a case involving the federal government, even if the services were performed by a firm in which the congressman had only a "residual interest."

Two years earlier, the short, wiry, slightly rumpled Landauer had exposed conflicts of interest by New York Republican Congressman Seymour Halpern, a senior member of the House Banking Committee.

While checking the backgrounds of banking committee members because of a tip about heavy lobbying behind a banking bill, Landauer found some of Halpern's recent voting to be out of step with his past positions. Probing more deeply, he discovered that Halpern was "up to his ass in debt" and had obtained bank loans at subnormal interest rates.

He went to Halpern's office and, bluffing, pretended to know more than he really did. A trick used frequently by skilled investigative reporters, it put Halpern on the spot. He had to choose between lying, with the risk of getting caught at it, and trying to sell the reporter on an innocent explanation of the truth. He chose the latter. He admitted to having borrowed more than $100,000 from seven banks, much of it in unsecured loans, despite an inglorious credit record. He had bounced checks at one of the banks and one of his credit cards had been cancelled due to nonpayment. Though several of the banks had various matters pending before government agencies, Halpern insisted his personal finances had no connection with his official duties, and therefore presented no conflict of interest. Landauer included the congressman's version in his story, but Halpern was defeated at the next election.

Landauer, who's been with the *Wall Street Journal* for fourteen of his forty-four years, doesn't like to base stories on anonymous sources. He prefers to work from records and thinks that Woodstein's reliance on anonymous sources in their Watergate reportage lowered the standards of proof for the newspaper industry. Landauer's 1965 article on sweetheart contracts between coal companies and the United Mine Workers came strictly from records, as did his later stories on the UMW's failure to enforce contract provisions on company contributions to the union's pension fund.

The pension fund story emerged from records at the U.S. Department of Labor and state reports on mine output in Kentucky, West Virginia, Virginia, Tennessee, and Illinois. From Labor Department records, Landauer made a list of mining companies that were supposed to contribute forty cents per ton to the pension fund, plus the actual amounts contributed by each company. Some amounts were so low that the companies could not have remained in business if the figures accurately reflected the production of their mines. Sifting assidu-ously through state records on mine output, Landauer then found that many companies had contributed only a fraction of their contract obligations.

As a result of his stories, lawsuits were filed against the pension fund. The disclosures also figured prominently in the growing rebellion among coal miners that eventually toppled W. A. "Tony" Boyle from the UMW presi-dency.

Records were also the chief source for Landauer's earlier disclosures on the outside activities of federal judges that won a 1963 Raymond Clapper Award.

Acting on a tip, he checked directories of corporate officers and directors for the names of federal jurists. Discovering that the chief judge of the southern district of New York was a director of the Equitable Life Assurance Society, he studied public reports filed by insurance companies in which the salaries of officers and directors are listed. The judge, he found, was getting $100 per director's meeting, even while a case involving Equitable was pending in his court.

In 1968, Landauer revealed that the Seafarers International Union had sent twenty checks for $5,000 each to Democratic presidential campaign commit-tees around the country after Secretary of State Dean Rusk had granted the union's request not to extradite a union official to Canada. The official had jumped bail to avoid a five-year prison term for hiring goons to beat up a rival union leader, and fled to the United States. This story also came from records, which Landauer tracked down in various parts of the country.

In 1969, he revealed how the Seafarers Union was forcing Japanese and Filipino sailors to pay up to $1,000 for jobs on U.S. ships and then using the money illegally for campaign contributions. Landauer got a list of the "con-tributions" and the seamen who had been forced to make them from a source inside the union who disapproved of the practice.

In 1971, he uncovered a $10-a-month shakedown of Marine Engineer Beneficial Association pensioners that raised $250,000 a year for the union's political fund. The figures were on the union's records. By talking to several of the retirees, Landauer determined that the $10-a-month donations to the fund were not actually voluntary.

Landauer is a firm believer in the jackpot of stories to be found in public records. "There are many stories lying around in file cabinets that no one is thinking about," he says. There also are a lot of "public-spirited guys in the bureaucracy" who are willing to point reporters in a fruitful direction, he says.

He's among those who contend every reporter should be an investigative reporter—be willing to spend the extra time and energy required to get to the bottom of a story, and not be afraid to make enemies. Investigative reporters also need a keener than average skepticism. Landauer, for instance, assumes that nothing happens by accident, especially if there's "a lot of money floating around."

Five weeks before the Spiro Agnew scandal broke in the *Wall Street Journal*, while America's attention was riveted on John Dean's televised story of White House skullduggery in the Watergate cover-up, Saul Friedman of the Knight Newspapers Washington Bureau wrote the real first story about Agnew's involvement in a corruption investigation.

Friedman's article was worded very guardedly, however. It said that federal investigators were questioning former cronies of Agnew in Baltimore and the investigation might lead to the Vice President. It did not say categorically that Agnew himself was a target of the probe. Friedman knew more than he wrote, but he didn't use material not confirmed by a second source, and he didn't use off-the-record information not backed up by an on-the-record source.

As a result of his caution, the national preoccupation with Watergate, and the fact that the Washington papers had run articles about a Maryland investigation affecting former Agnew associates, Friedman's revelations attracted no notice in Washington and little elsewhere—though his story was given prominent play in the Knight papers, including the Detroit *Free Press,* which Friedman represented in the Washington bureau.

Friedman had begun an inquiry after a lawyer friend whose firm represented one of the men under investigation hinted that his firm's client was implicating Agnew. Interviews with Baltimore area contractors and former Agnew associates, many of whom later became grand jury witnesses, convinced Friedman that the lawyer's hint was on the mark. Like Landauer, he also got a vivid view of blatant, taken-for-granted corruption. Some contractors described the devices they used for channeling payoffs, including phony Christmas bonuses for employes who passed the money along to officials. But no one would go beyond generalizations and name names.

Next he talked with federal prosecutors, who were cagey. Friedman was able to surmise that Agnew was indeed in deep trouble, but couldn't maneuver them into saying so directly. There was nothing on which to hang a solid story.

He combed through Baltimore newspaper files for background on dealings by Agnew and his friends, and on Agnew's relationships with others whose activities were under scrutiny. Investigative reporting is often like intelligence work, in which bits of information from various sources are assembled and fitted together to form a perceptible picture. Some facts take on meaning only after they are combined with others. Bringing together all the pieces he garnered from various records and the new information he had turned up on his own, Friedman wrote his story.

Friedman's spadework gave him a big edge when Landauer's story appeared. He contacted his sources again for the latest developments. Some would not talk to him now. They had since testified before a grand jury and had been told it was illegal to discuss their testimony. With what he already knew, Friedman had enough to write the first report on the details of Agnew's alleged involvement, including accusations of $1,000-a-week payoffs from the time he was the Baltimore County Executive until after he became Vice President.

A chunky, quiet-spoken man who started his newspaper career as a police reporter twenty-three years ago, Friedman also was ahead of everyone else on the impeachment story. As one who likes to spot trends and look ahead to their future ramifications, he wrote an article on the procedures for impeaching a president a year before Congress began seriously to consider it. This made him friends on the House Judiciary Committee who later helped him stay a step ahead of other reporters when the committee began its deliberations on impeachment charges against Nixon.

Friedman would go into the committee offices in the middle of the night to copy documents and trade suggestions with staffers on the next leads to pursue. Though this gave him several good scoops, Friedman acknowledges it wasn't really investigative reporting. It was more akin to the "leak reporting" he once denounced in a column as reporting that's passed off as investigative but isn't—because it's merely finding a source who's willing to disclose what government investigators are doing.

Friedman has practically specialized in being ahead of his colleagues, perhaps too far ahead, sometimes, to get recognition for his exploits.

He was writing about illegal campaign contributions by corporations in 1970, long before Watergate made them a national scandal.

While a reporter for the Houston *Chronicle* years ago, he worked nights as a nurse's aide for three months gathering eyewitness evidence for an exposé of filthy conditions and maltreatment of patients at a hospital. One of his jobs was to clean out tracheal tubes, in which he found cockroaches. He saw patients lying unattended in their own excrement. He discovered doctors performing unnecessary sterilizations on black women because someone had decided "they shouldn't have any more babies."

He became an undercover member of the John Birch Society, first in Houston, then ag in in Detroit after he joined the *Free Press* in 1965. In Detroit he was a section leader in the right wing extremist organization and was chosen for leadership training. His chief discovery about the Birchers, he recalls, was that their meetings were dull.

Though considered by Washington journalists as the best investigator in the bureau, now the Knight-Ridder Washington Bureau, Friedman works on investigative assignments only about twenty-five percent of his time. He believes all stories "should be more or less investigative," but, like most reporters, can never find as much time for thorough investigation as he would like.

Others in the bureau also have turned in noteworthy investigative work. Robert Boyd and Clark Hoyt won a 1973 Pulitzer Prize for uncovering the mental illness in Democratic Vice Presidential candidate Thomas F. Eagleton's past. This they did with enterprising investigation of an anonymous telephone tip (later revealed possibly to have come from Watergate trickster E. Howard Hunt).

Friedman is not sure he would want to be a full-time investigative reporter. They often get set apart from other staff members, he says. This can cause friction among the staff, and lead to inappropriate pressure on the investigator to produce frequent, rather than thoroughly investigated, stories.

Despite the greatest national corruption scandal in American history in recent years, Friedman believes the federal government is the most honest in the country. "It's full of people with axes to grind," he says, "and this makes for checks and balances." Many of them try to use the news media for their own purposes, and that's fine with Friedman. He even encourages his sources to use him. After all, it brings in information and stories.

Dan Thomasson of the Scripps-Howard Bureau in Washington has kept a skeptical eye on the federal government's Medicare and Medicaid programs ever since they began. They were obviously vulnerable to fraud and abuse, almost as if they had been designed to attract it. That proved to be no idle apprehension.

Thomasson had written to some extent about the cheating, the waste, and other problems, but as 1975 began he decided to do a thorough investigation.

Working with Carl West, another investigative reporter in the bureau, Thomasson went to sources on Capitol Hill, studied material compiled by the Senate Finance Committee, pored over records at the Department of Health, Education and Welfare, and talked to Government Accounting Office investigators. He and West interviewed government officials in Washington and Baltimore, then traveled to New York, Miami, Chicago, Los Angeles, and other cities for more interviews—with doctors, nurses, hospital administrators, patients, government officials.

They went meticulously through state and county records on the administration of the programs for the poor and the elderly. In some places they delved into the results of investigations conducted by civic groups, such as the Better Government Association in Chicago.

The result was some thirty stories over several weeks beginning on February 15, 1975. They spelled out in detail how the programs were losing $3 billion a year to a variety of fraud schemes from minor bill padding by doctors, to an alleged $10-million-a-year bill collection racket with organized crime connections in Illinois. Thomasson and West uncovered abuses among nursing home operators, hospitals, pharmacists, and lab operators as well as doctors. Their stories brought out that federal and state authorities were doing little to stop the plunder. As a result of their revelations, several congressmen initiated moves to impose tighter controls. One proposal called for a special inspector general to oversee the two giant health care programs.

Thomasson finds investigative reporting "more gratifying when you work it from the ground up," as he and West did on Medicare and Medicaid. But he's also developed many exclusives from leaks. "You have to have leaks," he says. "Since the press has no subpoena power, we need someone to provide the leads." A leak as a lead, however, is only the starting point, the stimulus that launches the investigation.

It was a leak that led Thomasson and two other reporters to the 1973 story that first revealed Lyndon Johnson's use of FBI agents as political spies at the 1964 Democratic National Convention.

Along with Jim Squires of the Chicago *Tribune* and Harry Kelly of the Hearst newspapers, Thomasson heard that the Senate Watergate Committee had obtained a copy of a memo from former FBI official William Sullivan to John Dean containing details about LBJ's use of the FBI. When they couldn't pry any information out of the committee, they got busy and interviewed nineteen former assistants of J. Edgar Hoover scattered around the country.

They made slight headway at first, but every little bit helped them get more from the next ex-aide they located. Soon they knew enough to draw a great deal out of some. The trio even got a second big story for their efforts—that the FBI had used such illegal tactics as surreptitious entry ("bag job"), wiretapping and mail snooping for twenty-five years until 1966, including break-ins at foreign embassies and homes of persons suspected of espionage or organized crime.

Few remembered this original work on FBI misuse two years later when indiscretions by the CIA and the FBI burgeoned into 1975's most sensational scandal. Nor did the story make much of a splash at the time. Like Clark Mollenhoff, Jack Nelson, Saul Friedman, and others who write for newspapers outside the New York-Washington orbit, Thomasson has frequently suffered the frustration of feeling his best material disappears somewhere in the hinterlands and is never seen by anyone. "I sometimes feel," he says, "like I'm pissing into the wind."

Among Thomasson exclusives that others managed to overlook have been an exposé of corruption in the Small Business Administration's program for minority businesses, disclosure of the contents of E. Howard Hunt's safe at the White House, a story four days before the actual event that Nixon would resign the presidency, and the CIA's involvement in an attempt to poison leftist Patrice Lumumba of the Congo.

"It takes a special kind of person to be an investigative reporter," says the forty-two-year-old Thomasson. "One who's willing to spend hours doing mundane work, getting bleary-eyed from looking at records, following trails that dead end.

"It's tough, demanding work. Most of the time it's a long ways from being glamorous. An investigative reporter who works an eight-hour day just ain't going to make it," says Thomasson, who is lean and athletic and dresses sportily. He looks more like a yachtsman than a determined twenty-one-year veteran journalist who once moonlighted full-time as a reporter while serving in the Army.

A good investigative reporter, he believes, must have an instinct to go for the jugular, yet can't be bloodthirsty or biased. He shouldn't delight in it, but feel it's necessary. He also needs a change of pace, an occasional escape from investigative drudgery and frustration to preserve his sanity. He works better alone than on a team, because he's an independent soul, and highly competitive. "Nothing gets a guy going faster," says Thomasson, "than to hear that Sy Hersh is working on something."

With a little less bad luck, David Kraslow might well be the most famous investigative reporter in America. Kraslow was the first to write a story about CIA-backed preparations for the disastrous Bay of Pigs invasion of Cuba. But his newspaper decided not to run it. He and a colleague disclosed Vietnam peace negotiations three years before secret documents about them were left out of the controversial Pentagon Papers because they were "too sensitive."

Though their revelations had considerable impact at the time, they were overshadowed by the Pentagon Papers controversy later. In 1974, Kraslow obtained information indicating President Ford was about to pardon his predecessor for Watergate misdeeds, but missed the story because Ford's press secretary persuaded him he was on the wrong track.

In the summer of 1960, several youngsters heard military orders blaring from loudspeakers in a Cuban exile camp near Homestead, Florida, a farming area thirty miles south of Miami. From outside the camp, they also saw Cubans marching in formation. The youngsters decided to have some fun. They threw firecrackers into the camp. The Cubans, believing themselves under attack, came out firing carbines. One of the American youngsters was wounded, charges were filed against several of the Cubans, and a brief account of the incident appeared in the Miami newspapers.

But nothing further happened, and that piqued the curiosity of the Miami *Herald's* courthouse reporter. He kept asking why the prosecution of the Cubans was not proceeding. He finally was told there had been a request by the U.S. State Department to "lay off." Now the *Herald's* city editor was curious. He called Kraslow, the *Herald's* Washington correspondent, and asked him to find out why the federal government was so concerned about the fate of a few Cuban exiles.

Kraslow spent five weeks rooting out the story from sources in the State Department, the White House, and the FBI. Accustomed to dealing with state department officials who handled Latin American affairs, he found their evasive responses to questions a bit odd. The same happened with White House sources. Something extra sensitive must be going on. Sources at the FBI told him he was onto something hot. He kept badgering them to tell him what it was.

FBI Director J. Edgar Hoover at the time was engaged in a bureaucratic struggle with the CIA over the CIA's training of Cuban exiles in Florida. Hoover claimed the CIA was violating the federal Neutrality Act, which the FBI was charged with enforcing on American soil. Hoover argued that it had to stop. A belief that a story exposing the training operation might help Hoover win the argument apparently prompted someone in the FBI to tell Kraslow the story.

Kraslow wrote 1,500 words saying the CIA had secretly been authorized by President Eisenhower's administration to recruit and train Cuban exiles for a military operation against Cuba. The story described pressure on Eisenhower by Hoover and Attorney General William Rogers to move the training operation out of the United States.

During the next several weeks there were several conversations in which Kraslow, Washington Bureau Chief Ed Lahey, Managing Editor George Beebe, and Executive Editor Lee Hills agonized over the question of whether the story would damage national security. Kraslow and Lahey were asked to sound out CIA Director Allen Dulles.

They went to Dulles' office in November, told him what the story contained, and asked for his reaction. Dulles sat quietly puffing on his pipe, looking like a college professor. "I'm not indicating whether it's true or not," Dulles said, "but if that story is published it would not be in the national interest."

After further soul searching, Miami *Herald* editors and John S. Knight, head of the Knight newspaper chain, decided they did not want to disclose national intelligence operations. The story was not run.

All this was several months before *The New York Times* got onto the story and gained recognition as being first. The *Times'* Latin America correspondent, Tad Szulc, stopped in Miami en route from Brazil to Washington early in April and learned that an invasion of Cuba was imminent. Szulc's story, contrary to some later reports that the *Times* suppressed it, ran on April 7, 1961. But it had been "toned down." References to CIA involvement and the imminence of the invasion had been removed. *Times* editors feared they would compromise national security, contribute to the failure of a military operation, and cause greater casualties among friendly forces by alerting Cuba to the time of an attack. President John F. Kennedy later told a *Times* editor that the *Times* might have prevented the "colossal mistake" of the Bay of Pigs invasion if it had run all of Szulc's story.

Kraslow's Vietnam peace talk story began six years later, in the spring of 1967. Rumors circulated in Washington that America's December 1966 bombing of Hanoi, the capital of North Vietnam, had sabotaged an effort to set up peace talks between the United States and North Vietnam. State Department officials insisted there was no substance to the reports. The Associated Press distributed a story quoting unnamed officials that the U.S. had made every effort to create an atmosphere for negotiations. It said the bombings had no connection with the peace initiative.

Kraslow, by then the news editor for the Los Angeles *Times* Washington Bureau, became intrigued by the story as he discussed it with Stuart Loory, the bureau's White House correspondent. They agreed someone ought to find out what had really happened. Had there been a communications breakdown between the military and the diplomats? Had the military hawks deliberately sabotaged a peace move? They approached bureau chief Robert J. Donovan with a proposal that they take two or three months off to investigate, then write a series. Donovan gave his approval.

The project, as it turned out, took eight months. And the story they uncovered was more momentous, and more fascinating, than they had suspected. It evolved into a book as well as a series.

They began to realize the larger dimensions as they started talking to diplomats and State Department officials. Progress was slow, however, and they turned for help to Senator Robert Kennedy, who kept close ties with developments in Vietnam diplomacy and who had many friends and allies in the State Department. When they told Kennedy they had heard some Frenchmen were somehow involved, Kennedy suggested they talk to Henry Kissinger, a Harvard professor with no visible connection to the government.

Though the public had not yet heard much of Henry Kissinger, Kraslow had. He had taken a course in defense policy from Kissinger when he attended Harvard on a Nieman Fellowship for journalists in 1961–62. However, Kraslow could not fathom what Kissinger might have to do with Vietnam peace talks.

When Kraslow went to see him, Kissinger inquired, "Who sent you?" Upon mention of Kennedy, Kissinger disclosed he was a consultant to the government on Vietnam diplomacy, but would say little else. A source had mentioned the word, "Marigold," to Kraslow, and now he flung it at Kissinger.

"What do you know about Marigold?" he asked.

The professor with the thick accent was unable to contain his surprise. His face reddened and he needed fifteen seconds to regain his composure. "I don't want to talk about it," Kissinger said. The incident convinced Kraslow that he and Loory were on to something stupendous.

"Marigold" was the code name for a five-month attempt by a young Polish diplomat in Vietnam to arrange secret peace negotiations. The detailed story of this ill-fated venture, its demise after the December bombing raids, and how the raids came to happen at such a disastrous time, comprises the first part of Kraslow's and Loory's 1968 book, *The Secret Search for Peace in Vietnam.*

The rest of the book is about other peace initiatives the two reporters uncovered during their investigation, which took them to several foreign countries and included interviews with scores of American and foreign diplomats, and U.S. government officials.

Since they never expected to get access to classified documents, the pair knew they had to wrest the story from the recollections of the people involved. Kraslow believes the fact they were working on a book, not just a newspaper series, convinced their sources that their undertaking was a serious, scholarly one, not just a bit of sensationalism. There was a problem of conscience, the feeling among government officials and diplomats that to disclose classified information would violate their oaths of office. Kraslow and Loory overcame this by contending that disclosure would serve the national interest better.

They also found, as investigative reporters everywhere know, that the more they learned, the easier it became to learn more. Once an official realized they already knew a great deal, he usually became helpful and candid. But it was not easy. It took a long time to wear down the resistance.

Kraslow and Loory conducted joint interviews in the United States, but split up the overseas chores, Kraslow going to Canada, England, and France, Loory to Italy, Czechoslovakia, and Poland.

They had just finished writing the book at the end of March, 1968, when President Lyndon Johnson made his surprise announcement that he would not seek reelection because of the Vietnam war controversy. Kraslow and Loory rushed to complete their newspaper series. It began April 4 with their timely revelation of Kissinger's secret role in peace initiatives, his series of communications to North Vietnamese President Ho Chi Minh through two Frenchmen, one a microbiologist and the other an old friend of Ho, that culminated in the Paris peace talks.

The disclosure of Kissinger's role caused a sensation. Both the series and the book were nominated for Pulitzer Prizes. The series made it to the finals in international reporting before losing to an account of brutality by U.S. Marines against Vietnamese civilians. The series did win the Raymond Clapper Award for Washington correspondence and the George Polk Memorial Award for international reporting. Kissinger later referred to the book as the most accurate account available of Vietnam peace negotiations. Kraslow regards the project as "the most satisfying piece of work" he's ever done.

The Kissinger aspect, however, overshadowed the "Marigold" disclosures. Three years later, when Daniel Ellsberg gave *The New York Times* the Pentagon Papers containing government secrets about America's Vietnam policies and strategy, he omitted four volumes that dealt with Vietnam peace initiatives, including "Marigold." He believed these documents were too sensitive to be exposed, even though most of the information had been reported by Kraslow and Loory. President Johnson later used the "Marigold" documents in his book, *The Vantage Point*, confirming the accuracy of Kraslow's and Loory's account. Yet, the pair's "Marigold" disclosures never aroused the controversy or achieved the notoriety that the Pentagon Papers generated.

In 1974, after serving as Washington Bureau Chief for the Los Angeles *Times* and assistant managing editor of the Washington *Star*, Kraslow set up a new national bureau in Washington to serve the Cox newspapers in Dayton, Atlanta, Miami, Palm Beach, and Springfield, Ohio. He was hired by Jim Fain, then editor of the Dayton *Daily News* and the Miami *News*, to stress enterprise reporting and investigative digging rather than conventional national coverage.

Though his main duties were administrative, Kraslow tried to keep his hand in reporting. In September, a month after Gerald Ford assumed the presidency that Richard Nixon had been forced to resign and Nixon had retired in disgrace to San Clemente, California, Kraslow learned that a Washington lawyer named Benton J. Becker had gone to San Clemente. Since Becker was a law partner of former Congressman William Cramer of Florida and Cramer was close to Ford, Kraslow suspected something out of the ordinary. It might be connected to negotiations for a pardon, by far the Number One topic for speculation in a capital still reeling from shock. In a phone call to Cramer, Kraslow got the same kind of reaction Kissinger had given to "Marigold" years earlier.

More phone calls turned up the fact that Becker was staying in the same San Clemente motel as Nixon's lawyer, Herbert J. Miller. Kraslow phoned Jerald ter Horst, the former Detroit *News* Washington Bureau chief who had become Ford's press secretary. He asked Ter Horst if Becker and Miller were discussing a presidential pardon for Nixon. Ter Horst called back in half an hour to say he'd been told by presidential aide Philip Buchen that the only topic of Becker's discussions with Miller was the disposition of Nixon's tapes and records.

"Why would Becker have to make a trip to California just to discuss the tapes with Miller?" Kraslow persisted. "They could do that in Washington."

Ter Horst insisted there was nothing more to it.

"I assume, Jerry, that if something as major as a pardon were being talked about seriously, you would expect to know about it."

"No question about it," said Ter Horst. "That is not the kind of thing I want to be surprised about."

Kraslow and Fain decided the story was too weak to run, in view of the White House denial. The surprise came two days later, on a Sunday morning, when Ter Horst called to advise Kraslow that Ford was going on television with an announcement. He said, "Dave, I'm very sorry."

"Don't tell me, Jerry."

"Yes," said Ter Horst. "If I knew on Friday what I know now, I would not have steered you away from that story."

Kraslow believes that Buchen's lie to Ter Horst was a factor in Ter Horst's resignation. Ter Horst, in an epilogue to his book, *Gerald Ford and the Future of the Presidency,* said his resignation was due to his disagreement with the granting of the pardon rather than the deception by Buchen that caused him to misinform a reporter.

Kraslow believes that the term, "investigative reporter," is a redundancy. All reporters should, by definition, be investigators who probe beneath press releases and surface explanations to get the whole story. Investigative techniques are tools to be used by all reporters, not just a special few. What others call investigative journalism, Kraslow terms "high risk journalism," because it often requires an extraordinary commitment of time and other resources to a project that carries a big risk of ending up fruitless. "Few papers," he says, "are willing to spend the money to do it right."

In Kraslow's case, the main risk seems to be nonrecognition. In November, 1975, he wrote an article saying Kissinger was likely to be the next major victim of a power struggle in the Ford Administration. Will anyone remember his story if his prediction turns out to be right?

Richard Dudman of the St. Louis *Post-Dispatch* was disgusted with *The New York Times'* coverage of the Vietnam War. He knew he could do a better job of reporting the truth about the controversial conflict.

He had already been to Southeast Asia several times, including 1959 when he took a plane into the jungle to learn from Laotians reported to have engaged Red Chinese soldiers in a major battle that the battle never actually took place. In 1970, he had been captured by Communists in Cambodia and held prisoner for forty days.

Now he resolved to get the inside story of North Vietnam's tenacious resistance against American military power, especially the massive bomb raids on their native land.

"Sometimes getting into a place is half the battle," says Dudman, a thin-faced, bald, forty-nine-year-old veteran journalist who's been a Washington correspondent for the *Post-Dispatch* for twenty-one years and bureau chief since 1969. His newspaper had editorialized against American involvement in the war, and that now stood him in good stead. For he got a visa even though it was a time of heavy bombing by U.S. planes and no other American reporter was gaining admittance to North Vietnam.

Dudman doesn't think of himself as an investigative specialist, but he's made effective use of investigative techniques in Washington and abroad. Now, during the first two weeks of September, 1972, he applied them to learning more than his hosts had in mind.

Though usually accompanied by two North Vietnamese escorts, Dudman managed to discover Hanoi's method of scattering ammunition dumps to avoid big losses to a bomb hit, and North Vietnam's use of small convoys to transport men and materials. He learned about their system of dispersing industry to minimize bombing losses, and their network of underground bomb shelters. He sneaked out of his hotel to take pictures before his escorts arrived in the morning.

He found the North Vietnamese candid about the heavy damage and casualties they suffered, but determined to outlast America's will to fight. His eight-part "Report from Hanoi" helped him win the 1972 Overseas Press Club Award for best reporting on Asia.

Dudman has exemplified the *Post-Dispatch's* traditional feistiness on the home front, too. When *The New York Times* began publishing the Pentagon Papers in 1971, Dudman quickly contacted sources that might help him get a piece of the story. Finally he got a call saying a reporter would be contacted if sent to a certain place. Dudman followed instructions and got parts of the documents, which the *Post-Dispatch* published after the federal government obtained a court order that briefly stopped *The New York Times*, the Washington *Post* and the Boston *Globe*.

His reward for his success, Dudman discovered later, was an FBI subpoena of his phone records to trace his sources. In 1975, he asked under the Freedom of Information Act to see FBI files on himself and his bureau, with special reference to material related to the subpoena. After his request, and a subsequent appeal to Attorney General Edward Levi, were denied, the *Post-Dispatch* filed suit to force release of the files.

"The *Post-Dispatch* likes to right wrongs more than most papers," says Dudman. The paper was founded by one of the greats of American journalism, Joseph Pulitzer, and continued in a tradition of "public service reporting" by Managing Editor Ben Reese. It once came to the aid of an Air Force major with twenty years of service about to be kicked out because he questioned an order.

More recently Robert Adams of the Washington Bureau exposed irregularities in the federal civil serice.

"Some accuse us of a moralistic attitude," Dudman observes. "But if we find an unfeeling approach toward people by government or business, we think it should be exposed."

Morton Mintz is admired by fellow Washington journalists as a topnotch veteran at investigative reporting. He won several national journalism awards, for instance, for his 1962 disclosures on the dangers of thalidomide, the drug that caused grotesque birth defects in Germany. His story revealed the heroism of a Food and Drug Administration doctor who kept the drug off the market in the United States despite fierce pressure by a drug manufacturer to force approval of thalidomide for use in a sleeping pill. The enormous impact of the story led to new legislation to protect the public.

Mintz was prompted to expand his investigation of the prescription drug industry. The thalidomide scare, he found, was but the tip of a frightening iceberg. He discovered widespread recklessness and disregard for safety among doctors and pharmaceutical companies, and dereliction of duty at the FDA. Patients who thought they were using safe drugs were being subjected to unnecessary risks, harmful side effects, even death. Mintz dug the evidence out of government records and presented it in his 1965 book, *The Therapeutic Nightmare*.

But Mintz, who covers federal agencies for the Washington *Post* while writing books and magazine articles on the side, doesn't believe in investigative reporting. To talk about investigative reporting, he thinks, is to miss the point.

The main thing, Mintz says, is spotting what the real news is. Reporters too often overlook matters of deep importance, such as the FDA's approval of oral contraceptives without adequate testing of harmful side effects. Mintz broke that story in 1965, then wrote a book on the dangers of the Pill. In 1970, he was among the few who were writing about the inordinate influence of corporate money on American politics through campaign contributions that broke or circumvented the law. He wrote a 1971 book about that, called *America, Inc.*

"You have to sacrifice something in order to do investigative reporting," says Mintz. "You miss a lot of other things, like investigations by others on Capitol Hill."

A favorite story about Mintz among the capital press corps concerns his reaction one day when he arrived to cover a committee hearing and found other reporters already in attendance. Turning on his heel, he went off to cover something that others were ignoring.

"Our function is to provide as best we can the facts that people need to know," Mintz says. "We ought to act like professionals and define our goals better, our standards of what news is."

3

Mr. Muckraker

ONE DAY IN DECEMBER, 1971, as American warships steamed into the Bay of Bengal to support Pakistan in its war against India, a high-ranking Washington official told columnist Jack Anderson the U.S. might provoke a war with Russia, who was backing India. Anderson expressed surprise. The Nixon Administration had stated publicly that the United States would not take sides in the conflict, which had started over East Pakistan's fight for independence with India's help. Anderson's source replied that, regardless of what the Nixon Administration said publicly, it was secretly aiding Pakistan. There were documents to prove it.

Anderson, who asks his most trustworthy sources for records or other proof, inquired about getting copies of the documents. The source demurred. He had in the past given Anderson information from top secret files, but had stopped short of letting the columnist quote from them directly, let alone see them. He wanted again just to give Anderson general information.

Anderson turned on more persuasion. It was a critical matter. The government was lying to the American people, placing the nation on the brink of a global war without the public's slightest suspicion. Public disclosure was vital to protect the national interest.

The source wavered. Well, maybe he could quote some parts of the papers.

Anderson insisted on copies. "This is important," he said. "I have to document it all the way."

At last, the source yielded. He turned over a few of the classified documents.

Now Anderson set in motion an investigative technique based on the principle of foot-in-the-door leverage. He played one source against another. Armed with partial information, Anderson contacted another in his vast network of sources. This one, Anderson figured, would talk freely when he realized Anderson already knew a good deal. The columnist was right. After some cajoling by Anderson, the source also gave him copies of secret documents.

Anderson then went to a third source and repeated the procedure, again with success.

Now he returned to the first source, equipped with more complete knowledge. In the end, Anderson got copies of all the classified intelligence reports, cables, and minutes of White House meetings that dealt with the Nixon Administration's secret "tilt" toward Pakistan.

As every investigative journalist knows, digging out the facts and publishing them is often not enough. Many a great exposé vanishes into oblivion for lack of attention. Anderson's first revelations of the Pakistan tilt appeared in unsensational fashion in his December 13, 1971, column. They followed several paragraphs about Drew Pearson, the man who had started the "Washington Merry-Go-Round" column that Anderson took over after Pearson's death in 1969. That day was Pearson's birthday.

The second half of the column disclosed that Henry Kissinger, then Nixon's chief adviser and personal envoy on foreign policy, had passed the word about an American commitment to Pakistan. Kissinger was saying the United States could not let Pakistan be overwhelmed by India with Russian aid.

In his next column, Anderson wrote about the "dangerous confrontation developing between Soviet and American Naval forces in the Bay of Bengal." He quoted from the minutes of White House strategy meetings by the Washington Security Action Group, composed of the nation's highest government leaders.

Two days later, he wrote about contradictions between the White House's public position on Pakistan and the private statements by Kissinger. He quoted a cable from Washington to Jordan with instructions to "keep open the possibility of authorizing King Hussein to rush several U.S.-supplied P-104 fighter planes to Pakistan."

Though these revelations were later to seem so sensational, none of them now caught anyone's eye among the news media.

Perplexed but determined, Anderson decided after Christmas to try a new twist on the old keep-pounding-away tactic. He would repeat the story, but this time he would make it thoroughly unmistakable that the documents from which he quoted were top secret. This time he would not pussyfoot around the gravity and magnitude of his disclosures.

Anderson wrote a second series of columns—four this time—beginning on December 30, 1971. The first wasted no time getting to the guts of the story. Referring to "highlights from secret White House papers" and "security labels used to hide . . . the blunders of our leaders," Anderson reported that Nixon had aligned the United States with Pakistan, overridden the advice of State Department experts, sent a naval task force to the Bay of Bengal "in a fit of petulance," and tried to circumvent laws against shipping arms to Pakistan.

Though it was really just a rehash of the earlier columns, this time the spark caught fire. *The New York Times,* after verifying the facts with sources of its own, ran a front-page story about Anderson's column. The *Times* followed with reports on the second and third columns. The wire services and TV networks picked up the story. A column by Tom Wicker in the *Times* entitled "The Anderson Papers" praised the columnist for his public service disclosures. Anderson gave copies of White House meeting minutes to the Washington *Post* for use as its own exclusive. Anderson found himself in demand for interviews and deluged with invitations to appear on television. Suddenly, after twenty-five years as a hardworking investigative journalist in the nation's most treacherous political jungle, Anderson was a celebrity.

Among the plaudits, however, were some sharp questions about the propriety of disclosing government secrets. It was the same issue that had racked the nation with tortuous debate several months earlier over the publication of the Pentagon Papers, secret documents on the government's handling of the Vietnam War.

Anderson responded by defending the public's right to know what its government is doing. He attacked the government for debasing security procedures by using them to cover up lies and blunders and protect personal power and prestige. "We can't let the government censor with a classified stamp," he says. In a *Parade* magazine article, Anderson quoted the late U.S. Supreme Court Justice Hugo Black: "The press was protected so that it could bare the secrets of government and inform the people. Only a free and unrestrained press can effectively expose deception in government."

Most of the attention was flattering, however. Magazines ran long articles on Anderson. Newsmen remarked how much more accurate, more impartial, and more serious at journalism he was than Pearson. Critics who had dismissed his muckraking as frivolous and erratic now recalled several noteworthy scoops over the years that perhaps had failed to get the recognition they deserved. Speech invitations came flooding in. The number of newspapers buying his column, already over 700, took another big leap. He got a $100,000 advance to write a book entitled *The Anderson Papers*.

It was an exhilarating time for the strapping, stern-visaged, forty-nine-year-old Mormon, who, in sharp contrast to the racy tone of his column, manages to look stiff and a bit severe even when his tie is loose, his shoes are off, and his manner is friendly. He doesn't drink, smoke, or work on Sunday, and his idea of a social event is to spend a day with his wife and nine children.

The sudden acclaim almost made up for all the times the column's exclusives had been ignored by the regular press. For example:

> Anderson's disclosures in 1967 and 1971 of attempts by the CIA to assassinate Cuban Premier Fidel Castro during the Kennedy administration with the help of underworld figures, a story that was finally recognized as important in 1975;
>
> His revelation in August, 1971, that Howard Hughes had given $100,000 to Nixon's campaign through Bebe Rebozo, Nixon's Florida confidante, a story that simmered for a couple of years until the Watergate scandal overcame the nation's indifference;
>
> Disclosure in 1960 of Hughes' $205,000 loan to Nixon's brother, Donald, at a time when Hughes Tool Company was a prominent defense contractor;
>
> A 1964 report questioning the Johnson administration's version of the Gulf of Tonkin incident, which became the justification for America's active intervention in the Vietnam War;
>
> 100-odd columns on the pocketing of political contributions and other misdeeds by U.S. Senator Thomas J. Dodd of Connecticut, a story that was nominated for a Pulitzer Prize but didn't win;
>
> A 1951 scoop on the historic Wake Island conference between President Harry S Truman and General Douglas MacArthur shortly before Truman fired the recalcitrant general, a story with which *The New York Times* won a Pulitzer Prize even though its version appeared nine months later.

This time, the committee that selects the winners of journalism's highest honors could hardly overlook Anderson. His achievement on the Pakistan story had received wide acclaim and publicity. That, to the dismay of many in a field that views itself as a profession, often plays as crucial a role in the winning of awards as the quality of the work. When the Pulitzer Prize winners were announced on May 1, 1972, there was Anderson on the list for the best in national reporting.

Not only was it a climactic honor for Washington's most prolific investigative journalist, it was also a sign that Anderson had at last been accepted by the high priests of journalism as an authentic member of the profession. Brit Hume, a reporter then working for Anderson, said in his 1974 book, *Inside Story*, it was "the breakthrough we had all been awaiting." Hume said it "gave Jack an instant and significant boost in standing both with the press and the public."

Anderson, according to Hume, remained coolheaded and relatively unimpressed by all the fuss. "Don't worry," he said. "Pretty soon they'll be giving us hell again. All of this was nice while it lasted, but the column has always been Peck's Bad Boy and sooner or later we're bound to do something they think is outrageous."

Though Anderson didn't know it at the time, among the attention his prize-winning story had attracted was the fury of powerful people who believed his behavior was already outrageous. Several White House officials and Nixon loyalists were so angry over the columnist's disclosure of secret documents that they began talking about ways to discredit Anderson or "get rid" of him.

Watergate conspirator G. Gordon Liddy, then an unknown lawyer working for the Committee for the Re-election of the President, was so agitated that he believed he had been ordered to kill Anderson. He was dissuaded only when deputy campaign director Jeb Stuart Magruder, another Watergate figure, convinced him the talk was not serious.

But early in 1972 Liddy and fellow Watergate conspirator E. Howard Hunt did explore the possibility at least of surreptitiously drugging the columnist. Hunt later told friends he had been ordered by a White House official to assassinate Anderson with poison, according to a September, 1975, story by Washington *Post* reporter Bob Woodward, of Watergate fame. After Woodward's story appeared, Hunt told *Time* magazine that he and Liddy had not contemplated murder, but only drugging Anderson so he would become incoherent on his radio show and be discredited. Hunt said the plot had been suggested by White House Counsel Charles Colson, but was discarded as impractical after Liddy and Hunt discussed methods with a CIA physician. Colson denied knowledge of any such plan.

Between the Pakistan policy disclosures at the end of 1971 and the Pulitzer Prize announcement on May 1, 1972, Anderson published his next bombshell, which transformed angry talk at the White House into a concerted campaign to ruin the columnist. This was Anderson's exposure of ITT lobbyist Dita Beard's infamous memo, the first solid evidence to be publicly revealed that the U.S. Justice Department, under Nixon crony John Mitchell, had given ITT a favorable settlement in an antitrust case in return for $400,000 to help finance the 1972 Republican National Convention. Publication of the memo's contents in three columns at the end of February and beginning of March triggered swift reaction by the news media and government officials. Partly because of all the attention on Anderson for the Pakistan story, the ITT memo was front-page news immediately.

The possibility of such a deal with ITT had first been published in a November 29, 1971, Washington *Star-News* article by investigative reporter Robert Walters. Walters attributed it to an accusation by a prominent California Democrat.

A December 9 column by Anderson had charged that an "aura of scandal" hung over ITT's acquisition of the Hartford Fire Insurance Company, a key issue in the antitrust case. The column questioned the Justice Department's approval of the acquisition after filing suit to stop it.

But Dita Beard's memo, which came into Anderson's possession on February 22, 1972, and which Mrs. Beard confirmed as genuine in two interviews with Hume, was the first solid corroboration of the story.

The two-page memo came to Anderson from one of two sources he had developed within ITT. Anderson's December 9 column, used partly as a "lure" to attract more information, apparently was a factor in prompting the source to give him the memo. The "lure" technique is used to reach people who have important knowledge and may be willing to reveal it if they are aware that someone has an interest in it. Stories are published despite incomplete information to invite unknown sources to come forward. This is a legitimate tactic as long as what is published is newsworthy, is sufficiently substantial to warrant publication, and is not unfair in its presentation of damaging allegations with incomplete proof. It's an effective way to develop a story a bit at a time, to chip away at it piecemeal, until a complete picture emerges from sources that otherwise would have remained unknown and unreached.

"There is a limit to what can be dredged up from interviewing obvious suspects and studying such records as are available to the public," Anderson wrote in his book. When the reporter "reaches the place where the trail vanishes, he is lost unless some unknown insider comes forward with the missing clue. I have never found anything unethical in trying to tempt the insider to come out into the cold. In this respect, muckrakers are like the sirens of Greek mythology, who, by their seductive singing, enticed unknowing wayfarers to abandon the cramped boredom of safe passage for a hazardous try at strange excitements and gratifications. Somewhere within ITT or the Justice Department or the SEC was a person who had access to the corroborating proof and a motive for revealing it. There is always someone somewhere." In his December 9 column, Anderson said, "We were singing our siren songs."

Disclosure of the Dita Beard memo raised embarrassing questions for attorney general designate Richard Kleindienst in his Senate confirmation hearings, since he had been involved in the case for the Justice Department. It also prompted the Senate to launch an investigation, and annoyed the White House into a determination to investigate, harass, and discredit Anderson.

Among the steps the White House took was to feed disparaging material about Anderson to the press and Republican members of the Senate committee investigating the controversy. FBI agents were assigned. Anderson learned he was being tailed and his house had been staked out. Neighbors noticed a car with two men parked nearby. Anderson's children thought it was great sport to spot men watching their house with binoculars.

It was neither the first time nor the last time that government officials tried to avenge Anderson's revelations by sicking the FBI on him. Years earlier, when Drew Pearson began exposing how the late Senator Dodd was misusing campaign funds and performing favors for a West German agent named Julius Klein, the FBI tried to determine how Anderson had obtained documents from Dodd's files for Pearson.

Aides of Dodd, an ex-FBI agent himself, were subjected to FBI interrogation, not about their employer's misconduct, but their possible involvement in helping Anderson. Four of Dodd's employes later announced publicly that they had given documents to Anderson during his twelve-month investigation.

Anderson learned from informants in the Justice Department that his telephone was tapped and that indictments were being prepared against him for theft of Dodd's papers.

Later, in 1973, Anderson's second-in-command, Les Whitten, was arrested by the FBI as he helped return stolen Indian treaty documents.

Anderson and his staff take for granted that their phones are tapped. They often talk with their sources in code.

While Nixon's aides were working feverishly to unhorse Anderson early in 1972, a Lehigh University student named Jeff Brindle, working for Anderson as an unpaid intern, pored through a pile of ITT memos, letters, and cables received from a source inside ITT. Though the papers had no apparent connection with the antitrust scandal, Hume thought they'd be worth checking. According to a public admission by ITT lawyers, a large quantity of records had been destroyed after it was known that Anderson had Dita Beard's memo. Perhaps some interesting documents had been overlooked and never got to the shredder.

As it turned out, these documents were the basis for a March 21 column breaking the story that ITT officials and the CIA had plotted to prevent leftist Salvador Allende from becoming president of Chile. Anderson revealed that ITT and the CIA had tried to stir up economic chaos in the hope of instigating a military coup, blocking Allende, and heading off the prospect of an anti-American government that might seize ITT holdings.

While the government and the public were still reeling from that disclosure, Anderson kept spewing out more. One column described how U.S. Ambassador to France Arthur Watson had made passes at stewardesses while drunk on a transatlantic flight. Anderson published parts of the Pentagon Papers that Daniel Ellsberg had not given *The New York Times*, segments that dealt with secret diplomatic moves to promote peace talks between the United States and North Vietnam in 1966 and 1967.

On May 1, 1972, the day that Pulitzer Prize winners were announced, Anderson's column revealed that the FBI for years had collected information on the sex habits, business affairs, and politics of movie stars, sports celebrities, black leaders (including Martin Luther King, Jr.), politicians, and newsmen who had dared to be critical of the FBI or its famous director, J. Edgar Hoover. When the newly appointed acting director of the FBI, L. Patrick Gray, denied that such information was kept in secret files, Anderson wrote that he would be glad to supply the file numbers so that Gray could see for himself. Anderson had obtained copies of the dossiers from a source who had access to them. This was another story, however, that did not get much attention until 1975.

Amidst the gratifying recognition and a continuing spate of major revelations, Anderson managed to miss the biggest story of all, the Watergate conspiracy. Though later he did publish several exclusives during the gradual emergence of the Watergate story, he missed three opportunities to get most of it far ahead of everyone else—at the time of the Watergate arrests in June, 1972, and possibly even earlier.

In April, Anderson had received a letter from William Haddad, a former investigative reporter and government official in the Kennedy Administration. Then in New York, Haddad wrote that a private detective had told him of plans to tap telephones at Democratic National Committee headquarters. Haddad said the people behind the plan were advertising experts connected with the Nixon campaign. Anderson learned later that James McCord, one of the five men caught red-handed inside the Democratic Party office, had been in New York City to test the security of telephones used by the advertising experts, known as the November group. While there, McCord had mentioned to someone that he had done wiretapping at the Democratic Party headquarters, and this got back to the private detective who told Haddad about it.

But, many other things were absorbing Anderson's time, especially the furor and follow-up coverage on Dita Beard's memo, the authorship of which the lady lobbyist had later denied. There were also appearances before the Senate committee investigating the matter. Though Anderson told Democratic National Chairman Lawrence O'Brien about the wiretapping tip, he made no effort to pursue the lead. The Watergate plot might never have proceeded to the break-in on June 17, Anderson wrote in *The Anderson Papers*, if he "had been a more diligent investigator."

Anderson's second chance to catch the Watergate story even while it was happening came on the day before the break-in. The columnist encountered Frank Sturgis, one of the burglars, at the Washington National Airport as Anderson was leaving for Cleveland to give a speech.

Anderson recognized Sturgis, whom he had known for years, especially in connection with the ill-fated Bay of Pigs invasion of Cuba in 1961. Sturgis was with several other Cubans and Anderson was curious about Sturgis' purpose in Washington.

"Private business," Sturgis explained cryptically.

Anderson noticed that all the Cubans were nervous. But all he did was make a mental note to check into the reason for their presence in the nation's capital as soon as he got back from Cleveland, where he learned the reason in the meantime from the newspapers.

At least he can say he tried when the third opportunity presented itself.

Back in Washington from Cleveland, Anderson went to the jail where the Watergate burglars were being held. His plan was to get to Sturgis by saying he was the prisoner's friend. Since Sturgis hadn't given his real name when he was arrested, Anderson described him to the jailer. Sturgis came out and talked briefly with Anderson, giving him some information but nothing earthshaking.

Anderson was sure he could get the Cuban to tell him more if he could get Sturgis away from there, maybe back to his home. So Anderson hung around until the burglars were brought before a judge and offered to vouch for Sturgis if the court would release him in Anderson's custody. Just when Anderson thought the ploy was going to succeed, a prosecutor objected, and the judge said no.

Failing like almost everyone else to recognize the true significance of the break-in, Anderson lost interest in the Watergate story. He later obtained a document concerning the CIA's efforts to restrict the FBI's Watergate investigation, but still didn't grasp the potential. Once Anderson almost secured Watergate records that Hunt had hidden in a friend's basement, records that Hunt told the Senate Watergate Committee he had destroyed, but his contact never delivered.

It was not the first time he had missed a big story. In 1960, after getting a tip about strange business dealings by Bobby Baker, clerk of the Senate and protégé of Senate Majority Leader Lyndon Johnson, Anderson dropped his investigation after confronting Baker and looking at income tax returns that Baker displayed with a flamboyant show of candor. The returns showed little income from outside interests. It wasn't until four years later, when the Baker scandal was exposed, not by newsmen but by the filing of a lawsuit against Baker, that Anderson realized he had been fooled.

After the unfolding of the Watergate story picked up momentum early in 1973, Anderson held his own. One night in January, 1973, he sat in a room in the Arlington Towers, across the Potomac River from the Watergate, while the four Watergate burglars from Miami met with Hunt in an adjoining room. The burglars discussed whether to accept Hunt's offer to pay their families $1,000 a month and seek executive clemency in return for their pleading guilty and remaining silent. When the meeting ended, one participant secretly reported to Anderson that the defendants accepted the hush money because they believed the operation had been ordered by the CIA. Anderson reported the details in his column.

Anderson was the first to report that McCord had sent Judge John Sirica a letter implicating top officials of CRP in Watergate.

In April, Anderson began publishing excerpts from testimony before the federal grand jury investigating Watergate, even though disclosure of grand jury proceedings is a violation of federal law. Someone had contacted Anderson's office to offer information and later brought in transcripts of grand jury testimony. Anderson published them because he feared that Nixon's efforts to conceal Watergate facts behind grand jury secrecy might succeed. Among the revelations and confirmations in the testimony were the facts that the June 17 break-in at the Watergate had been preceded by a similar break-in for bugging purposes three weeks earlier, and that top White House aide H. R. Haldeman had kept $350,000 in his safe until after the 1972 campaign.

Judge Sirica and the fourteen other judges of the District of Columbia federal district court ordered a separate grand jury to investigate the leak of grand jury testimony to Anderson. Though faced with the prospect of a contempt charge if he refused to identify his source, Anderson defied the judges and the grand jury by continuing to publish excerpts from the proceedings. While in private Anderson consulted with his lawyers, in public he claimed credit for pressuring the President to let his aides appear before the grand jury.

Finally, Anderson, accompanied by two attorneys who advised him to be cooperative, met with three Watergate prosecutors. Though the prosecutors didn't know it, Anderson had used up the grand jury testimony in his possession. He had no more new revelations.

One prosecutor maintained that Anderson's disclosures were discouraging witnesses from testifying, and this was hampering the investigation.

Anderson replied that he had the right to publish material from the transcripts. He argued his doing so had helped advance the case. He also insisted he had a constitutional right not to reveal his source. If the U.S. Supreme Court ordered him to reveal a source, he would have to conclude the court was in error.

Another prosecutor spoke at length on the need for secrecy by grand juries.

At last Anderson said he had no desire to interfere with the investigation. He would publish no more direct quotes from grand jury transcripts. He also agreed to return the transcripts if assured he would not be called to testify except as a last resort. Outside, Anderson told reporters he had consented not to print further verbatim excerpts because it "would not be in the best interests of the investigation." Considering he had no more to reveal anyway, it was a remarkable performance.

Anderson has never been forced to reveal a source, he says, and none has ever been found out. He takes great pains not to reveal apparently harmless details about the circumstances surrounding receipt of information or documents, either in the column or to his colleagues, lest a crucial clue slip out inadvertently. A Pentagon employe once was questioned and harassed as a suspected source when authorities tried in 1971 to make him an example of what would happen to a person caught divulging unauthorized information. But he was finally cleared by a grand jury, and Anderson says he wasn't one of his sources, anyway.

Protection of sources is vital to the ability of reporters to gain access to concealed information. Without the right not to disclose confidential sources, the rights of the press under the First Amendment would in practice be curtailed. Access to information would be hampered by the danger that journalists could be forced to expose their sources to retaliation. This is the theory behind the "shield laws" in some states that specifically acknowledge this right and provide that reporters cannot be required to disclose a source.

Protection of sources is especially crucial to Anderson and his staff. Their information and leads come mostly from a network of sources inside government, a network carefully cultivated and nursed along over a period of years. Some reporters rely on their ability to spot stories in public records. Others do best at coaxing facts out of reluctant people. Anderson, who periodically repeats in print that he would go to jail rather than reveal a source, owes his prowess as the nation's Number One investigative columnist to his great number of strategically placed sources—in the White House, the Pentagon, the FBI, the CIA, the State Department, the offices of senators and congressmen.

Anderson developed most of his sources during the twenty-two years he worked as a legman for Pearson. Since taking over the column after Pearson's death, he's kept in touch with old sources, but has added few new ones. He must spend most of his time in the office, writing, editing—putting the facts his staffers gather into the punchy, colorful idiom of the column—and tending to administrative responsibilities.

Another impediment is having his name out front as the columnist. "It's hard to develop sources when you're as notorious as I am," he observes. Breaking in new sources is easier for a reporter who can be inconspicuous. So the staffers take care of that.

Anderson prefers his sources to be high-level types, whether in government, business, or other organizations. "Low-level sources give limited versions." But he believes in being ever alert to opportunity from any direction.

Once, years ago when he was in New York gathering data on Frank Costello, then the top man in the American Mafia, Anderson got a call at his hotel room. Over a table in a dimly lit café, the man who called told Anderson that Costello was a great guy and a fine family man. He suggested that Anderson write only "friendly stuff." Though aware that he was being gently threatened, Anderson said he would publish the truth.

Though nothing further happened in connection with his Costello probe that Anderson could trace to that incident, the same man later called him again, this time from Miami. Anderson was working on a story about a Chicago alderman's ties to organized crime. The man offered to lead the columnist to a better story if he would forget the Chicago alderman. Anderson said he'd trade if the other story was indeed better.

The man told him a certain mob leader in Milwaukee would give him proof of gangland connections by the late Senator Joseph McCarthy, then a controversial figure on the national scene, if Anderson would go at once to meet him.

Anderson took a plane to Milwaukee without delay, but the mob leader denied knowing what Anderson was talking about.

But Anderson converted the man who had called into an inside underworld source, whom Anderson identifies only as a nongangster with close ties to mob leaders. One fruit from this source was Anderson's August 21, 1975, column saying that former Teamster Union president Jimmy Hoffa, who had disappeared, was killed to protect the mob's hold on the union.

What motivates a source is not as important to Anderson as the validity and significance of his information. If someone turns over confidential documents because he wants to hurt a rival or get his boss fired, that doesn't matter as long as the documents are authentic. A source's possible bias is evaluated for its distortion effects, however, and extra care is taken to double check for accuracy and completeness. Material from his most reliable sources is verified elsewhere, Anderson says. Even they are sometimes inadvertently misleading.

When a source becomes the subject of a damaging disclosure, his status as a source doesn't exempt him, unless the information he provides is better. Anderson sees nothing wrong with that. He regards it as similar to a prosecutor's granting a witness immunity in order to bag bigger game.

Anderson says he never pays informants because purchased information may be tainted, and he can't afford it anyway.

Most of his sources are motivated by good intentions and high ideals, Anderson believes. Like Senator Dodd's staff members who became disillusioned by his unethical behavior, they believe they are serving the national interest.

Anderson says his most reliable sources are public servants who see their prime loyalty as belonging to taxpayers, not their bosses. They are often torn between fears of being caught and conviction that the facts should get out. Sometimes they doubt their information would interest anyone or be taken seriously. These can be encouraged to "break the ice" by "lure" stories. "They clam up until they see it's being made public anyway," says Anderson. "Then their tongues loosen."

Anderson has an ability to put sources at ease. With politician-style backslapping and conviviality, he tells them it's common for people to give him confidential material, making an extraordinary request seem ordinary. Rather than press someone immediately with tough questions, he gets them talking casually. When his ear catches something of interest, he starts asking for details. He's been known not to discourage the idea that the column is reckless if that might make a source eager to set him straight. He's been accused of rough tactics, too, such as threatening an unfavorable reference in the column, which he denies.

Though his public image reflects an abrasive, uncompromising manner, Anderson in person is disarmingly amiable and sympathetic, even while looking stern.

After Hume rounded up evidence that cartoonist Al Capp had sexually assaulted coeds on campus speaking trips, Capp pleaded with Anderson not to write the story. Playing the nice guy while Hume came on strong—in the old hard/soft routine that police interrogators like—Anderson told Capp he would prefer not to run the story, but he couldn't let his personal feelings affect his decisions on what went into the column.

When Anderson got a tip that Senator George Murphy of California was getting a $20,000-a-year consultant fee from Technicolor Inc. while serving in the Senate, he got Murphy to admit it. Chatting congenially with Murphy on the phone, he led the senator to think he wouldn't consider it improper.

Anderson, who got his first reporting job at the age of twelve for a weekly in a Salt Lake City suburb, is unique among investigative journalists. He has no editor to overrule him, and he has to produce a column every day. He also writes regularly for *Parade* magazine, does radio and TV reports, and gives speeches. His staff regards him as a tolerant and generous, but demanding, boss. They respect him for his skill, his courage, and his indefatigability. Their offices on the second floor of an old red brick house on 16th Street are always full of commotion and charged with zeal, though his staffers are among the lowest paid reporters in the capital. He receives hundreds of applications from students for five unpaid internships in his office.

Chief assistant Whitten says it's the best job he's ever had. Where else can a journalist be so free to dig out and expose wrongdoing and blunders by public officials? Where else has the ruin of so many betrayers of the public trust been achieved? Anderson doesn't relish hurting people, he says, but the national interest comes first. He wouldn't be any good as a muckraker if he worried whether people liked him.

Being called a muckraker doesn't bother him, either. Though some reporters wince at the term, and like to view modern-day investigative journalism as a cut above old-time muckraking, Anderson takes pride in the designation. To him it connotes an obsession, not with sensationalism, but with reform. Among the honors he recalls with a special fondness is that accorded him in 1974 when he went to Boise State University in Idaho to make a speech. Several students costumed as mobsters met him at the airport and presented him with an oversized rake inscribed with the words, "Muckraking and Supersnoop Award."

Anderson views himself and his staff as among only a few investigative reporters in Washington who try to find out what's really going on, don't believe the official versions, don't curry favor with the mighty, and couldn't care less if they're cursed in the halls of the Capitol and are left off party invitation lists.

What does worry Anderson, he says, is his newly acquired respectability. His July, 1972, blunder in reporting that Senator Thomas Eagleton, then the Democratic vice presidential candidate, had a record of drunk driving arrests without verifying the story, tarnished his Pulitzer Prize illustriousness. And he still makes more errors than most top reporters, if for no other reason than that he publishes a lot more stories. But he is nevertheless firmly entrenched among the nation's most highly regarded investigative journalists.

"It's pleasant," says Anderson. "But it makes me wonder when too many people approve of what we do. I seem to do my best work when everybody hates me."

Les Whitten did not follow his usual routine on the morning of January 31, 1973, a Wednesday. Before he could leave for work, he received a telephone call from Hank Adams, a Sioux Indian who had been acting as an intermediary in negotiations between federal officials and several American Indians who in November had vandalized the Washington building that housed the Bureau of Indian Affairs. The Indians had spirited away boxes of paintings, artifacts, office equipment, and documents that later were dubbed the Broken Treaty Papers. Adams had been instrumental in returning many of the stolen items to authorities. Now, he told Whitten, he had arranged to deliver another batch of the papers to the government in about an hour.

It would be a good story, Whitten calculated, to witness the return of documents for which government agents had been scouring the country in vain—even though their contents were not newsworthy.

Whitten was familiar with the contents because he had spent hours examining the papers in Phoenix, Arizona, and Minneapolis, Minnesota. He had flown to Phoenix after the Indians agreed to show the documents to the Anderson column, though Anderson did not offer money and others had. Anderson believes this was because the column had demonstrated a concern for mistreatment of Indians and had a record of championing the downtrodden. In Phoenix, Whitten met furtively with the Indians at a bowling alley, a coffee house, and a parking lot because they feared the FBI might have bugged their motel room and car. In Minneapolis, Whitten holed up in a hotel room to scan thousands of documents while an Indian guarded the door.

The result was several columns on the defrauding of Indians, pollution of their land, destruction of their timber, violation of their treaties, and illegal diversion of their water.

Arriving at Adams' apartment not far from the White House shortly before ten o'clock that Wednesday morning, Whitten found that things were not going as planned. John Arellano, who described himself as a Pueblo-Apache, had not yet appeared with the red Volkswagen camper in which Adams planned to transport the documents to the BIA building, where an FBI agent was to pick them up. Adams had used the camper in the past to return documents, since he had no car of his own. He phoned the BIA building to say he would be late, but was on his way.

Whitten helped him lug three heavy cartons of papers down to the street. Since Arellano still hadn't shown up, they turned to Whitten's car. Arellano, they learned later, was an FBI informer.

As Whitten was about to load the boxes into his yellow Vega, several FBI agents rushed up and arrested him. When Whitten whipped out pencil and paper to take notes, an FBI man snatched them away and snapped handcuffs on his wrists. The reporter was taken to jail, where he remained for several hours until hauled before a magistrate and charged with illegal receipt and possession of stolen property, a crime for which the maximum punishment was ten years in prison and a $10,000 fine. Whitten was then released without bail pending grand jury action.

Though the grand jury declined to indict Whitten, he and reporters everywhere were nervous for a couple of weeks. To Whitten and Anderson, it was an obvious frame-up, a blatant attempt to intimidate Anderson and journalists in general. It would have been a dark omen for investigative journalism if the government had gotten away with it. In Anderson's view, the FBI would not have thrown any reporter in jail without an order from higher authority. Anderson believes such an order came from H. R. Haldeman, Nixon's top aide, perhaps tracing back to the all-out effort to "get" him after he revealed the ITT memo.

There was, of course, a sense of excitement overriding the fear of trouble. As quoted in *Time* magazine at the time, Anderson said he and his whole staff were ready to join Whitten in jail "before we stop digging out and reporting the news." Even while denouncing the FBI for illegal harassment, Anderson and Whitten seemed to be enjoying themselves. They were grandstanding a little, and, like many an investigative reporter under the threat of imprisonment for daring to publish government secrets or refusing to divulge a source privately half wished they would actually go to jail. That would make another good story, and bolster their status as heroes.

Whitten is the acknowledged workhorse of the office, a dynamo charged with boyish fervor. He careens around the office like a dervish, bounding from phone call to another room and back to a new phone call, simultaneously carrying on conversations with a visitor or two, while more phone calls stack up on hold. In between, he checks the mail for a good lead.

Relying largely on his own network of sources nurtured since he arrived in Washington in 1958 to cover the night police beat for the Washington *Post*, Whitten has turned up many of the exclusives for which his boss gets the credit (though the column also carries Whitten's by-line).

Among the exposés he's relished the most, besides the Broken Treaty Papers, were disclosures of staff kickbacks that led to the conviction of Pennsylvania Congressman J. Irving Whalley, the contents of secret documents on the Vietnam War and the CIA, and payola in the pop music record industry.

A former aide of Whalley told Whitten how his boss had made him kick back $1,200, forced other staffers to give money to the congressman's nephew, and required two congressional office employes to do work for his automobile dealership and coal company. Whitten got Whalley to admit getting money from the ex-aide, but the congressman maintained it was rent for an apartment he had subleased to his employe. Whitten also extracted an admission that two women employes did do work for his private firms.

The story of record industry payola came from an inside source whom Whitten persuaded over a period of time to give him details for publication.

Rather than fazing Whitten, the pressure of needing to fill a daily column turns him on full blast. In fact, it's not enough to keep him occupied. While driving to and from work, Whitten thinks out the books and articles he writes at home on Saturdays. So far, he's published four novels—the latest about an investigative reporter—a children's book, a biography of famed criminal lawyer F. Lee Bailey, translations of poems by the Frenchman Baudelaire, and numerous articles for newspapers and magazines.

Yet, no one accuses Whitten of being tense and hard driving. Tall and loose-jointed, with a lanky appearance, Whitten is gushingly friendly, soft-spoken, and reflective even when tottering on the edge of being harried beyond endurance. He's outgoing and a bit wide-eyed, which helps him look youthful. He doesn't look at all like a demon of persistence.

Whitten's relentless zeal for exposing corruption, however, does not propel him into careless or premature reportage. One of the favorite Les Whitten stories among Washington reporters, in one version or another, has him jumping up and down in frustration as he's encountered by a fellow reporter. According to the story, Whitten complains, "If I could just write the story before checking it out. I lose too many that way."

Whitten is recognized as one of the best in Washington. When Washington *Star* reporter Shirley Elder wrote an article in 1975 naming the ten best investigative reporters in the nation's capital, she included Whitten but not Anderson. "Whitten is a solider reporter than Anderson," Elder wrote, "less likely to go off on an emotional tangent or to pick at peccadillos."

Anderson takes no issue with the assessment. He says, "Whitten is the finest investigative reporter in the country. He can beat Hersh, Nelson, any of them. He'd get the story first and tie it down best."

As an example of Whitten's obsession with accuracy, Anderson likes to tell about a time he changed a column written by Whitten to say an old man "shuffled" instead of "walked." Whitten objected, saying he didn't know for a fact that the old man had "shuffled."

"What difference does it make?" Anderson asked. "It doesn't change the main point of the story. It's just a little touch to make it read better."

"I don't care," said Whitten. "I don't know if he shuffled. But I know he walked, one way or another."

In the end, Anderson yielded. "That's how scrupulous he is," Anderson says.

Behind all Whitten's enthusiasm is a conviction that he has the world's greatest job. In April, 1972, when the spotlight of publicity shone brightly on Anderson and his cohorts, Whitten was quoted in *Life* magazine, "This job gives me a chance to do what I wanted to do all my newspaper life, knock the bleeding crap out of the people who are corrupting this country, and there are plenty of them."

Three years later, his dedication hadn't dimmed. "Here I'm free to get to the people who really are the centers of power," he said. "I can pick the big ones. This is the best column in the country. There's a certain esprit de corps, sort of us against the crooks. I've never found anything to match this, for excitement, for usefulness, for fulfillment."

Unlike his boss, Whitten did not get printer's ink in his veins early in life. Born in Florida in 1928, he grew up in Washington and took journalism at Lehigh University, where he was editor-in-chief of the college paper. But he planned, as he graduated, to be a poet. Journalism was not his thing.

After hitchhiking to Mexico and working briefly for NBC in Washington, Whitten went to Europe because his girl friend did. He later married her in Paris, but in the meantime got a messenger boy's job with Radio Free Europe in Munich. He hoped to go into production, but the first opening came in news. He came back to New York for Radio Free Europe, but left in 1957 after discovering it was CIA-connected and went to work for International News Service in Washington. When INS was merged into United Press a year later, he worked briefly for UPI in Columbia, South Carolina, before going to the Washington *Post*.

Though he remembers his grubby year on the night police beat for the *Post* as the nadir of his career, that's when he became fascinated with investigative techniques, and the gap between surface news and what's really happening.

Promoted to the municipal court beat, Whitten began "to fall in love with this craft." After a man was killed on a construction job and he got a tip that safety inspection reports weren't accurate, Whitten dug into the case and found the corporation counsel's office for the District of Columbia was letting builders violate safety rules. He exposed collusion between slum landlords and housing inspectors, credit gouging by "debt consolidation" companies, and cheating among used car dealers.

The *Post* sent him to the American Press Institute's seminar on investigative reporting, but Whitten felt the *Post* was too fearful of stepping on important toes. (He now feels the *Post* has changed and is the greatest newspaper in the world.) He moved in 1963 to the Washington Bureau of the Hearst newspapers, where he felt he had more freedom. But when the Hearst paper in New York City folded up in 1969, there seemed little outlet for his work. Anderson talked him into joining the column.

Whitten considers his work the most important kind of reporting there is. "Nobody else," he says, "takes on the really tough cases like we do. We're on the front line." Whitten feels he must have an extra helping of something every investigative reporter needs to be effective, a compulsion to lay the villains low—or, in loftier terms, "a sense of outrage."

4

The Top Teams

BUMPING ALONG the dirt road in a 1956 Dodge taxi driven by a Turk named Genghis Husseyin, Robert Greene and two fellow reporters from *Newsday* drove into the tiny village of Degirmendere, deep in the Turkish hills 400 miles from Istanbul. They were carrying guns, partly to pose as hunters, but also to impress the villagers.

The villagers, however, were more annoyed than impressed. They herded the intruders into a mud hut and ordered them to lie on the floor while they decided what to do. Greene, a huge, imposing 300-pound man with modishly long grey hair, exchanged nervous glances with his companions, Knut Royce and Les Payne, as they listened to the villagers discuss whether to kill them.

The reporters had studied Turkish customs thoroughly before embarking on their journey. They were sure they hadn't done anything to offend the villagers. But they knew the Turks could be quick-tempered. They must have made some error, to be in this predicament. Would their grand investigation end so ignobly, squashed like a harmless flea in a remote, grubby little place where indoor plumbing and electricity were still unconfirmed rumors? Would they disappear beneath this distant turf, without anyone's knowing where to look for their bodies?

The villagers decided to be friendly. They let Greene and his companions stay for a couple of days and learn what they had come to learn—how Turkish farmers cultivated the poppy to get opium for sale to smugglers, starting the heroin trail that ended in the veins of American addicts.

It was June, 1972, time for the last legal opium harvest before the new government prohibition took effect, a ban that Turkish authorities had agreed to impose under pressure from America. Greene and his cohorts rose with the villagers at 4:30 the next morning for a breakfast of hard bread, cheese, a soup containing yogurt and chicken entrails, hot milk, and tea. At 6:30, they went to the poppy field with the village women while the men remained at the tea house to play cards.

The reporters watched as the women made cuts in the round pods of poppies with small sharp knives, stooping over the short plants as their wrists flicked. Opium gum oozed from the cuts. It would be left overnight to congeal into a clay-like form, then scraped from the pods the next day. The hardened gum would then be collected into round loaves for sale to smugglers and shipment to chemists who would convert it first to a morphine powder and then heroin.

Opium, as Greene and the others learned, is only one fruit of the poppy. Its oil was used in cooking, its leaves for salad, its seeds on bread. The pods were fed to livestock, and the stalks became part of the ceilings in the village huts. Aside from the village's age-old tradition of defiance of the central government, the poppy was too valuable a crop to be discontinued, regardless of the subsidy the government promised as compensation until a substitute could be found. The poppy was the only crop known to be hardy enough to grow in the area's poor, windblown soil. The villagers told the reporters about hidden caches of poppy seeds that would be planted if the government ban were to be lifted, or needed to be violated. When Greene asked for a look, a large bag of small, grain-like seed was shown him. He took a picture of it with a Polaroid camera.

Greene also snapped pictures of the opium loaves and the villagers, who were delighted to get some of the prints. A camera, he realized, was better for winning friends than a gun.

Greene, Royce, and Payne had arrived in Turkey on June 4, ostensibly to write travel stories and possibly set up an Istanbul bureau for their Long Island daily newspaper, while enjoying some hunting on the side. Their real mission was to trace the route taken by the scourge of American drug addicts from its origin in the poppy to its conversion to heroin powder in France and its distribution to pushers in the United States.

They had undergone intensive preparation. "The key to the whole thing," says Greene, "was the preliminary work." *Newsday* Publisher William Attwood had suggested an investigation of extraordinary proportions to determine why heroin kept flowing into the United States despite the massive efforts to stop it. Greene formed a team to conduct a two-month "sniff," as he calls it, to evaluate the potential.

A former investigator for the U.S. Senate Rackets Committee and the New York City Crime Commission, Greene had set up *Newsday's* first investigative team, which was called the "Greene Team" and "Greene's Berets," in 1967. He changed team members with each project to get the reporters he deemed best suited by experience and skill for that particular probe. The one common factor was that Greene led the team, made the assignments, analyzed the incoming information, and decided on tactics. This time he chose the thirty-three-year-old Royce because he was a native of Marseilles, where a great deal of opium is converted to heroin, and he spoke French. Payne, thirty-two, was a strong, husky black man who had been an Army Ranger captain in Vietnam.

The new Greene team read mountains of material on the heroin problem that plagued the United States, the unavailing efforts of authorities to combat drug traffic, the evidence of corruption among police and politicians in the United States and abroad, and the economics and politics of the foreign countries that figured prominently in the heroin trade.

Greene went to Miami to look up Sal Vizzini, a former narcotics agent who had worked for six years in Turkey and had once infiltrated Mafia overlord Charles "Lucky" Luciano's dope smuggling operations by posing as a military pilot. Vizzini gave him detailed insight into the workings of the heroin business and names of underworld sources in France and Turkey. Greene listened as Vizzini described raids on French labs known to be producing heroin, but which were curiously found clean, with no trace of such activity, when police arrived. Vizzini introduced the reporter to a former head of the

French secret police who explained how his agency dealt with drug smugglers. A heroin courier arrested by American authorities had claimed to be acting on orders from the French secret police. The Frenchman now told Greene, without confirming the man's claim, how involvement by the agency in the heroin traffic would fit into the picture if it were true.

Early in May, with the decision made to go full steam ahead, Greene, Royce, and Payne took three-week courses in Turkish. In Turkey, they rented a small villa on the outskirts of Istanbul, arranged for a housekeeper, and hired Genghis Husseyin as driver and interpreter. Between visits to poppy fields, they contacted underworld sources to learn how the smuggling was done.

Illegal opium was bought from the poppy growers, the team found, by collectors who often were prominent businessmen or powerful politicians. Greene and his crew were able to identify several collectors in the villages and provinces of the poppy farming region. One of the largest was a member of the Turkish parliament.

The collectors transported the opium, concealed under the floorboards of trucks or beneath mounds of food in baskets strapped to donkeys, to secret depots protected by armed guards. Much of the opium was converted to morphine powder in Turkey because only a simple process was required and it reduced the bulk and weight by ninety percent, making shipment much easier. Labs where this was done, and storehouses of the morphine powder, were more heavily guarded than the raw opium.

One smuggler told the Greene team, "If you know the name of someone big, you can go into a village and within five minutes they can produce 100 kilos of opium for sale. But the police never find anything. If they did, a little bribe would be paid, and the police would say that they found nothing. That's how it works down there."

Turkish authorities entertained little concern about America's heroin troubles, the reporters discovered. Heroin addiction wasn't a problem in Turkey and they couldn't understand why the United States was unable to control it. If there weren't a demand for the drug, there'd be no poppy growing. Before the new ban, opium could be legally sold only for medical purposes. But black marketing, smuggling and bribery had long been an accepted part of Turkish life. No one in Turkey seriously expected that to change.

Collectors, the Greene team learned, were financed by patrons in Istanbul. These were wealthy merchants who, in addition to legitimate business pursuits, arranged for clandestine export of raw opium or morphine powder to the French labs. Many had close connections with influential business and government leaders. They dealt with Corsican gang leaders operating on France's Mediterranean coast and hired smugglers to deliver them the opium or morphine from the storage depots in Turkish villages. Greene and his colleagues spent much of their three months in Turkey gathering information for a list of fifty patrons that was published as part of the Greene team's thirty-two Pulitzer Prize-winning articles on "The Heroin Trail" in February and March of 1973.

To compile that list, the reporters pieced together scraps of information picked up in restaurants, bars, hotel lobbies, and brothels. These tidbits had limited value, however, and the team had to turn down one chance to interview a patron because his price was $40,000. Then, one rainy summer afternoon, a tall man with wraparound sunglasses and only half a thumb on his left hand came to their villa and offered them details about every patron in Istanbul except himself. Over tea at a dining room table, the Turk fished a sheaf of papers from his jacket pocket. "I put everything down on paper," he said, "so I wouldn't forget anything."

Greene had no doubts about his visitor's knowledge. He recognized him as an exporter-importer known to police as a mastermind behind illegal drug shipments out of Turkey for twenty-five years. The patron gave the reporters names, routes, prices, dates of shipments, political connections, fine points on how the system worked. There was no Mr. Big, he said. "Everyone is a chief." Narcotics, he said, was the most profitable business in the world.

The interview completed, he walked to the fireplace and ignited his pile of notes with a gold-plated cigarette lighter. "If the wrong people found me with this," he said, "it would mean my death." He returned twice more, each time burning his notes. He never asked for anything in return.

Two smugglers named Ghassen and Samir told the reporters that a Bulgarian government agency guaranteed safe shipment of opium and morphine through Communist Bulgaria for smugglers who agreed to run guns to leftist guerillas in Turkey on their return trips. A police official in Istanbul confirmed their story. Bulgaria, the reporters had learned, lay on the main land route used by smugglers. Greene wrote the Bulgarian government for permission to enter the country and write travel stories, but received no reply.

Greene and Payne climbed into the Dodge taxi with Husseyin and drove to the Bulgarian border at Kapikule, Turkey. An estimated fifty percent of the opium and morphine that ended up as heroin in the United States was leaving Turkey at Kapikule's border checkpoint in false-bottomed suitcases, spare tires, hollowed-out axles, and other hiding places. After an hour's wait and a small bribe, the Greene team proceeded to the Bulgarian capital of Sofia without so much as a cursory check of their car for contraband opium.

Arriving about 3:00 A.M. at the Grand Sofia Hotel, Greene and Payne were told the visas they had obtained at the border were good for only twenty-four hours instead of the three days they thought. To get that straightened out, they had to go to the police station, which resulted in the assignment of a government press agency journalist to accompany them wherever they went. Greene and Payne had planned to meet Ghassan and Samir in Sofia, but now they would first have to ditch their escort. This they did by turning up the volume on the TV set in their hotel room and sneaking out to meet the smugglers on a street corner.

Arrangements were made for Greene to photograph other smugglers who were to meet Ghassan and Samir at an outdoor café table in front of the Grand Sofia Hotel. When Ghassan scratched his ear, that meant the man arriving at their table was a smuggler whom they would identify later, and Greene was to snap his picture. When the time came, several men came to the pair's table, Ghassan kept scratching his ear, and Greene kept taking pictures.

Failing to get an interview with a Bulgarian official or to verify the story about the helpful agency, Greene and Payne went back to Istanbul, where the team made plans to travel over the land smuggling route through Bulgaria, Yugoslavia, and Austria to Munich, Germany, and on into France. They concocted an experiment to see for themselves how easy it was to smuggle heroin past border guards and customs officials. They put some white powdered sugar, which looks like heroin, into two clear plastic bags and packed them in their suitcases in easy view of anyone who checked their luggage.

At the Istanbul airport customs inspection station, a man put out his hand, said, "How about something for the boys?" and accepted a dollar, but no one checked the reporters' suitcases. In Vienna, airport porters wheeled the suitcases through a door marked, "Nothing to Declare," without opening them. No one asked the reporters if they wished to declare anything. The team rented a car and, with the powdered sugar still in their luggage, drove south to the Yugoslavian border at the small Austrian village of Spielfield, a key entry point on the smuggling route. They were stopped by the Yugoslavs, but no one looked inside the car or inspected the trunk. On the way back into Austria, they were not even stopped for examination of passports.

Before reaching the Austrian-German border on the autobahn to Munich, the midpoint transfer station on the Istanbul-Marseilles opium route, the reporters set the plastic bags in open view on the back seat. They passed the border, where two sleepy guards lounged against a wall, almost without noticing it. They put the plastic bags on the front seat for the crossing into France over the Rhine River at Strasbourg. The German border guards waved as they drove by. The French border guards didn't even look up.

The next day, the Greene team drove back into Germany, this time with the plastic bags on the dashboard. No one at the border paid any attention. Driving south, they entered Switzerland. At the Swiss border, a guard stopped their car and asked, "Anything to declare?"

"No," said Greene.

The guard waved them through.

They were not stopped on their return into France, nor later when they drove into Italy from the French Riviera and back. They made ten border crossings altogether, without being searched or questioned.

In September, the Greene team set up shop for the French phase of their investigation in a seaside villa on the southern coast of France near the heroin labs of Marseilles. Greene went often to Paris to track down leads developed in the United States and Turkey, and Payne made frequent trips to Munich. Meanwhile, a second team of reporters headed by Washington correspondent Anthony Marro began delving into the American end of the heroin trail.

Marro's team concentrated on New York, Long Island, and Washington, but also traveled to Miami and Mexico.

In France, the Greene team abandoned its cover pretenses. Greene realized at once that the French authorities suffered no delusions about his team's true purpose. Their phone was tapped and they were followed by police. Baggage was twice misrouted, and film in the suitcases was later found to have been exposed. The team began to document ties between the heroin underworld and politicians. As French gendarmes dogged his steps in Paris, Greene began to wonder if he had more to fear from the government than the underworld. Greene didn't trust the French post office. Material was sent to *Newsday* by mailing out of Germany on Payne's excursions to Munich. Greene learned later that the French government asked American authorities to have *Newsday's* heroin articles delayed until after the French elections. What bothered French authorities the most was the team's acquisition of evidence about ties between the government and the underworld. These traced back to President Charles de Gaulle's use of gangsters for counterterrorist help against right-wing opposition to De Gaulle's granting of independence to Algeria.

When the two reporting teams met back in Long Island in December to write their series, they had been to thirteen countries. Fourteen reporters had taken part in the seven-month investigation. Arrests of heroin dealers, congressional hearings, and a cutoff in aid to Turkey followed publication of the articles, but Greene is skeptical about the probe's accomplishments. "As long as there is a demand for heroin," he says, "there will be a supply."

Marro, who later went to *Newsweek* magazine, still admires the endeavor's magnitude, but thinks the money could have been put to better use elsewhere. He believes the project was motivated by a desire to build a national reputation for *Newsday* and help it escape being "just a suburban newspaper." The paper's 1971 investigation of President Nixon's Florida dealings with Charles "Bebe" Rebozo and former Democratic Senator George Smathers had failed to achieve that goal. If Marro is right, "The Heroin Trail" project was a success. Besides the 1974 Pulitzer Prize for meritorious public service, it won a Sigma Delta Chi Award for distinguished public service and the National Headliners Club Award for investigative reporting.

Marro also participated in the Nixon-Rebozo-Smathers investigation, which culminated in a six-part, 70,000-word series disclosing new details about Nixon's Florida investments. One was that only Nixon made a sizable profit on the sale of stock in Fisher's Island Inc., a land firm dominated by Rebozo. Another was that a house rented for $18,000 a year by the U.S. Secret Service near the Florida White House at Key Biscayne had been purchased by a millionaire friend of Nixon, Robert Abplanalp, with the Secret Service's help. The articles also revealed that many of Nixon's dealings involved key figures in Florida's Democratic Party organization.

That project, which absorbed two and a half months in Florida and six months altogether, was conceived in a desire to expand *Newsday's* investigative horizons. The Greene team had won a Pulitzer Prize for exposés of suburban government corruption and Greene felt confident it could do as well on a national level. "The team was well-honed," he says. "We had the talent, the discipline, the know-how. There isn't that much difference between investigating a small town and a president of the United States."

Greene had read an article about Nixon's deal on Fisher's Island and was intrigued about Nixon's relationship with the millionaire wheeler-dealer, Rebozo. He and a team conducted a two-month "sniff," reading everything that had been written on the topic, checking court cases, contacting sources, and talking to other investigative reporters who had looked into Nixon's financial affairs.

Deciding to proceed with a full-scale probe, the team set up headquarters in Room 321 of the Royal Biscayne Hotel and began sifting through 40,000 documents in court files and property records, including many examined in Washington on shuttle trips from Key Biscayne. They conducted 400 interviews. It wasn't glamorous work, but "dismal slogging," according to Greene. The reporters hand-copied many of the records, and did endless cross-checking. Access to some records was obtained only after protracted hassles with state and federal officials. A few state bank records were never seen.

The team picked up hints of organized crime in some of Rebozo's dealings, but didn't report them because they couldn't be proven. "Others wrote about them later with no more evidence than we had," says Greene. "But if you can't prove it, it's just innuendo, and publishing it is a disservice to our profession."

The series produced little of positive value, but had two negative consequences. Martin Schram, *Newsday's* White House correspondent who assisted in the investigation, got the cold shoulder treatment for three months from Nixon's press secretary, Ron Ziegler, and was excluded from the list of newsmen approved to accompany the President on his 1972 trip to China though he met all the eligibility requirements. It was later revealed to the Senate Watergate Committee by former White House counsel John W. Dean III that the White House had arranged for Greene's income tax returns to be audited.

The Greene team had evolved from his 1967 investigation into payoffs to zoning officials in the Long Island town of Islip. Then a thirty-eight-year-old general assignment reporter who did occasional investigative stories on organized crime, Greene heard talk that *Newsday's* Suffolk County editor was mixed up in land deals with local politicians. His colleagues on the reporting staff told him they had been diverted to other assignments whenever they tried to check into it. Greene spent a fruitless month and a half going through property transfer records at the county clerk's office. One day he asked a lawyer if there was any place to look that he hadn't tried.

The lawyer suggested he try the records of land that had been sold at a tax auction at one time or another. Those, he said, were kept in a different room.

That's where Greene discovered that the Suffolk editor and local officials had bought land whose value had sharply increased after a town councilman engineered a decision to locate a new airport's entrance near the land. Articles about this led to several indictments and the councilman was convicted of promoting his personal interests through official acts. More importantly, Greene's success stimulated him to dig further beneath land use planning and zoning changes in Islip.

He found such widespread skulduggery that he needed help. He requested a room to keep his files secure, and clerks to help him with the elaborate FBI filing method, which starts a new file on each new name that crops up and each newly discovered incident of misconduct, plus sub-files for different aspects. Duplicates of all memos, documents and other information are put in each file and sub-file to which they are relevant. At first, Greene used part-time Kelly girls, but later was assigned staff clerks. He also requested and received two reporters to help him investigate and write stories on zoning payoffs to Islip officials, mostly by developers of suburban garden apartments.

Greene reasoned that the situation in the adjacent town of Brookhaven might be similar. It was undergoing the same kind of rapid growth and was dominated by the same political party. One of his preliminary "sniffs" sensed a comparable pattern. He persuaded his editors to make another major commitment and the Greene team became permanent. The team's Brookhaven stories led to more indictments of public officials.

One investigation often leads to another. While probing the zoning records in Brookhaven, Greene ran across hints that a state senator was arranging for profitable rezonings of land in his home county of Nassau in exchange for similar rezonings in Suffolk. Additional checking uncovered evidence that the senator, who served on the senate's banking committee, was getting unsecured loans from a Long Island bank to buy land and build shopping centers. Two reporters spent four weeks copying down bank deposits by the Town of Hempstead and three weeks examining the senator's record on bank legislation. The team reported that the senator, in return for the loans, had arranged for big deposits of Hempstead's public money in the bank and protected the bank's interest in the legislature.

Greene team exposés led to indictments of twenty-one persons, convictions of seven, resignations by thirty public officials, and a passel of journalism awards for *Newsday*, including the 1970 Pulitzer Prize for meritorious public service.

Not all investigations need to put people in prison, according to Greene. It's enough to inform the public how its government actually works. Nevertheless, he believes a good investigative reporter must have, in addition to extensive sources, an instinct for the jugular. "A lot of good reporters become very source oriented," he says. "When it comes time to write something nasty about a source, they go into a paralysis."

Greene has contributed to American Press Institute seminars on investigative journalism since 1969. He defines investigative reporting as the gathering of important information that someone is trying to keep secret. The information must be uncovered firsthand, not pirated from an assistant prosecutor or police investigator. "The essence of investigative reporting," says Greene, "is that it's your own work product."

To have an effective team, Greene says, it's necessary to have a strong leader, one who can direct and coordinate others as well as investigate expertly himself. Since Greene became Suffolk editor in 1973, long after the editor he exposed had died, *Newsday* has lacked strong leadership for its investigative team. Investigative reporting at *Newsday* has since been fragmentary, with Greene trying one team and then another in less ambitious probes until he hits upon the kind of team leader he wants.

Of the *Newsday* reporters who have worked on Greene's teams, the one who otherwise does investigative work most consistently is forty-eight-year-old Thomas C. Renner, *Newsday's* expert on organized crime and the New York Mafia since 1968.

In 1971, after two A&P supermarket managers were murdered and several stores were torched because the chain refused to buy an inferior detergent marketed by a Mafia-controlled distributor, Renner and fellow reporter Joe Demma surmised the Mafia might be pushing other products as well. Starting with public records on corporations and unions, they found evidence of extensive mob infiltration into the food industry, including the production and marketing of cheese, soft drinks, soaps, canned goods, eggs, meats, and pizza. Renner and Demma traveled across the country to piece together the proof, then called on mob figures for interviews. The gang chiefs, as usual, denied connections to any crime syndicate, but, to the reporters' surprise, freely discussed their food industry interests, providing an unexpectedly vivid perspective on the extent of underworld infiltration.

Earlier, in 1970, Renner exposed how the mob used infiltration of the U.S. Postal Service, and its ability to dictate airline hiring through control of the union, to steal mail worth $70 million a year from New York post offices and Kennedy International Airport. Mobsters, he revealed, pressured or paid postal and airline employes to help them steal credit cards, jewelry, stocks, money orders, and cash from the mail. Renner's articles led to improved security measures at post offices and the airport.

One of Renner's first investigations of organized crime identified 151 Long Island members of New York's five Mafia families. Assembling bits of information from police records, tax rolls, court files, property records, and interviews, Renner compiled such a complete and accurate picture of Long Island racketeering that the U.S. Justice Department's Organized Crime Strike Force in New York asked him for a list before publication so it wouldn't be embarrassed when it appeared. Within the next three years, 135 of the 151 were arrested. "We don't presume to take credit," says Renner. "But what we did was push law enforcement into action."

In 1972, Renner revealed the smuggling of 500 Sicilian aliens into the

United States to beef up the defenses of aging Mafia rulers against the challenges of young rebels. The aliens also were used to consolidate infiltration into restaurants, bakeries, food companies, and the construction industry. Though much of the information came from law enforcement sources, Renner's underworld informants also made vital contributions.

Renner, who has written three books on crime and the Mafia, is proud of his ability to develop sources who trust him "on both sides of the fence." He attributes it to his "penchant for accuracy as well as deliberate, careful check and cross-check." To report on organized crime, he says, "One absolutely must build a reputation for trust within both the underworld and the intelligence community." That means never breaking a confidence or exposing a source, no matter what—even if it means passing up a good story.

Donald L. Barlett and James B. Steele examined 20,000 tax liens filed by the Internal Revenue Service. Among the most intriguing cases were these:

A fifty-six-year-old Pottsville, Pennsylvania, doctor named Robert Erdman owed $906,453.38 in federal income taxes, held no real estate in his own name, and said the IRS was "very nice" and "not trying to push" him in negotiations on settlement of the tax bill. Erdman had once admitted delivering a bribe to a judge in a tax evasion case involving a Mafia figure.

Seymour L. Rosenfield, a fifty-year-old insurance executive who owed $2,091,487.04, was sentenced in 1972 to six months' confinement for a tax violation, but never served a day in jail because he didn't show up to serve his sentence and no one tried to find him.

The brains behind a multimillion-dollar complex of companies, Thomas A. Shaheen, Jr., forty-two, of Washington, D.C., owed $743,050.12 that was uncollectible because he had sold his $190,000 home, placed other assets in a trust, and shipped his belongings and himself to England before the IRS got around to making a serious attempt to collect.

Leo I. Bloom, a fifty-four-year-old financial consultant in Reading, Pennsylvania, owed $729,833.06, but the IRS had written off a third of it as uncollectible, and was "very accommodating" in negotiations on reducing the rest, according to Bloom's attorney, while Bloom lived comfortably on a five-acre estate and made frequent trips to the Caribbean.

These four cases figured prominently in Barlett's and Steele's Pulitzer Prize-winning 1974 series in the Philadelphia *Inquirer* on tax law enforcement that treats the rich delicately while pressing with inexorable harshness the middle-income taxpayers and the poor.

During a six-month investigation that took them across the United States, Barlett and Steele unearthed records showing that the IRS had failed to collect billions of dollars in taxes, and that most of it was owed by wealthy and prominent people who regularly were allowed to settle their tax bills for only a fraction of the original amounts.

However incredible the cases of Dr. Erdman, Rosenfield, Shaheen, and

Bloom might have seemed, they were not unusual. Movie stars, celebrities, people like Xaviera Hollander, the ex-prostitute who wrote a best-selling book, and Sidney R. Korshak, an attorney who represented Hollywood types and Las Vegas gambling casinos, could expect to get by with paying no more than a third of their taxes, according to the IRS' customary disposition of such cases. Well-publicized IRS toughness against visible figures like C. Arnholt Smith of San Diego, California, a millionaire friend of President Nixon, was not only rare, but little more than a propaganda ploy to deceive the American people.

The truth that Barlett and Steele extricated from mounds of records was that, contrary to the intent of federal income tax laws, the wealthy paid a smaller percentage of their incomes in taxes than the middle class or the poor. The more money one made, the more taxes he could get away with not paying. The IRS' administration of the tax laws, they discovered, actually encouraged upper-income taxpayers to avoid paying taxes. Failing to pay $200,000 in taxes, for instance, would normally result in no penalty at all and probably a profit. The omission was not likely to be spotted in the first place. If it was, negotiations would eat up five years and the eventual settlement would be about $80,000. During the five years, interest on the $200,000 would earn enough to pay the $80,000, leaving the well-heeled taxpayer $200,000 ahead.

Barlett and Steele, perhaps the most systematic and thorough investigative reporting team in the United States today, got no help from the IRS, even though most of the information for their articles came from public records.

"It was always a hassle getting government records," says Barlett, forty, who's short, chunky, and bald, has a quiet, unflappable manner, and seldom speaks except to ask a question.

"It wasn't a matter of someone overtly standing in our way," adds Steele, a thirty-three-year-old Kansan who's taller and more outgoing, has lots of thick dark hair, and seems a bit British. "It was just that no one could ever find what we wanted. We didn't have the right name of the report or something."

The two spent most of their time pulling together facts and statistics from several different sources, sometimes computing or estimating new statistics. Besides the 20,000 tax liens they analyzed in New York, Philadelphia, Chicago and Los Angeles, they read published IRS reports, studied 30,000 pages of court records and transcripts in eight states, and examined 5,000 pages of real estate records, probate reports, congressional committee files, medical licensing records, and government agency hearing transcripts.

They struck it particularly rich in a pile of documents obtained by a Seattle, Washington, couple after they won a Freedom of Information Act lawsuit in a court battle with the IRS over their tax bill. Among the stacks of papers was a computer printout that turned out to be a secret audit confirming that higher income taxpayers avoided taxes more often than others.

Their investigation uncovered the startling fact that the IRS could not interpret its own growing tangle of rules and regulations with consistency.

Besides winning several awards, Barlett's and Steele's "Auditing the IRS" articles stimulated serious new moves for tax reform in Congress where they have been gathering momentum ever since.

It was not the team's first award-winning venture into statistics and the new computer journalism pioneered by Philip Meyer of the *Inquirer's* Washington bureau, the author of the 1974 book, *Precision Journalism*. Meyer helped Barlett and Steele produce their 1973 "Crime and Injustice" articles based on investigation and computer analysis of 1,374 criminal cases in the Philadelphia courts.

Their investigation and analysis uncovered such facts as these:

> Jerome A. Wilson, nineteen, was placed on probation after beating his seven-month-old son to death; Malka Davis, thirty, got one to three years in prison for killing his girl friend's two-and-one-half-year-old son with a belt whipping; Ulysses Pratt, Jr., thirty, was sent to prison for three to ten years for slaying his two children; all less than the average sentence for robbery.
>
> Persons who committed a violent crime in a bar, restaurant, or grocery received stiffer sentences than those who committed violence on the street or in the victim's home.
>
> Judges were more lenient when the defendant said he was working and supporting a family, expressed remorse, was married to the mother of his children, was accompanied to court by his family, promised to enter the military, or admitted he was a drug addict and said he was enrolled in a rehabilitation program.
>
> Blacks were more likely to get prison sentences than whites for the same type of violent crime.
>
> Alfred E. Smith, a twenty-four-year-old black ex-con with a heroin addiction, was sentenced to prison for three to ten years for robbing a sixty-one-year-old loan collector, but William H. Douglas, a nineteen-year-old white ex-con with a heroin addiction, was placed on probation after his conviction for beating and robbing a fifty-five-year-old man.
>
> The prosecutor's recommendations were equally as responsible for leniency as the judges he criticized for it.
>
> A robber was more likely to go to prison than a rapist.
>
> Of three teenagers identified by the victims in a series of robbery-rapes, one went free with all charges dropped, one was acquitted on a directed verdict by the judge, and the third got three years in prison after making a deal with the prosecutor, all because of faulty police methods in obtaining confessions and identifications.
>
> One of every four persons later acquitted of a serious crime or freed by dismissal of charges spent time in jail because he couldn't post bail or bail wasn't set.

Barlett's and Steele's investigation of Philadelphia's criminal court system evolved from their first team project, an exposé of scandal in Federal Housing Administration programs. During their housing probe, they had dealings with District Attorney Arlen Specter, and were not favorably impressed. Specter complained about leniency by judges, and this was an absorbing public issue.

With the concurrence of Executive Editor Eugene L. Roberts, Jr., Barlett and Steele set out to determine exactly how justice was meted out to criminals.

They began by sorting through boxes of court records in a musty garret atop city hall, picking out 1,374 cases of murder, robbery, rape, and assault involving 1,034 defendants. In their housing investigation, they had devised a form to simplify the tedious culling of facts from documents. It saved a lot of time to just fill in the blanks for predetermined categories of information. Now they developed a new form for the criminal case data.

To get the full history of each case, they scrutinized indictments, bail applications, court hearing summaries, police complaints, prior arrest records, psychiatric evaluations, probation reports, hospital records, trial transcripts, sentencing records, defendants' backgrounds, prison records, and other records about each crime, its circumstances, and its victims. Approximately 100,000 pieces of information, including the age, race, and sex of defendants, victims, and judges, were put on 9,618 IBM cards and fed into a computer according to a program designed by Meyer.

The series won a 1973 Heywood Broun Award for public interest reporting. In the meantime, Barlett and Steele had submitted to Roberts a new list of proposed probes.

They selected the IRS, but after a month switched targets. It was March, 1973, and a national oil and gasoline crisis loomed. Home heating oil had run short in some parts of the United States during the 1972–73 winter, and that, according to the grapevine, was only the beginning.

Barlett and Steele read everything they could find on the oil business, including oil company reports filed with the Security and Exchange Commission, publications by the U.S. Bureau of Mines, and the British Petroleum Yearbook, the oil industry's bible. They made elaborate, detailed charts of oil production at home and abroad. Only when they were saturated with knowledge did they sally forth for interviews.

"You don't know what to ask," says Steele, "if you don't check all the records first. We can't tell if someone is lying or doesn't know what he's talking about unless we study all the available data ourselves."

They went to Washington, New York, Houston, and Tulsa to pore over records of government agencies, congressional committees, industry trade organizations and the oil firms themselves. Putting it all together over three months, the two reporters were able to prove that, while a fuel shortage was indeed on the way, it was not because supplies were running out. The real reason, they wrote in a three-part series in July, 1973, was a shortage in refinery capacity caused by bungling and shortsightedness in government and the oil firms.

They discovered, for instance, that the oil companies were expanding sales efforts, drilling new wells, and building new refineries in Europe and Asia even while telling Americans they had to cut back, because overseas operations were more profitable. The government had taken a number of steps, especially on import restrictions and tax rulings, that encouraged the oil firms not to expand refinery capacity at home.

This series won several national awards, and the team's analysis was substantiated by subsequent disclosures.

In the fall, the Arab oil embargo interrupted their IRS probe again. Barlett and Steele went to England, Holland, France, and Italy, where the Arabs had reportedly "turned off the taps" completely. The two reporters found that to be a fiction. More oil than ever was flowing into Europe from the Arab oil wells. They learned this from shipping records, from reports they were surprised to find open to them at the famous insurance firm, Lloyd's of London, and from port workers who laughed at the official government promulgation of "total embargo." By analyzing records of ship movements, the team was able to report that 103 oil tankers had sailed from the Arab skeikdom of Bahrain during December, in the midst of the "embargo," and this was forty more than in September, the month before the boycott supposedly had begun.

While probing behind the oil crisis, Barlett and Steele became as unfavorably impressed with U.S. State Department officials as they had been earlier by District Attorney Specter. It might be a good idea, they agreed, to check out the State Department's administration of America's foreign aid program as soon as they finished with the IRS.

First, as usual, they read everything that dealt with the foreign aid program, primarily State Department reports to Congress. They picked out for special attention several projects that received the most glowing descriptions. The countries involved were Thailand, Peru, South Korea, and Colombia.

The State Department had sponsored a $5-million housing development called Friendship Village in Bangkok, Thailand. Barlett and Steele asked Roger Ernst, director of the State Department's foreign aid program in Thailand, where in Bangkok the project was located.

"I don't know," said Ernst. "I have not seen any record of it."

They directed the question to William Ackerman, special assistant for the Thailand aid program.

Ackerman said he wasn't sure if project files contained an address.

Next they asked the American developer, William E. Miller.

"I wouldn't be interested in talking to you," said Miller. "Newspaper people are only looking to screw things up."

So they tried Miller's Thai partner, Kobchai Sosothikul.

"I'm very busy," Sosothikul replied. "I cannot talk to you."

Their curiosity now sharply whetted, Barlett and Steele resolved to find out why everyone was so uncommunicative about Friendship Village. They discovered that the cluster of 674 homes on the outskirts of Bangkok, supposedly a shining symbol of American know-how and beneficence, was in reality a fiasco, a costly administrative nightmare, and, in the words of a Bangkok newspaper, a "swindle." Though the aid program's purpose was to furnish housing for low-income families, the houses of Friendship Village were occupied by doctors, lawyers, merchants, supervisors, school teachers, military officers, and bankers. When plans had called for recreation areas and schools, the developers had built even fancier houses without government aid. Roads were narrow in the government-sponsored sections, but splendidly wide in the more expensive private area.

When buyers of the government-sponsored homes began protesting, AID program officials said it wasn't their problem and referred the complainants to the Thai government and the private developer. Soon there were defaults, foreclosures, deterioration. The State Department, Barlett and Steele discovered, made no attempt to monitor such projects or enforce its own guidelines. Instead it spent millions of dollars trying to clean up such messes after it was too late.

The reporters found a similar housing development in Bogota, Colombia, a pleasant cluster of brown brick homes behind white stucco walls not far from the city's ghetto. The homes were occupied by affluent tenants, not the poor. Project after project, they found, did more to enrich developers and produce luxury living for the wealthy than to provide housing for low-income families. Worst of all, the State Department's housing program was not an isolated debacle. It was typical of the deception, waste, profiteering, and corruption that riddled the entire foreign aid program.

Despite language difficulties, the *Inquirer* team accumulated more information in the foreign countries than in Washington, where they encountered obstreperous resistance. "The State Department," says Barlett, "is one of the least cooperative federal agencies we've ever dealt with."

Barlett's and Steele's first team endeavor, their FHA fraud revelations, had a casual beginning. Steele had joined the *Inquirer* as an urban affairs writer in 1970, coming to Philadelphia from the Kansas City *Star*. In the summer of 1971, shortly after release of a congressional report on abuses in an FHA program to insure home mortgages for low-income families, Steele discussed housing problems with Executive Editor John McMullan, Roberts' predecessor. Steele, they decided, would spend a few days in the deed room at city hall to see if a full-fledged investigation was in order. The reporter found an inordinate number of turnovers and transactions involving houses with FHA-insured mortgages. Many properties had been conveyed to George Romney, Secretary of the U.S. Department of Housing and Urban Development, FHA's parent agency, through foreclosure. It looked like a situation ripe for investigation.

Agreeing, McMullan asked Barlett to work with Steele. An investigative specialist who had worked for newspapers in Chicago, Cleveland, and Akron before joining the *Inquirer* in 1970, Barlett pitched in with his organized mind. The two reporters plowed through deeds and mortgages for two months. After a while, they detected a pattern. The same names appeared over and over again—the same mortgage companies, the same buyers and sellers, the same addresses.

Interviewing buyers who had lost their homes through foreclosures, the reporters were amazed to find that most of them had not wanted to buy a house in the first place. Mostly poor people, they had wanted to rent, but had been pressured into buying. They told Barlett and Steele the houses fell apart after they moved in, even though an FHA appraiser had inspected them.

Mr. and Mrs. Mario Cosme had been looking for a house to rent. They spotted a "Rent-Sale" sign on a house and inquired at Tower Real Estate. A salesman said they would have to buy it.

"He said it was much better to buy a house than to rent," Mrs. Cosme told the reporters, "because eventually it would be yours. He said you buy the house and you have something for your children.

"Mr. Tower said he wanted us to move in right away. He said he wouldn't fix it until after we moved in. He said anything wrong with it, he will fix it. He said you sign the papers, so I signed the papers. He told me it was FHA approved."

With $100 down, the Cosmes bought for $6,500 a three-story house that a partner in the real estate firm had purchased eight months earlier for $1,000. The couple and their five children moved in.

"After a rain," said Mrs. Cosme, "all of a sudden the water came down through the living room ceiling and down the steps." After Mrs. Cosme complained to Tower Real Estate, a man arrived who drilled holes in the living room floor to let the water out.

"After I signed the papers," Mrs. Cosme said, "the dining room ceiling fell down. And the ceiling in the kitchen. My husband was in the kitchen cooking when all the plaster fell down on his head."

The house had been approved for FHA mortgage insurance despite the fact that it had been cited by the city as "unfit for human habitation"—and despite the fact that federal law said a property approved for an FHA mortgage must meet "the requirements of all state laws, or local ordinances and regulations, relating to the public health or safety."

Things got so miserable that the Cosmes stopped making their mortgage payments. "When the water came up the cellar steps and the crap from the toilet all went into the basement and the dirty water from the kitchen went into the basement," said Mrs. Cosme, "I didn't pay nothing after that."

The mortgage was foreclosed, but no one lost anything except the Cosmes and the federal government. The mortgage company that had processed the loan had its fees, and the mortgage company that later bought the mortgage collected $7,143 from HUD under the FHA insurance for the unpaid principal, interest and attorney fees. HUD got the $1,000 house.

Barlett and Steele found hundreds of such cases. Speculators bought up the houses at miniscule prices, spent a few dollars on cosmetic repairs, and sold them at inflated prices to poor people on FHA mortgages with the connivance of FHA appraisers and officials. The speculators and the mortgage firms couldn't have cared less whether the buyers could afford the payments. Only

Uncle Sam could lose. One speculator named Theodore Clearfield bought eighty-five houses for a total of $220,000 and resold them, usually within three months, for $603,000. Another speculator was the husband of the Secretary of the Commonwealth of Pennsylvania. Profits ran into the millions and, by the time Barlett and Steele came onto the scene, HUD had been stuck with hundreds of decrepit houses in Philadelphia alone.

After talking to home buyers, the *Inquirer* team went to Washington. They found HUD officials and congressional committees on housing blissfully unaware of the fraud and corruption that was making a mockery of their well-intentioned program. Back in Philadelphia, Barlett and Steele explained it for them in a series of articles which brought in an avalanche of phone calls and letters about similar outrages.

In 1975, after it was disclosed that the CIA had retained a company owned by billionaire recluse Howard R. Hughes to retrieve a Russian nuclear submarine from the floor of the Pacific Ocean, Barlett and Steele set out systematically to examine all of Hughes' connections and dealings with the United States government.

For eight months they plodded through records—contracts, audit reports, court depositions, computer printouts, hearing transcripts, trial records, corporation documents, partnership agreements, financial statements—in government offices and court files from New York to Los Angeles. They compiled 10,000 pages of notes and documents.

The astounding facts unearthed by Barlett and Steele were published in a December, 1975, series of articles that were picked up by newspapers around the country. Samples: Hughes and his companies were receiving $1.7 million a day from the U.S. Treasury; over ten years, Hughes enterprises had been paid more than $6 billion on government contracts; most of the deals that produced this income were executed in secret, eighty percent of them without competitive bidding; federal agencies like the IRS, the Defense Department, and the Civil Aeronautics Board did more to help, protect, and enrich Hughes than to regulate him; the CIA admitted to thirty-two contracts worth $6.6 million with Hughes Aircraft Company, but refused to divulge anything about contracts with other Hughes companies; Hughes' personal foundation, the Howard Hughes Medical Institute, had been free from tax law enforcement for six years because the IRS hadn't made a decision on application of the 1969 tax reform law; the CAB had dished out $55 million in taxpayer money to subsidize a California airline owned by Hughes.

Getting records was often a bitter struggle. When Barlett and Steele submitted requests for Defense Department records under the Freedom of Information Act, word got to Hughes executives. The Hughes people filed Freedom of Information requests to see the reporters' requests and all information released to them. Barlett and Steele countered by filing requests to see the Hughes requests. Defense Department officials once refused to release documents after Hughes executives opposed it as "catastrophic." The IRS refused to release records on its dealings with Hughes despite court rulings that such records are public.

The team's most bountiful source was a mass of documents and testimony in a defamation suit by onetime Hughes aide Robert Maheu against his former boss in Los Angeles. The team also interviewed ex-employes of Hughes and his companies.

But the relentless investigators fared no better than anyone else in getting an interview with Hughes. Letters to Hughes company executives came back unopened or were not answered. Three requests mailed to Hughes came back marked, "Not at this address."

Every day at quitting time, William Mullen glanced around the office of the Chicago Board of Election Commissioners to see if anyone was watching him. If not, he stuck a bunch of ballot applications under his shirt.

For a while after Mullen began working as an election board clerk in May, 1972, someone had followed him every night when he left the office. Mullen had been appointed to the job by the only Republican on the three-man election board, and the Democrats, who held 196 of the 200 jobs, were suspicious. The tail put on Mullen watched him go every night to the Chicago *Tribune*. At first puzzled, the Democrats finally concluded he was visiting a girl friend. They never suspected he was on an undercover assignment for the *Tribune* Task Force of investigative reporters.

At the *Tribune*, Mullen took the ballot applications for the March, 1972, primary from under his shirt and handed them to George Bliss, the *Tribune's* leading investigative reporter for many years. Bliss had returned to the *Tribune* in 1971 after a three-year interlude as chief investigator for the Better Government Association, a civic organization that campaigns against corruption and malfeasance. Bliss now was director of the Task Force, which has made a specialty of undercover tactics.

Bliss made copies of the ballot applications. Many of the signatures appeared to have been made by the same hand. Bliss had them examined by a handwriting expert while reporters checked out the people. As they suspected, hundreds of signatures had been forged. At least one person had died before the primary. Another had been in a hospital on voting day. Most said they hadn't voted and that wasn't their signature.

Mullen discovered that Republican election judges actually had been voting in Democratic primaries, another election law violation. Over four months, Mullen slipped out evidence of more than 1,000 ghost voters, phony election judges, and ballot forgeries.

Task Force reporters were elated. Surely this was enough proof at last to get action against voting fraud by Chicago's indifferent authorities. Chicago newspapers had been exposing election irregularities for years, but never with much impact. Past exposés had been strong on allegations, thin on facts.

Politicians who rigged elections shrugged them off with sighs of annoyance and went back to business as usual.

This time it would be different. Bliss had proposed the investigation in December, 1971. "We figured there were about 200,000 votes stolen in every election," he says. "It was getting ridiculous." Bliss was sure that U.S. Attorney James R. Thompson, a Republican known to be smart, tough, and honest, would prosecute if the *Tribune* could produce solid evidence.

Before the March primary, Task Force reporters mailed registered letters to 5,495 voters in fourteen precincts where past investigations had pinpointed heavy cheating. About 700 letters came back. The addressees couldn't be found. Reporters discovered that many of the voters had died. Others had moved. Sixty-two addresses were vacant lots or abandoned buildings.

Bliss arranged with Republican leaders to have seventeen *Tribune* staffers and eight BGA investigators appointed as Republican election judges and poll watchers. On election day, the reporter-judges challenged votes cast under the phony names, but were overruled by Democratic precinct captains who weren't supposed to be at the polling places, but who in fact were bossing the poll workers and election judges. The undercover reporters witnessed campaigning in the polling place, distribution of campaign material, and multiple voting by election judges, illegal assistance to voters, and tampering with voting machines.

Bliss spied on one polling place from a third-floor apartment. Spotting a campaign worker giving money to voters, he chased the man down and got him to admit it.

Task Force stories began appearing two days after the primary. The findings were turned over to U.S. Attorney Thompson and a federal grand jury. But nothing happened. Despite an abundance of documentary and eyewitness evidence, more, apparently, was needed.

When Bliss heard about an election board opening for a Republican clerk, he approached Cook County Republican Chairman Edmund J. Kucharski. The only thing left, Bliss explained, was to get someone inside, just as the Task Force had done in the past. Kucharski agreed.

Mullen, a tall, portly, twenty-eight-year-old rewrite man chosen for the assignment because he hadn't covered politics and wouldn't be known to the Democrats in Mayor Richard Daley's powerful political machine, had done the job. Five days after Mullen's articles began to appear on September 10, 1972, and his new evidence was delivered to Thompson, the grand jury indicted forty election judges for fraud. Later, thirty-nine more were indicted. Within a year, twenty-seven pleaded guilty, three were convicted, the cleanest election in Chicago's history was held in November, and the *Tribune* won a Pulitzer Prize for local reporting.

The man behind the Task Force's enthusiasm for undercover tactics was William Jones, who had started it in 1970 when he became an ambulance driver for two months to investigate bribery of police by ambulance firms. Bliss, then working for BGA, received a call from an ambulance firm owner who complained about "a lot of wrongdoing." When Bliss and Jones went to see the man, he charged that his competitors were paying policemen to give them the ambulance business in accidents and emergency cases.

Jones, thirty-one, and a twenty-eight-year-old BGA investigator named Bill Recktenwald went through first aid training and obtained city licenses as ambulance attendants. Jones got jobs at two companies, Recktenwald at three. The sadism and mistreatment they witnessed shocked them beyond their grimmest expectations.

In one incident, an ambulance crew dragged an old man wracked with pain from cancer across the floor to a stretcher, ignoring his pleas for gentle handling.

A black girl suffering a miscarriage was told by a driver to walk down two flights of stairs to the ambulance.

An epileptic with a fractured hip waited two hours for an ambulance which police summoned instead of taking the victim directly to a hospital. Recktenwald saw the driver hand ten dollars to one of the cops.

Bliss and a BGA investigator posing as his friend staged a heart attack scene in an apartment. When a two-man ambulance crew arrived, Bliss was lying on the floor gasping for breath. One of the crew lifted him up, felt his pockets and found two dollars. He said they couldn't put the victim on the stretcher until they were paid forty dollars. The victim had only the two dollars, said his "friend." The crew put Bliss into a chair and left, snatching up the two dollars on their way out. A *Tribune* photographer in the next room with Jones took pictures of the incident.

His first day on the job, Jones was confronted by his employer, who suspected Jones was a private investigator working for a lawyer in a $1-million lawsuit against his firm. The owner asked to see Jones' ambulance attendant's license.

"Very well," he said. "Mr. William Jones—private investigator."

Jones laughed off the attempt to catch him off guard. "I'm really James Bond," he said.

"I had you pegged for a reliable, long-term man when I hired you," said the other. "But if you're a private investigator, you're going to wind up with a rap in the head. You understand what I'm saying?"

Jones laughed again.

The employer asked for his driver's license and compared it with the ambulance attendant's license. That seemed to satisfy him.

This firm had billed the state for more than $130,000 in Medicaid fees for welfare patients during the first four months of 1970. Jones received explicit instructions about welfare patients. Accept them. The state would pay. If the patient was not eligible for Medicaid, the policy was cash in advance. "No bread, no bed."

What if the family had no cash?

"Turn around and leave."

Before he wrote his stories, Jones conducted a thorough analysis of Medicaid billings to the state for ambulance fees. He found bill padding that inflated payments by as much as forty percent.

Though usually scornful of newspaper exposés, Mayor Daley ordered an immediate city investigation. The county public aid director banned three ambulance firms from transporting welfare patients and started a probe on his own. The state director of public aid halted payments to one firm and began a third investigation. Two months later a grand jury took up the case and in November indictments were returned against ten policemen and six ambulance company officials. Medicare officials decertified two companies, one of which was found to be controlled by crime syndicate figures. Next May, Jones won a Pulitzer Prize.

A blond, athletic-looking Midwesterner who wears a vest with a hint of Ivy League formality, Jones is now the *Tribune's* Managing Editor for News at thirty-six. He defends the undercover method as the only way to get some evidence. "It should be used very carefully," he says, "within ethical boundaries and under controlled conditions." In the ambulance investigation, Jones wasn't just posing; he was a bona fide licensed ambulance attendant. "In fact," he says, "one of the better ambulance attendants in Chicago."

The undercover method worked so well with ambulances that Jones was authorized to set up an investigative Task Force to use it in a steady program of probes. There was some notion of patterning the team after *Newsday's*, but *Tribune* editors wanted a unique concept. The Task Force would not concentrate on putting politicians in jail, but on exposing crooks and incompetents who directly victimized the average reader. It would be consumer oriented, and concerned with the taxpayer's getting his money's worth of government. Jones picked young, aggressive reporters rather than experienced veterans.

The first project was nursing homes. Pamela Zekman, a small, plainspoken redhead who had been a social worker and who later would become the Task Force's director, went to work as a nurse's aide in four nursing homes, using her real name but a false job background and phone number. Jones and two other reporters, Philip Caputo and William Currie, got jobs as janitors, medical aides, and kitchen helpers. Currie became an administrator briefly at one home. Bliss and other BGA investigators were placed as patients in homes where a job couldn't be obtained. Caputo entered one home as a mental patient.

Zekman remembers long hours of emptying bedpans and changing sheets for six weeks, and experiences that made her physically ill. "We never cleaned up after the patients," she says. "We were told to leave it for the night shift." Every day after work, Zekman and the others went back to the *Tribune* and wrote memos on the day's observations.

They saw two old women screech and claw over a ragged blanket. A nurse's aide told them, "Shut your goddamn mouths, both of you, or I'll take your blankets away and you can both freeze."

At a large North Side home, uneaten portions of food were scraped off patients' trays and served to other patients.

A man and a woman were taken for a bath at the same time to the same room and ordered to undress. After their baths, aides dried them with pillow cases because there were no towels.

A ninety-one-year-old man who asked two aides giving him a bath to "slow down, I can't bend my legs this fast," was slapped across the face.

Janitors were left to watch patients. Patient rooms were filthy, dimly lit dungeons. Skid row alcoholics were recruited to work as orderlies, nurse's aides, and cooks. Reporters got jobs without showing credentials or proof of experience. Nurse's aides were told to administer medications. Patients who complained were threatened. Beds reeked of urine, plumbing was broken, plaster was falling out of walls. Rats and roaches scampered about.

Yet, the nursing homes managed to keep their licenses, and were receiving hundreds of thousands of dollars in state payments for welfare patients.

"Thousands of our senior citizens are spending their last days," the Task Force wrote in its first article on February 28, 1971, "wondering why it all must end in the indignity of filthy, rat-infested rooms, physical abuse, wretched food and caretakers who can't see beyond the next welfare or Social Security check."

Working undercover, says Zekman, was the only way to get the evidence. "There is only one way to tell the story," said the first article, "and that is to live with them, bathe them, feed them, watch and listen to their 'keepers' and then report their story of rage, confusion, and frustration as they live out their days in a warehouse for the dying."

Within days of the first article, the Illinois Public Aid Department began withholding payments to nursing homes. The Cook County Public Aid Department assigned thirty investigators. The City Council ordered a probe. Mayor Daley called for a new ordinance to upgrade standards for nursing home employes. A federal grand jury issued subpoenas. Authorities began to close some of the worst homes. The state senate began hearings. A new system of surprise inspections was inaugurated, resulting in the closing of more than a hundred nursing homes across the state. Two nurse's aides were arrested for striking patients.

In the fall of 1971, with the gray-haired, grandfatherly Bliss back from the BGA, the Task Force investigated waste and mismanagement in Cook County government. This time the tactic was surveillance. Reporters following work crews discovered bricklayers who never laid bricks, plumbers who never touched a wrench, and heating engineers who didn't work at heating plants. They calculated the county was losing $14,228,000 a year, $36,497 a day. Cook County ordered an outside study and 108 jobs eventually were abolished.

In 1973, Bliss, now working independently of the Task Force, wanted to investigate police brutality. There had been talk of it for years. 1972 statistics showed that only twenty-nine of 827 complaints against policemen had been sustained by police department investigations. Jones, who had become City Editor, assigned Zekman and two other reporters to work with Bliss as a team separate from the Task Force, which was busy with another investigation.

The police department would not let the reporters see its records on brutality complaints. Bliss' background as police reporter and investigative journalist since 1937 came to the rescue.

Bliss had been on the scene in the old days when reporters failed to see any news value in the fact that policemen moonlighted as bouncers at gambling joints. On his first investigative assignment, Bliss had trouble infiltrating the gambling spots because the moonlighting cops recognized him. Later he became what he calls the *Tribune's* "first spaghetti editor," writing about the Mafia and the underworld with Sandy Smith, who later went on to nationwide recognition as an investigative writer for *Life* magazine. Bliss and Smith put together one of the first charts of organized crime's hierarchy, before law enforcement agencies had much zeal for the topic. They were among the first to expose underworld infiltration of legitimate business. In 1953, as the *Tribune's* labor editor, Bliss exposed an attempt by racketeer Joey Glimco to take over the Chicago Conference of Teamsters, meeting helpful union members on deserted roads in the middle of the night to get the story. Over the years, investigations by Bliss had resulted in the imprisonment of more than 100 persons.

By the time his police brutality probe faced collapse for lack of access to police files, Bliss had a lot of friends in the Chicago Police Department. One, a high-ranking official who did not approve of his department's handling of complaints, succumbed to Bliss' appeals. He took a batch of records and met Bliss in a hotel room. Bliss made copies and the police official put them back before they were missed.

The team delved into 500 cases, locating and questioning victims and witnesses, often arranging for lie detector tests. Many victims were afraid to talk. Medical records were inspected.

The reporters found that police brutality was not confined to slum areas. Race was not a factor, as some of the most brutal officers were black. Thirty-seven cases were selected for a lengthy series of articles. It was "probably the most thorough examination of police brutality ever published in a U.S. newspaper," said *Time* magazine.

A grand jury indicted several policemen. The police department was ordered to train recruits better, set up a program to spot and discipline unstable officers, and improve its attitude toward brutality complaints.

In 1974, with Zekman heading the Task Force, it exposed illegal and unscrupulous practices of bill collection agencies by getting jobs in eight of them. Task Force reporters posed as potential investors to probe fraud amongst the growing number of franchise business opportunities. In 1975, they went to work as salesmen for career schools to get inside evidence of misrepresentation and fraud.

About three months before the November 5, 1974, election, thirty-two-year-old Task Force reporter William Crawford rented an apartment and started hanging around Democratic Ward headquarters at 5242 North Sheridan Road. He said he was a landscape foreman out of work and he'd do anything for a job.

"You have to see Sam," he was told. "You never go over your precinct captain's head."

Sam was seventy-six-year-old Sam Herr, precinct captain and engineer in the city's Bureau of Sewers. One day Herr said to Crawford, "I talked to the boss, and he said he had a couple of slots, but I want you to do a little job for me and we'll see how you work out. If you do okay, we'll have something for you, but first I gotta see how political you are."

Crawford joined Herr and a sheriff's office clerk in "working" the precinct. That meant ringing doorbells, hanging posters, exhorting residents to vote straight Democratic.

Whenever Crawford asked about prospects for a city job, Herr said they were good, but their main concern was the election. On October 28, Crawford was given a sealed envelope by ward boss Martin Tuchow, who said, "You take this to Room 603 in City Hall in the morning and they'll take care of you."

Within forty-eight hours, Crawford was earning $520 a month stamping burial forms for the Board of Health without benefit of going through the city's personnel office.

The job wasn't free, however, a fellow city employe said. "You have to pay dues," he said. "$200 to $300 a year. Tuchow will assess you at the ward dinner in November."

From his vantage point inside city government, Crawford saw firsthand how the patronage system worked, how city offices were overstaffed with workers who had nothing to do but look busy, how patronage employes took time off whenever they felt like it, how some didn't show up at all except to get their paychecks. The patronage system, the Task Force wrote in its articles on padding and waste in city government, was "perhaps the single most important factor accounting for $91 million in waste uncovered during a three-month investigation."

The investigation dealt with nine bureaus in three major city departments. It found that five men were used to change a light bulb in a street lamp. Many of the "temporary appointees" who comprised a fourth of the city work force had been on the payroll for years. $317,684 was spent every year to wash street signs, which other cities let the rain do. The probe included surveillance of city work crews and visits to other cities.

In 1975, Task Force reporters investigated health care again, this time getting jobs as nurse's aides and janitors in city hospitals to expose patient abuse, filthy conditions, assembly line tonsillectomies, dangerous understaffing, Medicaid bill padding, and numerous other violations.

William Gaines, a chunky, professorial-looking reporter, posed as a skid row bum with a Medicaid card for three weeks to learn firsthand how hospitals recruited and mistreated welfare patients. One hospital sent out a van to scout for them. As a janitor in one hospital, Gaines was asked by a nurse to stay in an operating room and watch over a six-year-old girl who had just gone through a tonsillectomy and hernia surgery. After the Task Force's revelations were published, Gaines and Crawford testified on their experiences before the U.S. Senate's Special Subcommittee on Aging.

"Doctors don't rat on each other and hospitals won't let you in," says Zekman. "Infiltration is the only way to get irrefutable evidence." The real story, she says, is that health authorities don't do their job until newspapers force them to. The hospital probe was one of two that won a 1976 Pulitzer Prize in local reporting for the *Tribune*.

Bliss returned to the headlines in 1975 with the other Pulitzer Prize winner, a seven-month investigation of the FHA's 235 program of mortgage insurance to help poor people buy houses. Working with a young colleague named Chuck Neubauer, Bliss went beyond the usual FHA exposé showing fraud, collusion, and kickbacks among brokers, developers, builders, appraisers, and government officials. Bliss and Neubauer revealed how mortgage companies were costing taxpayers millions of dollars by violating FHA guidelines and engaging in such fraudulent practices as certifying fire-damaged houses as undamaged.

A Pulitzer Prize-winner in 1962 for exposing ghost jobs and political payroll padding in the Metropolitan Sanitary District of Greater Chicago, Bliss dug out evidence that the main beneficiaries of government housing programs for the poor and the elderly were not the poor and the elderly, but real estate brokers and mortgage companies who knew how to hogtie FHA officials in their own red tape. He showed that FHA and its parent agency, HUD, encouraged fraud with a "hands off" attitude on violations. Top government officials, Bliss and Neubauer discovered in hard-to-get records, tried to conceal the $4 billion in losses rather than implement reforms, and blocked attempts by employes to stop the waste. Mortgage companies had amassed such influence among HUD officials that even the most unscrupulous continued to get FHA approvals.

Real estate brokers and mortgage companies, the reporters learned, actively sought out home buyers who would not be able to keep up their payments on FHA mortgages. They couldn't lose. They had their commissions and fees, and if foreclosure occurred, the FHA insurance. As a result, HUD was stuck with 3,579 vacant and dilapidated houses in Chicago, and expected soon to foreclose on 5,000 to 7,000 more.

Congressional investigations were launched. HUD secretary Carla Hills, who called Bliss to congratulate him on the articles, announced tougher regulations on foreclosures.

Bliss chuckles over the idea that investigative reporting is a new fad. He's been doing it so long he finds it hard to distinguish from his other reporting. It's all a matter of finding out what's going on.

Jones doesn't dispute the contention that all reporting is investigative, but doesn't consider it worth arguing. "Sure, you can waste time on semantics," he says. "But it's something to be debated in journalism schools, not newsrooms."

Jones believes "investigative reporting" is a good term. "It enjoys a special category of respect in the minds of young people and the public. Maybe there's too much romanticism attached to it, but it tends to explain more clearly what newspapering is all about—investing money and manpower to serve the community."

The records had been crammed haphazardly into a small, dusty storeroom in the basement of the Public Works building. Rain had seeped in the windows and some of the documents were wet. Three reporters of the Boston *Globe's* Spotlight investigative team surveyed the mess with chagrin, but began crawling over boxes to lift out papers to be sorted.

They found the invoices they were after, bills paid by the suburban city of Somerville for services and supplies from several companies during the 1960–70 decade. But that wasn't good enough. The bills were bundled without regard to date, job, or other common element. To determine how much had been paid for one job, for one batch of materials, or to a single supplier over a period of time, they would have to make copies of the bills and collate them.

That presented a problem. Team leader Timothy Leland solved it by slipping a few invoices into his notebook every day as they left and sneaking them out to a copy machine. The next day he brought them back and spirited out some more. One day he forgot about the contraband in his notebook and opened it to check something as he was passing a secretary on the way out. The invoices fluttered to the floor. Leland caught his breath, sure he was in big trouble. But the secretary let him off with a reproving look and went back to her work. She must have suspected what the reporters were doing, Leland concluded later, but did not disapprove.

A phone call prompted by the Spotlight team's first investigation had brought the reporters to Somerville.

Leland, a slender thirty-three-year-old with thinning hair, a mustache and diversified background in journalism, organized the team in September, 1970, after studying the London *Times'* famous Insight team for six months and taking a look at *Newsday's*. The Spotlight team, the *Globe* announced, was to "reconstruct major news events as rapidly and comprehensively as possible, with an emphasis on the 'why' rather than the 'what' of an event. The unit will also seek to expose public corruption and malfeasance."

Besides Leland, the charter members were: Gerard O'Neil, twenty-seven, a reporter who had covered city hall and state government and had won a UPI award for exposing a school board member's relationship with a contractor; Stephen Kurkjian, a short, dark, twenty-six-year-old reporter who was also a lawyer; and Ann DeSantis, twenty-three, a secretary-researcher.

Casting about for a project worthy of its ambitions, the team followed up a suggestion by the real estate editor to investigate a parking lot on city-owned land. By standing outside with a counter for several days, the reporters discovered the city had made a bad deal by leasing the property for only $132,000 a year without benefit of public bidding. After this first Spotlight report, the parking lot lease was canceled, and a young radio reporter in Somerville telephoned the team to say, "You think that's bad, you ought to come out here."

"Why?" he was asked. "What's going on in Somerville?"

Illegal contracts, said the radio reporter. Totals kept below $1,000 to circumvent the bidding law. Jobs split into several bills under $1,000. A school was painted and the bills came in for one wall at a time.

The officials allegedly responsible for this no-bid business were no longer in office. The current administration in Somerville gave the reporters access to the records.

Copying and collating, the reporters made some eye-catching discoveries.

On July 8, 1969, a plumbing company owned by two brothers named Sillari had done $3,984 worth of drinking fountain repairs at city playgrounds. But the company had not sent a bill for that amount. I had sent twelve bills, each for less than $1,000. There had been no bidding for the work.

In 1969, the city water department had purchased $20,479 in plumbing supplies from a Sillari firm without taking a bid. A Sillari company had also done "emergency work" totaling $10,037 at the city's central heating plant in 1969. "Emergency work" was exempt from bidding requirements, but the company kept all the bills below $1,000 anyway.

The Sillari brothers had done $329,604 in no-bid business over a ten-year period. One of the brothers had a son who was a partner with a former Somerville mayor in an insurance agency.

Within a three-week period in 1962, a company owned by Luigi Analetto, a contractor who had served two years in prison for defrauding Somerville on previous contract work, did $9,041 worth of no-bid sidewalk construction. The firm had billed the city in fifteen separate invoices, the largest for $986. Analetto's company had received $777,756.44 in no-bid business from 1960 to 1970.

The city had paid $481,063 for no-bid work to three companies owned by a former public works commissioner, including an automobile service station that got $34,682.

A painting contractor had submitted thirty separate bills totaling $27,154 for painting various rooms in the Somerville High School. He had done $130,864 worth of no-bid business over ten years.

Almost $2.2 million had been paid to a construction firm in no-bid business, including $1.6 million on an "emergency" contract to repair a fire-damaged junior high school.

Altogether, the city had spent $4.3 million on no-bid business with five contractors—$2 million for jobs and materials billed piecemeal in amounts under $1,000, and $2.3 million in "emergency work."

The city charter required that public bids be taken when a job or contract was expected to exceed $1,000. It also said, "No bill, contract, or lease shall be split or divided for the purpose of evading any provisions of this section."

After the team sorted 6,000 documents, it was time for interviews. "We do the paper investigation first," says Leland. "Then the people." Interviewing is done systematically. "We start on the perimeter," says Leland, "and work in. First, the enemies of the key people, who don't report back that we're asking questions. Then we tighten the circle, begin talking to cronies and colleagues. If they're part of the malfeasance, we promise to keep them out of it if they cooperate. We figure they'll report back what we're up to, and that makes them increasingly nervous.

"Sometimes one of the key figures will call and say he'd like to straighten it out if we would talk to him. We say yes, we want to talk to you, but not yet. We want to know everything we can first. Then when we finally walk in, maybe with a lawyer and a tape recorder, he's dying. That's part of our strategy."

This time, the strategy did not produce results as conclusive as the billing records, but it did yield a few gems. Said one former mayor: "You must remember that when you're sitting in the mayor's chair there are a million things to do with little time to do it; you can't study each and every bill." Another former mayor said, "I don't climb up on every roof every time somebody fixes a roof and I don't go into a room every time it's painted."

The Somerville articles prompted a state investigation that culminated in 119 indictments against four companies and nineteen persons, including three ex-mayors of Somerville. The Spotlight team, less than two years after its birth, won a Pulitzer Prize.

Meanwhile, events were brewing at the Massachusetts Turnpike Authority that would become the subject of the team's next probe.

Philip A. Graham, one of three Turnpike Authority members, was driving along a turnpike stretch that was being resurfaced in the summer of 1970 when he noticed that new pavement was being laid in long strips. One strip of asphalt would cool before the adjoining strip was put down. Knowing that the $5.5-million contract for thirty-three miles of resurfacing specified that both strips be at least 150 degrees when joined together to assure durability of the seam, Graham stopped his car to investigate. He discovered no effort to reheat the edge of the asphalt before workers formed the joint. "If that asphalt is 150 degrees," Graham told the engineer in charge, "I'll sit on it."

Graham reported his discovery to the other Turnpike Authority members, Chairman John T. Driscoll and Albert P. "Toots" Manzi. A flurry of memos and conferences ensued. The Authority's consulting engineers, which had drawn up the contract specifications, decided that "hot joints" weren't necessary, after all.

Four months after the work was completed, cracks and crevices began to appear over the joints. In some spots, the seam became so loose that chunks of pavement could be lifted out by hand. Graham tried to have payments withheld from the contractor, Bayer & Mingolla Industries Inc. "If it's this bad now," said Graham, "I hate to think what it will look like in a couple of years."

Manzi and Driscoll were not fazed. On November 12, 1970, they voted to give the contractor another $5.6 million worth of turnpike resurfacing work, overriding Graham's vehement objections. There was no bidding on the contract because Massachusetts law exempted the Turnpike Authority from the usual public bid requirements.

When the Spotlight reporters learned about the situation, they conducted a preliminary "smell" to determine if a full-scale investigation was likely to produce newsworthy results. Manzi, they heard, was a close friend of Cosmo Mingolla, executive vice president of the contracting firm. If their relationship was behind the awarding of the contract, that would be a good story, even if it were not technically illegal.

Getting the basic facts was easy enough. The *Globe* hired a paving expert to examine the resurfaced turnpike and he said the cracks appeared "to be the result of weakened joints and the stress of subsurface conditions." Graham was helpful and much information was in the public record. The snag was a lack of hard evidence that Manzi and Mingolla were friends.

Implementing their interview strategy, Leland and his crew talked to enemies, associates, and friends of both men. Though they turned up some supporting information, unassailable proof eluded them. They would have to get an admission of the friendship from Manzi or Mingolla.

The team went to the Turnpike Authority office in Boston and confronted Manzi. Trying to conceal their anxiety, they planned to throw out the question casually, pretending it was a minor point. If Manzi denied the friendship, their story would be wobbly, perhaps dead. It was important that he not suspect how crucial an admission would be. In the middle of the discussion, Leland said offhandedly, "Mr. Manzi, you're a very good friend of Mr. Mingolla, right?"

The reporters fidgeted in suspense, but did not have to wait long. Manzi, who had no idea how much the reporters had learned but knew they'd talked to a lot of people close to him, said, "Sure, I'm a close friend of his. There's no secret about that. I've known him all my life. What's the big deal? I have a lot of friends."

Well, did that have anything to do with awarding $11.1 million in no-bid resurfacing contracts to Mingolla's firm?

"Positively not," Manzi said.

Mingolla also admitted the friendship with Manzi, but also denied it was connected to the contracts.

After the team's disclosures about the case in May, 1971, the state legislature changed the law. It made the Turnpike Authority subject to the bidding law. Manzi resigned.

Spotlight reporters were fast becoming experts on no-bid contracts. Later that year, the team exposed improper procedures in contract awards and land purchases by the Redevelopment Authority in the city of Woburn. As a result, the state refused to pay its share of nine land acquisitions and $750,000 in construction contracts for an industrial park. The following year, a former Woburn mayor and the city's superintendent of public works were indicted.

The team then delved into the reasons why an auto towing company owned by a convicted bookie had a monopoly on towing disabled, stolen, and illegally parked vehicles ordered removed by police. Reporters spent hours watching the tow firm's main lot. They saw several policemen stop by. One cop was there all during his duty shift. Though he told a reporter his job was to check out stolen cars, he was observed moving cars and talking to customers. The team discovered the company's vice president shared an apartment with a police lieutenant.

One policeman they interviewed said, "Look, I'll level with you. There are towing kickbacks all over the city. It's been going on for years." Another cop said, "When the old-timers broke me in, they told me, 'When you send a tow job in, pick up your money.' "

A tow company owner told the reporters, "I quit Boston towing years ago because of the graft. Everyone was at your door looking for the dollar." Another signed an affidavit saying he made payoffs to police. Others said they had been chased from accident scenes by police who ordered other firms' tow trucks.

The owner of the tow firm that got all the city business denied making payoffs to police. As to how he obtained the business, it "just fell into place." There had been no public bidding. A city attorney could not explain why the city's bid law was not being enforced. After the Spotlight report appeared, it was enforced.

The Spotlight team has done other kinds of investigations, too. It revealed the state had paid $1,275,000 for a building closed as a public health menace after the state bought it for use as a youth service facility.

Spotlight reporters uncovered a probate judge's hidden interest in land deals with attorneys to whom he was channeling lucrative court appointments in estate cases.

They posed as potential customers to investigate several career schools that were bilking veterans and young people with misrepresentation and bullying sales tactics.

A salesman for an unaccredited dental assistant course told a Spotlight team member posing as a prospective student that she'd "be able to clean teeth, take mouth impressions, take X-rays, and all that, once you finish our course." Such work by a dental assistant, however, would have violated the law.

On a test to determine if she was eligible for the course, she deliberately gave more wrong answers than right ones. No matter. "You're pretty smart," said the salesman, who received a $100 commission on each $2,000 enrollment. "You're going to make a lot of money from this course."

Graduates, however, discovered they could not get jobs as dental assistants.

The team likes to do four major investigations a year, plus a "couple of quickies," according to Kurkjian. To do that, it must operate efficiently. One way, the team has found, is for every member to write a memo on each day's findings. Files are set up for every name, place, and incident. Copies of each memo are cross-filed wherever they may be useful.

"We have to keep everybody closely attuned to what the others have learned," says Leland. "We tape-record interviews because it allows all to sit around and listen. Someone may spot something the interviewer missed."

"By some standards, we over-research," says Kurkjian. "But we have it down to a formula. We know what can be done, what we'll be able to find, who will talk, how long it will take."

A successful team, says Leland, must have energy and team spirit. Most of all, it needs a strong leader, according to Leland, who turned the team's reins over to O'Neil in 1972 when he moved up to assistant managing editor.

There must also, he says, be a minimum of prima donna egoism. One reason for the team concept and the Spotlight name was to downplay individual by-lines and make the *Globe's* investigative journalism semianonymous. It was hoped the name would develop a mystique and become a symbol for uncorruptible, fearless public service.

Team members are convinced it has worked out that way. "We get an enormous volume of calls," says the team's newest member, Peter Cowen, "from people who recognize us as an agency of last resort in Boston."

The big story was slipping away, disintegrating out of their grasp. James Savage and Mike Baxter of the Miami *Herald* were stymied. About to disclose that a campaign fund raiser for U.S. Senator Edward Gurney had offered to help a Gainsville builder get approval for FHA housing projects in return for $5,000, they were informed of a statement by Gurney that he had no connection with the fund raiser, Larry Williams of Orlando. Gurney's statement, prompted by a list of questions submitted by Savage and Baxter, said he had met Williams only a couple of times.

Williams also denied any relationship with Gurney. All the reporters had was the word of the builder, Philip Emmer.

Emmer had phoned Baxter in 1972 after reading the team's articles about a curiously large number of FHA approvals obtained by an inexperienced Miami home builder named John Priestas. Emmer said he had been approached by Williams and asked for $5,000 for Gurney. "He said they would help me get approval on FHA projects," Emmer said. But Emmer would not grant permission for his name to be used in a news article.

Savage and Baxter decided not to write about an isolated allegation if they couldn't quote its source by name. They didn't know Emmer or anything about his credibility.

Then they heard that Priestas, by then under investigation as a result of their stories, had confessed to the FBI. Priestas told the FBI he had given money to Williams to get FHA approvals. According to Priestas, Williams turned the money over to James L. Groot, Gurney's administrative assistant in Washington. Groot put pressure on FHA officials in Washington and three regional FHA directors in Florida, including William Pelski in Miami, who had approved Priestas' applications.

Emmer's story suddenly seemed more significant, more valid. They phoned the builder several times, imploring him to let his name be used. It was an important story that had to get out, they pleaded. It was up to him as a good citizen.

No, said Emmer, Talk to some other builders. He wasn't the only one. "Who?"

Anyone. Anyone who's doing FHA stuff.

During the summer of 1973, fifteen months after Emmer had first contacted Baxter, Savage decided to make one last try at cajoling the builder into going public. They had not been able to ferret the story out elsewhere. As it happened, Emmer had been watching Gurney wax righteous on TV as a member of the Senate Watergate Committee. He was irritated. "The hell with it," he said. "Go ahead."

But there was no corroborating proof that Gurney and Williams knew each other, let alone that Williams was the senator's bagman. Savage and Baxter had no doubts, but they had no concrete evidence, either, to refute the denials.

The Emmer story was published, but the reporters knew it was weak. Gurney was lying, and they had to find a way to prove it. Otherwise, this might be the end of the investigation they had started two years ago when a friend of Assistant Managing Editor Steve Rogers tipped the *Herald* to Priestas' peculiar good luck with FHA applications.

The two reporters had been refused access to records of Priestas' projects at the FHA office, a rebuff guaranteed to heighten a good reporter's determination. Persisting, they found names of fictitious corporations and individuals, falsified documents, forged signatures. From contractors and developers, they learned that Priestas had a reputation for shoddy construction.

It was the first time that Savage and Baxter teamed up. Savage, a soft-spoken, sandy-haired man of thirty-two, returned to the *Herald* in 1967 after an ill-fated five months on an investigative team at a Boston newspaper with Hank Messick and Nick Gage. The Boston paper refused to publish the team's discovery that a prominent community leader had underworld ties.

In Miami, Savage had reported on organized crime and Teamster pension fund loans in Florida, deriving much of the information from law enforcement sources, but also digging up a good deal on his own. He wrote the first story revealing that a Miami country club luminary named Louis Rosanova had been identified by Chicago police as a Mafia boss.

Savage exposed kickbacks to the manager of the city-owned Miami Beach Convention Center by the restaurant concessionaire. A tip had sent him searching through the convention center's records. Ten percent of the concession's gross income was to go to the convention center, but the payments looked small. The concessionaire refused to show Savage his books. Temporarily thwarted, Savage hit upon the tactic of getting food expenditure figures from organizations that had rented space in the convention center. Most of them had kept no such records, but one had, and Savage persuaded it to cooperate. The figures showed the concessionaire had been cheating. Confronted with the evidence, the man confessed to making payoffs to the convention center's manager. A state investigation begun after Savage's story appeared uncovered additional kickbacks.

Now, on the Gurney story, Savage was stymied again. For Baxter, a tall, rangy Nebraskan born in 1944 who had joined the *Herald* in 1968, such frustrations were relatively new. It was his first major investigative story.

The pair decided to interview everyone who might have seen Gurney and Williams together, or had knowledge of their dealings. This took them as far away as British Honduras, where one source said the senator and the fund raiser had once vacationed together. The reporters located a pilot who had flown Gurney and Williams around Florida. They got a tip that a baby-sitter at Williams' home had once answered a phone call there from Gurney. Savage and Baxter tracked down the baby-sitter, who said it was true.

This story revived the federal investigation, which had fizzled out after Gurney gave FBI agents his denial about knowing Williams. Now Gurney's story was that he hadn't known Williams had raised $233,000 in his name from FHA developers.

Another builder contacted the reporters with a story similar to Emmer's. The federal probe gained momentum.

Priestas and Pelski were indicted, pleaded guilty, and went to prison. Williams pleaded guilty to channeling a bribe, got six months in prison, and became the chief witness against Gurney. On July 10, 1974, a federal grand jury indicted Gurney on charges of bribery, conspiracy, and perjury. Six others also were indicted, including Groot and the FHA regional directors in Tampa and Jacksonville. In August, 1975, a jury acquitted Gurney, by then an ex-Senator, on all but the conspiracy charge and one perjury count. It could reach no verdict on those. A new trial was to be scheduled in 1976.

Savage and Baxter won a 1974 George Polk Memorial Award for metropolitan reporting, and the 1974 Public Service Award of the Associated Press Managing Editors Association.

It was all done, the reporters say, with no help—no information, no leaks, no cooperation—from any law enforcement agency or source. Savage and Baxter got it first, and then the authorities got into the act.

Gene Miller, a Miami *Herald* investigative reporter who prefers to work alone, is known for saving people who have been wrongfully convicted of murder. His most recent case came to a happy conclusion in September, 1975, when Freddie Pitts and Wilbert Lee walked out of a Florida prison as free men after twelve years on Death Row.

Two months before Pitts and Lee were scheduled to go on trial for the second time in February, 1972, Miller went to the state capitol in Tallahassee for a final try at finding proof of the pair's innocence. Miller, the defense attorneys, and polygraph expert Warren Holmes, who had brought Miller into the case in 1966, had no hope for an acquittal without a miraculous stroke of luck. Pitts and Lee were black. That, in the small town of Port St. Joe in Florida's northern panhandle, had been the most damaging evidence against them from the beginning. The new trial was to be held in nearby Marianna, where the atmosphere was the same—bitter resentment toward Miller and the *Herald* for taking the side of two no-good "niggers" who had admitted the August 1, 1963, murders of two white gas station attendants.

Pitts, then nineteen, and Lee, twenty-eight, had admitted the crime. It availed them little that they later recanted, saying they had been beaten by a deputy sheriff and advised by a court-appointed attorney to plead guilty as the only way to escape a death sentence. They had pleaded guilty in open court. And got a death sentence, anyway.

The other mainstay of the state's case was the testimony of Willie Mae Lee, a young woman who had been in a car with Pitts, Lee, and several others when they stopped at the gas station the night of the murder. Willie Mae testified she had accompanied Pitts and Lee (no relation to her) to a clump of woods where they shot the two white men, Jesse Burkett and Grover Floyd. The problem with Willie Mae's testimony was that it kept changing. Discovery of that had won Pitts and Lee the new trial.

Miller had learned of a contradictory story by Willie Mae from a Tallahassee reporter. The reporter said the prosecutor, J. Frank Adams, had showed him a statement in which Willie Mae accused a soldier named Lambson Smith instead of Wilbert Lee. It was known that Willie Mae had been in jail for several days before she accused Pitts and Lee, but not that she had accused someone else. Adams, who had concealed this evidence, now conceded the statement's existence. Florida Attorney General Robert L. Shevin was persuaded that the suppression of evidence would cause a reversal of the conviction in the federal courts. Shevin filed a motion "in confession of error" to the Florida Supreme Court, where an appeal was pending, and the court ordered a new trial.

Adams refused to drop the charges, although another man had by now confessed to the murders. The appeal courts had given this confession little credence because the man refused to repeat it in court unless he was granted immunity.

The other man was Curtis Adams, Jr., whose arrest for robbery in Key West had touched off a series of events that led to Miller's involvement in the case.

Adams' sentence for the Key West robbery had put him in prison where he told cellmate Jesse Pait about killing a Fort Lauderdale gas station attendant named Floyd McFarland. Remembering a Miami *Herald* offer of $15,000 for a solution to the McFarland murder, Pait contacted a Fort Lauderdale police detective and told him that Adams also had admitted two murders in Port St. Joe for which "two niggers were going to be executed."

Adams' girl friend, Billie Jean Akins, corroborated Adams' involvement in the McFarland murder, for which Adams was then charged. Believing Billie Jean had squealed on him, Adams accused her of the Fort Lauderdale and the Port St. Joe killings. Adams agreed to plead guilty in the McFarland case in return for a life sentence, and a lie detector test by Holmes was arranged for Billie Jean. The woman told Holmes that Adams had admitted the Port St. Joe murders to her. Holmes then administered a polygraph test to Adams, who had lived in Port St. Joe until the night of the murders. Adams gave Holmes a detailed confession of the murders.

Holmes went to Miller. The two had worked together on previous cases of false convictions for murder. In one case, they proved that a woman who had confessed to two slayings in Louisiana had been several hundred miles away at the time. She was released from prison in 1966. In another case, they had dug up evidence showing that a U.S. airman convicted of killing an airline clerk in Miami had been on duty at a West Palm Beach Air Force Base eighty miles away when the murder occurred. The airman got a new trial and was acquitted in 1966. Miller won a 1967 Pulitzer Prize for his work in those two cases.

Miller and Holmes contacted the attorneys who had kept the Pitts and Lee appeal alive. Miller began writing about the case in February, 1967. Four years later, the state supreme court ordered a new trial.

Now, that trial was soon to begin, with little chance for a new outcome. Miller sat down in the attorney general's office in Tallahassee and began reading through the thick court file one last time, in the desperate hope that some new crack in the case would magically appear. Page after page, however, revealed nothing he hadn't already known. Then, suddenly, there it was. A report by an attorney general's investigator.

It read: "The writer and J. Frank Adams questioned Willie Mae Lee in Port St. Joe on February 20, 1968 . . . at which time she changed her story and said that none of her previous testimony was true, that Pitts and Lee did not kill Burkett and Floyd, and she wasn't along, and had no personal knowledge of it. She further stated that she wanted to tell Mr. Adams on other occasions but just couldn't bring herself to do it."

The February 20, 1968, date meant that Willie Mae's retraction had happened before the new trial hearing that had begun the appeal process. Another crucial piece of evidence concealed by the prosecution.

However, this discovery, to Miller's outraged consternation, failed to produce an acquittal at the new trial. Willie Mae testified against Pitts and Lee again, giving an evasive explanation of the 1968 retraction. That was good enough for the jury. Another conviction, another death sentence.

But Miller's new evidence took hold elsewhere. It inspired defense attorneys to a new resolve in preparing yet another appeal. It put new voltage in the public spotlight on the case. An assistant professor at Florida Memorial College in Miami organized a letter-writing campaign that sent 600 protests to Governor Reubin Askew. Chris Burkett, the oldest son of one of the murder victims, wrote to Askew saying he had long assumed Pitts and Lee were guilty, but had changed his mind. "I can think of no greater tribute to my dead father," Burkett wrote, "than to make sure that the blame is placed on the right person and remove from prison Wilbert Lee and Freddie Pitts for a crime I'm sure they did not commit."

Black students began picketing the governor's office. The governor assigned a legal aide to look into the case. The aide and Askew's general counsel concluded something was wrong.

Meanwhile, the U.S. Supreme Court threw out the death penalty, changing the sentence to life in prison, but on February 3, 1975, the Florida Court of Appeals upheld the conviction. An attorney for Pitts and Lee petitioned the U.S. Supreme Court to intervene.

Askew got another letter from Chris Burkett urging a pardon. Finally, in September, the governor acted. After twelve years in prison, Freddie Pitts and Wilbert Lee, thanks to Gene Miller, Warren Holmes, and several dedicated attorneys, went home. And in 1976, Miller was awarded another Pulitzer Prize.

When the Senate Watergate Committee recessed its public hearings in the summer of 1973, most reporters covering the story took the opportunity to go on vacation. But not Brooks Jackson, a member of the Associated Press Special Projects Team in Washington. Jackson decided to use the lull to probe deeply into political contributions by the dairy industry.

References to the topic had surfaced during the televised Watergate hearings, enough to suggest a buried treasure of scandal for anyone who bestirred himself to dig. Frank Wright of the Minneapolis *Tribune* had written in 1971 about the Nixon Administration's turnabout cave-in to the dairy industry on higher milk price supports after sixteen industry spokesmen met with Nixon for fifty-eight minutes on March 23, 1971. It was known that dairy co-ops contributed $437,000 to Nixon's reelection campaign. But the White House and the dairy lobby denied there had been a deal, and no one had produced any public evidence to the contrary. Wright had not even hinted at a deal; he had attributed Nixon's switch to the dairy lobby's clout in Congress through $1 million in contributions to the 1970 campaigns of key congressmen and senators.

An easygoing, direct, thirty-one-year-old journalism school graduate, Jackson read everything he could find on the dairy industry and its political machinations, especially court records on several lawsuits involving the Associated Milk Producers Inc., the nation's largest dairy cooperative.

He found information substantiating that Attorney General John Mitchell had rejected recommendations by Justice Department antitrust attorneys to launch a criminal investigation of AMPI. His December, 1973, story on this was verified later in an affidavit by a former head of the antitrust division.

In March, 1974, Jackson went to Little Rock, Arkansas, for proceedings in a multiple antitrust action against AMPI by the Justice Department and private plaintiffs. AMPI had retained Little Rock attorney Edward L. Wright, once a president of the American Bar Association, to investigate illegal political contributions by former AMPI officials. Wright's report had been subpoenaed in the lawsuit.

Jackson was not the only reporter to secure a copy of Wright's report, but only he had done enough homework to perceive the significance of many details and understand the importance of studying it carefully. Combined with material he had already unearthed, information in Wright's report enabled Jackson to report illegal campaign contributions of $125,000 to Senator Hubert Humphrey by AMPI, and lesser amounts to other prominent Democrats, including Congressman Wilbur Mills.

According to Wright's report, a law firm retained by AMPI turned out to include U.S. Secretary of the Treasury John Connally, who was under investigation for allegedly accepting a $10,000 bribe from AMPI lawyer Jake Jacobsen to help engineer an increase in the milk price support. One day at lunch, a congressional committee investigator remarked to Jackson that Charles "Bebe" Rebozo, whose caretaking of a $100,000 Nixon campaign donation from Howard Hughes was under investigation, had been much smarter than Jake Jacobsen, who had said he put the $10,000 in a bank vault after Connally refused it. Pursuing that, Jackson learned that the serial numbers on the bills were not in existence when Jacobsen said he had put the $10,000 in the vault. Jackson's story described it as evidence that Jacobsen, who was supporting Connally's story, was lying. Connally was later indicted and acquitted.

As a result of his exhaustive probes all over the country into records that other reporters overlooked—what the AP described as proceeding "like a paleontologist reconstructing a dinosaur, fitting new finds into old until the beast emerged"—Jackson was among the first to report several aspects of the milk money scandal. These included the milk producers' promise of $2 million in campaign contributions during that fifty-eight-minute meeting with Nixon, Mitchell's knowledge of that pledge when he squelched grand jury investigations of AMPI, and a request by a Nixon emissary that the milk producers reaffirm the $2 million promise just before the price support decision was announced.

The AP's Special Projects Team, which Jackson joined in 1972, was formed in 1967 to undertake investigative assignments. Among early members who went on to achievement and fame elsewhere, besides Seymour Hersh, are James Polk of NBC in Washington, and Jean Heller of *Newsday's* Washington bureau. Dick Barnes, however, stayed with the AP team through 1975, producing some of its top stories.

One was the exclusive report on June 18, 1972, that James W. McCord, Jr., one of five men arrested in the Watergate break-in, was employed by the Committee for the Re-election of the President. This was the story that embarrassed Washington *Post* reporter Bob Woodward into a resolution never to be scooped on the Watergate story again. Another AP reporter had obtained a CRP report on expenditures that listed CRP employes. On a hunch, Barnes checked through it to see if any names matched those of the Watergate arrestees.

In 1970, during an investigation of pension funds around the country, Barnes uncovered some of the first evidence that Teamsters pension fund loans had financed the plush southern California resort of La Costa, and that La Costa had connections with gamblers from Las Vegas and the Bahamas.

In Las Vegas to glean information from property records about $60 million in pension fund mortgage loans to gambling casinos, Barnes heard about a Beverly Hills, California, land development that had Teamsters pension fund money in it. Traveling on to Los Angeles to learn more about that, he encountered talk about Teamster pension fund loans in San Diego. That led him to records showing $22 million in loans to La Costa, and then to a discovery that the FHA had insured $30 million in loans to companies in which the pension fund held stock.

In 1975, Barnes became irritated by stories about federal employes looking forward to cost of living increases because their pensions would go up. He got out a calculator and found that their pensions went up faster than the cost of living under a formula approved by Congress to keep pensions in step with inflation. The formula provided that pensions would rise an extra one percent every time they were adjusted to new cost of living levels. Barnes calculated this would cost taxpayers an extra $100 billion by 1990, and pensions would be far ahead of inflation in a few years.

His story attracted yelps of protest, but government officials later conceded that Barnes was right. Legislation was recommended to scale back the unintended bonanza. No one except Barnes had bothered to compute the formula's consequences.

5

Madness and Methods

EVERY GOOD INVESTIGATIVE reporter has to be slightly mad. Not only must he manifest the customary skills and characteristics of a journalist, he must do so to excess, and be ever ready to attempt the impossible.

An ordinary reporter is persistent. An investigative reporter never gives up, no matter how insurmountable the obstacles, or how hopeless the prospects. When failure is inevitable and further work will be a waste of time, because the truth or the proof, to be realistic, is unattainable, the investigative reporter can't accept it. He argues, rants, and pleads against surrender. He knows it's time to cut the losses and move on to another investigation, but he's not going to admit it. In fact, he secretly keeps the case open. He resolves to check out remaining leads in his spare time, confident that someday, somehow, he will turn up something that will break it wide open. There's no such thing as defeat.

Every good reporter is a skeptic who questions the motives of public officials and fears that people lie to him. But that's too timid an attitude for the investigative reporter, who's on the lookout for conspiracies and corruption almost everywhere. Tempered by a professional commitment to accuracy, this cynical turn of mind begets swifter detection of hidden truths.

A reporter in his normal routine encounters unpleasant types who treat him rudely and try to thwart his quest for information. It takes pluck to be a reporter in the first place, to approach strangers with questions they might not like. An investigative reporter, however, spends most of his time dealing with unsavory or hostile individuals. He occasionally faces danger to his life. An average endowment of courage is by no means enough.

To keep such difficulties from unhinging his professional performance, an investigative reporter must have extraordinary self-control. He can't lose his temper no matter how severe the provocation. He's not to behave abrasively, make threats about "getting" anyone, or boast of his "kills." He must remain polite and businesslike, and keep his emotions in check. Otherwise, he generates more difficulties for himself than the abundance that already exist.

To work his long, often irregular hours and withstand the diverse pressures, the investigative reporter needs an extra measure of stamina. Persevering against obstacles consumes energy enough, yet more is required when the subject of an investigation fights back with smears and slurs, advertising cancellations, police harassment, threats of violence, and multimillion-dollar lawsuits. In addition, the investigative reporter is sometimes resented by fellow staff members who think he gets favored treatment and lots of freedom. And his wife gives him hell for not spending enough time with his family.

Making sense out of a chaos of information is a reporter's normal function. It's his job to separate wheat from chaff quickly, and tie several threads neatly into a concise, cogent communication. An investigative reporter, however, copes with inordinate complexities. He's expected to extract needles of pertinent fact from haystacks of material, see quickly through tangled knots to the core of a case, deftly avoid digressions and pitfalls, sort, compare, analyze, and spot connections between facts with speed and acuity, and put it all into a form that readers can understand without becoming bored. Having an organized mind is not good enough; he has to be a human computer.

When the known techniques don't work, the investigative reporter is called upon to show his true mettle. Resourcefulness, the ability to come up with a new way to succeed when the old ways fail, is the most essential quality of all, the one asset that an investigative reporter can never afford to leave at home in the morning.

All would be for naught, however, if he weren't able to take the last clinching step. The investigative reporter must have what's called the "killer instinct" or the "instinct for the jugular," though it's not directed at hurting anyone. It's the capacity to summon the last ounce of courage to overcome the lone remaining obstacle or inhibition. The investigative reporter can't let his judgment be clouded, or his resolution softened, by claims that unpleasant revelations will upset the community or hurt a crook's wife and children. He must grit his teeth, get the decisive evidence, and write his story.

Though most investigative journalism takes aim at wrongdoing, its main objective is not putting someone in jail. It's to promote reform, expose injustice, enlighten the public, and discourage knavery. It also may find out why an institution doesn't do its job, reveal how a government really works beneath the platitudes and rhetoric, give voters important information on the people who woo their support, or reconstruct a momentous event.

Investigations often originate in a decision to look into long-standing conditions, recurrent rumors or new suspicions, or a desire to delve behind a current story. Many are prompted by tips from long-time sources or anonymous callers. A news organization or writer known for aggressive investigative journalism is a magnet for unsolicited leads. One probe frequently leads to several more. Keeping a sharp eye when checking court documents, congressional committee files, and other public records often catches something that should be probed.

Once a project is chosen, a "smell" or "sniff"—a quick scrutiny of published materials and a preliminary survey of records and sources—helps to evaluate potential results and costs, plan strategy, and pinpoint possible "fallback" stories short of the maximum goal. When a decision is made to go, specific goals should be set and a system arranged for progress reviews with editors.

Whether a team or a lone reporter takes on the assignment depends on the investigation and the people available. Members of a team can complement each other's talents, bolster each other's spirits, and offset each other's weaknesses. They can double up at interviews to provide an extra witness. But they must be able to work well together without undue friction. If the team has more than two members, a strong leader is essential to resolve disagreements over tactics and assignments. One drawback to a team is that members duplicate or overlap each other's work. A reporter working alone, though, needs more staying power and more time. Much depends on whether a team already exists, who's available, and how quickly the job is to be done.

The next question is where to start—in a stack of records, a thorough backgrounding in the subject matter, or a beating of the bushes for sources. It's usually best to check records and printed materials before conducting interviews, but some cases require early interviews to determine which records to check, fill in gaps, or shed light on their implications. Some apparently innocent or merely suspicious records become wellsprings of scandal when combined with explanations by the people involved. Donald Barlett and James Steele grasped the full extent of the villainy behind FHA mortgage manipulations in Philadelphia only after talking to home buyers who said they hadn't wanted to buy.

A tentative plan for the entire investigation should be mapped out, specifying the techniques to be used, the individuals to be interviewed, the records to be examined, and the order in which it's all to be done. The basic techniques are few in number, but there's a rich variety of application. Each investigative reporter has his own unique refinements. Here are the basics:

Public Records

1. *Where They Are:* Know what records exist, which are likely to have the information you want, and where to find them. If you don't know, know how to find out. One invaluable guide to both public and private records, reference works, and other information sources is a book entitled *Where's What,* compiled by the CIA but recently declassified and published in book form by Warner Books, Inc., of New York City. The Federal Register is a good source on the federal government. Each government department or agency also can offer information on the records it keeps. A newspaper clip file and occasionally the public library are good places to begin, but the most fruitful repositories of public records are government offices.

2. *What's Available* In rough order of likely value in yielding useful information:

   Criminal court files and trial transcripts; prosecutor's case records; arrest records; criminal records; complaint reports and other police records; coroner's records;

   Civil lawsuit files, transcripts of testimony, exhibits, depositions, pleadings; probate court records on estates and appointments; divorce court pleadings, transcripts, financial statements;

   Minutes of meetings by governmental bodies;

   Contracts awarded by governmental agencies for materials and services;

   Rezoning applications; planning commission records; building department and housing inspection records;

   Government payrolls, budgets, purchase vouchers; travel expense vouchers;

Election records and campaign finance reports;

Records, reports and hearing transcripts of state and federal government regulatory agencies and commissions (such as those regulating utilities, insurance or atomic energy); files and hearing transcripts of state legislative and congressional committees;

Property records, including transfers, deeds, mortgages, and land contracts; chattel mortgages;

Tax assessments, tax payment records, tax liens; U.S. Tax Court cases; state tax department records;

Corporation charters, reports, and franchise tax statements filed with the state; partnership and business name records, usually filed with the county; Securities and Exchange Commission records;

County and state auditor's office records;

Health department records;

Federal grant applications and records of applicant agencies;

Some records of federal agencies and programs such as FHA, SBA, IRS, FBI, HUD, HEW, etc.;

Licensing records, especially for liquor sales and horse racing;

Reports filed by lobbyists;

Vital statistics: births, marriages, divorces, deaths;

Automobile and drivers' licenses;

Veterans' records;

Labor union reports filed with the government.

3. *Gaining Access:* Most government offices make public records available for inspection and copying without ado. State laws vary on definition of public records, but the general rule is records that document official actions, unless explicitly exempted by state law. The Federal Freedom of Information Act has opened up many records previously kept under wraps, but has also produced a great deal of red tape. A pamphlet explaining how to request information under the FOI Act can be obtained from the Freedom of Information Clearing House, P.O. Box 19367, Washington, D.C., 20036, a project sponsored by Ralph Nader's Center for Study of Responsive Law, or the Reporters Committee for Freedom of the Press, 1750 Pennsylvania Ave., N.W., Washington, D.C. 20006.

When a bureaucrat or elected official denies access to a public record, throws up obstacles or tries to stall, first apply friendly reminders of the . law. If that doesn't work, a suggestion of a court order might help, though this threat is often weak because lawsuits take so long. Sometimes a compromise can be negotiated. If the problem is that someone's privacy would be violated, perhaps the name can be blocked out and the rest of the file seen. Be firm and persistent, but avoid emotional confrontations. Outside help may be available from the prosecutor, the state attorney general, another official or legislator, or a citizen organization that can apply pressure. Insiders might be recruited to slip the records out secretly. Publication of an official's refusal to release public records often does the trick. It makes him look as if he has something to hide. If one story won't do it, several might.

4. *Tracing Connections:* Information in one record is often more revealing

when juxtaposed with information from others. A person's connections with politicians on one hand, and underworld figures on another, can be traced through different sets of records—campaign contribution lists, for instance, and corporation reports or court testimony.

Non-Public Records

1. *Governmental:* Police intelligence files; criminal records (in some jurisdictions); police investigation reports; parole and probation records; FBI and other federal law enforcement agency records; income tax returns and investigation reports; internal memoranda and letters; juvenile court files; welfare case records; state hospital patient records.
2. *Private:* Credit bureau reports; telephone call records; bank records; insurance investigation reports; private investigators' files; business records; employment records; hospital records; union records; real estate development plans; personal finance records.
3. *Gaining Access:* Since there's no inherent right to these records, they can only be reached through sources willing to get the information, provide copies or sneak out the documents themselves, or by inducing someone to arrange access through persuasion, pressure, trickery, or payment of money. Much information about industry can be obtained, however, from corporation and trade directories, stock reporting and advisory services, trade magazines and publications of trade associations, and materials published by industrial and commercial corporations. There also are a number of private organizations whose business is to provide information on businesses, such as the National Investment Library in New York City, which distributes information from reports filed with the SEC, and the Foundation Library Center in New York City, which publishes a directory of private foundations.

Sources

1. *Existing Network:* Cultivating loyal sources willing to supply information when needed, and who volunteer tips and leaks at propitious times, is an art. It requires a delicate touch and constant attention. To convert a police lieutenant or an assistant department head into a source, a reporter may become his friend or treat him to frequent lunches. More often, he wins the source's respect with his integrity, professionalism, and effectiveness, especially among sources motivated by public-spiritedness. Sources who use the news media for their own purposes are easily recruited, but their information requires more careful evaluation. The main advantage of long-standing sources is an established track record on credibility.

Anyone a reporter talks to in the course of his work is a potential source. It can be a top official, an assistant, a middle-echelon bureaucrat, a strategically located secretary or clerk. It can be an insider, a peripheral figure, an enemy. Concentrate on people who are in a position to have information or access to records, and who seem most likely to succumb to blandishments. Then weed out the embellishers and deceivers.

Sources produce a variety of yields—tips, leads, basic information, pieces to fill in gaps, corroboration, other sources, documents, guidance on where to look in the public records.

2. *Acquiring New Sources:* Approach those most likely to possess useful information and most likely to divulge it among the people directly involved: neighbors, friends, associates; government authorities and private groups interested in such matters; rivals, ex-employes, former partners, ex-wives, others with a possible grudge. Knock on doors to talk to scores of people if necessary to find those who know and will talk. Many who won't reveal much themselves may refer a reporter to others who will. Publishing stories lets potential sources know that someone would like to hear from them. Many exposés are done piecemeal, with each story chipping away at the target while flushing out new sources until the whole truth is out. Buy information only as a last resort, in a way that enables its validity to be tested before the money is handed over. It sets a troublesome precedent, however. Other sources will stick out their hands, too.

3. *Off-the-record and Anonymous Sources:* Don't reject information offered off-the-record, meaning you can't publish it unless you obtain it independently from another source. Once in possession of the information, a reporter is better able to identify another likely source. He's also better equipped to persuade the source to put it on the record, or at least permit its use on a nonattribution basis as an anonymous source. Never violate an off-the-record agreement, but there's no prohibition on trying to get it changed. The main thing is to get the information, then address the problem of how it can be used.

4. *Trading Information:* Sources in law enforcement agencies and congressional investigating committees often are willing to exchange findings on an off-the-record or nonattribution basis. Be careful, however, not to reveal any confidential sources or pass along information that might lead to discovery of your source. Some investigative reporters, such as Clark Mollenhoff, even prod authorities into digging out facts and documents for them, or putting information on the public record to facilitate publication. Getting cozy with sources, however, entails a danger of their becoming so valuable, or so close, that the reporter exempts their conduct from exposure or probing. That's the wrong way to protect sources. A good reporter can make a source understand that it's his job even to expose the source if necessary and still keep him as a source.

5. *Protection of Sources:* Steadfast refusal to disclose a confidential source, even in the face of a contempt citation or possible imprisonment, is essential. A reporter who can't be trusted is soon without sources. Shield laws in many states appear to give reporters more specific protection against legal compulsion to reveal sources than the First Amendment, but they are subject to varying interpretations. Without the right and ability to protect the identities of sources, the news media would lose access to a vast reservoir of information and help. A proposed new federal antileak law would discourage many sources inside government with the threat of stiff penalties for disclosing government secrets, but its impact might be limited

as long as reporters can't be compelled to reveal their sources. Such a law nevertheless would constitute a serious threat to the news media's ability to exercise its freedom.

Interviewing

1. *Selecting the Subject:* Seek people who have the information and may be willing to reveal it, because they're disgruntled or can be persuaded.
2. *Thorough Backgrounding:* Learn as much as possible beforehand about the subject matter and the interviewee, especially for final confrontation interviews.
3. *Bluffing:* Pretending to know more than you do sometimes works, but do so only by implication, in case the bluff is called.
4. *Skillful Questioning:* Be precise. Don't let the subject stray, divert, or evade. Patiently rephrase or repeat the question until he answers it. Prepare questions carefully in advance, but also be alert to new lines of inquiry that open up during the interview. It's surprising how people feel compelled to give a direct and truthful answer to a direct question. Disguising one's true aim is useful when the subject will not give the information if he suspects it's critical. If it doesn't work, nothing is lost.
5. *Manner:* A friendly, sympathetic, even helpful ear often works miracles, even with hostile subjects. Gentle persuasion can melt away reluctance, especially if the subject can be shown that cooperation will benefit him as well as perform a public service. This is his opportunity to give his version of the facts, perhaps counter his enemies more effectively by getting his side before the public. Remaining silent, on the other hand, might not look good. Don't cross the line, however, into threats to make him look bad if he doesn't cooperate. With many, a straightforward, businesslike manner is most productive. Others respond to a friendly, bantering pressure. Play it by ear. Cajolery, badgering, bullying may work as a last resort, but is rarely necessary and often counterproductive.
6. *Whipsawing:* When more than one source is potentially available, the situation is ripe for exploiting the inclination to reveal more to someone who already seems to know a lot. Use what's learned from the first source to impress the second, then the additional material from the second to appear knowledgeable to the third, and so on.
7. *Publication:* Obstinate sources sometimes relent after a story or two appears in which their refusal to discuss the matter reflects on them unfavorably, or when every side of the story is well represented except his.
8. *Tape Recording:* Individual preferences vary. It's advisable for important interviews in which there's a possibility of dispute over what's said, or if the subject matter is intricate or complex. Another reporter might spot something the interviewer missed. But transcribing takes up a great deal of time.

Special Tricks

1. *Surveillance:* Following government work crews to check their loafing time or tailing a politician to see whom he meets has appeal for the cloak-and-dagger oriented, but is seldom appropriate.

2. *Impersonation:* Can be effective if there's no false representation that may produce false information. Posing as a medical patient is not pretending to be something a reporter is not qualified to be. Or a waiter or sales clerk. But information received by a reporter posing as a mechanic or lawyer might be distorted because the person giving it assumes the recipient has specialized knowledge which he, in fact, doesn't have. Corroboration or checking back may overcome such a problem, however. Information about a person's phone calls, credit records, airline reservations, or utility bills can be obtained by a telephone call requesting the information in a manner implying the caller is the person in question or someone acting on his behalf. Some news media organizations prohibit this tactic as unethical, but there's little agreement on the point among investigative journalists. It violates no law and doesn't produce false or tainted information.

3. *Undercover Tactics:* Sometimes called infiltration, this usually involves getting a job in the place or institution to be investigated. A highly effective technique, it usually requires some falsification of background. It may border on invasion of privacy in cases involving private businesses, groups, or individuals rather than government. Some news media organizations consider it unethical or at least improper.

4. *Outside Experts:* Hiring an accountant or a structural engineer to help in an investigation can furnish guidance and documentation.

5. *The Squeeze:* Like the prosecutor who offers immunity to turn a defendant against bigger game, reporters can convert a key figure's silence into a torrent of words by promising to omit or downplay his guilty participation. This is especially potent when the subject suspects, or can be led to suspect, that his companions in crime are throwing him to the wolves. A reporter might even offer to help seek immunity for him from the prosecutor.

6. *Cozying Up:* This is similar to infiltration except there's no concealment. The idea is to insinuate into a situation, or get close to people, until you're taken for granted and everyone lets down his guard.

7. *Ethics:* Most investigative journalists and news gathering organizations say they wouldn't break the law, and agree there's no need to. Surreptitious wiretapping, for instance, is not done. If the news media are to monitor the ethics of government and business, they must see to the impeccability of their own. Otherwise, however, methods are limited only by a reporter's resourcefulness. There's little hesitancy to accept the fruits of lawbreaking by others. Some who spurn undercover tactics as unethical have no qualms about encouraging sources to break laws on grand jury secrecy or release of classified documents.

A good filing system is indispensable. The best files have folders for every name, incident, transaction, and other major element, plus subcategory folders for each. Copies of documents, transcripts, articles, memos, and other material are filed in every relevant folder. If a memo on an interview mentions fifteen people, at least fifteen copies are needed. If there are files for only twelve, start three new files. When files become voluminous, it's time to set up cross references on index cards.

File memos should be written after each interview, or at least at the end of each day, especially if it's a team probe, so that other members can be brought up to date. Don't include the names of confidential sources in the memos, or information that can lead to discovery of their identities. Even in states that have shield laws protecting sources from direct revelation, it's not clear whether records containing information that might lead to revelation are also protected.

One discovery leads to another, but be wary of temptations to strike out in new directions or get bogged down in fringe areas. In a team investigation, frequent conferences are usually needed to coordinate decisions on which leads to pursue and keep the probe on its track. Strong leadership may be required to resolve disputes.

Frequent analysis is essential. Facts are pulled together from several sources to determine how they affect each other's meaning and significance. If large amounts of similar information are to be combined, check the feasibility of a computer. One device that's useful for spotting gaps is a chronology that charts the flow of events. Another is to write an analysis of an incident, one person's involvement, or other aspect. Evaluate the material for fairness, thoroughness, and accuracy of perspective. Make plans for filling holes and conducting final interviews. If the matter may be one for criminal prosecution, consider whether to place the findings before the appropriate law enforcement agency before publication. If the agency promises to investigate, that's a news angle.

Decisions must be made on adequacy of corroboration, documentation standards, use of anonymous sources. Much depends on who the sources are and what's known about their reliability. A police chief seems clearly a more credible source on activities in his department than a patrolman, but it's not necessarily so. Each instance has to be judged in its own circumstances. A review by libel lawyers is often not the last step it's expected to be. More gaps are found. Lawyers should be consulted earlier if any of the methods used may involve invasion of privacy. Don't forget that effective presentation and display enhance an exposé's impact.

Once the exposé is published, some believe, the investigative reporter's work is done. Let the prosecutor or the public pick up the ball and take it from there. Most investigative reporters, however, take the opposite view. They insist that follow-up pressure is necessary to overcome inertia and produce the result intended from the beginning. A barrage of stories on related aspects or new developments is one way to maintain pressure. So can interviews of authorities on what they plan to do about the situation, or comments of outrage from public officials. The editorial page can intensify the pressure by demanding action. Some, like Mollenhoff, go personally to authorities and demand that they do something. Over a period of time, an exposé becomes a crusade.

If a grand jury takes up the case, have no reluctance to testify as long as it's consistent with the original purpose, and there's no attempt to learn confidential sources. It makes little sense to refuse cooperation to authorities you've forced to act.

Nonpublication pressure—a phone call from the editor to a prominent citizen to enlist his help in prodding authorities to act—is viewed by some journalists as out of bounds. But the purpose of publishing exposés in the first place is to provoke change, not to produce idle reading if no one responds immediately. Perhaps publication alone should be sufficient to the purpose, but often it's not. Hesitating to apply whatever follow-up pressure it takes to achieve the goal is self-defeating, a madness of the wrong kind.

6

Probers on the Air

LT. COL. ANTHONY HERBERT, who claimed he'd been railroaded out of the Army for trying to expose atrocities by friendly forces in the Vietnam War, was the subject of the show. The purpose was to find out if he was lying.

"In almost all the cases that you claim you reported war crimes, either to Colonel Franklin or General Barnes," said Mike Wallace to Herbert in their bristling confrontation on CBS' "60 Minutes" show of February 4, 1973, "we have only your word against theirs. Nobody else was there."

"Mm-hmm," said Herbert.

"So what we decided to do was to zero in on the one case where there's a possibility, anyway, of proving who's telling the truth, without relying on your word against their word."

Producer Barry Lando had spent an entire year tracking down men who had known Herbert in the Army or who had been mentioned in Herbert's book, *Soldier.* One of the places Lando visited was Hawaii, where he checked Colonel Ross Franklin's version of a Valentine's Day incident in 1969.

Herbert's story was that he had spoken with Franklin twice from the field on that February 14, then had flown back to tell Franklin personally about the killings of captured Vietnamese by South Vietnamese police while an American adviser watched.

But Franklin told Lando that Herbert had never said anything to him about war crimes, and that Franklin had been in the Ilikai Hotel in Honolulu on that Valentine's Day. He had not returned to Vietnam until February 16.

"I say he was there," said Herbert.

"And that he's lying?" asked Wallace.

"If he says he wasn't there, I say he's lying."

"Can you prove it?"

"No, I cannot."

Wallace told viewers that the hotel in Honolulu confirmed a registration by Franklin and his wife from February 7 to February 14, which was February 15 in Vietnam. CBS had found two Army officers who had accompanied Franklin on the trip and they confirmed Franklin's dates. There was also a check, signed by Franklin, dated February 14, and made out to the hotel.

"Therefore," said Wallace, "he could not have been where you said he was on the fourteenth of February."

"I can probably find you a hundred checks," Herbert countered, "that I have either dated for another reason, wrote after the fact, misdated, what have you. I don't know. All I know is I saw Ross Franklin there and talked to him. I know that. I know what I saw. I know what I did. And I stick by it and I still say it. And I swear to it and I've sworn to it under oath and I'll swear to it again, you know?"

Wallace explained that Herbert had provided the names of several men who could testify that Franklin had been in Vietnam on that February 14, but none of them would confirm Herbert's claim. Nor could any of them remember that Herbert had ever reported the February 14 killings.

He asked Herbert if he had any documents to show that he had reported a war crime prior to his return from Vietnam, where he had been relieved of his command.

"I'm not going to say we have documents or not," said Herbert. "I just say we have statements, sworn statements, and testimony that will prove that I reported war crimes in Vietnam."

"Have you published them in your book?"

"I don't think so."

"Why?"

"I didn't—I had no reason to. It was already in the paper, other things. I don't know why. I have lawyers, just like you have lawyers. We didn't put everything out we have."

At one point, Herbert tried to shift the issue.

"Let's say I didn't, just for the sake of discussion. It would make absolutely no difference if I waited five years to do it. The motive would make no difference whatsoever. The question is: did the crimes occur or didn't they?"

"Oh?"

"Were Colonel Franklin and General Barnes well aware of them or weren't they? I say they were and I say I reported them, and it's still there and it still stands."

Wallace wasn't taken in. "No. The point is there's no dispute that war crimes occurred in Vietnam. The dispute, it seems, is this: you've called Franklin a liar."

"Yes."

"You've called Barnes a liar."

"Yes."

"You said the Army, really, deprived you of your military career because you insisted upon reporting war crimes and they wanted them covered up. And that's really what the issue is here."

"And I still say it," said Herbert.

Another officer named by Herbert as one to whom he had reported war crimes was a military lawyer and judge who told Lando that no such thing had ever happened. Several men who knew and admired Herbert, Wallace reported, said Herbert had not mentioned his trying to push war crime charges at the time he was relieved of his Vietnam command. Others who had known Herbert in the Army said Herbert had been brutal with prisoners, and careless with the truth. One of Herbert's company commanders told Lando that Herbert was "the best battalion commander I've ever had, but for some reason he's become a liar."

Wallace's tough questioning of Herbert was typical—of Wallace, of "60 Minutes," of CBS. Brit Hume of ABC-TV's rival documentary show, "ABC

News Close-Up," describes Wallace's interviewing as "brutal and tough, but done with style and polish."

Wallace is even tough on CBS. As he made a point to mention during the Herbert show, the publisher of Herbert's book was a CBS subsidiary. In a 1974 show on trips, discounts, and other free gifts showered on reporters by companies in search of publicity, Wallace pointed out that while CBS News employes were forbidden to go on junkets, the public relations people in another CBS division were arranging all-expense-paid trips for television critics.

As Wallace and Morley Safer use it on "60 Minutes," tough questioning is a device for showing viewers part of the investigation in process. Only on TV can the confrontation interview with the subject of the investigation be witnessed by the public. The subject's manner and reactions become part of the information that's uncovered and transmitted, an element that's often more revealing than the bare words. This the print media can't offer.

The TV camera has other unique investigative powers as well. When "60 Minutes" went to Chicago to do a February, 1976, report on kickbacks paid to doctors by medical laboratories in search of Medicaid lab business, a camera was hidden behind a one-way mirror in an apparent doctors' office set up by three investigators from Chicago's Better Government Association. As medical lab representatives showed up and offered to rent nonexistent space or pay secretary salaries to get the lab business, the camera filmed the proceedings. Though only the words of the "doctors" were taped, Wallace listened in and reported what was said. During a second round of visits by the lab reps, Wallace and the camera emerged from behind their cover in the midst of the sales pitches. Some of the lab representatives tried to back off from what they had been saying, but others were so stunned they admitted the kickback scheme.

Now nine years old, "60 Minutes" carries on the legacy of toughness established in the 1950s by Edward R. Murrow's "See It Now" documentaries on CBS. Wallace's incisive but unabrasive interrogation technique has won him respect and renown as the sharpest, most formidable interviewer in all of TV.

CBS Washington correspondent Daniel Schorr is just as tough, but also abrasive. Along with fellow CBS newsman Dan Rather, Schorr was among the reporters most bitterly hated by the Nixon White House. Schorr has been investigated by the FBI on White House orders, and Nixon aide John Ehrlichman used to call him Daniel P. Schorr, though L is Schorr's true middle initial. When finally asked what the P was for, Ehrlichman said, "Prick." After Schorr found out that President Ford had expressed off-the-record fear to *New York Times* editors that the Rockefeller Commission might uncover CIA assassination plots, and broke the story on the air in February, 1975, former CIA Director Richard Helms called him "Killer Schorr" and "that cocksucker." The gray-haired, pipe-smoking, fifty-nine-year-old Schorr is no less abrasive with fellow CBS employes, who find him grouchy and far too tough in the competition for air time.

More controversial than ever in 1976 because he gave a secret congressional committee report on the CIA to the *Village Voice*, Schorr is sometimes disparaged by other journalists, perhaps out of envy, as not a true investigative reporter. Hearing talk about President Ford's remark at a luncheon with *New York Times* editors, or getting a copy of a congressional committee report before it's declared secret, his critics contend, is not genuine investigating. They also cite such flubs of competitive haste as Schorr's rushing a retired Air Force officer on the air who falsely identified former White House aide Alexander Butterfield as a CIA spy.

But other investigative reporters rely no less heavily on sources, and sometimes make mistakes. No one denies that Schorr is aggressive, persistent, and resourceful. However he got it, the CIA assassination plot exposé was one of 1975's biggest stories. Once revealed, the plots could not be ignored by the Rockefeller Commission.

The scene opens with James Polk on a snow-covered mountaintop. "This is Mount Snow," says Polk, "in the winter a playground for two U.S. senators."

The scene shifts to skiers on the slope. Polk's voice continues, "Their ski vacations—on the cuff—were paid by a resort corporation in federal trouble."

Senator Birch Bayh of Indiana appears on the screen. The senator, says Polk's voice, spent the New Year's holiday at Mount Snow. His bill was $1,239, but Bayh didn't pay a cent.

Now there's a shot of Senator Mike Gravel of Alaska. Gravel, says Polk, enjoyed a free vacation at Mount Snow that ordinarily would have cost $1,148. Gravel, he adds, has accepted free ski trips for four years. Both Bayh and Gravel said they were personal friends of an executive in the Mount Snow company, Polk reports.

In this NBC-TV network news report, Polk reveals that the Mount Snow company needs government approval of a sewer system in Vermont to sell vacation houses and escape financial straits. Two of Gravel's aides, Polk says, made phone calls to the U.S. Environmental Protection Agency to inquire about progress on the sewer project approval and mention that a friend of the senator would benefit. Gravel appears on the screen to deny that a conflict of interest is involved. He's just trying to be of assistance to a taxpayer. The issue, says Polk, is what free gifts members of Congress should be allowed to accept.

Another time, another filmed report: Polk is standing on an open beach in front of a housing development. "This spit of beach poking out into the Gulf of Mexico at Destin, Florida," he says, "was once a deserted stretch of sand owned by the federal government. Now it is a multimillion-dollar oceanside housing development called Holiday Isle. The congressman from Florida's panhandle—Robert Sikes—pushed through the bill that smoothed the way for development. But Sikes never told Congress that he was a founder and officer of two corporations holding leases on this former federal land." In 1976, the House Ethics Committee found Sikes guilty of using his office for personal gain.

Placing Polk on a mountaintop and a beach was NBC's solution to one of the biggest problems faced by investigative reporters in TV; namely, the need to convey complex stories in pictures, with dramatic impact, and in easy to understand form.

Another problem, says Polk, a Pulitzer Prize winner at the Washington *Star* before he joined NBC in April, 1975, is the small amount of time into which a TV story must be compressed.

"Newspapers can string a story out in bits and pieces, but we can't," says Stanhope Gould, the forty-one-year-old head of NBC's TV investigative unit. "We have to boil it down, pull it all together in a coherent picture, and still be accurate. Lots of time we have backup evidence that we don't use to avoid confusion. If we have five documents, we use one. We do as much investigating as the print guys, but we have to work hard to get it right and easy to understand, too, in a lot fewer words."

Gould describes his job as "dreaming up ways to dramatize complicated things." A report on Teamster pension fund loans, for instance, might show a flashily garbed mob leader who got a million-dollar loan, then switch to a retired trucker in a tattered old jacket who can't get his pension. A three-part series on the sale of American wheat to Russia fixed on the theme that two groups of people had been ripped off, the farmers and the taxpayers. "We should be doing more stories," says Gould, "that show where the system breaks down and focus on an individual who's been victimized. Investigative reporting is most successful on TV when there's a victim the viewer can identify with."

Part of the time problem, says Polk, is the speed with which a story moves through a viewer's attention. A report flows by too rapidly for total absorption and there's no written record to pick up and read again for a better understanding. "Since it's so transitory," says Polk, "there's a limit to how well it can inform. It's the nature of the medium, and I'm not sure how to overcome it."

Another difference Polk has found in TV is its "strong tendency," as he puts it, "to report the obvious." He says TV is reluctant to create news, to get into what he calls an "exposed position" where it might be accused of affecting events rather than just reporting them. TV, he says, prefers to investigate a piece of a story that's already been broken elsewhere. It's cautious about breaking new ground.

Polk, whose deep voice is a natural for broadcasting, won a Pulitzer Prize in 1974 for his articles on illegal contributions to Nixon's 1972 reelection campaign, especially the secret $200,000 cash donation by financier Robert Vesco.

Polk had just quit the Associated Press in 1971 and was negotiating with the

Washington *Star* when he was approached by Philip Stern of the Fund for Investigative Journalism. Stern proposed a grant to cover a year's investigation of presidential campaign funds. Polk had been probing into political finances as a member of AP's special projects team. He had exposed Congressman Gerald Ford's failure to report $11,500 in contributions he had forwarded to a Republican committee, which in turn had sent $12,233 back to Ford's campaign. Polk accepted Stern's offer and arranged to sell the fruits of the investigation to the Washington *Star*.

Among his first successes was exposure of Herbert Kalmbach, Nixon's personal attorney, as a surreptitious fund raiser. Another was a disclosure that Wall Street financier John L. Loeb had concealed a $48,000 contribution to Senator Hubert Humphrey's campaign. Loeb became the first political donor to be convicted under the new campaign disclosure law.

By the time that Stern's grant ran out and Polk joined the *Star's* staff, Polk had accumulated a storehouse of material, but some key pieces were missing.

One day while drinking with a White House source, Polk had thrown some names at him, including that of Vesco, whose name he had seen on 1968 campaign finance reports.

"Oh, yeah," snapped the source. "That son of a bitch."

Though the source would say no more, Polk knew that Vesco was known, and disliked, at the White House.

Later, at the *Star*, he heard about a stock fraud investigation of Vesco by the Securities and Exchange Commission. He dropped by SEC offices to look through six boxes of records for information on campaign contributions. On page 115 of a hearing transcript, he found a reference to $250,000 from the Bahama Islands on April 6, 1972, which was the day before the new campaign disclosure law had taken effect. When the SEC refused to give him access to additional testimony, Polk pursued another lead he spotted in the records of a lawsuit, a mention of a New York private investigator.

The detective told Polk he had been the armed guard for a briefcase stuffed with $250,000 in cash, but wouldn't reveal the money's destination or purpose. Vesco attorney Harry J. Sears, a Nixon campaign official in New Jersey, refused to discuss it.

But Polk had enough for his January 26, 1973, story describing the money's mysterious trip from the Bahamas on the last day of Nixon's secret fund-raising drive.

Five days later, Nixon's campaign organization refunded $250,000 to Vesco—$200,000 that had never been reported, and $50,000 that had. A Vesco associate became a government witness, and a grand jury probed the case. In May, former Attorney General John Mitchell and former Secretary of Commerce Maurice Stans, Nixon's chief fund raiser, were indicted on charges of perjury and obstruction of justice. The $250,000, said the indictments, had been given in exchange for pressure on the SEC to halt its investigation of Vesco. Mitchell and Stans later were acquitted.

The thirty-eight-year-old Polk prefers the friendly approach when coaxing information out of people. "If something's not right, I show bewilderment rather than call him a liar," says Polk. "I ask him to explain, saying that I don't quite understand this contradiction. Most people like to talk about their work if you're a sympathetic listener and you don't try to argue with them. You have to make a friend of your source, convince him he can trust you. I may get him a little off guard as to what I'm really interested in, or imply I have proof when I don't, but I never lie. It's also important to have enough information to ask the right questions, or it shows that you're fishing."

During its first year, NBC-TV's investigative unit—NBC's "noble experiment," as Gould calls it—consisted of just Gould and Polk. But there were plans to expand, and regular correspondents have done occasional investigative reports, such as Ford Rowen's story on government computer information banks in operation despite official denials of their existence.

A producer at CBS-TV News for ten years before switching to NBC, Gould says NBC's approach is unique. It's not locked into a particular program with deadlines to meet or time slots to fill. The flexibility permits tailoring a story to the most suitable of several outlets, including the network's "Week End" magazine-format show as well as documentary programs and daily newscasts.

Polk has reservations about the new wave of interest in investigative reporting. "It's creating a star system," he says. "Investigative reporters are opportunists who will pick their topics according to what will attract attention. But there aren't that many stories of Watergate dimensions around."

NBC-TV was attracted to investigative reporting by Watergate, says Polk, because it "had to hold its own in the prestige game." But he believes TV nevertheless has enormous potential for investigative journalists.

Gould, who agrees the potential is great if management "has the guts," sees nothing wrong with the prestige motivation. In fact, he asks, what else is there to get out of it? "It'll never be cost effective. The expenses are too great. You do it for image."

―――――――――――――――――――――――

First there's a view of the devastation caused by the collapse of the coal slag dam at Buffalo Creek. West Virginia Governor Arch Moore appears, vowing to get rid of dangerous dams. Next are several aerial shots of coal slag dams. Then the scene shifts to an office, where Brit Hume hands a sheet of paper to a man behind a desk and says, "Here's a list of the dams. Can you say which ones are safe?"

"Well, ah," says the man, "you've got me at a disadvantage on specific dams."

"Isn't there information available," Hume asks, "on which dams may still be in danger of collapsing and causing a flood?"

"Well, I'll not try to guess the results of nature."

"Surely your office has some information."

"Ah, I don't think I could comment. I'm not knowledgeable or expert in that field."

"Well, sir," says Hume, driving the last nail in the poor man's public coffin, "aren't you the state official who's responsible for the dams?"

"Well," the man gulps, "yes."

The scene is from the first documentary produced by the "ABC News Close-Up" show, a program of investigative reporting that Hume helped start after he left the Jack Anderson column. The show launched Hume on a new career as a TV interviewer who elicits truth with well-backgrounded, carefully drafted questions asked while the camera is rolling.

"My role as an investigative reporter at ABC," says Hume, "has been secondary to my role as an interviewer." He's found that an interviewer can achieve unique results on camera. "You can't capture the drama of someone blowing his top in print like you can on film," he says. "The camera really puts people on the spot."

It's vital, of course, that the interviewer be well prepared. "You must be well steeped in the subject matter," says Hume, "so you can spot an evasion or inconsistency and keep cutting away until you get the truth." In a 1975 show on food, Hume put a question about the stability of farm prices to an Agriculture Department economist twelve times. The economist evaded the issue the first eleven times, but finally gave up. "Developing the use of the camera for the hardball interview," says Hume, "is an important contribution to journalism."

The aggressive confrontation interview by a reporter who's well versed in the subject, said executive producer Av Westin in 1975, "is the secret of Close-Up's success." The program has won several awards since it began in 1973. Some of its shows have been compared to documentaries by the pioneer of hard-hitting investigative journalism on TV, Edward R. Murrow.

Making the interviewer as knowledgeable as his subject is where the investigation comes in. For the food show, producer Pamela Hill slogged through "tons of records" for five months at the Agriculture Department, the Food Aid Program, and several other agencies. "It's slow, long, hard, drudge work," says Hill, "but I do it myself because I'm not comfortable unless I know every line is right."

Hill turned up several new disclosures in her food show. One was that a great deal of food was being sent to military allies rather than needy countries. Another was that American food policies were exacerbating world food problems. She also showed that government controls resulted in more benefits for industry than for consumers.

Documentaries are more suitable for investigative reporting than the nightly news show, says Hume, because the complicated subject matters require more time. "Close-Up's" 1974 show on oil, he says, "proved you can take a complicated topic and give a lucid, effective presentation on TV. We gave a clear picture of what the oil crisis was all about."

Tall, lanky, and still looking boyish at thirty-three, Hume believes TV can do some kinds of investigative stories better than the print media, and have a greater impact. Yet TV, he feels, is generally less well suited to investigative journalism than the print media where he made his fame as the man who interviewed Dita Beard.

That began one February day in 1972 in Jack Anderson's office. Handed a two-page memo on the letterhead of the International Telephone and Telegraph Corporation, Hume saw that it was addressed to W. R. Merriam, head of ITT's Washington office, and signed by D. D. Beard. Topic of the memo was "San Diego Convention." It said, in part, "I thought you and I had agreed very thoroughly that under no circumstances would anyone in this office discuss with anyone our participation in the Convention, including me. Other than permitting John Mitchell, Ed Reinecke, Bob Haldeman and Nixon (besides Wilson, of course) no one has known from whom that 400 thousand commitment had come. . . . I am convinced, because of several conversations with Louie re Mitchell, that our noble commitment has gone a long way toward our negotiations on the mergers eventually coming out as Hal wants them. Certainly the President has told Mitchell to see that things are worked out fairly. . . . Mitchell is definitely helping us, but cannot let it be known."

Though Hume did not recognize all the names, he understood the gist. ITT lobbyist Dita Beard was telling Merriam to keep his mouth shut about the $400,000 that ITT was giving the Republican National Convention, then planned for San Diego, in return for a favorable settlement of a government antitrust case against ITT acquisition mergers. There had been much talk and a couple of stories about such a deal, but this was the first solid evidence. It had come from inside ITT.

The memo's authenticity had to be established. Hume decided on a confrontation with Dita Beard. If he tried to check it with anyone else, Beard might hear about it and, with time to think, brand it a fake. She had to be caught off guard. She mustn't realize that the memo's genuineness was a crucial point. Hume had to act as if that were taken for granted. The tactic he picked was to ask for clarification on several aspects.

Dita Beard was a large, gray-haired woman with a brassy manner and a raspy voice. Hume met her at a conference table in ITT's Washington office the next morning. Also in attendance were two public relations men. Hume explained he wished to afford Beard an opportunity to place the contents of the memo in context. He took it out of his coat pocket and slid it across the table to her.

After a moment, the lady lobbyist began shaking her head. "It didn't work at all," she muttered. She went on reading and denying, flustered. But she was denying the memo's implications, not her authorship of it. She referred to a penciled initial at the top of the first page as her "own little D."

Beard and the two PR men gave Hume the official ITT version of the convention donation. Sheraton Hotels, an ITT subsidiary, had merely tried to help secure San Diego as the convention site. Nothing had been expected in return from the Justice Department or elsewhere in the Nixon Administration.

Hume offered to wait a couple of days while they checked their files for anything that might prove the memo was misleading.

The next night, Hume learned that Beard had tried to reach him. He phoned her at her home. "I'd like to talk to you," she said.

It was late, but Hume drove to her modest, red brick home in suburban Maryland. She embarked on a long, rambling plea for faith in ITT's innocence and a promise not to destroy her. She said there was no point in trying to fool him about the memo. "Of course I wrote it," she said. She implied, however, that it had been exaggerated. The convention money was totally unrelated to the antitrust suit.

Hume kept pressing, gently but relentlessly. Why would she refer to a deal if there hadn't been one? There had been one, hadn't there?

Finally she told him about seeing Mitchell at a Kentucky Derby party given by Governor Louis Nunn in 1971. Mitchell chided her for lobbying against the antitrust provisions in Congress instead of coming to him; Nixon had told him to settle the ITT case. Then Mitchell asked her what ITT wanted, and she told him.

But she still insisted that ITT president Hal Gineen had known nothing about this when the $400,000 was pledged for the GOP convention.

With the addition of a few corroborating details, that was enough to give Hume the biggest story he ever wrote. Beard later claimed the memo had been forged, and denied having told Hume it was hers. Hume passed a lie detector test on his version of their interviews. Beard was not up to a lie detector test because of poor health.

"The ITT affair," Hume wrote in *Inside Story,* his book on his experiences with the Jack Anderson column, "was the best thing that ever happened to my career. I was virtually unknown before it began, despite several years with Jack and the publication of my book (*Death in the Mines,* on corruption in the United Mine Workers union). Now I was well known through the news business and even known to some outside it."

Producer Pamela Hill's first "Close-Up" effort was a natural for TV. Its topic was fire. Written with Science Editor Jules Bergman and aired in 1973, it showed polyurethane insulation advertised as fire resistant burning fiercely, plastic baby cribs bursting into flames, and other fire hazards that helped give the United States the highest fire death rate among industrialized nations.

The network has given "Close-Up" producers a great deal of investigative freedom, says Hill, a tall, willowy blonde who formerly worked for eight years at NBC News, where she won a Peabody Award for a documentary on organized crime. "The only restriction we have is that we have to prove it."

"The problem," says another "Close-Up" producer, James Benjamin, a soft-spoken fifty-three-year-old veteran of commercial and educational TV, "is that there's never enough air time to do all there is to do."

What TV can do, says Benjamin, "is put a little light on a problem" by "getting the facts together and finding ways to make them visual." His 1974 documentary on lapses in air safety showed a stewardess' uniform bursting into flame, then compared it with a fabric that wouldn't ignite. This was important, the show explained, because most air crash victims die from fire and smoke after the crash.

Benjamin spends up to nine months on a show with an associate producer and sometimes a researcher, in addition to a camera crew when needed. During a 1973 investigation of agriculture as big business, his team traveled around the country to observe food inspection procedures. In the poultry business, they found inspectors who said they'd been forced to pass unclean chickens. Benjamin persuaded some to make their allegations on film. Acting on a tip that processors were violating a ban on giving arsenic-tainted feed to chickens within seven days of slaughter, associate producer Debbie Kram followed feed trucks to the feeding troughs and scooped up some overflow for analysis.

"It's tougher for us than the print media," says Benjamin. "We have to wrap it all up at once. We have greater momentary impact, but we don't have the air time to keep pounding away. But if we can shed some light, someone else can pick up the ball."

Hume believes TV can have mass-scale impact and is mostly optimistic about its potential, but has some doubt. "TV basically is an entertainment medium, rather than a news medium. Investigative journalism stirs up controversy and trouble that TV doesn't usually want. The likelihood of significant contributions in investigative journalism is not great."

Executive Producer Westin, who won several awards at CBS News before he joined ABC in 1969, displays more confidence. "There's a fundamental change under way in broadcast journalism," he said last fall before he left ABC. "We have begun to throw off some of our old limitations.

"We're breaking away from the need for pictures, for instance. We're not afraid to show documents, like a ledger or an affidavit. We get the story first and then address ourselves to illustrations. Illustrations are no longer Number One.

"We don't care if a program is dull if it reveals important facts," he said, pausing to consider the implications of his words. "But in fact," he added, "our shows are not dull."

Clarence Jones became a frequent sight at the walk-in bookie parlors and after-hours liquor joints in Louisville, Kentucky. The operators and other customers became used to the short, friendly businessman from Indiana who always carried a lunch box under his arm. A nice guy, they figured. A regular. Around for eight months or so, altogether.

Then one day in February, 1971, they saw him on WHAS-TV, showing pictures of them plunking down two bucks on Number 5 in the eighth. Jones, it was clear, wasn't a businessman and he wasn't from Indiana. And inside that lunch box had been a camera.

WHAS had hired Jones away from the Miami *Herald's* Washington bureau to do an undercover investigation. His mission was so secret that he wasn't put on the station's payroll, and not even his children knew where he really worked.

A few months after his Louisville probe, WPLG-TV lured him back to Miami, where he'd been before going to Washington, to do hidden camera tricks in the Sun City.

Jones filmed a meeting outside a warehouse between Dade County State Attorney Richard Gerstein and a notorious local fixer by setting up a camera in a van parked in a service station. In 1975 he got pictures of longshoremen looting a ship by smuggling a camera aboard. When a state senator and the speaker of the house boarded a plane for Costa Rica with a racetrack lobbyist, Jones was there with his camera rolling inside an attaché case. He once went to Las Vegas to get a shot of the Florida Supreme Court's chief justice at a craps table.

By tailing bookies in the fall of 1973, Jones saw Judge David Goodhart go to a Miami Beach men's store regularly on Saturday mornings just before a bookie and a Las Vegas gambler close to crime syndicate mogul Meyer Lansky also entered the store. A former assistant to Gerstein, the judge once met Gerstein in front of the store and handed him some money. Jones, naturally, took a few pictures.

He was not alone, however. There was also John Camp of WCKT-TV, who, in addition, filmed a breakfast meeting between Lansky and the Las Vegas gambler, Hymie Lazar, at Wolfie's Sandwich Shop in Miami Beach. Camp later took some footage of another judge as he left a barber shop near the men's store a few minutes after Judge Goodhart and Lazar were seen talking inside.

In Camp's April 28, 1974, report on a federal investigation of illegal gambling and corruption, he disclosed also that both judges frequented a golf club known as a hangout for gamblers and organized crime figures.

Goodhart said he met Lazar and the bookie by chance and he did not know they were gamblers. The money he gave Gerstein was just a ten dollar loan. Called later to testify before a grand jury, Goodhart cited the Fifth Amendment and refused to answer questions. He later resigned from the bench.

That story, which won a Peabody Award for investigative reporting for Camp, was his first big exposé after he moved to Miami in 1973 from Baton Rouge, Louisiana, where his background was in radio. In Baton Rouge, Camp had exposed a bribery scheme in which a state official got more than $100,000 from a bank for arranging deposits of state money in a non-interest-bearing account.

The sources he cultivated in his first Miami investigation led to 1975 stories identifying twenty-four organized crime figures who had fled to the Miami area to escape a New Jersey crackdown. These disclosures led to a special state probe.

Camp develops most of his stories from tips by law enforcement sources and attorneys. He often trades information, though this often involves no more than "passing along information from one law enforcement file to another. Different levels of law enforcement have terrible liaison, particularly between federal and state agencies. Investigative reporters sometimes provide a conduit for intelligence information."

Yet Camp, who's forty-one, revealed a confidential memo about allegations that the special agent in charge of the Miami FBI office had accepted gratuities from persons under investigation by other agencies. The agent was transferred to Oklahoma City. He also disclosed a congressional probe to determine if Gerstein had been behind allegations of IRS spying on taxpayers' sex lives and drinking habits as a scheme to discredit the IRS because it was investigating him. Despite his rapport with lawmen, Camp didn't flinch at exposing a few of them.

7

Slick-Paper Sleuths

IT WAS TOO LATE to be first with the biggest story of 1975. So Anthony Marro of *Newsweek* did the next best thing. From the billowing CIA scandal, he picked out one thread to run down: CIA-owned businesses.

Mention of CIA front operations had popped up from time to time, but no one had taken a serious crack at ascertaining precisely how many business ventures the CIA had set up to camouflage its spying. This would be a good time to do so.

Marro and *Newsweek* colleague Evert Clark read everything on the CIA they could dredge up from the files in *Newsweek*'s Washington bureau. They made two lists. One contained the names of people mentioned in connection with the CIA. These were compared with names in Standard and Poor's directory of corporations and officers. The second list had all the companies ever named in articles about the CIA. From this they compiled a third list —directors and officers of CIA-connected companies. Soon they could discern a pattern of businessmen, lawyers, and bankers who were working for, or willing to help, the CIA. The next step was to investigate their backgrounds, then approach them for interviews.

If you talk to enough people, says Marro, you will find one who has valuable information and is willing to part with it. "Out of twenty-five, maybe two will talk," he says, "and one will tell you the truth."

Marro and Clark found enough talkers to uncover an "old boy" network of businessmen and lawyers who had responded eagerly when old college chums came around to reminisce and ask a bit of assistance for Uncle Sam. An Arlington, Virginia, lawyer named L. Lee Bean, for instance, had agreed to set up two companies to help the government with national security work at the request of a former University of Virginia classmate. Anderson Security Consultants and Zenith Technical Enterprises were soon in operation, with Bean's office as their address. Both were wholly owned subsidiaries of the CIA. Anderson Security performed such services as destroying classified documents and investigating employes. Zenith set up the CIA's training of Cuban anti-Castro forces in southern Florida.

These were only two of many. The CIA, Marro found, had been secretly running one of America's most diversified corporate empires. Among its enterprises were several airline companies, an aircraft repair firm, an engineering company that built airstrips, Radio Free Europe for broadcasting propaganda into Communist countries, and a flock of small shops set up at home and abroad to provide cover for spies or channel bribes to public officials. Other companies, such as the Robert R. Mullen & Company public relations firm in Washington, D.C., were not owned by the CIA, but furnished cover for CIA activities by putting agents on their payrolls.

The most surprising fact the *Newsweek* reporters uncovered as they traced the CIA's cloak-and-dagger trail through the business world, was that the CIA had begun to close down many of their businesses.

When Marro and Clark were finished, they not only had an exposé for the May 19, 1975, issue of *Newsweek*, they also possessed a massive file on the CIA that included the name of anyone ever mentioned in connection with the agency. Material and sources acquired during the investigation helped lead to another *Newsweek* exclusive, the operations of an American intelligence agency even more secret than the CIA. This was the Defense Department's National Security Agency, which uses sophisticated computerized equipment to eavesdrop on international cables and phone calls and deciphers the diplomatic codes of other countries.

Before Marro moved to *Newsweek* from *Newsday* in the fall of 1974, the thirty-three-year-old dark-haired reporter with the neatly clipped mustache and the open, friendly manner had been more a records man than a source man. At *Newsweek*, he found that sources in such agencies as the CIA and the FBI were behind the prowess of his competitor at *Time* magazine, Sandy Smith. Marro worked hard to catch up. By the summer of 1975, he not only had the CIA well in hand, he was learning the details of illegal break-ins by the FBI's "black bag boys" from former agents and sources inside the bureau. As he disclosed in a July issue, the break-ins had been conducted over a period of years to ransack files and install electronic bugs at foreign embassies, mob hangouts, and extremist group headquarters.

When Marro headed up the American end of the Greene team's heroin trail investigation for *Newsday*, sources among narcotics agents, customs officials, government prosecutors, and defense attorneys gave him a great deal of help. But he relied mostly on records. He set up a file system and put into it information from police reports, court files, customs records, statistical reports, and reporters' memos.

Marro brooks no violation of the daily memo rule. The investigative reporter, he insists, must commit his finds to a written record at the end of each working day. Copies are cross-filed wherever they may be needed. This way, another reporter can take over an investigation or write the story if necessary. "In order to be a good investigative reporter," says Marro, "you have to maintain good files and keep them up to date."

Marro had learned about files from Bob Greene during *Newsday's* 1971 probe of President Nixon's financial dealings in Florida. The facts in that investigation were so complicated, says Marro, that it took three months to find out what questions to ask. Much time was spent prospecting through land records. Marro earlier had spent four weeks hand copying bank deposit records in the Hempstead town clerk's office on Long Island in an investigation of favors done for a bank by State Senator Ed Speno in return for unsecured real estate loans. All that ended up as two paragraphs in the story, Marro recalls wryly. On the other hand, "Every time you work a story, you come across clues for eighteen more."

Nothing is more important in an investigation, says Marro, than the chronology, the putting of the facts in chronological order to see what's missing and get a clear view of the contradictions. "I like to take a story," he says, "and pinpoint the holes, the unanswered questions, the contradictions." Then the final interviews can be conducted effectively.

"I'm no good at matching wits, or parrying, or drawing someone out," says Marro. "I've never had any success or enthusiasm for bullying people. What works for me is to be well grounded in the facts. That way I know what to ask."

When Sandy Smith heard that two Teamster Union organizers from Cleveland had obtained a charter to set up a local in another union for Las Vegas casino dealers, an eyebrow lifted behind the glasses. He knew from years of covering the underworld that something perfidious was afoot.

Under questioning by Smith, the lawyer who had helped the two Teamsters get the charter from the International Office and Professional Employes Union revealed that he represented the son of Cleveland Mafia boss Frank Milano. Smith uncovered a Mafia plot to facilitate extortion schemes against casino operators by unionizing their dealers. After Smith relayed this information to the OPEU's chief counsel, the charter was quickly revoked.

When Chicago police ran roughshod over hippies and demonstrators at the 1968 Democratic National Convention, Smith had a ready explanation in *Life* magazine. Chicago police were uncontrollable because they had been crooked for so long. Smith knew well enough. For twenty-five years he had covered the police beat for the Chicago *Tribune* and the Chicago *Sun-Times* before he joined *Life* magazine's new investigative team in 1967.

In 1975, when the news broke that President Ford had spoken of CIA assassination plots, Smith remembered an old column by Jack Anderson on a mobster's involvement and knew exactly where to get details. Smith had been writing about the Mafia's inner workings long before it had been fashionable. He probably knew more about Sam Giancana, the Chicago Mafia boss rumored to have been involved in the assassination plots, than any other reporter in the country. He had once crashed a Giancana daughter's wedding, talking his way past the guards at the door of the reception room. He started writing down the names on the place cards. Giancana rushed up, furious. But Smith calmed him down and coaxed him into an interview. Smith revealed Giancana's role in the CIA assassination plots in the March 17, 1975, issue of *Time* magazine, where he had become the magazine's chief investigative reporter after *Life* magazine folded in 1972.

Smith wrote about mobsters and corruption for *Life*, mostly in 1967 and 1968 when fascination for investigative journalism and organized crime stories flourished among national magazines. Based largely on information in police files across the United States, Smith's article delineated the Mob's activities and described its leaders in vivid, voluminous detail. He explained how millions of dollars were skimmed off the top of the take in Las Vegas, how gangsters had seized control of corporations, how they ran their rackets, eliminated troublemakers, corrupted politicians.

Smith's skill at establishing sources in the FBI and other law enforcement organizations is legendary. The late J. Edgar Hoover was believed to have been one of Smith's sources. *Time* magazine ranked second only to the Washington *Post* in media critic Edward Jay Epstein's assessment of Watergate coverage, thanks largely to Smith's rich lode of old sources and his awesome ability to get new ones in a hurry. Anthony Marro of *Time's* competitor, *Newsweek,* recalls running up against Smith's virtuosity while working on an article about Watergate conspirator G. Gordon Liddy. "Everywhere I went," says Marro, "Smith had been there two days earlier."

Since newsmagazine journalism seldom permits long-range investigations, Smith's job is usually to round up exclusive subsurface facts for important current stories, or probe one angle in depth. The no-byline aspect of *Time's* group journalism is fine with Smith. A big, jovial man in his fifties who enjoys lounging for days at a time on his sailboat, Smith would just as soon be as anonymous as his sources. He declines to be interviewed, himself. Publicity, he says, might make his job harder.

Another member of *Life's* investigative team, William Lambert, held the record for toppling the highest-ranking public official with an exposé until Woodstein came along. Lambert revealed in a 1969 article that U.S. Supreme Court Justice Abe Fortas had received $20,000 from the family foundation of imprisoned financier Louis Wolfson. The story led to Fortas' resignation, and a Heywood Broun Award for Lambert.

That same year Lambert disclosed the energetic influence peddling of seventy-one-year-old Nathan Voloshen from the office of John W. McCormack, Speaker of the U.S. House of Representatives. Described by Lambert as "among the classic Washington fixers of all time," Voloshen, and McCormack's chief assistant, Martin Sweig, had been able to operate under the cloak of McCormack's office without McCormack's knowledge. Both Voloshen and Sweig were indicted.

Lambert's 1970 exposé of Maryland Senator Joseph Tydings' failure to list all his assets on a voluntary financial report despite his public pronouncements in favor of full disclosure by politicians led to the senator's defeat at the polls. Lambert had been tipped to the story by White House Special Counsel Charles Colson, a Nixon aide whose motive was to oust Democrat Tydings from the senate. Lambert said later that the source of the tip was irrelevant; the story was factual.

Lambert won a 1957 Pulitzer Prize with fellow Portland *Oregonian* reporter Wallace Turner for exposing an attempt by Teamster Union leaders from Seattle to take over Portland's rackets.

Denny Walsh was the *Life* team's other Pulitzer Prize winner. Walsh was at the St. Louis *Globe-Democrat* when he won a 1969 Pulitzer with fellow reporter Al Delugach for exposing corruption and illegal political contributions by a Steamfitters Union local in St. Louis. The local and three of its officers were convicted of conspiracy to violate federal laws against use of union funds in federal election campaigns.

At *Life*, Walsh exposed the underworld ties of St. Louis Mayor Alfonso J. Cervantes, disclosed that Ohio Governor James Rhodes had made a Mafia murderer eligible for parole by reducing his sentence after Mafia leaders had put up $300,000 for his release, and revealed that a U.S. Attorney in San Diego had intervened to hamper a bribery investigation involving a firm controlled by millionaire C. Arnholt Smith, a financial backer of President Nixon.

After *Life* went out of business, Walsh landed at *The New York Times*, and later moved to the West Coast to join the staff at the Sacramento *Bee*. Lambert, meanwhile, had gone to the Philadelphia *Inquirer*. But as 1976 began, the only member of the old *Life* magazine investigative team still performing the brand of reporting that made *Life* the lion of American journalism in the late 1960s was Sandy Smith.

Nicholas Pileggi was about to saunter down to Columbus Circle to take a look at the Italian-American Day rally when the ringing of his telephone stopped him.

"Don't go to the rally," said a man's voice.

"Why not?" asked Pileggi. He knew there was unrest in Mafia circles over the rally and he wanted to see if anything newsworthy developed.

"There's going to be trouble," said the voice.

"What if I just drive by in a car?"

"Don't go by in a car."

"Okay. I'll just go out and get a copy of the *Post* after a while."

"Don't go out and get a *Post*," said the voice. "Get out of town."

Pileggi's article on the Mafia's exasperation with Joseph Colombo had appeared in *New York* magazine just two weeks earlier. The other Mafia family leaders had long been known to be displeased with the antics of Colombo's Italian-American Civil Rights League, but Pileggi's story had a new twist to report.

Entitled "Merciful Heaven, Is This the End of Joe Colombo?" it revealed that a group of house painters had beaten up an official of the League with lead pipes and slapped Colombo around when he tried to intervene. It was hard to imagine a bunch of painters getting into a street brawl with the head of a New York Mafia family, Pileggi wrote. Indeed, that wasn't it at all. Pileggi's sources in the Mob had told him that Colombo's rival, Joseph "Crazy Joey" Gallo, had ordered the attack. That Gallo would do such a thing meant he had the approval of the top Mafia brass. It had been a message to Colombo that the boys were serious about their advice to cut down on his public visibility and fade into the background of the rally organizing.

Colombo had ignored the warning, and Pileggi's article had as much as fingered Gallo as the Number One suspect if anything happened to Colombo. Gallo wasn't called Crazy Joe for nothing. He wasn't the average rational gangster who knew better than to mess with a journalist. The man on the phone had been giving him a friendly warning.

So, Nick, what did you do?

"I got out of town."

Pileggi learned about the shooting of Colombo at the June 28, 1971, rally while reading a newspaper the next day at the home of relatives some distance from New York.

He knew his way around the underworld because he'd been covering the police and the Mafia since 1952. For sixteen years he was a crime reporter for the Associated Press who phoned in his stories to a rewrite desk. "I didn't write a story myself until I was thirty," he recalls. But he learned a great deal about crime and police work, and acquired a lot of valuable sources. "I got to know cops and court clerks, rather than judges, and fingerprint men and shyster lawyers." The reality of the system, he found, did not match the descriptions in the textbooks.

In the mid-60s, Pileggi began writing about crime and corruption in a sophisticated style for *Esquire* magazine. His 1966 piece entitled "The Lying, Thieving, Murdering, Upper-Middle-Class, Respectable Crook," revealed underworld infiltration of legitimate businesses. "The Long Palm of the Law" described the intricate methods devised by cops to get on the take. To do "We Burned a Bum Friday Night and We're Going to Burn Another One Tonight" in 1967, Pileggi tracked down two teenage boys who had set fire to a couple of derelicts, killing one of them. He pieced the story together by talking to their schoolmates and neighbors. His 1966 article on electronic surveillance was years ahead of public awareness. "Investigative reporters are always far ahead of the public interest," observes the easygoing, debonair Pileggi. "By the time Joe Valachi came along and got people interested in the Mafia, I was bored with it."

New York magazine Editor Clay Felker induced Pileggi to leave AP in 1968 and write full time for his magazine as a contributing editor. Pileggi produced more articles on the Mafia and in 1973 listed the city's top heroin and cocaine dealers. He later revealed the prosperous narcotics business run by several New York police detectives with the drugs they seized in raids.

Boredom with the Mafia and police corruption overcame him in 1974. He began probing into another milieu of power, the world of business and politics. He started with Bill Shea, a little-known New York lawyer and behind-the-scenes manipulator, and a Brooklyn Democratic Party dinner in Shea's honor. Pileggi uncovered a copy of the guest list and, with a few phone calls, learned who else had attended. There were 1,200 names altogether. Pileggi investigated their business interests, political connections, and arrest records.

The result was his November 11, 1974, article entitled, "No Matter Who

Loses the Election, Bill Shea Wins." Shea, it said, was "the city's most experienced power broker, its premier matchmaker, a man who has spent forty years turning the orgies of politicians, bankers, realtors, union chiefs, underwriters, corporation heads, utility combines, cement barons, merchant princes, and sports impresarios into profitable marriages." Shea was the "most powerful manipulator of political influence in the state," the "unofficial chairman of the state's unofficial permanent government," the head of "the consortium of businessmen that has run New York for years, though it can be neither censured nor dislodged by a vote." The article was accompanied by a chart showing the tentacles of Shea's connections with several of New York's biggest, most powerful corporations. There was also a Shea remark from the past: "I don't practice law. I'm a broker. I bring together various forces."

That was his breakthrough article, Pileggi says. "That made people stop thinking of me as a rackets and mob reporter."

He next took on New York's new governor, Hugh Carey, and his oil tycoon brother, Edward. He revealed how mysterious, unknown Edward had made politician Hugh a governor with huge chunks of cash filtered through election law loopholes into his brother's campaign. "It was a virtuoso performance of tricky campaign financing," Pileggi wrote. He spent days poring over contribution lists to unravel how donation limits had been circumvented by funneling money through different individuals and groups.

Having discovered Edward Carey's unsuspected power in the oil industry as one of the nation's largest independent importers, refiners, and distributors of petroleum products, Pileggi hastened to Washington to examine the files of the Senate Subcommittee on Multinational Corporations and see what more he might learn. On page 510 of a hearing transcript, he spotted a reference to a dispute over Bahamian crude oil between Carey's firm and the giant Standard Oil Company of California.

From there, it was all downhill to his October article disclosing how Standard Oil of California had tried to squeeze Carey's company out of its Bahamian refinery, and how, in coping with that, Carey ended up under investigation by a grand jury for allegedly overcharging New York utility companies for oil.

Investigating the complex machinations of business is similar, says Pileggi, to investigating the complex machinations of crime. "Every time an organized crime guy got arrested, I made a file card," he says. Now he does the same with references to businessmen and politicians that he clips every day from several newspapers. "I use the same techniques. I chart their connections and get to know their names. The key is to cover these guys the same way I cover mobsters."

It came to him one day in the shower.

As the water splashed over him, Robert Walters reflected on testimony before the Senate Watergate Committee that a friend of White House Appointments Secretary Dwight Chapin had spied on Senator George McGovern's presidential campaign by posing as a reporter. No name had been mentioned, but a vague sense that he should know who it was kept nagging at the edges of his thoughts. Suddenly he remembered.

"Investigative reporting," says Walters, "is often like a jigsaw puzzle." The key piece had just popped into his mind.

Every time Walters had traveled on McGovern's campaign plane, there also was Lucianne Cummings Goldberg. Other reporters drifted in and out of the news media entourage, but Lucy Goldberg was always on hand, never missing a thing for her employer, which she had identified as the Women's News Service.

Goldberg was now in New York, Walters discovered. He picked up the phone and invited her to lunch.

He was writing a story on Chapin's friend for the Washington *Star*, he told her at lunch. He implied he knew the whole story and just needed her comments to flesh out his article.

Goldberg sighed. "I knew that sooner or later someone would ask me about that."

She had been hired by Murray M. Chotiner, a former political adviser to Nixon, to accompany the McGovern campaign and report to the Nixon reelection committee on the personal habits of the campaigners. "They were looking for really dirty stuff," she said. "Who was sleeping with who, what the Secret Service men were doing with stewardesses, who was smoking pot on the plane—that sort of thing." She had been paid $1,000 a week.

Spying was a new phase of politics for Walters. His specialty had been money. A small group of reporters had begun around 1970 to probe deep beneath the surface of political contributions and detect the true sources of campaign funds, and Walters had been one of them.

He was among the first to reveal a possible connection between political contributions by the dairy industry and the Nixon Administration's turnabout decision to increase price supports for milk. It was Walters who first reported that a $400,000 contribution by Sheraton Hotels to help lure the 1972 Republican National Convention to San Diego might be connected to the Justice Department's sudden willingness to settle an antitrust suit against ITT, the hotel firm's parent company.

Walters left the *Star* in 1974 after ten years to write for *New Republic*, *The Nation*, *Ramparts*, the *Washingtonian*, the *Washington Monthly* and other magazines willing to publish investigative work. A thin, earnest, scholarly-looking man, he negotiated a contract for regular contributions to *Parade* magazine and arranged for desk space at the *National Journal*, a monthly magazine on congressional happenings.

A Virginia murder case introduced Walters to investigative reporting shortly after he joined the *Star* in 1964. Sent seventy miles to Winchester, Virginia, to cover an arrest in the slayings of two elderly women in their Shenandoah Valley home, Walters encountered a defense attorney who convinced him that thirty-five-year-old Otho Howard was innocent. According to the attorney, the other defendant in the case, twenty-two-year-old Luther Durham, Jr., had implicated Howard to get revenge. Howard had fired Durham from a job at the farm that Howard managed.

Walters asked for time to look into the case.

"You've got a lot to learn," shrugged the city editor. "But, all right."

Back in Winchester, Walters began talking to scores of people—"scut work," he calls it. He discovered that Durham was the state's chief witness in several other murders and burglaries around the state. In each case, Durham said he was at the scene of the murder but did not participate in it. Digging into a few of the cases, Walters found several instances in which the defendant had done something Durham hadn't liked. Further probing unearthed evidence that two of the murder defendants had been miles away at the times of the killings. One prosecutor dropped murder charges against five persons accused by Durham. All the murder charges against others eventually were dropped, and Durham pleaded guilty to one of the killings. Walters pieced the story together over a four-month period. Durham had begun confessing and accusing after he was sent to prison for stealing an outboard motor from the farm managed by Howard.

That story was satisfying, says Walters, because of the tangible results. "By contrast," he says, "most instances of dealing with the federal bureaucracy are comparable to punching a bowl of Jello. It quivers briefly, then surrounds your fist—and returns to its original shape almost immediately after the hand is removed."

Much of what passes for investigative reporting isn't, really, according to Walters. *Life* magazine's exposés, he maintains, weren't dug up by the reporters, but handed to them by prosecutors whose own investigations had been thwarted. Walters says he knew when the Tydings story broke that it had been prompted by White House Special Counsel Charles Colson, but he couldn't publish that fact because he had acquired the information on an off-the-record basis.

Investigative reporting "is a lonely thing," he says. A practitioner is unwelcome at social events, is "looked upon with scorn" even by other reporters, and spends most of his time off by himself buried in a stack of records. "Myself, for instance, I have a fixation with documents. If it's on paper, it's got to be good."

Not that he turns away sources. "I'll insist on verifying and documenting information from a source, and finding out what his motive is," says Walters, "but I'm willing to talk to the devil himself."

More than 120,000 Vietnamese refugees were streaming into the United States in the spring weeks after South Vietnam's 1975 collapse. It occurred to Michael Drosnin, a young free-lance writer, that hundreds of them must be criminals, assassins, torturers, heroin traffickers, and officials of Saigon's dreaded secret police. Editor Jonathan Z. Larsen said *New Times* magazine would pay expenses for an investigation.

Starting with names culled from published materials, Drosnin got on the phone to see how many of them he could locate in the refugee processing centers on Guam, at Camp Pendleton in California, and at Fort Chaffee in Arkansas. He called refugee program officials, refugee camp workers, refugees themselves. The CIA, which Drosnin discovered sneaking Vietnamese ex-employes into the United States under phony names, would not tell him how many refugees were veterans of the CIA's controversial antiterrorist program, Operation Phoenix, which was known to have tortured and assassinated civilian Vietnamese suspected of being Communists.

Some second and third level officials in the refugee program gave Drosnin the names of refugees who weren't on the official lists. By matching these and the lists against the names of known secret police, drug traffickers, and Phoenix program operatives from his other sources, Drosnin produced his May 30, 1975, article, "A Rogues' Gallery of Refugees."

Among the refugees in the processing centers bound for a bright new future in the United States, Drosnin discovered, were: Nguyen Ngoc Loan, the secret police official who had executed a suspected Viet Cong with a bullet in the head in front of TV cameras; Trang Si Tan, a former Saigon police chief known as a master torturer; Nguyen Mau, head of a notorious interrogation and torture center; Loi Nguyen Tan, a jailer who liked cells too narrow for prisoners to do anything but stand or squat; Nguyen Minh Chau, a warden who crammed prisoners into the infamous "tiger cages" and starved them; Dang Van Quang, reputed to be a leading heroin merchant; and Chung Tan Cang, a heroin smuggler. Ngo Dzu, an army general described before a congressional committee as one of the chief heroin traffickers in Southeast Asia, had already been cleared through the Fort Chaffee processing center.

Drosnin also gleaned new details about the Phoenix program and the name of a former CIA official who would tell him more. Now intent on a second article, one that would expose in full the true savagery of Operation Phoenix, he embarked on a cross-country trip to locate Vietnam refugees and Americans who had participated in Phoenix and would discuss their experiences. To find the few dozen he did persuade to talk, Drosnin spoke to several hundred.

"The business of investigative reporting," says Drosnin, "is convincing people who should keep their mouths shut that it's in their best interests to tell you what you want to know." He admits to no remorse of guilt about misleading them. He explains the possible consequences, he says, and persuades them to talk anyway.

"Many people feel compelled to talk to a reporter. They seem to think they don't have any option, and I use that. I've found that wearing a suit will make me seem a figure of authority to some people. The Vietnamese who worked for the CIA responded to that. They began to feel I was just another bullying American."

Some thought he was a CIA agent checking on their pledges not to reveal anything. Others were eager to discuss their work for the CIA, displaying more pride than qualms or guilt. Drosnin nodded and agreed as long as that produced information.

For knowledgeable persons who resist, like former CIA Director William E. Colby, Drosnin has a different technique—the "just one more question" line.

When Colby wouldn't respond to a phone call at his office, Drosnin called him at home.

"I don't think I should talk to any reporters," Colby said.

"I know a lot more about the Phoenix program than the Senate committee," said Drosnin. "It would be irresponsible of me not to speak to you before I write a story, don't you think?"

They discussed that for a few minutes and Drosnin would throw in another question to keep Colby talking. Every time Colby tried to end the conversation, Drosnin would say, "Just one more thing." Before Colby realized it, he was talking to a reporter.

"There's almost no one who you can't get to talk to if you try hard enough," says Drosnin, who's tall, thin, articulate, and intense.

His *New Times* article on the Phoenix program laid out the grisly details of what Drosnin called "the only systematized kidnaping, torture, and assassination program ever sponsored by the United States government"—the executions of women and children, the slicing off of ears, the CIA-built network of interrogation centers, the shooting of old men in their beds, the torture of prisoners with electric wires attached to ears, nose, breasts, and genitals, the killing, altogether, of 40,000 civilians. Drosnin considers it one of the most important stories of the Vietnam War.

He raised a bigger ruckus, however, with a 1975 story about the hazards of spray can fluorocarbons, an article he stitched together with strands from published sources and a couple of crucial new seams. "Some investigative reporting," Drosnin explains, "is not disclosing new facts, but pulling together what's only been reported so far in little squibs."

Several articles had appeared on the subject of fluorocarbons in the propellant gases of aerosol sprays. The fluorocarbons don't decompose when they're released. Instead they float up into the stratosphere where they accumulate and over a period of years destroy the ozone layer that protects the earth from the sun's ultraviolet radiation. But no one had fully explored the true severity of the implications, which Drosnin found to be potential annihilation of the human race, or determined if anyone was doing anything to head off the catastrophe, which, Drosnin found, no one was.

A former Washington *Post* reporter and *Wall Street Journal* staffer, Drosnin began free-lancing in 1971. He finds it more satisfying. "It's not the most rewarding financially," he admits, and he spends almost as much time selling articles as writing them, but he can write what he wants if he can interest someone in buying it.

He likes *New Times* because "it's not afraid to run anything I can back up."

Founded in 1973 by former *New York* magazine publisher George A. Hirsch as a weekly "feature news magazine," *New Times* bills itself as the "Mighty Mouse of Magazines"—"a tough magazine that gets to the guts of the issues" and "holds nothing sacred." It has published a variety of investigative articles and evidences a radical counterculture slant, yet appeared still to be groping for a clearly definable character as it passed its second anniversary last fall. Some critics called it too predictable. Others said it was too spotty or too superficial. No one, however, accused it of being too timid.

Another investigative contributor, Robert Sam Anson, became intrigued by the John Kennedy assassination case when he saw the Zapruder film of the tragic incident for the first time while watching television early in 1975. Anson had never been attracted to conspiracy theories; in fact, he'd been "turned off" by most of their advocates. But he had seen men shot while a *Time* magazine correspondent in Cambodia, and the Zapruder film made one of the conspiracy arguments look sound. Kennedy's body movements under the impact of the fatal bullet did indeed support a contention that the missile had come from the front, not the Book Depository Building where Lee Harvey Oswald worked.

Anson called *New Times* the next morning and got a go-ahead to write an article about the assassination. He contacted people whose criticisms of the Warren Commission's lone assassin conclusion had seemed relatively sensible. He visited Dealey Plaza in Dallas, dug into the National Archives in Washington, interviewed countless numbers of people, and wrote an April article saying there was new respect for evidence of a conspiracy and cover-up. By now, however, the conspiracy logic he found most cogent was that the "magic bullet theory" was untenable. The time gap between Kennedy's reaction to the first shot, which went through his neck, and Texas Governor John Connally's reaction to his wounds in the car seat ahead of Kennedy, as shown in the Zapruder film, convinced Anson that one bullet could not possibly have hit both men.

The article brought him a proposal from Bantam Books to write a paperback summarizing the evidence against the lone assassin finding. Though busy as special events producer for New York's public TV station, WNET, Anson took on the project. His book, *They've Killed the President!* was on the stands before the end of the year. A thorough collection of the case's chief points of dispute, the book presented a concise, coherent, highly readable analysis. It concluded with a call for a new national investigation, perhaps by Congress, to resolve for all time the question of whether a conspiracy by the Mafia, the CIA, Cubans, or anyone else was behind Kennedy's untimely death.

Anson should not have been surprised to find himself eventually attracted to the Kennedy assassination puzzle. He's always liked to tackle stories that are obviously incomplete. Another one like that was a sex scandal at his Alma Mater, the University of Notre Dame, where he had started a student newspaper before he was graduated in 1966.

Six black football players had been accused of gang rape by an eighteen-year-old white high school girl. Anson thought it strange that the punishment had been only a year's suspension from school. It also struck him as odd that interest in the story had quickly subsided. The girl's attorney had announced that she would not press charges.

Back on the familiar campus, Anson found few people connected with the case who would talk to him about it. There was widespread belief among students that the girl had submitted voluntarily, even solicited the sex.

Anson found the truth to be somewhere in between. The girl had gone to one of the player's dormitory room for intercourse. When he left her there alone afterward, another player happened by. It was someone with whom she had quarreled earlier. The argument flared anew and ended in a rape. Four others came by and joined in. The girl's parents did not wish the incident to be aired publicly in court.

Anson worked six years for *Time* magazine after graduating from Notre Dame. While in Cambodia, he was captured by North Vietnamese troops and Cambodian guerillas, an experience he later recounted in the magazine. Tall, strapping, fair-complexioned, and straightforward, Anson vents his investigative compulsions by churning out frequent magazine articles, including one a month for *New Times*. Other *New Times* pieces he's done have revealed extortion of "organizing money" from political candidates by black community leaders, and uncovered evidence of corruption in the administration of Boston Mayor Kevin White.

Ron Rosenbaum, best known for his cloak-and-dagger interview of narcotics case fugitive Abbie Hoffman while a frustrated FBI floundered around trying in vain to find him, describes himself as a storyteller rather than an investigative journalist. A slight, red-bearded free-lancer whose prolific writings appear in *New Times* and *Esquire*, Rosenbaum is a twenty-nine-year-old Yale graduate who confesses he went into reporting because it looked romantic.

While at the *Village Voice* from 1969 to 1975, he exposed Robert Mullen & Company, the Washington public relations firm that employed Watergate conspirator E. Howard Hunt, as a frequently used CIA front. He uncovered "checkerboarding" maneuvers by the New York construction trade unions in which black workers were juggled from one site to another to fool inspectors checking compliance with a racial integration program.

In *Esquire*, he exposed "phone freaks" who gyped the phone company on long distance calls by using "a little blue box" full of electronic gadgetry that enabled them to bypass the phone company's billing mechanisms. For *New Times*, he probed into the curious circumstances behind the 1975 firing of Federal Drug Enforcement Administrator John Bartels, Jr. as a Senate committee prepared to examine allegations that he blocked an investigation of a fellow DEA official for consorting with criminals and prostitutes.

Rosenbaum left the *Village Voice* in 1975 because he felt the Greenwich Village weekly was lapsing into conventionality under its new owner, *New York* magazine Editor Clay Felker. The *Voice* was becoming too concerned about trends, Rosenbaum explains. "If you're concerned about keeping up with trends, you're already behind them."

Utility bills kept going up, yet utility executives insisted it wasn't their fault. "We're just passing through our higher fuel costs," they said. "There's not a penny of extra profit."

Something about that didn't sound right to Stan Sesser, the West Coast editor for *Consumer Reports*. He decided to take a closer look.

California utilities were indeed permitted, under a "fuel-adjustment clause" approved by the state, to make their customers pay their rising costs. But it was not just a local phenomenon, Sesser discovered. The same was true in most parts of the United States.

The flowering of consumer organizations across the country gave his investigation a welcome assist. "You used to have to do business and consumer stories all by yourself," says Sesser. "Now you can get at least one consumer group in every state to help." Sesser also contacted state agencies that regulate utilities. "There's always someone on the staff who will talk."

Though the utilities' explanation appeared on the surface to be right, Sesser uncovered the hooker underneath. Some utilities, he found, owned their own fuel companies. Ohio Power Company, for instance, buys coal from its coal mining subsidiary, Central Ohio Coal Company. The unregulated subsidiary could raise the price of its coal without first getting the state's okay, and the parent utility firm could pass it on to consumers automatically under the fuel-adjustment clause. Instant profit. Not for the utility directly, true enough, but for its subsidiary. The next thing, he wrote in his November, 1974, article explaining it all, would be cost pass-throughs to the consumer for pollution control costs, taxes, etc., etc.

That article, Sesser says, "got more reaction than anything else I've ever done." Several states rescinded their fuel-adjustment clauses.

Business is more difficult to investigate than government because its records aren't public. But it can and should be done, says Sesser. A good, thorough knowledge of an industry can compensate for the records problem. Sesser has found it not that difficult, anyway, during five years at the *Wall Street Journal* and two with *Consumer Reports*. He says, "It's amazing, the extent to which you can get corporate executives to give you information that's damaging."

During his probe behind the locating of a nuclear power plant near a major earthquake fault, a vice president of the utility bragged to Sesser that the firm was monitoring the electricity usage of the plant's critics. That made an even better story.

Once he had trouble getting verification for a story that food companies were selling surplus cyclamate products overseas after the United States government banned them. Sesser called Libby-McNeil-Libby's vice president for international sales and engaged him in a chat about the problems he encountered because of the cyclamate ban. Sesser commiserated with the executive. After a while, he said casually, "It's lucky you've been able to sell your cyclamates in Europe."

"Well, we haven't been able to sell all of them," said the vice president.

"Really?" said Sesser. "How many have you sold?"

The vice president told him, and that was the story.

Sesser believes there's been too little investigative journalism directed at America's corporate establishment because reporters feel they don't understand business and their editors won't let them take time to become informed.

They should, he says. "If any area needs investigative reporting, it's business."

8

Supersnoops West

WHEN GEORGE REASONS went to a friend's cocktail party one day in 1966, he had no idea it would change the course of his newspaper career and lead to a Pulitzer Prize for the Los Angeles *Times*.

Between sips of martini, one of the guests dropped a mention of crooked practices in the city's planning commission.

"Oh?" said Reasons.

Yes, said the other. A friend of his, a former city administrator, had evidence of connections between planning commissioners and businessmen who appeared before them to request zoning changes.

Until then, the *Times* had displayed little appetite for investigative reporting and none at all for probing into the administration of Democratic Mayor Sam Yorty. But Reasons, a veteran newspaperman of forty-three who had been working as a relief man on the rewrite desk three days a week, was looking for a project to keep him busy the rest of the time.

He dove into the zoning records, scanning thousands of applications for rezoning and variance permits. He delved into the backgrounds and business interests of the planning commissioners, developers who made frequent requests for rezoning, and lawyers who showed up repeatedly on behalf of applicants. He combed through civil suits, credit records, divorce cases, corporation reports, property documents. Reasons soon found himself working on the project every day. Before he knew it, he was a full-time investigative reporter.

Six months after he started, Reasons broke the story on the front page of April 30, 1967. Among his revelations: One planning commissioner had an interest in a land development company that had obtained several rezonings for high-priced gas station sites; four commissioners were friends or business partners of developers who sought zoning changes; one commissioner had solicited campaign contributions for Mayor Yorty from developers; the commission had granted service station zoning in violation of the city's land use plan for property owned by a commissioner's mother.

Reasons' probe led to resignations by two commissioners, the transfers of two others, and changes in the zoning ordinance. It also gave him a taste for investigative work.

"We got a look inside the Yorty administration," he says. "We could see it was riddled with favoritism and corruption." He requested and was assigned four reporters to help him dig deeper into zoning cases and city contracts. Reasons prefers a team approach on complex stories. "When you're dealing with complicated stuff, it's helpful to have another head to compare different perspectives and interpretations," he says. "Also to figure out methods to get information people don't want you to have."

Reasons found that poking around for mischief stirs up pet peeves. "Why don't you take a look at the Harbor Commission?" suggested one tipster.

Okay, said Reasons.

He spent a couple of weeks test probing to see if it was worth a big commitment of resources. There were signs of something fishy about a $12-million contract for construction of a World Trade Center. Reasons put his team on the story for six months, most of it spent immersed in court files and city records.

They broke their findings on October 18, 1967, disclosing that the $12-million contract had gone to a developer who teetered on the brink of insolvency. The developer had made big stock purchases in a savings and loan association headed by a member of the Harbor Commission, and had helped another commissioner get a hefty bank loan. Two former commissioners, after the contract was awarded, had joined a medical lab venture with an associate of the developer.

The day before the savings and loan commissioner was scheduled to testify before a grand jury, his body was found floating in the Los Angeles Harbor. Police ruled it an accident, however. They said the dead man had fallen from a boathouse, struck his head, and drowned. Three other harbor commissioners were convicted of bribery. The $12-million contract was canceled.

Reasons' next target was the Recreation and Parks Commission, where he uncovered impropriety behind a $165,000 food concession contract at a golf course and an architectural contract awarded to a business partner of two commissioners. As a result, the commission adopted a new code of ethics prohibiting commissioners from ruling on contract proposals by business associates.

Then Reasons discovered that the rapid transit system had sold trolleys worth $350,000 to a friend of the system's manager for only $37,450. The friend resold them to a firm owned by the manager which in turn sold them at a big profit to a Mexican company that had offered the transit system $250,000 for them earlier.

These and other investigations by Reasons and four other reporters—Art Berman, Gene Blake, Robert L. Jackson, and Ed Meagher—won the *Times* the 1969 Pulitzer Prize for meritorious public service.

The team drifted apart but Reasons remained a full-time investigative reporter, sometimes working with a colleague or two. He and Robert Rawitch discovered widespread cheating on $211 million in Small Business Administration loans for repair of homes damaged by a 1971 earthquake. They had heard that much of the money was being used to make improvements rather than repairs on homes that had suffered little or no damage. Loans under $2,500 required no inspection of damage. Since SBA loan records were confidential, Reasons posed as an SBA auditor to interview home owners on how they used the money. He also found a cooperative contractor who let him go along while he estimated improvement jobs. The story named none of the home owners who cheated, but pointed up the gaping flaw in SBA's emergency loan system, which the SBA later changed.

A tip from a police source in 1974 prompted Reasons to investigate why a state senator had arranged a concealed weapon permit for a George J. Hatcher, who had served a jail term for writing bad checks. A check of what Hatcher did for a living alerted Reasons to a bigger story. Hatcher was running an ambulance chasing racket that preyed on poor Spanish-speaking residents of Los Angeles. He had set up a phony charity and installed a Catholic priest as its figurehead to get his men inside hospitals, where they solicited auto accident victims as clients for a group of damage claim lawyers. Hatcher's ring also monitored police calls, bribed auto body mechanics, towing firms, and junkyards, and got referrals from the legal officer in the Mexican Consulate. The lawyers filed false insurance claims, forged signatures, and refused to turn over insurance money to accident victims. Hatcher had even set up a firm to supply the lawyers with fraudulent medical reports. Reasons and reporter David Rosenzwieg wrote a five-part series that led to indictments of eleven persons, including the Mexican diplomat.

Now a trim, white-haired fifty-three, Reasons likes his life as an investigative reporter, though it's "marked by long dry periods." Sometimes, he says, he keeps coming up empty-handed. "You feel depressed, terrible, and you can't get a handle on anything." That's when he's most in favor of having more than one investigator, someone to bolster the spirits as well as share the work. "If I had a newspaper," he says, "I'd have a team."

The *Times* used the team approach in 1975 to investigate the virtual takeover of the trans-Alaska oil pipeline project by organized crime and a Teamster Union boss named Jesse L. Carr. A four-man team spent two weeks in Alaska after a preliminary scouting expedition by reporter Mike Goodman. They came back with evidence of widespread lawlessness, frequent violence, wholesale theft, hoodlum infiltration, wide-open prostitution and gambling, and refusal of police to do anything. The Alaskan boom, they found, was largely an illusion. Pipeline workers making $1,000 a week spent most of their work time sleeping. The consortium of oil companies building the pipeline ignored featherbedding and theft because completing the pipeline with a minimum of trouble was more important to them than standing up to the union, regardless of cost. The Anchorage (Alaska) *Daily News* won the 1976 Pulitzer Prize for meritorious public service with a similar investigation of Teamster power in Alaska.

Four years earlier, the *Times'* investigative business reporter, Al Delugach, had revealed the underworld connections of a mysterious entrepreneur, Phillip J. Matthew, who had bought 500 acres of Alaskan land that turned out to be located along the pipeline route when the route was announced later.

Delugach, who has written extensively on Teamster pension fund loans and manipulations by Las Vegas casino owners for the *Times*, won a Pulitzer Prize in 1969 while at the St. Louis *Globe-Democrat*. That was for exposing corruption and illegal political contributions by a Steamfitters Union local with fellow investigative reporter Denny Walsh, who later went to *Life* magazine and *The New York Times*.

One member of the 1975 Alaska probe team, William Endicott, was borrowed for the project from the *Times'* state capital bureau in Sacramento, where he's applied his investigative skills to exposing such matters as the legislature's frittering away of a million dollars on plans for a new capitol building that was never built. There is no secret formula for good investigative reporting, according to Endicott. "What works on one story—perhaps digging into court records and public documents—won't work on another." Endicott says, "Any good journalist should be equipped to do investigative work."

The *Times'* Bill Hazlett relies mostly on scores of sources in local, state, and federal police agencies. Most stories of major significance, Hazlett believes, end up as law enforcement stories sooner or later. A former city editor in Long Beach, public affairs radio writer in Hollywood, and police reporter in Wichita, Kansas, and Denver, Colorado, Hazlett exposed organized crime's takeover of Los Angeles' pornography business in 1975.

Hazlett and Washington Bureau correspondent Jack Nelson wrote the first article published by the regular press alleging ties between President Nixon and organized crime. Their May 31, 1973, story quoted a reference in a federal investigative report to a "love affair" between the White House and Teamster Union President Frank Fitzsimmons. It reported that an FBI agent had said, "This whole thing of the Teamsters and the mob and the White House is one of the scariest things I've ever seen."

The article described how Fitzsimmons had joined Nixon aboard the Presidential plane a few hours after meeting with a major Mafia leader at the crime syndicate's La Costa Country Club near San Diego, an incident first mentioned in a *New York Times* story by Denny Walsh a month earlier. Nelson and Hazlett added this remark by a California lawman: "I can stand crooks, but it bothers hell out of me when a guy meets with mobsters and then with the President." The reporters disclosed that the Justice Department had been lax in prosecuting Teamster Union corruption and schemes to loot Teamster pension funds. A second article laid out in detail the crime syndicate's invasion of southern California.

The *Times'* national editor, Edwin Guthman, is an old hand at probes of Teamster corruption. While a reporter for the Seattle *Times* in 1948, he started a file on Dave Beck, president of the Western Conference of Teamsters, after he was shocked to discover that Beck had lied to him in an interview.

"Oh, don't you know?" said labor reporter Paul Staples. "Beck lies all the time."

"But why?"

"Well, for one thing, I'm pretty sure he's stealing money from the union."

Guthman checked real estate records and Teamster welfare fund documents for information on Beck. Staples had cultivated sources inside the union who said Beck diverted union funds to his own use. Guthman and Staples began writing articles in 1953 about Beck's real estate ventures, the union's purchase of his lakefront home for $163,000, and large insurance commissions paid to a friend of a Beck protégé.

At Harvard University for a Nieman Fellowship reunion in 1954, Guthman met reporter Clark Mollenhoff, who was investigating Teamster corruption in Minneapolis. They arranged to keep in touch and exchange information. Early in 1956, Guthman helped Portland *Oregonian* reporters Wallace Turner and William Lambert expose an attempt by Seattle Teamster leaders to take over juke boxes and rackets in Portland. When the chief counsel for the U.S. Senate Rackets Committee, Robert Kennedy, came to Seattle that same year to ask his help, Guthman agreed to cooperate. He and Staples concluded they could advance no further into Teamster records without subpoena power, and Mollenhoff had said Kennedy could be trusted. Guthman later served as Kennedy's special assistant for public information from 1961 to 1965 when Kennedy was U.S. Attorney General.

Guthman stresses investigative enterprise in the paper's Washington bureau. "It's such an integral part of knowing what's going on in Washington," he says. Most important of all, he adds, is knowing how to check public records—how to get them, read them, interpret them—and spot the knavery that others miss.

Wallace Turner was the first investigative reporter for a major American publication to write a detailed exposé of organized crime's stranglehold on the plush, unreal world of Las Vegas gambling. In a five-part series on the front pages of *The New York Times*, Turner disclosed how the fast-growing, multimillion-dollar gambling industry was poisoning America with its corruption of politicians and show business celebrities, its infiltration of legitimate businesses and Wall Street, its use of gambling profits to finance other criminal operations, and its easy access to a billion-dollar Teamster Union pension fund.

Turner described how profits were skimmed off the top of casino earnings before taxes were computed. He revealed how gamblers and bootleggers from New York and Ohio, men like Meyer Lansky and Moe Dalitz, had muscled into control of hotel-casinos on the gaudy, garish Las Vegas Strip. Singer Frank Sinatra had been forced by Nevada authorities to sell his casino interests because he became too open about his friendship with Chicago Mafia boss Sam Giancana. One article explained an elaborate stock scheme in which underworld owners of a casino had swindled the public of $10 million. Turner disclosed how organized crime front men had obtained $20 million in loans from the Teamsters Union's Central States, Southwest and Southwest Areas Pension Fund to finance gambling casinos, and got loan guarantees from the Federal Housing Administration in their real estate ventures.

It was quite a story, but any impact it might have had was diluted by a far more immediate calamity. The last of Turner's articles appeared on November 22, 1963, the day that President John F. Kennedy was shot down in Dallas.

Ironically, the series had been ready for publication earlier. Turner, who had joined *The New York Times'* San Francisco bureau after several turbulent years of exposing corruption in Portland, Oregon, had been assigned to investigate what happens when people who've been doing something illegal get a license to do it legally. Turner's experience in probing the activities of gamblers at the Portland *Oregonian* in the 1950s had prompted the idea.

After weeks of travel across the country, interviewing casino operators, Wall Street financiers and victims of swindles, plowing through records in courthouses and government offices, and writing his articles with meticulous attention to detail, Turner had been told the series couldn't run because there was "no news peg."

Then the Bobby Baker scandal hit the headlines. Vice President Lyndon Johnson's protégé was forced to resign as Secretary of the Senate by disclosures about outside business dealings. A Washington *Post* article said Las Vegas gamblers had come to Baker for help in a business deal. Turner investigated and wrote a November 7 story about Baker's attempts to get gambling concessions in the West Indies for a Las Vegas casino owner who dealt frequently with underworld figures. Since Las Vegas gambling was now in the news, Turner's series was scheduled.

Though overshadowed by Kennedy's assassination, the articles made Turner a recognized expert on gambling. He wrote a book called *Gambler's Money* and in the spring of 1964 turned up in the mountain resort of Hot Springs, Arkansas, to expose what he termed "the biggest illegal gambling operation in the United States." Authorities in Hot Springs, he reported in the *Times*, made no effort to close down illegal casinos.

Embarrassed, Arkansas Governor Orval E. Faubus ordered Hot Springs officials to shut down the gambling or he'd send in state troopers to do it. The casinos did close, but when Turner went back a year later for a follow-up check, they were going full blast again. This time his article produced a grand jury investigation. In the meantime, Turner had visited the Bahama Islands and disclosed the channeling of underworld money through Bahamian banks. He also revealed the political maneuvers behind the opening of a new casino.

A blunt-spoken, craggy-featured veteran of newspapering, Turner had first learned about gamblers during his first months on the night police beat for the Portland *Oregonian* in 1943. The city's gambling boss once tried to give him money. "I was writing about hoodlums and crime all the time," says Turner. "You drift into it and it becomes your focus."

His first investigative assignment was to dig into the background of a young sheriff who had sued the newspaper because a columnist wrote that he got drunk at a party. Turner discovered the sheriff was three years younger than he admitted, had never finished high school though he claimed to be a college graduate, and had been dishonorably discharged from the Marines after he was caught bootlegging. His investigative instincts aroused, Turner began "really digging." He learned the sheriff had gone to Lake Tahoe, Nevada, with a prostitute and stayed in a hotel with a notorious gambler. The local citizenry organized a recall and booted the sheriff out of office.

Turner's biggest story began in 1956 when he was asked to check the background of a used car dealer who was running for mayor. He called upon a local hoodlum named James B. Elkins who had been a sometime source. Elkins didn't look good.

"What's the matter?" Turner asked.

"I've been having a lot of trouble with the Teamsters," said Elkins, but he refused to elaborate.

Turner sought out Elkins again and badgered him to say what it was all about. Elkins finally told him. Two Teamster Union racketeers from Seattle had conspired with the Portland prosecutor to put Elkins in jail and take over Portland's gambling and prostitution rackets, illegal liquor joints and juke box business. Elkins gave the reporter tape recordings of conversations between the prosecutor and the Teamsters. "I wouldn't have believed it otherwise," says Turner.

Turner and reporter William Lambert began a probe that resulted in a five-part series. Like most investigative articles, they were reviewed by the newspaper's attorneys before publication. Turner asked that they not be shown to one attorney in the firm because he also represented the city's pinball machine operators. His request was denied. Turner discovered later, after the attorney suddenly died, that the attorney had been leaking the stories to his pinball machine clients and had been planning to have Turner and Lambert killed.

The articles touched off a storm of controversy, libel suits, and grand jury investigations. Turner and Lambert became the first witnesses to testify at Senate Rackets Committee hearings on Teamster Union corruption.

Turner became the *Times'* San Francisco bureau chief in 1970, but still spends much of his time reporting and probing such West Coast blockbusters as Patty Hearst's kidnaping and the attempts on President Ford's life. He doesn't like the term, "investigative reporting." Good old plain solid reporting is supposed to dig beneath the surface of every story, he says.

Don Bolles walked past the big camper, glancing inside to get a glimpse of George Harry Johnson, the man who had tapped his telephone. The camper belonged to Arizona Congressman Sam Steiger, to whom Johnson had first spilled out his story. Steiger spotted Bolles and invited him in to meet Johnson.

Johnson repeated the story for Bolles, relating how he also had obtained information about the reporter's bank account, telephone calls, credit records, and personal life. Johnson had done a thorough investigation of the Arizona *Republic's* investigative reporter. He also had tried to dig up material to smear Steiger.

Johnson had been hired to do all this, he revealed later, by Arizona's prominent Funk family, which ran several dog racing tracks around the state, and by Emprise Corporation, a Buffalo, New York, conglomerate that operated food and drink concessions at race tracks and sports stadiums all over the world and had far-flung financial interests in horse racing and professional sports.

Ten months earlier, in October, 1969, Bolles had launched a five-month investigation of Emprise for his Phoenix newspaper after discovering that Emprise owned more of the Funk family's dog tracks than the Funks. Several Arizona greyhound breeders had filed a suit alleging the dog tracks were trying to run them out of business by using out-of-state dogs. A routine background check of racing commission records revealed Emprise's presence as the true controlling owner. A legislator's assistant gave Bolles a report on an investigation of Emprise's involvement in an Arkansas race track. The report mentioned ties with organized crime. Bolles sold his editors on a thoroughgoing probe.

His investigation included a ten-day trip to Denver, Chicago, Boston, New York, Washington, and Miami. He read all he could find on Emprise in newspaper files, inspected court records, and interviewed state racing officials. He found that Emprise and its founder, Louis Jacobs, had a long history of dealings with men identified by law enforcement agencies as crime syndicate leaders, especially in connection with race tracks. Piecing together facts from several sources, Bolles discovered that Emprise had acquired control of race tracks and professional sports teams with huge loans to financially beleaguered owners. Without the public's knowledge of its manipulations in the sports world, the giant complex of concession companies had amassed immense power in American horse racing and professional baseball and basketball.

When Bolles testified at hearings by the House Select Committee on Crime on the influence of organized crime in sports, he said Emprise's clout in the sports world, combined with its habit of doing business with underworld operators, was "a very disturbing thing." Bolles went on: "If they are in ownership positions, they, in my opinion, are in a position to affect the outcome of the contests. I just feel that it is absolutely essential, with millions of dollars changing hands on private bets and otherwise on every major sports contest in this nation, that we be absolutely assured that we have clean, honest sports."

In Arizona, Bolles uncovered business dealings and other connections between Funk family interests and three racing commissioners. All three resigned.

After Bolles began writing about Emprise, Congressman Steiger began a personal crusade for a congressional investigation, which he finally got from the House Select Committee on Crime in 1972 after Emprise was convicted in a Los Angeles federal court of conspiring with three Mafia bosses to conceal their ownership of a Las Vegas gambling casino.

When Johnson revealed how Emprise and the Funks had struck back, the Arizona *Republic* ran articles about that. The Funks sued Bolles and the paper for libel. Bolles countered with a suit charging invasion of privacy. He told the Select Committee on Crime that Emprise intimidated and harassed its critics, threatening lawsuits at every turn. It had "a very chilling effect," he said.

Reporters need a great deal of stamina to withstand such counterattacks by subjects of investigation. Many aren't able or willing to do so for long. "After a while," says Bolles, "you get tired of all the retraction demands and efforts to damage your own reputation."

Bolles had been an investigative reporter since 1964 when he uncovered evidence that two state tax commissioners had taken bribes to overlook bill padding by a Phoenix printing firm on tax form and envelope business. That led him to expose similar bribes and irregularities in the state Corporation Commission. Bolles also revealed a multimillion-dollar land fraud scheme, the Mafia's invasion of Phoenix, and a con man's near-successful promotion of an $82-million public bond issue to finance a phony device claiming to convert black and white TV into color for ten dollars.

But the Emprise experience soured him on investigative journalism. "The harassment by Emprise was the turning point of my career," he said in November, 1975. "I thought, 'This isn't worth it to me or my family' of seven children. Also, we have an incompetent county attorney here and after years of seeing our investigations die at his doorstep, I told my editors, no more. I'm no longer in investigative reporting."

Two months later, however, it became clear that Bolles couldn't make it stick. There were new scandals in city government and several arrests had been made. "I tried not to be active in investigative reporting," he said, "but I was forced back into it."

The Bolles story took a tragic turn in June, 1976. A bomb exploded in Bolles' car while he was investigating land frauds. The reporter died eleven days later. "They finally got me," Bolles said before he died, naming the Mafia, Emprise, and a thirty-two-year-old hoodlum and dog racing figure who was later charged with Bolles' murder.

The publisher of the Arizona *Republic* vowed that the reporter's death would be avenged, several investigative reporters went to Arizona to pick up the trail, and authorities finally put aside their indifference to the goings-on that Bolles had been revealing.

9

Ms. Investigators

IN MIAMI TO COVER the 1972 Democratic National Convention, Jean Heller met a reporter friend from San Francisco who was on her way to an African vacation. The friend mentioned a story she hadn't time to pursue, a story about a research project on syphilis at the U.S. Public Health Service's Center for Disease Control in Atlanta, Georgia.

Would Heller be interested?

She was.

A few facts about the syphilis study had reached Heller's friend from a former employe of the Public Health Service in San Francisco. The former employe had heard of a syphilis study that used black males as guinea pigs, and had sent a letter to Atlanta requesting details. The reply told him not to become alarmed, there was nothing wrong with it.

A member of the AP Special Projects Team, Heller telephoned her friend's San Francisco source as soon as she returned to Washington. The source had learned additional facts by telephoning Atlanta, he said, and was appalled. Heller made a call of her own to a CDC official in Atlanta. The official confirmed the existence of a syphilis study and said it was conducted in Tuskegee, Alabama, but would give no details. He brushed it off as nothing new, a study that had been discussed at length in medical journals.

"Would you send me copies?" Heller asked.

Certainly, he said.

No single article contained a full description of the project, or revealed what it really involved. But several together gave Heller a clear picture of a forty-year atrocity perpetrated on 200 black men in the name of scientific research.

More calls to Atlanta turned up CDC officials who had been upset by the study. They sent her more material. Heller discovered that the study, started in 1932, was still going on. One object had been to determine the long-range effects of untreated syphilis on the body through autopsies, and seventy-four of the men were still living.

Heller learned enough by phone and through the mail to write her story, which went out on the AP wire onto front pages across the country on July 25, 1972. "For forty years the U.S. Public Health Service has conducted a study," it began, "in which human guinea pigs, denied proper medical treatment, have died of syphilis and its side effects." At least seven men had died, Heller revealed.

The experiment had involved 600 black males, mostly poor and uneducated, in Tuskegee—400 with syphilis and 200 without. Half of the 400 had received treatment; the others had not. Though the study began ten years before penicillin was discovered, the drug might have saved some of the subjects later. But it had not been used, according to the doctor now in charge of the experiment, who admitted he had serious doubts about the project's morality.

Heller went to Atlanta and located doctors who confirmed that none of the subjects had been informed of his syphilis. In Tuskegee, townspeople were in a state of shock. "This used to be a real friendly town," one resident told Heller. "But now everybody's suspicious of everybody else. Folks are all trying to figure out who the people in the study were."

U.S. Senator William Proxmire of Wisconsin called the study "a moral and ethical nightmare." He suggested Congress pay compensation to the families involved. Senator Birch Bayh of Indiana called it "sickening and outrageous." Senator Abraham Ribicoff of Connecticut condemned it as "a frightening instance of bureaucratic arrogance and insensitivity."

Several investigations were started. Heller kept the story alive with sixteen follow-up articles. One disclosed her later discovery that at least twenty-eight, and possibly 100, had died. She wrote a three-part series on the ethics in human experimentation. The federal government created a panel to determine whether human rights were adequately protected in health research projects. The stories won Heller the 1973 Pulitzer Prize for investigative reporting. In 1975, the federal government agreed to pay $37,500 to each survivor whose syphilis had not been treated, and lesser amounts to the estates of those who had died. But, it was too late for effective medical treatment of those still living.

Heller, who had started with the Associated Press as a radio news writer in 1964, left in 1974 to join a newly formed Cox Newspaper National Bureau in Washington, where she soon unearthed another exposé.

During a conversation at a dinner party in her home, an official of the Federal Energy Office complained about politicians who called him with things they wanted done. One name he mentioned was Hugh Carey, then a congressman. During lunch with another FEO official a month later, Heller asked about Carey. Her luncheon companion said Carey was under investigation in connection with an export deal. But he would tell her no more, and asked her not to write about it yet. Heller agreed, but occasionally checked export records at the Commerce Department.

She ran across two published items in April, 1975, that shed light on the hints. One was contained in a newsletter published by a Ralph Nader organization. It mentioned an "off-the-record" session with Vice President Nelson Rockefeller and quoted Rockefeller as saying the oil embargo of 1973–74 would have been worse had it not been for a "secret deal by my brother." When Heller called Rockefeller's office for details on the secret deal, she was told the reference had actually been to someone else's brother, whose identity could not be divulged. Then an article appeared in *New York* magazine on the financing of Congressman Carey's successful campaign for governor in 1974 by Carey's oil magnate brother, Edward. In the middle of the article, Heller found a telling nugget of information. Carey's brother, Edward, had made a secret oil deal with Libya. That sent Heller back to the FEO, asking questions and checking records, now working furiously to dig out the story. She found helpful sources and soon had enough to publish.

The story, which ran June 22, 1975, in Cox Newspapers in Dayton, Ohio, Atlanta, Georgia, and West Palm Beach, Florida, began, "With the backing of powerful political allies, an old friend of Alabama Senator John J. Sparkman and the brother of Governor Hugh Carey of New York reaped millions in profits in a secret oil deal at the height of the Arab embargo last year."

Sparkman acknowledged that he had interceded at the White House and the Commerce Department to get approval of three oil export licenses for a company owned by an Alabama oilman. The licenses permitted the oilman to sidestep a price limit of $5.10 per barrel on domestic crude oil by exporting it. He sold a million barrels to a Bahamian oil refinery owned by Edward Carey for $13.51 per barrel—$8 million more than he could get under domestic price controls. Carey's refinery later shipped the oil back to the United States and sold it to New York utilities for up to $23 a barrel.

When the FEO learned about the first export license in December, 1973, it tried briefly to block further approvals, but capitulated under political pressure. One former FEO official told Heller that Hugh Carey, then a member of the powerful House Ways and Means Committee, had contacted him personally. He had written a memo on the incident for his files. Another source in the FEO said he had seen the memo. But FEO officials said they could find no such memo. Hugh Carey denounced the story as a lie.

The FEO and the Justice Department ordered investigations. In February, 1976, Attorney General Edward H. Levi announced that a federal grand jury had failed to uncover "credible evidence" that Hugh Carey had contacted the FEO to help unblock the oil export license. A New York grand jury was still investigating.

Heller had picked off a spicy piece of a national exposé in 1969. The Los Angeles *Times* revived its 1966 story about U.S. Supreme Court Justice Williams O. Douglas' $12,000-a-year post as head of a private foundation supported by a mortgage on a Las Vegas hotel and casino. Heller got a tip that Douglas was involved in a Dominican Republic casino with a Florida gangster and Albert Parvin, the man who set up the foundation with proceeds from his sale of the Flamingo hotel and casino. She met a state government investigator in Florida, however, who told her the story she was chasing was in Las Vegas. There she got a lead that sent her to Reno, where she went to lunch with a friend who brought along another friend.

"I've got something that would be dynamite," said the friend's friend.

"How can I get it?" asked Heller.

"I'd like to give it to you," said the man, "but I can't."

Heller contrived to visit his home, where she was served drinks, but no information. They dined at the Harrah Club in Lake Tahoe, where Heller tried to inveigle the dynamite out of him during the Bobbie Gentry show. Heller is not a good bluffer, she says, but she can be persistent. Finally, at 4:30 in the morning, the man left, instructing Heller to meet him at his office at 9:30.

She showed up on the dot and he pulled out of a desk drawer a copy of a contract between Parvin and Meyer Lansky, the national crime syndicate's chief money man. The contract, as Heller disclosed in her October 22, 1969, story, gave Lansky a $200,000 finder's fee for setting up the Flamingo sale, the sale that financed a foundation headed by a U.S. Supreme Court Justice.

That was the twist, Heller believes, that gave the story its hell-raising power. She received a call from Robert Hartmann, the chief assistant to House Republican Leader Gerald Ford. Hartmann said Ford was preparing an impeachment resolution against Douglas and would like to know more about the Lansky connection. But Heller didn't know any more than what she had written. Ford's impeachment move failed.

Stories like that are valuable to an investigative reporter even if they don't produce tangible outcomes. They build a reputation that attracts tips. "The more stories I write," says Heller, "the more I get."

It was a frustrating time for Bette Orsini of the St. Petersburg *Times*. More than a year had gone by since she had disclosed connections between Florida Education Commissioner Floyd Christian and a corporate network behind companies that had been awarded $912,000 in state board of education contracts. Christian had denied getting any money out of it. "Not a nickel," he said. A state legislative committee named to investigate Christian had displayed little sign of activity. Orsini felt stalemated because the important evidence was missing. She had not been able to show that Christian had received a payoff.

She had proven quite clearly that Christian had lied.

Orsini's first story, in August, 1972, had disclosed that the principal figure behind the companies awarded contracts for a reading test system, mobile classroom design, and construction of the mobile classrooms, was Robert N. Bussey, a "longtime friend and on-and-off banking associate" of Christian. Christian said he had signed the contracts in 1970 and 1971 routinely, without knowing much about them or that Bussey had anything to do with the companies. He said he had had no other dealings with the companies or their principals.

In Washington, however, Orsini learned that Christian had contacted federal officials to urge approval of a $1.5-million federal grant for a five-state reading test project. The project included an $884,000 subcontract for Motivations Systems Inc., a company that held the $400,000 reading test contract with the Florida board of education. Orsini discovered that Christian had arranged a meeting of educators from several states during a convention of school administrators at Atlantic City, New Jersey, in the spring of 1971 to promote participation in the federal grant application and explain the Motivation Systems reading test. Christian had been accompanied to the Atlantic City meeting by the president of Motivation Systems Inc., James T. Glisson, and a Mr. Bussey.

In pursuit of details about the Atlantic City meeting, Orsini telephoned school administrators and university professors around the country. A University of Texas professor mentioned there had also been a 1970 meeting in Luxembourg.

"Did Mr. Christian stay with you there?" Orsini asked.

"No," said the professor. "He was in a different hotel."

Christian admitted his attendance at the Luxembourg meeting, which concerned an investment fund controlled by Bussey. He said it had nothing to do with the $400,000 reading test contract he signed five months later.

These disclosures caused embarrassment for Christian, and trouble for Orsini. Christian called her an irresponsible reporter on a vendetta against him and demanded that her editors pull her off the investigation. Orsini was still on the investigation as 1974 began, but discouraged by her failure to pin down proof of a payoff.

Orsini had been drawn into the investigation after a neighbor of an editorial writer complained about school reading tests. Orsini found a great deal of confusion and agitation among teachers over such procedures as teaching the test to children before they took it. The reporter wrote an article about that, but also decided to look at the contract for the tests. Once she was in the records, one thing led to another.

The corporation that held the reading test contract, she found, had the same address as the corporation that was to design the mobile classrooms. She attacked the records in earnest. State board of education employes were uneasy, but the white-haired, self-possessed reporter handled them smoothly. "I've found I get more by being polite and firm," she says, "than by courting confrontations."

Orsini had no inside sources to help her, said St. Petersburg *Times* Editor Eugene Patterson in a March 16, 1975, column. She was "on her own, without guidance," and "found herself plunged into a bewildering jungle of dead ends." But, she "noticed certain tracks kept crossing" in a "maze of seemingly disconnected corporations" that had been "erected deliberately to confuse even a certified public accountant."

Orsini pressed on, Patterson wrote. "Equipped only with a reporter's skepticism and an uncommon tenacity, she tracked the corporation addresses back one by one to a common address in St. Petersburg. She matched up recurring names on various boards of directors and found them interlocking. She traced each of the companies' dealings with the state's commissioner of education. She began asking questions of Christian and others and met a stone wall."

During the investigation, stories had surfaced in the *Wall Street Journal* about a lawsuit accusing Bussey of looting a recently collapsed Bahamian bank. Orsini searched assiduously through some of the bank's records for a connection with Christian, but couldn't get access to all the records. She reaped little more for her efforts than a few stories about Bussey's woes in the Bahamas.

She kept in touch, however, with the lawyers handling the bank's liquidation and investors who had been victimized. One day early in 1974 a letter arrived from an investor saying he had heard about a mysterious bank account that liquidators were trying to trace. Orsini found the liquidators puzzling over $130,000 in certificates of deposit issued to Zera R. Tom. Several complex transactions had been involved and some files were missing. It had been established that at least $10,000 of the money had been transferred from the Robert N. Bussey Trust Account. The liquidators had no idea, however, who Zera R. Tom was.

Orsini did, though. She knew that Christian had a daughter named Zera and a son called Tom.

Four days after Orsini's disclosure of the secret bank account, Christian admitted to the legislative committee that the account was his. Three months later he was indicted on nineteen counts of bribery, conspiracy, and perjury. As state legislators organized an impeachment investigation, Christian resigned. A year later, he pleaded no contest to three felony charges, admitting to $29,000 in kickbacks. He was sentenced in April, 1975, to seven years' probation and ordered to pay $43,273 in fines and reparations. Before the month was over, he also pleaded guilty to federal income tax evasion.

Orsini, wrote editor Patterson, "gave nearly three years of her life to the fulfillment of a free press's investigative function—to scrutinize government officially, independently and steadfastly, from the outside, as a part of the public and acting to inform it.

"And she did it without sources and without help, under pressure, alone," said Patterson, a former editor of the Atlanta *Constitution* and a former managing editor at the Washington *Post*. "I have never seen this piece of work excelled."

Ushered cordially into Bennett Cerf's plush office in New York, Jessica Mitford almost felt bad about the purpose of her visit. But not bad enough to desist.

The subject of the interview was the Famous Writers School, a mail-order outfit that advertised Cerf and several other American literary lights as members of its "Guiding Faculty."

What, asked Mitford chattily, did Cerf do as a member of the guiding faculty?

Not much, Cerf allowed. "I know nothing about the business and selling end and I care less. I've nothing to do with how the school is run." Cerf, Mitford discovered, did no teaching, recruiting of teachers, setting of standards, or grading of student work. But he assured her it was a good company. "It's been run extremely cleanly," he said. "I mean that from the bottom of my heart, Jessica."

Did he do anything at all in his guiding role?

"I go there once or twice a year," said Cerf, "to talk to the staff." He also had contributed a section on preparation of manuscripts for a textbook.

Well, said Mitford, phrasing an innocent-sounding time bomb, how many books by the school's students had been published by Cerf's publishing company, Random House?

"Oh, come on, you must be pulling my leg," said Cerf. "No person of any sophistication whose books we'd publish would have to take a mail-order course to learn how to write."

My goodness, what, then, was the purpose of the school?

It served an extremely valuable purpose, Cerf explained, in teaching professors, lawyers, and businessmen how to write intelligibly. Sure, mail-order selling had some built-in deficiencies, like a hard sales pitch to ensnare the gullible, but that was unavoidable in the cold-blooded world of business. "Don't quote me on that 'gullible' business," he said.

"Would you like to paraphrase it?"

"Well, you could say in general I don't like the hard sell, yet it's the basis of all American business."

"Sorry," said Mitford. "I don't call that a paraphrase. I shall have to use both of them. By the way, why do you lend your name to this hard-sell proposition?"

"Frankly," said Cerf, with his most charming grin, "I'm an awful ham. I love to see my name in the papers."

And the compensation for the use of his name?

That was a private matter.

Cerf was pained to discover his words in Mitford's exposé of the school in the July, 1970, issue of the *Atlantic Monthly*. "I told her I was suspicious of direct mail advertising," he complained to a *Time* magazine reporter. "Now I'm even more suspicious of people who go out and do hatchet jobs and get paid for it."

Mitford's article led to the closing of the school. It revealed that the "Famous Writers" contributed little more than the use of their names in advertising that implied they would grade students' work and give advice. Several of the "Famous Writers" told Mitford that people who believed advertising were naive. The school's profits were based on a large dropout percentage and an aggressive dunning program to collect the full $785 to $900 fee from the dropouts.

Mitford had embarked on the investigation after her husband, Oakland, California, lawyer Robert Treuhaft, had tangled with the school's intransigence over a course sold to a seventy-two-year-old immigrant widow who could hardly speak English, let alone write it. Mitford put an ad in the *Saturday Review* asking persons who had taken the course to contact her. After discovering by telephone and personal visit that the "Famous Writers" did not know much about the school, she called at its office in Westport, Connecticut.

Acquiring the facts that scandalized the literary world proved no trouble at all. "People have faith in what they're doing," she says. "They will tell you a great deal. They think that what they are doing is right, and have no reason not to tell you."

An engaging, witty Britisher, Mitford broke into muckraking with a smash hit in 1963, her book, *The American Way of Death*. The book's revelations about the inflated cost of funerals captivated an American public that had been wondering when someone would muster the courage to mention it.

Her husband had put her on to that one, too. For many years the executive secretary of the Civil Rights Congress in the East Bay area of San Francisco, Mitford found herself with nothing to do when the organization folded in 1956. She had no formal education or job training, and was thirty-eight. The younger of her two children was nine. She decided to write a book. That was *Daughters and Rebels*, an account of her childhood in England as one of an eccentric baron's six daughters.

About the time she finished the book in 1960, she became aware of her husband's grumblings about morticians. They seemed to know exactly how much to charge for a funeral so that it used up every last penny of a man's union death benefits. He had helped organize a group to work toward lower funeral prices with collective bargaining. Mitford started reading the funeral industry literature that Treuhaft brought home, copies of *Mortuary Management* and the *National Funeral Service Journal*. They were filled with advice on maximizing income from casket sales and inducing bereaved relatives to think they needed services they didn't. She found the publications, she says, "riveting."

Having taken up writing, she tried her hand at an article about the mortuary business. Because the subject was too morbid, however, no one would buy it, except a small, obscure magazine named *Frontier*. It was reprinted by a funeral directors' organization and Mitford was invited to debate the issue on TV, which caused a local uproar. Writer Roul Tunley dropped by to interview her for a *Saturday Evening Post* article entitled, "Can You Afford to Die?" Deluged with letters, Mitford wrote to Tunley suggesting he write a book on the subject. He wrote back, saying, "Why don't you write one?" Why not, indeed.

Mitford has written countless magazine articles and taught courses in investigative journalism at Yale University and San Jose State University, but she's known mostly for her books. Her others are *The Trial of Dr. Spock*, and *Kind and Usual Punishment*, which exposed the barbarities and absurdities of America's prison system.

The prison book grew out of an *Atlantic Monthly* article in 1971 on indeterminate sentences. The American Civil Liberties Union had asked her to write it, so she asked the ACLU to mail 150 copies of the magazine to the libraries of thirteen penal institutions in California. She was identified in the front of the magazine as the wife of lawyer Treuhaft and she knew prisoners could correspond confidentially with attorneys. She hoped to attract letters from inmates on prison life and conditions. It worked, she says, very nicely.

Mitford found out for herself about prison life, however. As part of an eight-day conference on crime and corrections at Shenandoah in Virginia, conferees were required to spend a day and a night in a jail. Mitford and eight other women served their sentences in the District of Columbia Women's Detention Center. Despite the brevity and superficiality of her encounter with the prison system, Mitford came away shaken by the humiliation, self-disgust, and depression she had been caused to feel. There must be some other way, she wrote in her book, to protect society from crime.

"You folks interested in buying a car?"

Miriam Ottenberg pulled out the newspaper and showed the salesman the first item in the ad, an almost new Chevrolet for $1,235.

"We don't have that one anymore," said the salesman, though the news-paper had come off the press only a few minutes earlier. He ran his finger down the list of "repossessions" to a year-old Chevrolet for $1,070. "We have that," he said, "but you wouldn't want it. It used to be a police car."

When Ottenberg and a companion insisted on seeing some of the repossessed automobiles in the ad, the salesman took them on a tour of crumpled fenders, flat tires, and missing headlights. "All these repossessed cars are like that," he said. "Even if they look all right on the outside, you can't tell. A man can ruin an engine in twenty minutes driving without oil. It would cost more to repair one of these repossessed cars than to buy one of our good cars. Here, let me show you something you'd like."

He tried to interest them in a new Chevrolet at $1,895. They decided to test drive a three-year-old Mercury on sale for $1,495. Back at the lot, the salesman took them into an office, pulled out a form and started asking questions about Ottenberg's credit. She protested she didn't want anything written down until she knew how much it was going to cost.

"This doesn't mean anything," said the salesman. "We do it all the time. After I get this down we can talk terms."

Ottenberg gave him the credit information.

The salesman left and came back with another man. Ottenberg said she wanted to know how much it would cost per month.

The second man began filling out papers. He said he could explain easier when he had it down on paper. When he had the papers ready, he asked about the down payment.

"Your ad," Ottenberg reminded him, "says one dollar down. I have it with me."

"Of course," he said, "that's only where people's credit is good. Now I'm sure yours is good, but can't you make a down payment? Don't you have anything?"

Ottenberg finally conceded she had $100 in a savings account.

How soon could she bring it in?

Well, she guessed, when the bank opened.

At last he showed her the documents. There was a price of $1,495, a down payment of $1, a "pickup payment" of $100, and a balance due of $1,394, with one payment of $394 and a final payment of $1,000 both due within a week.

"I can't pay $1,394 in a week," Ottenberg protested. "I don't have all that money."

"Oh, we'll arrange that. We get you a second mortgage, just like on a house, and that takes care of the $394. Then we get the $1,000 financed through a bank."

She asked about finance charges and insurance.

"That's all arranged by the bank," he said. "We have nothing to do with that."

"Well, how much would I have to pay a month?"

"How much can you pay?"

She told him fifty-five dollars.

He said that would be all right. Fifty-five dollars would cover both loans.

"Could you just give me an idea of how much it will all be?"

The salesman did a series of rapid calculations on a sheet of paper, then threw the sheet away. He never did give her a specific amount for a monthly payment.

But Ottenberg, with the help of information she had acquired earlier, already knew the answer to the real question: how buyers of used cars were fooled into thinking they paid one amount and found out later they were actually paying a lot more. It was a sleight of hand trick, done with two contracts. Once a buyer signed the $1,394 contract for the Mercury, he would be taken to a small loan company to borrow $394. Then the used car dealer would say he couldn't get a bank loan and had to go to a finance company, without pointing out that the finance charges would be much higher. He would write a new contract, with a new set of figures and charges making a total for the whole deal about $500 higher. If the buyer balked at signing the second contract, he would be reminded he already was committed to the $394 loan and obligated to pay the rest under the first contract he had signed. Though this wouldn't be true, the customer wouldn't know it. Feeling unsure and helpless, he would sign the second contract.

Ottenberg learned nothing at the next lot. As she approached, a man ran up, saying, "Hold it, Sam! This little lady is from the Washington *Star*. She's an investigator."

Ottenberg's investigation of fraud and trickery among used car dealers, years ahead of America's consumer movement, won a Pulitzer Prize in 1960. This was twenty-three years after her first newspaper investigation, in which she and a fellow reporter posed as a married couple to uncover a baby broker ring. In the years since, she had exposed narcotics traffic, gangland operations, phony marriage counselors, and a scheme by the postwar Navy to discourage young sailors from leaving when their enlistments were up.

In 1963, she became intrigued by a line in a speech by Attorney General Robert Kennedy: "We're about to have a breakthrough against crime." No one else took particular note, but Ottenberg suspected it was the tip of something big. Intensive questioning of Justice Department sources led her to the discovery that someone in the Mafia was spilling a sensational story to federal agents. Several sources finally told her the details after she agreed not to write a story without obtaining Justice Department clearance.

She sat on the story from April to August, until she got a call that the story had been given to Peter Maas for an article in the *Saturday Evening Post*. Moving quickly, Ottenberg got into print first with her scoop on Joe Valachi, the mobster who turned canary because he believed he had been mistakenly marked for death as an informer.

It was the 1959 series on used car cheats, though, that started Ottenberg on the road to fame. Under the title, "Used Car Buyer Beware," the articles drew such an astonishing response from readers that the next year Ottenberg did "Homeowner Beware," an investigation of home improvement swindles. Then came "Investors Beware" on shady stock issues, and "Debtor Beware" on exploitation by debt consolidation firms. Ottenberg was the toast of Washington as the "Beware Girl."

Consumer investigations became so much a specialty that when Ottenberg retired in 1974, she was given the first Honorary Postal Inspector certificate ever awarded by the Post Office. *The Postal Inspection Service Bulletin* pointed out that as an investigative journalist, Ottenberg had been "involved in this unique type of reporting long before it came in vogue." It said the award was for helping the Postal Inspection Service protect the public from victimization by fraudulent mail schemes.

"Investigative reporting has been my whole life," Ottenberg says. "My purpose has always been to expose the bad and promote the good, not to destroy anyone. I've gotten a bunch of new laws and new regulations passed, and a lot of bad guys have left town."

She never ran out of things to investigate. When it came time for the big retirement party in September, 1974, Ottenberg tore herself away from her current probe to attend. Then she went back to finish the investigation, and after that wrote for the *Star* as a freelancer. She was retired from the *Star*, but not from investigating.

Fraudulent vocational schools might be duping thousands of young Americans out of millions of dollars, but Jean Carper gradually realized they couldn't do it without the federal government's help.

This came into focus as she interviewed administrators at the U.S. Office of Education for a magazine article on vocational school rip-offs. The OE administered the government's student loan program that made it possible for poor young people to attend the schools. Without the money from the loan program, Carper came to understand as she talked to the people at OE, many of the schools couldn't stay in business.

There were hints of worse. The OE had its own collection bureau. When a student dropped out of a school, as many did, he still had to repay the government. The banks didn't dawdle when a loan became delinquent. They whipped out their government loan guarantees and collected the money. Then the government was stuck, unless the OE collectors could wring it out of the ex-students. It mattered not if the school they attended was a fraud. The student borrowed the money; the student had to repay it. This, it occurred to Carper, was a better story than her original one.

Better, perhaps, but not as easy to get. The OE was not so generous with information about itself. Student loan records were not open to the public. A frontal assault demanding access to the records would clearly be counter-productive. A short, unassuming blonde freelancer, Carper insinuated herself into the scenery.

"I'm very low key," she says. "I get much more from infiltrating. I spent a lot of time at OE quietly, looking through files and records. People began to think I worked there. I found by talking to people where to go for further information. If you talk to people long enough, they tell you things. I even got into nonpublic records."

Carper's article, which appeared in the Washington *Post* of April 27, 1975, described several poignant cases. One was George R. Dominquez of Rosemead, California, who had taken a management course in an airline school on a federally insured $1,200 loan. He was being forced to pay even though the course had been dropped by the school and he was on welfare. Linda Leslie of Oneanta, Alabama, was being dunned for $1,500 despite having dropped out of a commercial college course that had disillusioned her. There were 1,200 students like Dominquez and Leslie, many of them victims of fraudulent schools. OE had organized an army of 235 collectors to "persuade" students to pay up.

Consumer affairs and health subjects are Carper's specialties. She coauthored the book revealing the dangers of food additives, *Eating May Be Hazardous to Your Health,* with Food and Drug Administration biochemist Jacqueline Verrett, after she discovered Verrett's findings on the perils of cyclamates. Earlier she had written *Not With a Gun,* a case history of a home-improvement swindle; *The Dark Side of the Marketplace,* a catalogue of consumer frauds and product hazards coauthored with U.S. Senator Warren G. Magnuson; and *Bitter Greetings,* one of the first noteworthy attacks on the military draft.

Bitter Greetings contained previously undisclosed information from a secret Pentagon study that not even Congress had been able to get. Carper spotted a copy on the desk of a U.S. Labor Department official as she was winding up her research for the book. She cast feverishly about for a way to get a look at it. They were talking about statistics. Could he get her copies? He left the room.

Carper scanned the report, rapidly taking notes. It said a phaseout of the draft was feasible. There were figures that differed from others released earlier by the Pentagon. It was a satisfying scoop.

A bit lucky, perhaps. "But," says Carper, "the important thing is to be alert."

No, said the young men, they didn't know anything about the former tenant, except that she had a roommate called Mizmoon Soltysik. Maybe the lady who lived upstairs knew something.

Marilyn Baker climbed the steps and asked the woman if she had any information on Patricia Soltysik.

"I wouldn't tell any pig reporter if I did," snapped the woman.

"Look, lady," Baker snapped back. "This is what I get paid to do. Maybe I'm not clever, but I don't live off food stamps or welfare, and I sure as hell pay the taxes that let people like you live off them. Now all I want are some simple answers to some straight questions."

The woman blinked. "Oh, what the hell. Okay. The other girl moved out last week. The feds have been around here. They were looking for this Soltysik. I didn't know her myself, but some of the neighbors say she was a heavy lesbian."

Baker found the landlord at his flower shop. His thick accent was hard to understand, but Baker gathered that tenant Soltysik had been visited frequently by black men.

Most of the neighbors around Soltysik's previous residence in Berkeley, a rundown apartment converted into a commune, wouldn't talk to Baker. But the forty-four-year-old blonde from KQED-TV in San Francisco had never been known to give up easily during twenty-eight years as a reporter. She kept knocking on doors, extracting scraps of information that gradually formed a vivid portrait. Soltysik was obviously a dominant force in the Symbionese Liberation Army, the group of would-be revolutionaries who had kidnaped Patty Hearst, the daughter of newspaper publisher Randolph A. Hearst.

Baker had traced Soltysik through voting records after a telephone caller whispered a name that sounded like "Sol-tie-sick." The caller said the name belonged to a woman who was "the brains of the SLA." Baker searched through hundreds of voter registration cards for names starting with "Sol-" before she found it.

Patricia "Mizmoon" Soltysik fitted perfectly into the picture of the SLA that Baker had been patching together well ahead of other reporters. Her first exclusive disclosure about the SLA, broadcast three weeks before the Hearst kidnaping, had been based on materials she found inside a burned out former headquarters that police forgot to guard after arresting two SLA members for killing Oakland School Superintendent Marcus Foster. That report said the SLA's leaders were women. Now Baker knew the identity of one.

Another whose identity Baker had uncovered was Nancy Ling Perry. When the two arrested SLA members were first stopped by police while cruising in a van, they said they were looking for Mrs. DeVoto's house. Baker later traced Mrs. DeVoto to a city in the East through the real estate agent who handled the rental of the burned out house. When Baker described to Mrs. DeVoto the short, dark-haired woman who had been seen running from the burning house, Mrs. DeVoto said it sounded like Nancy Ling, whom she had known in school.

Street people sources in Berkeley cultivated by Baker's long-haired, twenty-six-year-old son, Jeff, produced leads to Gilbert Perry, Nancy Ling's ex-husband. Baker interviewed him for the first exclusive revelation of an SLA leader's name.

Her next big scoop was the identity of the two black men who helped kidnap Patty Hearst on February 4, 1974. Like the Soltysik story, it originated with an anonymous telephoned whisper. "The two blacks are Wheeler and De-----, escaped cons." The second name sounded like Defis or maybe Debreeze. But the important clue was "escaped cons."

Baker phoned a prison official she'd known for years, and told him the names. Try Vacaville for Wheeler, he said, Soledad for the other. A report came in from another KQED reporter about talk in Berkeley of a "black dude" who said he had escaped from Soledad prison and called himself "Cinque." A source at Soledad said the name must be De Freeze, Donald D. De Freeze, who had escaped almost a year earlier. Did he have a nickname? As a matter of fact, yes. "Cinque."

Calls to the Vacaville prison, a medical and psychiatric facility, unearthed details about Thero Wheeler. He had been a member of a revolutionary group called the Venceremos and had received visits from a white woman connected with the law firm representing Joseph Remiro, one of the men arrested for the Foster murder.

Baker held up her scoop for two days until the Hearst family gave its okay. In the meantime, she learned that De Freeze had been hated by fellow inmates at Soledad as an informer, had put a criminal companion in prison in a deal with police for a lighter sentence, and had beaten and robbed a black prostitute when she asked to be paid. He was the SLA's token black, Baker wrote in her book on the Patty Hearst kidnaping and the SLA, *Exclusive!*

By March 22, with the help of son Jeff's street contacts at the University of California in Berkeley, Baker was able to broadcast the identities of all the people at SLA's core—Soltysik, Ling-Perry, De Freeze, Wheeler, Angela Atwood, William Wolfe, Emily and Bill Harris, Camilla Hall.

Baker got plenty of attention for her successes, and not just from fellow reporters. After her De Freeze–Wheeler disclosure, KQED got a call saying there was a plastic bomb in the studio "meant for Marilyn Baker." Police arrived for a search. Then they tore Baker's car apart looking for the bomb. No bomb, but much sweating.

A few days earlier, another caller had said, "Shut Baker up, or else!" Baker had a police guard for a week.

Shortly before police discovered the SLA's hideout in Los Angeles, Baker got messages that Tania, formerly known as Patty Hearst but now a full-fledged convert to SLAism, would kill Baker "in living color" at the KQED studio. Police surrounded the studio hoping to catch the revolutionaries. But nothing happened.

Ironically, Baker was not at the scene when six SLA members were trapped in a burning Los Angeles house and killed. KQED, a public TV station, couldn't afford to send a camera crew to Los Angeles when they got word that morning that police were staking out a house. Baker refused to go without a camera crew. She had to settle for enterprising coverage by telephone.

She got an address from a Los Angeles police source, and had the KQED librarian make a list of phone numbers near that address from a Los Angeles cross-reference directory. Dialing frantically, she located a man who lived next door to the object of the police siege. He gave her a blow-by-blow account. Baker was ahead of everyone even when she wasn't there.

10

Little Giants

JACK WHITE MET a man in 1973 who suggested that White would find it interesting to know exactly how much income tax President Nixon had been paying. Newspaper and magazine articles had said Nixon must have paid little or no federal income tax since becoming president in 1969, but offered no facts, figures, or proof.

White was winding up a probe of the U.S. Navy's decision to cut back operations at Rhode Island naval bases. He told his editors at the Providence *Journal* he'd like to pursue the Nixon tax tip in Washington. White's work as Newport bureau manager had been impressive and he had demonstrated a flair for investigative persistence. The editors gave their approval.

Much of White's three weeks in Washington was spent floundering. But his search for someone in the federal government who would show him cold, hard, indisputable figures on an official document finally paid off.

His October 3, 1973, story revealed that Nixon had paid $792.81 in federal income taxes in 1970, $878.03 in 1971. These figures, moreover, represented the President's final tax bills after receiving refunds of $72,614.43 and $58,889.41, respectively. White attributed the information to "documents provided by government sources," stating he had not seen Nixon's complete tax returns for those two years.

White is still surprised that journalists have expected him to identify his source. A *Time* magazine reporter became distraught when he refused to reveal who had shown him the documents. Three months after his story appeared, the IRS announced the resignation of an employe it said had given the information to White. The IRS did not release the employe's name and White offers no further word on the matter.

The story touched a deep and angry nerve in the body public. White was buried under an avalanche of phone calls from newspapers, TV networks, wire services, and radio stations. Though drained by the Watergate scandal, Americans reacted with a new surge of indignation. A columnist calculated that Nixon, on a presidential salary of $200,000 a year, had paid the same amount of tax as a worker who made $7,000 a year and had one dependent.

Pressure mounted on the President to defend himself. In a televised appearance before the Associated Press Managing Editors convention in November, Nixon confirmed he had paid only "nominal amounts" of taxes in 1970 and 1971.

Nixon made his tax returns public on December 8, 1973, an act unprecedented in American history. A congressional committee began a probe of the President's taxes. Nixon said he would pay any tax the committee said he owed. The IRS reopened the case. It was disclosed that Nixon had claimed a $576,000 deduction for vice-presidential papers donated to the public, a deduction later ruled illegal because the gift had been made after the effective date of a new law prohibiting such deductions. Criminal charges later were brought against Nixon tax advisers and accountants for back-dating the gift to make it appear legal.

White remembers thinking in wonderment, "This one story did all that?"

As investigative reporting, the Nixon tax story was no spectacular effort, White concedes, even though it won a 1974 Pulitzer Prize for national reporting.

A stocky former construction worker and tugboat captain with bushy red hair and piercing blue eyes, the thirty-one-year-old White had been pushing for a full-time investigative team at the *Journal*. After the Pulitzer Prize, and with New England's Mafia boss, Raymond Patriarca, about to get out of prison, the editors took him up on the idea. They assigned thirty-year-old Randall Richard, a former Washington correspondent and assistant city editor, to work with White.

White and Richard posed as patients in a 1975 investigation of "scribblers"—doctors who sold prescriptions for amphetamines, barbiturates and other dangerous drugs for the price of an office visit. One needed only to know the right way to ask, usually by claiming to be overweight.

On the first visit to one doctor, the reporter was greeted, "So, you want to go on a diet?" The reporter was weighed while wearing combat boots and a black leather jacket. Others in the waiting room talked freely of being there just to get drug prescriptions, some for resale on the street.

Over a five-month period, White and Richard got prescriptions from the doctor for 150 doses of amphetamine. When they later returned, identifying themselves as reporters, the doctor stressed his strictness about prescribing amphetamines for weight control. He said the reporters, for instance, would not qualify. Informed he had earlier prescribed amphetamines for these same reporters when they posed as patients, the doctor calmly checked his files and observed that he "must have been impressed" by their sincerity in desiring to lose weight.

The articles described the reporters' experiences with three known "scribblers" and seven other doctors from whom they had obtained prescriptions. A past president of the state medical society deplored the situation, but said the society could do nothing about it. The state health director said he had insufficient authority to act against unethical prescription practices, but the attorney general ruled that he had plenty. The health department's medical examining boards then scheduled 1976 hearings on revocation of licenses.

White and Richard, meanwhile, had turned up fascinating facts about an August 14 armed robbery at a private vault company in which safe deposit boxes had been looted of cash and valuables eventually estimated to be worth as much as $3 million. The reporters located a list of box holders, which revealed that one was a business associate of Mafia boss Patriarca. Two other box holders were under investigation for income tax evasion. Further checking revealed that one of every five box holders had underworld ties. One of the pair's articles disclosed that organized crime figures had known about the robbery in advance, indicating an inside job and possibly an insurance fraud scheme.

In another organized crime investigation, a mobster gave White the details of an assassination attempt, but White never ran the story because it might have gotten the source killed. "It's a great story," says White, "but we don't want to be responsible for someone getting hurt."

Newspaper investigations of organized crime, White believes, are still in their infancy. He's developing sources and building files on the underworld because he believes its cancerous spread into countless facets of American life may turn out to be the biggest story he ever writes.

As they methodically analyzed the records of more than a thousand land rezoning cases in Florida's fastest growing county, Christopher Cubbison and Robert Hooker of the St. Petersburg *Times* noticed several abrupt switches in outcome. An owner of eighteen acres, who had been turned down twice on requests for trailer park zoning, met success on his third attempt when two of the five Pinellas County commissioners changed their votes. Five months after the commissioners rejected a developer's application for rezoning of forty acres on a 3–2 vote, one of the no votes became a yes.

Sure they were on the right track, Cubbison and Hooker dug deeper into the details of the flip-flop cases, made a list of attorneys and developers who sported high percentages of success in their rezoning requests, and probed thoroughly into the backgrounds of everyone involved, especially the commissioners. Hooker, who says, "The public records turned out to be a gold mine," also studied campaign contribution reports. Then the two reporters interviewed developers, attorneys, real estate brokers, politicians, and government officials.

They learned enough in ten weeks to begin writing stories. Their first articles in February, 1974, outlined several switch cases, described the clique of lawyers, engineers and developers—many of them friends of the commissioners—who always got the rezonings they wanted, and exposed the commission's frequent disregard for environmental warnings by the county's planning and zoning staff. In one case, close friends of Commissioner A. Oliver McEachern made $1.6 million on a 365-acre tract after the commission hurriedly rezoned 120 acres of it without the usual staff review, and against guidelines the staff had recommended earlier. One article disclosed that four commissioners had switched their votes to approve a rezoning after a friend of McEachern bought the land.

One of the commissioners, Realtor George Brumfield, was already under investigation by Pinellas-Pasco State Attorney James Russell for trying to sell forty-five acres to a developer while the county was trying to buy the land for a park. Cubbison's and Hooker's articles prompted Russell to expand his probe.

"If we didn't have complete documentation," says Hooker, "we had enough to get authorities to investigate."

Their investigation had been inspired by recurrent rumors of wrongdoing in Pinellas County government. Cubbison, twenty-six, had attended an American Press Institute seminar on investigative reporting in the fall of 1973 as part of the paper's campaign under editor Eugene C. Patterson to specialize in investigative journalism and win recognition as the best medium-sized newspaper in the country. Cubbison was looking for a suitable project and Hooker, twenty-seven, had been frustrated by the lack of time to check into the corruption rumors about Pinellas County government, his regular beat.

The two reporters made a careful outline for the project. They wrote down their aims—examine all rezoning cases since 1969, check backgrounds and business dealings of all commissioners and their associates, probe possible connections between consultants and commissioners, end up at least with articles giving readers a clear view of how county government works. They listed all the people who might be helpful, set up a file system, and located a place to keep the files secure.

They kept probing after their first series. "We like to think we not only prompted an investigation," says Hooker, "but also helped sustain it." One article revealed how commissioners overruled the staff five times as often when a land development conglomerate controlled by several brothers named Green was involved. One of the Greens had contributed to a commissioner's campaign. Another story exposed a prominent politician's secret interest in a land deal that produced a $1.4-million profit after it was rezoned.

When it was all over, three of the rezonings had been reversed, four of the county commissioners were out of office, and eleven arrests had been made. After a conviction for taking payoffs, Brumfield helped the prosecution by strapping a recorder to his body for conversations with fellow commissioners and developers. Commissioner William D. Dockerty was sentenced to two years in prison. McEachern admitted taking five payoffs. Former commissioner W. E. Taylor confessed to accepting $5,000.

In the meantime, chief state capital reporter Martin Dyckman and education writer Bette Orsini maintained investigative pressure on other fronts. Because of St. Petersburg *Times* investigations, the state commissioner of education had pleaded no contest to three counts of bribery and perjury, the Judicial Qualifying Commission was investigating two state supreme court justices, and another state official was the target of a grand jury probe in Tampa. Editor Patterson's ambitions were making a deeply felt impression.

Hank Greenspun went to the safe in the corner of his office at the Las Vegas *Sun* and twirled the combination dial. "Don't watch," he said.

Presently Greenspun reached into the safe and extracted an attaché case, which he took to his huge desk and snapped open.

Inside was a sheaf of lined yellow sheets containing handwritten notes addressed to "Bob." Greenspun identified the handwriting as Howard Hughes'.

"That," said Greenspun, "is what caused Watergate."

Sam Dash, chief counsel for the Senate Watergate Committee that unraveled the scandal in front of a national television audience in 1973, has agreed with Greenspun.

It began, says Greenspun, at a Nixon press conference in Portland, Oregon, in August, 1971. Columnist Jack Anderson had just disclosed Hughes' $100,000 contribution to Nixon's campaign through Nixon's Florida friend, Bebe Rebozo. Several months earlier, Greenspun had revealed Hughes' sudden and mysterious departure from Las Vegas. When Greenspun saw White House Communications Director Herb Klein at the press conference, he told Klein that these Howard Hughes developments, combined with Anderson's earlier disclosure of Hughes' $205,000 loan to Nixon's brother, Donald, might sink Nixon's chances for reelection in 1972. Greenspun hinted to Klein that he was saving additional explosive material on Nixon-Hughes relationships for publication later.

Herbert Kalmbach, Nixon's personal attorney, paid a visit to Greenspun in October. Kalmbach tried to pry from the crusty, sixty-one-year-old publisher what he knew about Donald Nixon and the $100,000 delivered to Rebozo. Greenspun was not informative.

In a telephone conversation the following April with Wallace Turner, chief of *The New York Times'* San Francisco bureau, Greenspun mentioned that his collection of Howard Hughes memos was no doubt the world's largest. Turner put that in an article.

Though Greenspun didn't learn it until later, Attorney General John Mitchell assigned E. Howard Hunt and G. Gordon Liddy of the White House's special intelligence squad called the "plumbers" to get from Greenspun's safe and files what the publisher had on Donald Nixon and other Hughes connections with the President.

When Greenspun arrived at his office one early summer day in 1972 and discovered someone had broken into his office through the front window and tried to crack the safe, he figured it for a routine burglary attempt. Not until the following summer, while watching Senate Watergate Committee hearings on TV, did he know the truth.

According to committee counsel Dash, the purpose of the Watergate wiretaps on Democratic Party telephones was to detect calls from Greenspun or former Howard Hughes aide Robert Maheu to give the Democrats information on Nixon-Hughes connections for use in the presidential campaign.

Greenspun has published numerous Howard Hughes exclusives, using Maheu as a frequent source. The notes in Greenspun's attaché case were addressed to Maheu. Greenspun came to know so much about Hughes that when Hughes fled his Desert Inn penthouse and left Las Vegas suddenly in

November, 1970, Greenspun was convinced it wasn't voluntary. When Clifford Irving's "autobiography" of Hughes was announced, Greenspun turned to free-lance investigative writer James Phelan, who was in his office at the time, and said it must be a fake.

Phelan, who later was to prove that Irving had used a pirated copy of Phelan's own manuscript about Hughes to perpetrate the hoax, did not then agree with Greenspun. "It's no doubt authentic," he said.

"No way," said Greenspun. "Hughes would never meet anyone face to face."

Greenspun called Noah Dietrich, Hughes' right-hand man for many years, and asked his opinion. Dietrich thought it was genuine.

"No way," said Greenspun. "It's a fraud."

He turned to Phelan and said, "Jim, I'll kiss your ass one hundred thirty times in the middle of the Vegas Strip if that book isn't a fake."

Another time Greenspun got a call from an uncle in Canada telling him Hughes was connected with a new uranium mining company that was selling stock in Montreal. Greenspun phoned Phelan at his home in Long Beach, California, and asked him to investigate a fraudulent stock sale in the offing. Hughes, said Greenspun, would never let his name be used that way.

Phelan's investigation revealed the mining company had been formed by four of Hughes' personal aides. While publicity about a Hughes connection and plans to mine uranium sent the price of the stock soaring on the Canadian Stock Exchange, Phelan discovered the company's mining operations in Arizona to be a phantom. There were only untested mining claims and the company had no income except from the sale of stock. The Arizona headquarters was a back room in a small real estate office. Phelan's disclosures in Greenspun's newspaper led to tremors of scandal in Canada. The stock exchange chairman, also an official in the brokerage firm that had backed the stock, was suspended. Several investigations started up. The chairman of the Quebec Securities Commission went to Italy and telegraphed his resignation. Another stock exchange official committed suicide and two were indicted. Greenspun wasn't surprised.

He says he has a few surprises, however, in his attaché case, including Hughes' extraction of a promise from Hubert Humphrey, in exchange for campaign contributions, that Humphrey would do all he could to get atomic testing stopped in Nevada. Early in March, 1976, Greenspun published a story saying he had evidence that Cuban Premier Fidel Castro was behind President Kennedy's assassination.

Investigative swashbuckling and feisty independence have been Greenspun's trademarks ever since he bought a small Las Vegas newspaper from the International Typographical Union in 1950 and renamed it the *Sun*. He started a column that made blistering attacks on Nevada's most powerful politician, U.S. Senator Pat McCarran, and Wisconsin's Communist-hunting demogogue, Senator Joseph McCarthy. The *Sun* began probing into local corruption and conditions in the city's black ghetto. When the famous Kefauver hearings exposed the underworld backgrounds of gambling casino owners, Greenspun gleefully revealed their connections with McCarran's political machine.

McCarran and his friends struck back in 1952 with an advertising boycott by the hotels and casinos. Greenspun filed a $225,000 lawsuit alleging a conspiracy to drive him out of business. When Greenspun located a former hotel employe who testified she had taken a call from Washington the day the boycott had been arranged, the hotel-casino operators made a cash settlement and agreed to "continue present advertising policies" without trying to interfere with editorial policy.

In a 1954 investigation of a county sheriff's hand in local prostitution profits, Greenspun brought in an undercover agent named Pierre LaFitte to pose as a well-heeled hoodlum interested in buying a brothel. LaFitte was approached by Madame Roxie, who wanted to sell one of hers. LaFitte requested assurance that his investment would be protected from police interference. Several meetings were arranged with prominent attorneys and officials, including the sheriff and Nevada's lieutenant governor, who assured LaFitte he "wouldn't have any trouble." As LaFitte met with an attorney in a hotel suite to complete the arrangements, *Sun* reporter Ed Reid and an assistant district attorney hid in a closet with a tape recorder. The *Sun* ran a twelve-part series. The sheriff was indicted.

Greenspun won another extraordinary court victory while crossing swords with a leading Las Vegas attorney, George F. Franklin, Jr. He accused Franklin of making deals when he was city attorney that would have gotten him indicted except for the statute of limitations. Franklin sued for libel. Greenspun responded with articles alleging Franklin was involved in a black market adoption ring. Franklin filed more lawsuits. Greenspun disclosed that the judge in the case also was involved in the adoption racket, but the judge refused to disqualify himself.

When Greenspun was socked with a $190,000 judgment against him, the *Sun's* insurance company offered Franklin $75,000 to drop the case before Greenspun appealed. Greenspun refused to okay the deal. The insurance company insisted. An agreement was devised in which the insurance company paid $75,000 and washed its hands of the case. Greenspun would pay any final judgment in excess of that. When the judgment was overturned on appeal, Greenspun kept the $75,000.

Before becoming a newspaperman, Greenspun had lived an equally adventurous and colorful life. He had smuggled guns from Hawaii to help Israeli freedom fighters establish a new Jewish nation in 1948, seizing a private yacht in California and posing in Mexico as an agent of China to get the arms aboard a ship and the ship on its way. For this he was convicted of violating America's neutrality act, but President Kennedy pardoned him in 1961.

He once worked as a publicity man for Benjamin "Bugsy" Siegel's Flamingo Hotel, quitting after Siegel was murdered by his underworld compatriots in 1947. Greenspun then put his money in the New Desert Inn being built by a friend, Wilbur Clark, only to be squeezed out by Moe Dalitz and other Cleveland gangsters to whom Clark had turned for financing. Greenspun handled the Desert Inn's advertising and public relations until Dalitz told him one day to cancel advertising in the union-owned paper. Greenspun refused and soon quit to buy the newspaper.

Greenspun's latest investigative coup was the *Sun's* 1974 exposé of fraudulent silver certificate business by the American Independent Party's candidate for governor, James Ray Houston. A gas station operator had turned up at the *Sun's* office complaining that Houston's company refused to give him silver bullion for $52,000 worth of certificates he had bought. Greenspun sensed a rip-off.

Sun reporters found that Houston was operating a Ponzi scheme, in which money received from new investors is used to pay promised returns to earlier investors until sales fizzle out and everything collapses, with the schemer having absconded in the nick of time with his ill-gotten millions. Houston's company was selling certificates supposedly redeemable in "inflation-proof" silver bullion in ninety days, but had only a fraction of the bullion needed to meet the obligations. Investors were put off with excuses about trouble at the silver smelter.

Greenspun persuaded a security guard to look the other way while his men sneaked into Houston's main office, photographed the empty vault that Houston said contained vast amounts of silver, and made copies of the company's financial records. Confronted with evidence that his company was $2.4 million in the red and that nearly $2 million collected from investors had disappeared, Houston insisted he had silver and money to meet his obligations, but refused to say where it was.

In true Greenspun style, the *Sun* broke the story the day before the election. Noting that Houston had offered to give Nevada voters 25 million shares of stock in his company if he were elected, the story said, "Mr. Houston is giving nothing away because the stock is worthless." Houston, as might be expected, was not elected.

At the San Diego airport waiting for a plane to Los Angeles in April, 1973, Jim Drinkhall heard that Allen Dorfman had just left for Deming, New Mexico, in a twelve-seat Grumman Gulfstream jet owned by the Teamsters Union Central States Pension Fund. Why in the world, Drinkhall wondered, would the national crime syndicate's chief liaison with the pension fund be going to a small, out-of-the-way town in New Mexico?

Back in his office the next day at *Overdrive* magazine, the trucking industry publication that specializes in exposing Teamsters Union corruption and underworld connections. Drinkhall phoned Deming to verify that Dorfman's plane had landed. It had. He surmised that Dorfman had visited the La Costa

Country Club near San Diego, a plush resort built by the crime syndicate's Las Vegas gambling interests with a Teamsters pension fund loan, before heading for Deming. Posing as an employe of Dorfman, Drinkhall called the telephone company in San Diego and got the long distance phone numbers Dorfman had called from La Costa.

The people on the other end of the phone numbers were Chicago gangsters. More calls informed Drinkhall that the only place in Deming visited recently by Chicagoans was a small plastics factory. Drinkhall hastened to Deming to see what it was all about. There was scant information in the public records, but the mustachioed, thirty-two-year-old editor of *Overdrive* learned from workers at the factory that the company had big problems with money and faulty machinery. Drinkhall conned his way into the confidence of the company's pilot, who told him about trips to Las Vegas.

Though Drinkhall had been investigating the Teamsters and their pension funds on a full-time basis for only a few months, he had been probing intermittently since joining the magazine in 1961, the year it was founded by former trucker Michael Parkhurst. During those years, Drinkhall had cultivated a rich crop of sources inside the highest levels of the union and the pension fund. Now he called on one of them to check for a pension fund loan to the Deming plastics factory, and to get him copies of any documents relating to it.

The pension fund, Drinkhall discovered, had loaned more than $4 million to an Indiana toy manufacturer that had operated the factory until it went bankrupt. In 1971, a new Illinois company had been formed to reopen the plant and take over the indebtedness to the pension fund. The men behind the new company were close associates of Dorfman and the Chicago crime syndicate. One, Ron DeAngeles, was known as the Chicago mob's electronics expert and was a suspect in a 1967 bomb killing of a mobster who had turned government witness.

The new company had borrowed another $1.4 million from the pension fund on the basis of a letter from a Panama firm agreeing to buy the factory's products. Drinkhall knew from another investigation that the same company official had sent a letter to Bally Manufacturing Company of Chicago, a maker of slot machines and other gambling equipment. Obtaining a copy of the Bally letter, Drinkhall saw that the signatures on the two letters were different. The Deming letter, he concluded, was a fraud. His January, 1973, article exposing the deal concluded with this prediction: "Those involved may be about to engage in bankruptcy fraud. The company will proceed normally for a time, then 'problems' will arise, forcing it to go out of business. The loan will not have been paid off, of course, but the assets will have vanished."

Drinkhall's article caused the Justice Department's Organized Crime Task Force in Chicago to investigate. A year later, a grand jury indicted Dorfman, DeAngeles, Chicago Mafia leader Anthony Spilotro, and four others on charges of conspiracy to defraud the pension fund. Although the company went out of business in 1973 as Drinkhall predicted and all the money had been siphoned off, the defendants were acquitted at the end of their 1975 trial. One reason for the outcome was the murder of a key government witness by four men wearing ski masks and carrying shotguns who surprised the witness as he entered his office in a Chicago suburb with his wife and son. Another reason was a suspicion among jurors that the pension fund was a party to the scheme rather than a victim.

Driving to work one morning on the freeway, Drinkhall saw a truck from the "America on the Move" organization. He had been saving newspaper clippings about the "Move" program, a publicity campaign organized by Ed McMahon of TV's "Tonight Show" to boost the Teamsters Union's image. Drinkhall jotted down the truck's license number.

When he heard later that McMahon had been sued by someone, Drinkhall thought the "Move" program might be worth looking into. Tracing the license number to an office building, he found a business that had recently lost an account with the "Move" organization. The proprietor was angry. The result was Drinkhall's December, 1973, article exposing how McMahon and a partner had diverted $1.5 million of union funds intended for the publicity campaign into their own corporations, including one that was filming a movie in Israel, while America on the Move Inc. was besieged by lawsuits for nonpayment of bills. A few days after the article appeared, the Teamsters Union filed a $6.75 million damage suit against McMahon.

Eighteen months after Drinkhall's 1974 revelation that a thirty-four-year-old real estate man from San Diego named Allen R. Glick was organized crime's new front man in Las Vegas, other news media had yet to catch up with the story. In 1971, Glick was a salesman for a San Diego developer. Then he moved to another development firm and soon owned forty-five percent of its stock. In 1972, he borrowed $2.3 million from the corporation to join some friends in a $9 million purchase of the Hacienda Hotel in Las Vegas. By 1974, Glick was able to get a $62.7 million loan from a Teamsters pension fund to buy Recrion Corporation, owner of two hotel-casinos. Glick got another pension fund loan in 1975 to buy the new Airport Marina Hotel & Casino, giving him and his companies a total of $111 million in pension fund loans.

Drinkhall disclosed Glick's associations with such crime syndicate leaders as Dorfman, Spilotro, Meyer Lansky henchman Edward Buccieri, Frank "Lefty" Rosenthal, and Anthony "Fat Tony" Salerno of the New York Mafia. He also revealed that professional football players had invested in real estate ventures with Glick's San Diego corporation.

Already the nation's acknowledged Number One investigator of Teamsters Union iniquity and pension fund mischief, Drinkhall expanded into new territory in 1975 with a fifteen-month investigation of a complicated international swindle attempt, in which a bank was flimflammed by a flurry of Telex messages into granting a billion-dollar line of credit to finance the purchase of nonexistent platinum. The bank did issue the credit, but realized its mistake and hired a private investigative agency that retrieved it before the swindlers could use it.

Drinkhall took special pride in the story. A double agent for the CIA and the Russian secret police was involved, but not a single Teamster.

Corruption in a church social agency? Too far-out to believe. But that's what the caller said. Check into the low-income housing projects of the Catholic Church's Mount Carmel Guild. Talk to the black contractors who were supposed to be among the beneficiaries of the federal government's housing subsidy program, but who actually were being ripped off. It sounded unlikely to Bruce Locklin, the investigative news editor for the *Record* in Hackensack, New Jersey, but he decided to check into it.

Locklin called on the two contractors, Gilbert Bryan and Scott Oates, who operated a firm called Omart Construction Company. They had built a thirty-two-unit apartment project sponsored by the Mount Carmel Guild in nearby Englewood.

Bryan and Oates would discuss it only off the record. Locklin agreed. Omart, they said, had been squeezed. The Guild hadn't paid them but they had to pay their subcontractors. Worse than that was the way they had been treated when they asked for payment.

One day Bryan had complained to the Guild's housing division chief, Joseph A. Brown, and the Englewood project's construction manager, Frank Sproviero, that payments to Omart were past due. Bryan said his company might have to stop work until it got paid.

"No, you can't do that," Sproviero replied. "All of your bodies, they'll float in the goddamned river."

Oates didn't take this seriously when Bryan told him about it, but Bryan did. He had heard that Sproviero was a friend of a mobster. Sproviero, in fact, had sent workmen from the Englewood project to help install a swimming pool at the mobster's home.

The contractors didn't know the mobster's name, but they thought one of the workers who had been sent out to the house could be found at the Englewood project. He lived there and was the janitor.

The worker had only a vague recollection of where he had been taken to work on the pool. Locklin prevailed on him to get in his car and they drove around, taking streets that looked familiar to the janitor. The chances of finding the house seemed remote, but find it they did. Locklin recognized it as the home of Frank "Butch" Miceli, who police said was an operations boss for the Mafia family of Carlo Gambino. Locklin realized he was onto an extraordinary story.

He teamed up with a twenty-two-year-old black reporter, Lovett S. Gray, to interview as many subcontractors and workers as they could find, most of whom were black. They found more rascality than even Bryan and Oates had suspected—widespread payroll padding, diversion of labor and materials to private uses, threats of violence when contractors complained.

Locklin also got an earful from Janet Upjohn Stearns, sixty-five-year-old heir of the Upjohn Pharmaceutical Company family, who had donated $220,000 to the Guild to buy the land for the minority housing in Englewood out of sympathy for the plight of the city's slum dwellers. Mrs. Stearns said she had suspected something was wrong when she discovered the Guild had obtained a $78,000 mortgage insured by the Federal Housing Administration to buy the land that had already been bought with her donation. FHA officials said it was unusual, but not illegal. Mrs. Stearns also distrusted Brown, but had no evidence of wrongdoing.

Brown had been installed as housing division chief by his uncle, Monsignor Joseph A. Dooling, the head of the Guild for twenty years until a new archbishop took over the diocese in the fall of 1974 and hired a professional administrator to run the housing program. Monsignor Dooling, then seventy, resigned. The new administrator fired Brown and Sproviero. Guild officials knew the housing program was in bad shape, but were shocked by the evidence Locklin showed them of criminality and infiltration by friends of mobsters. They gave the reporter access to some of their records. Locklin discovered a similar pattern of bill padding and irregularities in other housing projects. Brown and Sproviero had milked the Guild for more than a million dollars, leaving it holding the bag for $11 million in debts. Locklin and Gray revealed the astonishing case of "corruption in an unlikely place" in a four-part series in June, 1975.

A grand jury investigation was ordered. The Catholic diocese later discontinued the housing program and did away with the Mount Carmel Guild, absorbing its operations in a reorganization of service agencies.

The thirty-eight-year-old Locklin began full-time investigative reporting for the *Record* in 1972 with a series that provoked an embarrassing libel suit. The articles described how a real estate broker who served on the Bergen County tax board and a lawyer who won most of his cases before the board, had used their power and connections to make big profits in land deals together. The lawyer filed suit, complaining the articles neglected to mention the cases in which the tax board member had voted against him. The jury agreed with the lawyer.

Locklin's next probe concerned day-to-day indiscretions by officials in the town of Paramus—things like having a boat motor repaired free by a city contractor and contriving to channel the city's tire business to a particular store. The articles attempted, said the newspaper, "to explain the situation in human terms, to tell how and why it happened. There are no black and white villains and heroes here, only real people."

Locklin usually prefers, however, what he calls "the white knight approach." He says, "I honestly believe that my job, simply put, is to expose the bad guys." Among the bad guys he's exposed are a promoter of a nursing home fraud scheme, a crooked lawyer who fronted for mobsters and wrote bad

checks, and a thirty-two-year-old wheeler-dealer who enjoyed stock manipulations. All were subsequently indicted and convicted on various fraud charges.
One got eleven years in prison, another eighteen months, and the third probation.

It's important to be fair, says Locklin. "We try to tell their side of the story as
fully as possible. We try to understand them, and let the readers understand
them." But the main point of it all, after the facts are investigated, double-
checked, reviewed by a libel lawyer, and published, is to nail the villain to the
wall.

So many people showed up for the meeting that loudspeakers were set up in an
adjacent room for the overflow. Reporters, photographers, and TV cameramen
had come to Knoxville from Louisville, Memphis, Atlanta and as far away as
Washington, D.C., for this historic occasion on January 16, 1975. It was the
first time in the forty-two-year life of the Tennessee Valley Authority, Franklin
D. Roosevelt's monument to grass roots democracy in technological action,
that the TVA had opened its meetings to the public.

In the first row sat twenty-eight-year-old free-lance writer James Branscome, the man most responsible for the event. If it was a victory for anyone, it
was a victory for Branscome, his investigations, and his crusade to put an end to
the TVA's secrecy.

Branscome had made his first assault on the TVA's closed-meeting policy in
July, 1974, showing up with Knoxville TV newsman Mark Engel to demand
admittance to a regular meeting of the three-man TVA board. TVA officials
were numb with disbelief. Such a request was unheard of. Branscome made a
move toward the meeting room, but a secretary leapt from behind a desk to head
him off, shouting, "You can't go in there!" Engel found an opening and darted
into the meeting room with his camera, only to be ejected by TVA Chairman
Aubrey Wagner.

TVA Public Information Officer Paul Evans upbraided the upstart reporters. Instead of explaining the need for secrecy, Evans burned their ears with an
attack on Branscome's articles on the TVA in the *Mountain Eagle,* a small
weekly newspaper of 5,000 circulation in the Appalachian mountain town of
Whitesburg, Kentucky. Evans suggested the reporters emulate the fine work of
Knoxville *News-Sentinel* reporter Carson Brewer. Branscome knew about
Brewer. He had exposed TVA's payment of $11,000 to Brewer and his wife
for work on a book sponsored by TVA.

The Knoxville TV station lost interest, but Branscome, who lives in Sevier-
ville, Tennessee, went back to every subsequent TVA board meeting, demanding in vain that the giant public utility open its proceedings to the public. To
more potent effect, Branscome uncovered TVA activities and plans despite
strenuous efforts to thwart him. TVA officials rejected his unprecedented
requests to see records. When he filed formal requests under the Freedom of

Information Act, they said the clerical costs involved would cost him $6.75 an hour. One bill, for information on TVA's projected purchase of coal reserves, came to $108. But none of it stopped Branscome.

Starting out early in 1974, Branscome revealed that the TVA had planned to strip-mine coal in the Daniel Boone National Forest before pending legislation could be passed to prevent it, had lobbied for federal law amendments to let it avoid $1.6 billion in air pollution equipment costs, had set up surveillance and dossiers on TVA critics, and had secretly tried to buy the nation's largest coal company.

Branscome did not get much information from interviews or press conferences, he wrote in a December 19, 1974, article, but from TVA files under the Freedom of Information Act and "from stumbling onto information from other sources." He once learned of an important TVA move from papers left on a table in the men's room at TVA offices.

In the midst of Branscome's campaign, the *Mountain Eagle's* office burned to the ground. Editor Tom Gish and his wife, Pat, put the paper out from their home until new quarters were found in November. Since the paper had made enemies with its investigations of strip mining and mine safety hazards, Gish asked the state police to investigate. The state seemed more interested in investigating Gish. After kerosene-soaked envelopes were found in the debris, however, state investigators arrested four men, one of them a Whitesburg policeman. Two of the four pleaded guilty to setting the fire.

Now, as the TVA opened its meetings to the public at last, Branscome wondered how real the victory was. Board chairman Wagner said, "There never was any interest expressed in opening them before." He said the meetings were being opened because friends of the TVA had said "there was maybe something going on at the meetings which we weren't willing to tell the public." That, said Wagner, "isn't the case at all."

Though TVA general manager Lynn Seeber said the format of the meetings hadn't changed now that they were open, the board moved briskly through a forty-one-item agenda with only perfunctory discussion. Officials conceded that twenty-one matters had already been disposed of. It was clear that little had changed. The real decisions were still being made behind closed doors, and merely repeated in the public session as window dressing.

Instead of beaming with pleasure over the new openness, Branscome and other reporters questioned whether it was genuine. The battle was far from over.

In Madisonville, Tennessee, a quiet little town of 3,500 in the foothills of the Great Smoky Mountains, Editor Dan Hicks, Jr. of the weekly *Monroe County Observer* takes at least three things with him when he goes out to cover a story: a camera, a tape recorder, and a gun.

Shortly after Hicks bought the paper in 1967, he published an exposé of corruption in the county road department that led to embezzlement charges against the supervisor. On the first day of the trial, Hicks was beaten up by two young toughs who did it for thirty dollars and a gallon of moonshine.

Undaunted, Hicks went right on exposing local corruption, bootleg whiskey operations, Ku Klux Klan intrigues, unsafe equipment in the volunteer fire department, and deficiencies in the water system. His office was blasted with shotguns in 1968 and burned down in 1969 and 1972. "I've been told I'll be killed the next time," he remarked as he poked through the ruins of the second fire.

The stocky, wavy-haired, fifty-four-year-old Hicks was jailed in July, 1975, for violating a judge's order not to publish stories about a seventeen-year-old boy's fatal shooting of his cousin, but was released after three hours. He continued to write about the case in defiance of the gag order and filed a suit against the judge. He was already a party to several court actions—defendant in two libel suits and plaintiff in suits charging local officials with holding illegal secret meetings.

Hicks has won several journalism awards, including the John Peter Zenger Freedom of the Press Award in 1972 and the Elijah Parish Lovejoy Award for Courage in 1969. It bothers him little that he must keep an eye peeled for trouble and has no social life. He's doing what he wants.

Joseph H. Weston, the sixty-five-year-old, white-haired, granite-visaged editor of the *Sharp Citizen* in the Ozark Mountain town of Cave City, Arkansas, often answers the door at his home with a rifle in his hand. Since starting his weekly newspaper in January, 1972, because retirement bored him, Weston has made a shambles of the town's former tranquility with his attacks on the "crooked sheriffs," "sadistic judges," and "corrupt bosses" of Sharp County and the state of Arkansas.

It all began ominously when the county's political boss, seventy-one-year-old Eagle Street, decreed that Weston could not start a newspaper. Weston made it his first order of business once he was publishing to brand Street the "Bastard Tyrant of Sharp County" and write articles about Street's crooked business deals and prodigious sexual exploits. Within a month, Weston was getting obscene phone calls, threats, and attempts to run his car off the road.

One threat to kill him was delivered by a nearby town's police chief after Weston revealed police in his department were helping to run a wife swapping club. Weston also angered local and state police with frequent articles alleging police brutality. He accused police of killing a teenager at the Batesville jail and making it look like a suicide, of beating another teenager to death and dumping his body alongside a highway, and of deliberately murdering a fifty-two-year-old mentally retarded owner of a coveted parcel of land.

Not one to shrink from offending powerful politicians, Weston hurled charges of "brutal dictatorship" at Senator John McClellan and Congressman

Wilbur Mills. In 1973, one of his unique handwritten headlines blared: "Calling Himself 'The Strongest Man In The United States'—And Acting The Part—U.S. Senator John L. McClellan Ordered More Than 30 Million Dollars Of R.E.A. Loans Made To His Own Company In Conflict Of Interest So Colossal It Staggers The Imaginations Of Even The Cynical Top News Men Of Washington, D.C., Who Are Working With Editor Weston To Tell The People Of America What Has Happened To Our Government." The story concerned Rural Electrification Administration loans to the Alled Telephone Company of Little Rock, in which McClellan owned stock.

One of Weston's bitterest enemies was his next-door neighbor, whom Weston had accused in print of owning a moonshine still. In what Weston claims was a conspiracy by crooked officials to put him in jail where they could kill him, the neighbor filed a complaint of criminal libel against Weston in September, 1972. Tipped in advance to the plot, Weston fled the state and put out his paper from exile. It was the best thing that ever happened to him.

He became a national celebrity, a gutsy freedom fighter of journalism. *The New York Times* did a feature on him, he was invited to make speeches, and he wrote an article for the *Bulletin* of the American Society of Newspaper Editors. Returning to Cave City to face arrest, he arranged for friends to crowd the jail and keep watch until he was released on bail. One judge dismissed the charge, ruling the criminal libel law unconstitutional. But the prosecutor appealed and the state supreme court reinstated the case.

In the meantime, a county sheriff brought another criminal libel charge against Weston over an article saying he was protecting a narcotics racket. The second charge came to trial first and Weston was convicted. But his appeal led to an October 20, 1975, ruling by the Arkansas Supreme Court that the law was unconstitutional.

Weston reported the happy event in the *Sharp Citizen* under a typical headline: "After Four Long, Weary Years Of Beatins, Jailings, Bush-Whackings, Boycotts, Terrorizing Of His Family, And Near-Starvation, Embattled Editor Joe Weston Of The Famous Sharp Citizen Has Defeated The Infamous John McClellan-Wilbur Mills Police-State Dictatorship On Its Home Grounds In Arkansas, And, In Doing So, Has Scored A National Victory Over The Criminal Libel Law."

11

Mid-American Diggers

AS ROBERT COLLINS left the interview, he could hardly contain his elation. The contractor had laid it all out—names, dates, figures, the details of how the big companies got together in a Springfield hotel and cut their deals for highway construction contracts in Illinois. The state's bidding process was a farce. The contractor for each job was decided in advance. The price he wanted, everyone agreed, would be the low bid.

Months of searching through records at the Division of Highways had convinced Collins that bid rigging was swindling taxpayers on a million-dollar scale, but until now the proof had eluded him. Patterns of collusion had become evident as he analyzed bids covering a seven-year period. The same group of contractors did all the bidding. One would get one job, another the next, then a third, and the order would be repeated. But that wasn't proof. "Sometimes you can dig the proof out of the records," says Collins, "but this wasn't one of them."

It had to come from inside, a contractor who took part in the collusion, or an outsider who resented it. The highway contractors, however, were a tight-lipped bunch. Some gave him a nervous look when he brought up the subject of bidding. Others said he was "on the right track" and urged him to keep investigating because he "could perform a real service here." That bolstered his determination, but gave him nothing concrete to put in his newspaper, the St. Louis *Post-Dispatch.*

Collins kept badgering those who had encouraged him. A few agreed to meet with him at night in out-of-the-way places, but were too fearful to divulge specifics. But now, after Collins gave solemn assurances never to disclose his name, one of them had opened up. At last he could start writing.

That, however, was wrong. Two days later Collins received a letter from the contractor's lawyer. Forget he had ever talked to the contractor, said the letter. If Collins used any of the information the contractor had given him, the contractor would deny having spoken to Collins and there would be "legal disaster."

Collins shrugged off the setback and went back to work. His reputation for trustworthiness gradually took effect. Contractors began to give him the story in dribbles. Though he didn't have solid evidence against individual contractors, Collins and managing editor Evarts A. Graham decided to start publishing the general outlines of the collusion in March, 1970. Collins' first story said, "Some highway contractors have been rigging bids on projects involving millions of dollars in federal and Illinois highway construction funds." The article described how the bids were negotiated in advance, but named no contractors.

"Some think that's unfair," says Collins. "They say you must have it all buttoned up before you publish anything. But the story was legitimate and we figured it would turn up new leads. There were scores of people out there, maybe hundreds, who'd been wondering if anyone would ever do anything about it. They read the paper and say, 'Here's someone who's interested,' and they contact you. It's a technique I've used for years."

The story did bring in more leads and Collins wrote more stories. He revealed that mechanical and electrical contractors were fleecing Illinois taxpayers with bid rigging on state building construction. Collins disclosed that a former director of the state's Public Works and Buildings Department, in which the highway division was located, had received $10,000 when he retired from a group of highway contractors. Two public works department officials and their wives had enjoyed a week in Hawaii at the expense of the Illinois Asphalt Pavement Association. The gaudiest indiscretion of all was a six-acre lake built free of charge for a highway division engineer who was overseeing the lake-builder's performance on a $3.8-million freeway contract.

Collins met with two federal district attorneys and turned over his evidence to the FBI. At the FBI's request, he asked his sources to become government witnesses. Before the end of 1972, a federal grand jury indicted nine construction firms and four officers of road-building companies.

That was just the beginning. In January, 1976, with not all the results yet in, the score was: 225 articles by Collins, five grand jury investigations, fraud and antitrust indictments against sixty-six individuals and firms, eighteen guilty pleas, fifteen no-contest pleas, fifteen consent decrees providing for fines and injunctions against further violations, eleven trials ending in convictions, two acquittals, five pending trials, two prison sentences, $721,000 in fines, treble damage suits against twenty-seven contractors by the state of Illinois, stiffer penalties in state and federal law for collusive bidding, and a letter from Illinois Attorney General William J. Scott to *Post-Dispatch* editor and publisher Joseph Pulitzer, Jr. saying, "I salute you, your editors and Bob Collins for an extraordinary public service."

It was the most spectacular achievement in a long career of remarkable investigative accomplishments. A dapper, gray-haired gentleman who wears 1950-style business suits and likes to work alone, Collins had been probing into graft and corruption since 1946 at the Atlanta *Journal*.

In Atlanta, Collins touched off two congressional investigations by uncovering waste and corruption in the disposal of war surplus materials. He became city editor and then an editorial writer and columnist, but couldn't stay away from investigating. To prove that bootleg liquor sales and prostitution were flourishing, Collins enlisted two ministers to accompany him on a round of nightspots. While at it, he found illegal gambling as well. Two gambling house operators were convicted.

At the *Post-Dispatch* since 1951, Collins has reeled off one exposé after another. He pulled his gambling probe caper at the Corona Club, a lavish casino run by crime syndicate hoodlum Frank "Buster" Wortman north of East St. Louis, Illinois. He got past three guards by contriving to look like a big spender from Texas. After he wrote about the mink-draped women and tuxedo-clad dealers around the craps and blackjack tables, state police closed the club.

When a nursing home fire killed seventy-two elderly residents, Collins investigated hazardous and unsanitary conditions in Missouri nursing homes, which led to the closing of 150 and enactment of new safety requirements. He cost a federal conservation official his job with an exposé of illegal political activity. Voters in Independence, Missouri, adopted a new city charter and elected a new batch of officials after Collins revealed conflict-of-interest connections between the mayor and the city's gasoline supplier, and missing records and money at the police department. Collins wrote seventy stories disclosing mischief by the John Birch Society and other extremist groups. Joseph E. Ragen, a penologist with a national reputation, was fired as Illinois Public Safety Director after Collins uncovered law violations in a state penitentiary and irregularities in trucking invoices. The superintendent of an Illinois institution for retarded children resigned after a probe by Collins unearthed the fact that he had misrepresented his professional background.

When a tip came in that there had been "something wrong" with the 1966 Chicago jury that acquitted three doctors of fraud charges in the promotion of the controversial cancer drug, Krebiozen, Collins was assigned to investigate. He got a list of the jurors and tracked them down. Most refused to talk at first, but he kept going back. One finally remembered a magazine containing pro-Krebiozen articles in the jury room. He thought it was the *Butcher Worker*, a monthly magazine of the Amalgamated Meat Cutters & Butcher Workmen in Chicago. Collins located back copies at the University of Chicago's Industrial Relations Center. They contained several articles and editorials touting Krebiozen's fine qualities. He discovered that one of the jurors, Joseph S. Bukowski, had been an executive board member for the meat cutters union. Bukowski admitted he had discussed the articles with other jurors.

"Wasn't this a violation of the judge's orders?" Collins asked.

"How are you going to avoid it?" Bukowski replied. "I received the magazine at home. I have no control over what anybody puts in a magazine."

Bukowski got three years in prison for jury tampering.

Editor and Publisher Pulitzer got a letter from U.S. Attorney Thomas A. Foran that said, "Without Collins' untiring efforts and dedication, this defendant would have gone unpunished and our jury system dealt a severe blow."

Another full-time investigative reporter at the *Post-Dispatch*, Louis Rose, likes to plunge into public records and come up knowing everything that's going on. In a 1972 probe, however, success hinged on an interview.

A tipster had told him that real estate broker Anthony F. Sansone, a friend and political ally of Mayor Alfonso J. Cervantes, had made a handsome fee on a sale of land to the city for its airport expansion. There was nothing in the land records or airport files, however, to show that Sansone had a connection with any airport land purchase. The best Rose could do was to list six parcels that might include the one in question. Then he heard through a source in a federal agency that Sansone had made $83,000 on the deal, but still he didn't know which deal it was.

Selecting a half-acre parcel that best fit the few sketchy facts he had managed to scrape up, Rose delved into the background of the man from whom it had been bought, oil company entrepreneur Louis M. Levin. He learned everything imaginable about Levin—business dealings, political connections, zoning applications, driving record, credit rating, family life. At the interview, Rose was able to toss off the knowledge that Levin owned exactly 128 gas stations. Glancing at a photograph of Levin's daughter on the wall, he identified the horseback-riding prize in the girl's hand. "Now," said Rose, "Let's discuss the Sansone deal."

Disconcerted, Levin felt it would be futile to lie or evade. He gave Rose the details. The city had offered him $150,000 to $160,000 at first, so he had retained Sansone to get him a better price. Sansone had handled previous real estate transactions for him. Levin had agreed to pay Sansone as a commission whatever he could get from the city in excess of $175,000. The final price paid by the city was $258,161. Sansone confirmed the transaction, but maintained he had neither sought nor been accorded special treatment at city hall.

In another airport land probe, Rose tried to verify a report that only $800,000 of $1 million paid by the city for a parcel of cemetery land had actually reached the owner. But, the owner wouldn't speak to Rose. The investigation lay dormant until the reporter heard that the owner was getting a divorce. Inspecting the exhibits and depositions in the divorce case file, Rose found an income tax report with a reference to a $200,000 consultant fee paid with a cashier's check in connection with the land sale. The payee's name was not given, but the date of the check and the name of the bank were there. The city counsel's office refused to let Rose see city records on the transaction, but when Mayor Cervantes, a Democrat, went vacationing in Spain, Rose persuaded the Republican acting mayor to get the records for him. Along with a source in the bank, they led Rose to the identity of the $200,000's recipient. It was Sansone.

A short, amiable fellow with a restless air, Rose came to the *Post-Dispatch* in 1964 after seven years at the Providence *Journal-Bulletin* in Rhode Island, where he had turned into an investigative reporter while managing one of the newspaper's suburban bureaus. Rumors of political corruption involving the Mafia sent him rummaging through North Providence city records. He discovered that the city was permitting illegal trash dumping at a site owned by Mafia boss Raymond Patriarca, that city officials were using city employees to do work on private property, and that the police chief had kept traffic fine money he was supposed to turn over to the city.

"I like to take every major agency in a city government," says Rose, "and learn how they handle their paper work, the whole process from the beginning, step by step. I want to know what records are kept, how many copies are made, where the copies go, who handles them. If I don't get a record in one office, I can try another one that gets a copy. Or I can look up a duplicate record in revenue collecting if I don't want the assessor to know what I'm investigating. I'll take a specific piece of property and trace its complete tax history to see how the system works. I like to become a layman expert on all kinds of records: property, tax, business, banking, personal.

"A person generates an enormous number of records during his lifetime. He can't help leaving tracks. Records flow from the things we do, our car, our driver's license, marriage, school, property, utility bills. And I know most of them."

There's no record he can't get, Rose believes, regardless of apparent impossibility. During a 1975 investigation to determine if St. Louis City Treasurer Paul M. Berra had connections with a bank where the city had been keeping interest-free deposits, Rose was refused access to bank records. Learning that a national bank is required by law to provide a stockholder list to any stockholder who requests one, Rose bought a share of the bank's stock and discovered that Berra owned $50,000 worth.

Art Petacque knew who had killed Valerie Percy, but he couldn't publish the man's name. For eighteen months, he'd been hunting for a person he believed could provide the additional evidence he needed, but in November, 1973, seven years after the twenty-one-year-old daughter of U.S. Senator Charles Percy had been stabbed to death in the family's seventeen-room suburban mansion, Petacque had exhausted all leads.

He had learned the killer's name early in 1972. A Chicago crime syndicate loan shark and fence named Leo Rugendorf, whom Petacque had met in his early days as a Chicago Sun-Times reporter, called to say he had information on a case.

"The last time I tried to talk to you," Petacque said, "you got pretty abusive."

"Wait a minute," said Rugendorf. "This is about the Percy case. That big enough for you?"

"Why do you want to talk about that?"

"I'm dying," said Rugendorf. "I want to get it off my chest. Ain't you got ten minutes?"

Hurrying out to the mobster's home, Petacque found him ailing with diabetes and heart disease. The killer, said Rugendorf, was one of four men who had broken into the Percy home. The men had belonged to a Mafia-backed gang of burglars who preyed on wealthy suburbs across the nation. Rugendorf had helped plan many of the burglaries and dispose of the loot. One of the men, said Rugendorf, the same one who had squealed on him in a federal case, had killed the Percy girl. His name was Francis L. Hohimer, a forty-four-year-old career burglar whom Petacque had identified in 1970 as a prime suspect in the case.

Hohimer, said Rugendorf, had come to him after the Percy slaying and said he wanted to "go straight" because he couldn't "take the heat" any more and "they'll get me for the Valerie Percy murder."

According to Rugendorf, Hohimer said he and two other gang members had entered the Percy home through a back door. The Percy girl had been killed because she woke up while they were in her room.

"Is there anyone who can corroborate this?" Petacque asked.

"Yeah," said Rugendorf. "Hohimer's brother."

Harold "Wayne" Hohimer's whereabouts were unknown, however. And the most determined manhunt of Petacque's long newspaper years had failed to track him down.

During his search, the forty-nine-year-old veteran reporter made contact with many of Wayne Hohimer's friends and acquaintances. Word eventually reached him that Petacque was looking for him. He asked around about the reporter, wanting to know what kind of man he was. Among those he asked was an agent for the Alcohol, Tobacco and Firearms Division of the U.S. Treasury Department who had once done him a favor and who knew Petacque. Yeah, said the agent, talk to Petacque.

Petacque got the call in November, 1973. Wayne Hohimer came to the office for a taped interview by Petacque and fellow *Sun-Times* reporter Hugh Hough.

Wayne said he had seen his brother in a tavern the day after the murder and Frank had been "real nervous and uptight." Frank told his brother he had killed a girl because she had "made a lot of noise and they got in a fight." Wayne asked what burglary he was talking about, and Frank said, "It's all in the newspapers and on the radio today."

"He was talking about the Valerie Percy thing," said Wayne.

The reporters took Wayne to confront his brother in an Iowa prison where Frank was serving a thirty-year term in an unrelated case. Frank denied any part in the break-in or killing, or ever telling his brother he had taken part. Frank said Miss Percy had been killed by Frederick Malchow, another member of the gang who had died in 1967 from a fall off a railroad trestle during a prison escape in Pennsylvania.

According to Frank's story, Frank had been home in bed and Malchow came to his apartment with two other gang members to ask for clothes to replace his blood-soaked garments. Frank said he burned Malchow's clothes in an incinerator. His ex-wife, Holly, had been there, he said, and she could corroborate the incident. Frank said that Malchow had later admitted killing the Percy girl.

Now the challenge was to find Holly, who had remarried and whose new name was not known. Petacque found her by tracing her children's movements through the Chicago school system. Holly said she knew nothing about the Percy case. But she could not recall the bloodstained clothes incident and said Frank had not been home in bed that night.

The brother's testimony, combined with Rugendorf's, which the racketeer had given to police before he died, gave Petacque enough for a story. Hough helped him write it and they both won a 1974 Pulitzer Prize.

Though prosecutors need still more evidence before they can charge Frank Hohimer with Valerie Percy's murder, they say they're sure he did it.

It was by no means Petacque's first award. After joining the *Sun-Times* as a copy boy in the early 1940s, he showed up one day with an exclusive angle on a sensational murder story and was straightway made a reporter. Since then he's exposed police shakedowns, a Ku Klux Klan cell in the police department, fraudulent pyramid sales of "distributorships" by a California cosmetics firm called Holiday Magic, and a stock swindle by President Nixon's 1968 campaign manager in Illinois, William H. Rentschler, who was subsequently convicted of fraud.

Except for a Pulitzer Prize, which he's determined sooner or later to win, the *Sun-Times's* other full-time investigative reporter, thirty-three-year-old Ed Pound, has run up an equally impressive record of exposés in only seven years, usually by coming up with an inside source at the crucial time.

While investigating Chicago Alderman Thomas E. Keane with reporter Thomas J. Moore in 1973, Pound discovered that Keane had sponsored inconspicuous ordinances permitting the city to make fractional settlements on tax-delinquent properties. Several hundred such properties had been purchased by two secret land trusts and resold for big profits. Pound suspected that Keane had an interest in the trusts, but couldn't prove it—until he turned up a source who gave him the evidence. Keane was convicted of conspiracy and mail fraud and sentenced to five years in prison.

During his Keane investigation, Pound happened across a document revealing a connection between Cook County circuit court clerk Matthew J. Danaher and Chicago builder John T. Ahern. A source in a federal agency told him that Danaher and a brother-in-law owned a firm named Garden Realty and Investment Company. "The most important thing in investigative reporting," says Pound, "is to establish a good network of sources, in law enforcement, in politics, and on the street." Probing into Ahern's dealings, Pound learned about a falling-out with a partner named Arch Hermanns, who had moved to Florida. Pound grabbed a flight to Fort Lauderdale and Hermanns told him about $250,000 in payoffs to Garden Realty over a five-year period in return for

Danaher's help on zoning changes for a 900-home subdivision. Danaher had been Mayor Richard Daley's top aide and then an alderman during that five years. Danaher was indicted on federal conspiracy and income tax charges, but died before his trial was to begin.

Pound collaborated with *Sun-Times* political reporter Joel Weisman and columnist Jerome Watson in an exposé of questionable contributions to pay off deficits from Illinois Governor Daniel Walker's 1972 campaign. The donations had come from accounting and architectural firms, and an investment banking company that later got a state contract as a bond issue consultant. Pound's source was a campaign worker who had copies of contribution records.

Pound and Weisman had uncovered a bigger scandal together when both were reporters for *Chicago Today* in 1971. After getting a tip, Pound discovered in state racing board records that a daughter of Illinois Secretary of State John W. Lewis owned stock in Cahokia Downs racetrack and two horse racing associations. Their story broke three months after Federal Appeals Court Judge and former governor Otto Kerner had been reported to be under investigation for a racetrack stock deal. A fierce competition flamed up among Chicago's news media for exclusives about politicians who made big profits in racetrack stock.

Trying to keep up, Pound and Weisman phoned everyone who had any connection with racing. One racing industry insider struck them as susceptible to pressure. On the fifth try, Pound persuaded him to furnish the records that produced their Kerner blockbuster.

The judge, they disclosed, had made $22,400 on racetrack stock acquired secretly while he was governor. Subsequent articles revealed secret racetrack holdings by other public officials who obtained them at special low prices from racetrack interests. A federal grand jury indicted Kerner and several others. Kerner served seven months of a three-year term in a federal penitentiary. The stories won a Jacob Scher Award, Chicago's top prize for investigative reporting, and a National Headliner Award.

Pound's first investigative success had helped knock two state supreme court justices out of office. While covering the state legislature for the Alton *Evening Telegraph* in 1969, Pound met citizen activist and gadfly Sherman Skolnick. Skolnick alleged that Justice Ray I. Klingbiel had received a gift of bank stock shortly after writing an opinion that upheld dismissal of criminal charges against one of the bank's organizers. Pound and colleague Ande Yakstis traced stock transfers in state banking records to document the gift as having originated from the banker. They also found a similar gift for state supreme court chief justice Roy Solfisburg after he had concurred with Klingbiel's ruling. The two justices resigned.

Pound tackled Chicago's most invincible public figure, Mayor Daley, in 1974. He and fellow reporter Moore were checking records on Daley's summer home in Michigan when they spotted an unfamiliar name, Elard Realty. Elard, which they discovered to have assets of $200,000, appeared to be owned by Daley and his wife. But no one connected with the company would acknowledge it and there was no verification on any public record. They'd have a good story revealing that Daley was worth far more than he had said, if they could prove that he owned Elard Realty. An inside source came to the rescue again, conveying details from Elard's financial records. No lawbreaking on Daley's part was found, says Pound, but the story induced Daley to make a public disclosure of his finances.

Daley's chief newspaper nemesis has been Weisman, who set up a Chicago bureau for the Washington *Post* in 1975 after he left the *Sun-Times*. Browsing through appointments of circuit court receivers one day in 1973, Weisman jotted down names to be checked out. One of them, Tom Flanagan, ran a new insurance agency called Heil & Heil, and was a good friend of Mayor Daley's sons. What's more, Weisman learned, the city had just switched $1.5 million in annual insurance business to Heil & Heil on Daley's orders.

A phone call to the agency that had lost the business produced a tip that Daley's twenty-five-year-old son, John Patrick, was employed at Flanagan's new agency. Weisman called Heil & Heil and asked for young Daley. Daley wasn't in. In response to several phone calls over several days, secretaries at Heil & Heil took messages for John Patrick and said he called in regularly. Several persons told Weisman they were aware of John Patrick's involvement at Heil & Heil. But Weisman couldn't pin down the exact relationship. In his story, he said Daley's connection "has been kept vague intentionally."

Weisman and the mayor confronted each other a few days later at dedication ceremonies for the city's new Democratic Party headquarters. As Weisman came through the reception line and shook Daley's hand, he congratulated the mayor on the elegance of the new party digs, then leaned forward and whispered, "By the way, when will you be releasing your promised statement on your son's economic interests?"

"When I do," Daley barked, "I sure ain't going to give it to you or your newspaper. You never printed a true thing in your life."

"I'll print every comma and period," replied Weisman. "And I presume it will be true."

As Weisman walked away, Daley yelled after him. "Reporter, huh? If you're a reporter, I'm a ballet dancer."

Weisman struck again the following year. First he disclosed that John Patrick had received a $90,000 "soliciting" fee from Heil & Heil after the insurance business switch, though he had done no soliciting except to engage in a general conversation about insurance with former city controller David Stahl.

Then came the article that led to a grand jury investigation.

Though given a passing grade on his state insurance broker's test, John Patrick had not answered enough questions correctly to deserve the passing grade. A score of 70 out of 100 was required for passing, but young Daley had done no better than 35.

The next day, Weisman revealed that another of Daley's sons, William M., had received a passing grade on the insurance test despite scoring only 55.

The examiner who had passed John Patrick had been fired, Weisman disclosed, but had obtained another state job at a higher salary. A grand jury found that William Daley's test had been altered, and indicted a former grading supervisor for perjury.

Weisman wouldn't want it thought that the Daleys are the only people he investigates. He's exposed illegal reductions in personal property tax assessments for political contributors, and deposits of Cook County funds in interest-free accounts at banks with the right political connections.

He does relish his Daley marksmanship, however. "I shattered the myth that Daley was personally honest and aboveboard," he says. "I was the first to ever lay a glove on him."

Almost a year had passed since Richard Cady and William Anderson singled out police corruption as the first order of business for the Indianapolis *Star's* new investigative team. Disclosures of bribery, extortion, and thievery by police had burst on an unsuspecting public six months later, in February, 1974. The mayor and the county prosecutor had vowed to investigate. The *Star's* team had turned out dozens of follow-up exposés amidst police department denials and denunciations of the newspaper. By September, the police scandal was Indiana's leading topic of conversation, and all sides looked with suspense toward a report by the grand jury. Then, on September 12, an indictment was announced: against Richard Cady and William Anderson.

Behind this surprise development was a chain of freakish events going back to an anonymous phone call the team had received shortly after its first articles appeared. The caller said he had information on narcotics deals. He asked for a reporter to meet him at an abandoned service station. Interested but wary, team leader Cady decided the whole team would go. Cady and reporter Harley Bierce took one car. Anderson, reporter Myrta Pulliam, and photographer Gerald Clark went in another.

Cady and Bierce were approached by a short young man wearing blue jeans, a white T-shirt with a cigarette pack rolled up in a sleeve, and long blond hair. His name was Larry Keen and he was nineteen years old.

Keen climbed in the car and they drove around. Keen said he knew who had committed a 1971 triple murder in which the throats of three young businessmen had been slashed. He said the killer was a bootlegger who had once dealt in stolen goods under the protection of a prominent West Coast governor. He promised to supply the reporters with information on the 1971 murder and bootleggers' payoffs to Indianapolis cops.

Cady and Bierce found the young man a trifle absurd. They told him he'd have to show them documents—pictures or records—to establish his credibility. They suggested he take his story to the FBI. The reporters accorded the incident so little significance that they made no notes on it when they returned to their office.

Keen appeared at their office a week later. "I will sell you the knife used in that murder," he said. It was a machete, and he'd take $100 for it.

Cady told him they weren't interested. They didn't buy information or evidence.

Keen asked for money to go to Louisville.

Cady said they couldn't help him.

Keen left, but came back later. "Just to prove that I know what I'm talking about," he said. "I'm going to pay off a policeman and let you guys watch."

The reporters laughed.

By then they had acquired some facts about Keen. He had a record of burglary arrests as a juvenile and was a snitch for the police department's burglary squad, known as the Crime Action Team, or CAT. CAT was among the police operations that the *Star's* investigative team was investigating.

Keen told Lieutenant Lawrence Turner, head of CAT, that he was being pressured by reporters to "set up" a policeman. Turner dismissed it as some of the youngster's fantasizing.

But when Keen brought it up again, Turner wasn't so sure. "Those guys want me to set you up," said Keen.

"What are you talking about?" Turner asked.

"Bill Anderson is pressuring me," said Keen.

Suddenly apprehensive, Turner consulted Prosecutor Noble Pearcy, one of the scandal's most controversial figures. In addition to assurances that the reporters would never reveal their identity as sources, twenty-eight policemen who had helped Cady's team had made him promise never to give their names or evidence to Pearcy. Many of them had been harassed and threatened for trying to combat corruption on their own. They did not trust Pearcy and would cooperate with the *Star* only if the newspaper promised to seek an "outside" investigation, such as by federal authorities. Cady, in fact, had contacted Justice Department officials three months before the first articles were published, and an FBI investigation had begun.

The reporters next heard from Keen at 10:30 A.M. on March 12, 1974. Anderson took his phone call, which, it turned out, was recorded.

"Bill," said Keen, "this is Larry."

"Yeah," said Anderson. "Hello, Larry."

"You still want me to set up the policeman?"

"Yeah, sure, Larry, go ahead."

"I'll be at the White Castle on Virginia Avenue at twelve-thirty. Will you be there?"

"Yeah, sure, Larry."

Anderson mentioned the call to Cady and Bierce. When lunch time arrived, they decided to park in the White Castle lot for a few minutes before going on to John's Hot Lunch. As they watched, Keen appeared and entered the diner.

Bierce went in to buy cigarettes. "My man's going to show up," Keen told him. Bierce returned to the car.

As the reporters prepared to drive on to John's Hot Lunch, they saw Turner and a sergeant drive up. The two police officers walked into the White Castle. A few minutes later, Keen came out and left. Inside, Keen had handed Turner an envelope.

Over lunch at John's, the reporters discussed their observations. Nothing much had happened, they concluded.

Keen phoned that afternoon to ask if the reporters had witnessed his payoff. "Yeah," said Bierce. "We were there."

The team thought no more about the incident until the grand jury released a report saying it had turned over to the FBI information that certain newsmen "have contacted known law violators seeking to have them involve policemen solely for the purpose of providing news stories whereby possible intrusion of the civil rights of totally innocent policemen may be involved."

The reporters had been followed, warned, threatened, and secretly taped on hidden recorders, but this was the first sign that corrupt officials in powerful positions would tamper with legal processes to stop them.

An interview with Turner relieved their apprehensions, however. The lieutenant explained what had happened, and all agreed it had been a misunderstanding. They had been manipulated.

In the beginning, the investigation had concentrated on visits to bars and nightspots, and interviews with cab drivers and gamblers. But then the reporters noticed a proliferation of massage parlors and decided to check into that. They wrote several articles raising questions about the freedom with which the massage parlors operated, but failed to uncover proof of police protection. After a few more weeks of frustration, they shifted their focus. They would seek out sources inside the police department.

They knew of a few officers who had spoken out against corruption. Anderson, a forty-seven-year-old veteran crime reporter, already had good sources in the department. Cady, thirty-three, an aggressive, precise reporter who had been an assistant city editor, and Bierce, thirty-two, who had covered science and medicine, could establish dialogue with the young policemen who were trying to remain honest. Their new strategy produced the February revelations.

Mayor Richard Lugar named a seven-member commission to examine police department administration, created a "truth squad" of police to investigate their fellow officers, and appointed a new police chief. The grand jury began calling witnesses.

Aided by the *Star's* public demonstration of serious purpose, Cady's team recruited more policemen willing to give firsthand evidence. Results were meager, however. The head of the police finance branch was fired. A deputy chief was demoted. Two policemen were indicted for robbing card players during a raid. The *Star* published a series explaining how internal investigations of police corruption in other cities had produced only whitewashes. The standard reaction to scandal, that there were just a "few bad apples," was a cover-up. The *Star* published articles alleging manipulation of the grand jury by Pearcy and his assistant prosecutors.

Cady learned that federal authorities had found no federal law violations to prosecute. Near the end of August, Cady and Anderson were subpoenaed to appear before the grand jury and asked to waive their rights. When they refused to do so, they weren't called to testify. They suspected something unusual was in the works.

Their indictment charged them with conspiracy to bribe a police officer. It said they had conspired with Keen to give Turner money so that Turner would not press a burglary charge against Keen. It did not mention that the envelope which Keen handed to Turner had contained only a grand jury subpoena.

After Pearcy was defeated for reelection, and his successor, James Kelley, took office in January, 1975, the indictments were dismissed. "There is no evidence that a crime has been committed," Kelley said.

The team's first investigation won a 1975 Pulitzer Prize, a George Polk Memorial Award, a Sigma Delta Chi Award, the Drew Pearson Award for investigative reporting, and a host of other prizes.

Yet, Cady and Anderson were not thrilled. There had been only a few minor indictments and several of them had been dismissed. In February, 1975, they wrote that victory over corruption had been "small, tentative, and shaky." A year later, Cady said, "We are extremely frustrated. There's just too much corruption, and the right people aren't doing anything. The powers that be don't want to change the system. We don't feel we're making much headway."

But, stop investigating? Never.

No more information, said the U.S. Army, will be released to the *Daily Oklahoman*.

Has the Army decided, asked Jack Taylor, that public information will no longer be made public?

No, that's not the case, said Lieutenant Colonel Leonard F. B. Reed of the Army Information Office. This affects only the *Daily Oklahoman*.

No information at all?

Well, if Taylor were to make formal written requests, then maybe. But the information office would no longer reply to telephone inquiries from the *Daily Oklahoman*. Reed explained, "This office can't be subjected to the slings and arrows that you're casting at us which are, in my view, unnecessary and without cause."

Two days earlier, the Oklahoma City newspaper had disclosed that the Army had been investigating possible war crimes by an infantry company in the vicinity of the My Lai massacre in Vietnam.

Taylor spread the word about the Army's special treatment of his newspaper to officials of several news media organizations, who complained to Congress, the Pentagon, and the White House.

Reed issued a new statement the next day. The order to withhold public information from the *Daily Oklahoman*, he said, had been rescinded.

It was another victory for Taylor in his long battle with the Army over release of records and information. The battle had begun in December, 1969, when Taylor asked for the daily morning reports of the principal unit involved at My Lai and two other infantry companies in the same task force. Though Taylor's request was made under an Army regulation directing the release of such information, it was rejected. Releasing the records, said the Army, would violate the privacy of prospective witnesses in courts-martial and prejudice the rights of the accused.

Taylor bided his time until the My Lai court-martial of Lieutenant William Calley ended in a conviction on March 31, 1971, and charges against others had been dropped. Then he renewed his request, and asked, in addition, for a full, uncensored copy of the report issued by the war crimes investigation panel headed by Lieutenant General William R. Peers.

The Army replied that the material would be released only after all trials were concluded.

Taylor tried again at the end of 1971. When he finally got the morning reports in April, 1972, they were in a "highly excised" condition. He counted 401 censored items, including information the Army had previously made public, such as the names of soldiers killed in action.

Taylor filed an appeal for the deleted information and the Peers report with the Secretary of the Army, and wrote a story based on the records he had received. These records, he wrote, revealed that Calley might have been sent to Vietnam illegally, that reports of heavy casualties in Calley's unit had been exaggerated, and that the heavily censored summary of the Peers report released to the public was replete with errors. The Army admitted that Calley had been sent to Vietnam in violation of an Army regulation prohibiting deployment of inexperienced officers.

Though Taylor had by now been investigating for almost three years, he was merely tuning up for what lay ahead.

In September, he exposed an illegal program of administrative punishment imposed on soldiers exonerated of My Lai massacre charges in the military courts. He disclosed that the American troop commander in the My Lai incident suspected orders to destroy the hamlet and its inhabitants had come from higher headquarters, and possibly from the CIA. Taylor located evidence to support this contention in Army investigative records, especially a report on a lie detector test given to Captain Ernest L. Medina, who had been acquitted of massacre charges. The polygraph expert who administered the test, Taylor revealed, said Medina had lied when he denied having told a South Vietnamese army sergeant that, he, Medina had been acting under orders to kill the civilians.

Taylor next uncovered a Pentagon conclusion that the CIA had planned the massacre. One source said Army investigations after public disclosure of the My Lai incident had been manipulated to conceal CIA involvement. Peers had been named to head the probe panel, said the Pentagon source, because he was a former CIA official who could be relied upon to keep the inquiry a "smoke screen." Taylor revealed that the Peers panel had uncovered other atrocities by the soldiers at My Lai, and that not even Peers could get a copy of his report from the Army.

Taylor's successes against the Army's suppressive mentality won him several state journalism awards in 1973 and a national citation from the AP Managing Editors Association.

Perhaps the nation's most exhaustively organized investigative reporter, Taylor submits annual reports on his activities and successes to his editors, complete with statistics on the hundreds of Freedom of Information requests he's submitted to a passel of federal agencies.

Between reports, he's unearthed America's involvement in forcing millions of Russian refugees to return to Russia against their will after World War II, spotted organized crime's inroads into Oklahoma, conducted a thorough survey of the state's parole system, and won investigative reporting awards for exclusive disclosures in several campaign fund scandals centering on former Oklahoma Governor David Hall.

There's so much to do, in fact, that Taylor wishes he were a team. He's recommended to his managing editor that he be expanded into one.

When Gene Goltz and Jay Smith arrived at the Ohio State Racing Commission office in Columbus, executive director Pete Fleming and his assistant, Marge Selo, didn't know what to do. In all the years they had worked there, never before had a reporter asked to see the commission's records. They didn't know what records the reporters had a right to see, if any. The issue had never come up. Fleming was not about to make a mistake. Besides, he had no idea what the reporters were up to.

Goltz and Smith took the friendly approach. They patiently explained they were researching the history of Ohio horse racing for the Dayton *Daily News* as part of an investigation into the nationwide operations of a sports concession company called Emprise, which had food and drink concessions at several Ohio racetracks.

Fleming and Selo remained apprehensive, skeptical. They were sorry, but they couldn't let the reporters see the records.

Under Ohio law, the reporters said gingerly, public records must be made available for inspection and they wanted to see only those records that were public.

"Well, I don't think so," said Fleming.

The reporters looked at each other. It wasn't going to be easy. They sat down, prepared for a long campaign to convince the two race commission employes that they had nothing to fear, that the reporters were good, God-fearing people who intended them and the racing commission no harm.

It was a tough sales job. For one thing, Goltz, a cigar chomping veteran reporter of forty-two, was known to be a Pulitzer Prize winner. That, says Smith, worked against them. "They were afraid we'd find something damaging." Pulitzer Prize winners don't waste their time unless they can put someone in jail, do they?

At the end of the day, the reporters drove seventy glum miles back to Dayton. They resolved to try again the next day. "Jay, I think Marge has the hots for you," said Goltz. "Let's play on that a little."

Smith blushed. A twenty-two-year-old reporter less than a year out of journalism school at Ohio State University, Smith was on his first big investigation. One reason he had gotten the assignment, despite his youth, was his resourcefulness. If it took a little flirting to get a story, well, what's wrong with that?

They went back to Columbus the next day and the day after. Finally relenting, Fleming and Selo led the reporters into a conference room and brought in three large boxes of files. Goltz and Smith spread the papers on the table. The reporters examined, studied, analyzed, and copied them for two-and-a-half eye-straining weeks.

Selo came in from time to time to ask, "What are you looking for? What are you trying to prove?"

The reporters found what they had expected to find. Throughout the reports and racing license applications that no reporter had previously bothered to inspect, were the tracks of Emprise's tentacles and references to known underworld front men. The giant concession conglomerate had wielded immense power in Ohio horse racing with million-dollar loans and long-term concession contracts. It had taken control of several tracks, and had frequently associated with members of the Cleveland crime syndicate.

Goltz and Smith had begun investigating Emprise and its chief subsidiary, Sportservice Corporation, after Emprise was convicted along with three Mafia bosses for concealing their ownership of a Las Vegas gambling casino, and the House Select Committee on Crime announced it would take testimony on the concession empire's ties with organized crime. The two reporters took ten months to pull together from all over the country a complete picture of the company's farflung power in sports and dealings with the underworld. Their findings were published in a June, 1973, series that began, "A vast business conglomerate with direct links to organized crime figures and extensive dealings with publicly owned sports facilities has established a secret and powerful hold on the horse racing industry and large segments of professional sports."

The articles won a 1974 Heywood Broun Award honorable mention. They also emboldened the Ohio State Liquor Commission to revoke nineteen liquor permits held by Emprise-Sportservice at Ohio racetracks and sports arenas, only to have the action undone by a court appeal.

Goltz, who was an accountant in Iowa before he became a reporter, won a Pulitzer for a 1964 exposé of illegal kickbacks and fees among officials of a Houston suburb. A Houston *Post* reporter at the time, Goltz suffered a broken nose from a police commissioner's fist during his investigation. He headed an investigative team at the Dayton *Daily News* from 1971 until 1975.

Shortly before the Emprise assignment, Smith worked undercover briefly at a Dayton children's home to investigate reports of brutality. When another *Daily News* reporter made an appointment through channels to visit the home, Smith was on hand to witness the preparations. "Wear your coat and tie tomorrow," said a resident counselor. "The newspaper is coming and I want this place looking spotless." The children were instructed on what to say and how to behave. Afterward, the counselor crowed that he had fooled the newspaper. Smith reported it all, along with the beatings and abuse he had observed.

Wes Hills, an investigative reporter with a talent for loosening tongues by listening sympathetically, inadvertently ran Dayton's biggest heroin dealer out of town.

Hearing from police that the city's top dope trader was thirty-five-year-old George Lewis, Hills took a direct approach to verification. He asked Lewis. A flashy dresser with a diamond in his tooth and a house guarded by dogs and TV cameras, Lewis said, on-the-record, not any more, but off-the-record, yes. Hills' story prompted federal agents to get serious about Lewis and he shortly was arrested for selling heroin to an undercover agent. At his trial, a city cop testified that, unknown to the feds, Lewis was an informant for Dayton police. Before the day was over, Lewis disappeared. True or not, identification as an informer had put his life in danger. Lewis later reappeared and was sent to prison.

The Cleveland *Plain Dealer's* I-Team sent two reporters to pose as patients in 1973 to investigate doctors who freely dispensed prescriptions for dangerous drugs. At one doctor's office, they found, it was possible to get a prescription for Quaalude, a trade name for methaqualone, without seeing or talking to the doctor, without providing medical background information, or for that matter, without asking for one. A patient just plunked down fifteen dollars for the office visit and departed with a prescription for forty-five tablets.

That doctor pleaded guilty to a federal charge of dispensing a drug without a valid prescription, and his medical license was suspended for four months. Another doctor pleaded guilty to aiding and abetting the unlawful possession of Quaalude and was fined $5,000.

Principals in a Cleveland nursing home were indicted for grand theft and larceny-by-trick in 1975 after the I-Team revealed a double-billing scheme in which the nursing home collected Medicaid reimbursements from the state and then billed the families for the same services. They were accused of illegally collecting $32,000.

Gerald White, the Cincinnati *Enquirer's* full-time investigative reporter, says "investigative" is the wrong word. He prefers "documentation." He says, "I want to see the ledger, the memo, the log. I don't want somebody telling me what it says. I am extremely nervous about writing an investigative story in which I rely entirely upon the spoken word. I use a tape recorder and I use affidavits. But I still prefer the public document."

The public record was the first place White looked when he got a tip in 1970 that a machinery company worker had been improperly confined in a state mental hospital. He found that Morris Garvey had been taken there by two sheriff's deputies after his wife signed a probate court affidavit saying he was mentally ill and dangerous. The judge had ordered detention without investigating, though he had the authority to do so. Especially disturbing, White discovered, was that this was the normal procedure.

Garvey had not been allowed to call a lawyer or send out a sealed letter despite state laws giving him both rights. Garvey finally was released after seventeen days when a hearing was held. Then he got a $152 bill from the institution.

White spent six months sifting through court records and parking tickets for his 1971 exposé of policemen who fixed parking tickets for themselves, relatives, and friends. They had the help of judges who exempted them from paying fines on tickets for which the policemen took responsibility. White discovered that many of the parking tickets which the policemen presented to the judges as their own actually had been issued to cars of relatives and friends.

Articles disclosing that a probate judge gave favorable divorce rulings to lawyers who were his friends or business associates required three months of divorce record analysis. White also uncovered the judge's predilection for seeking campaign contributions from parties in pending divorces.

"I devote my full efforts to probing activities of public officials," says

White, a veteran reporter who has worked for several newspapers. "I try to give performance audits to public agencies—how well they are spending the public's money, what their work habits are, how well they perform. I am the public's man at city hall."

12

Mavericks and Lone Wolves

HANK MESSICK WAS WORRIED. The November election was fast approaching but the federal grand jury had not acted. Four years of crusading against crime and corruption in Newport, Kentucky, were about to go down the drain.

A group of ministers and citizens had prevailed upon George Ratterman, a thirty-four-year-old former quarterback at the University of Notre Dame, to be the reform candidate for Campbell County sheriff. Messick's investigations for the Louisville *Courier-Journal* had helped get grand jury indictments of city officials and the police chief, but the scandal would blow over and corruption would return to normal unless Ratterman won the sheriff's office.

That was so clearly the key to the battle that the underworld had tried to ruin Ratterman with a frame-up. Enticed to a Cincinnati restaurant across the Ohio River to meet a gambler pretending to turn informer, Ratterman was given a drugged cocktail. Groggy, he was taken to a Newport hotel room. A striptease dancer in a transparent nightgown was brought in. Arrangements had been made for a photographer, but when he failed to show up, the plotters switched to an alternate plan. Police arrived and arrested Ratterman.

The citizenry knew a frame-up when they saw one, and charges against Ratterman were thrown out when the photographer testified about the role he had been expected to play. But the federal grand jury investigating the frame-up had been strangely quiet for months. It was now October, and April Flowers, the stripper in the hotel room, had not yet testified. Newport gamblers spread the word that the grand jury's failure to act was proof that Ratterman hadn't been framed.

One rumor had it that Frank Sinatra's friend, actor Peter Lawford, had persuaded Lawford's brother-in-law, U.S. Attorney General Robert Kennedy, to keep hands off Newport. Messick contacted a few sources in federal law enforcement agencies and found the truth to be less sinister, but just as troubling. Someone in Washington had decided the grand jury shouldn't act until after the election, in order to avoid any appearance of meddling in local politics. Messick resolved to get that changed.

He tracked down April Flowers in St. Louis and persuaded her to tell her story. Published two weeks before the election, it gave April's version of the frame-up and said she feared for her life until she could testify. The Justice Department changed its mind and promptly convened the grand jury to hear April's testimony. On October 27, six men, including three policemen, were indicted for conspiracy to violate Ratterman's civil rights. Ten days later, Ratterman won a landslide victory at the polls.

Messick's investigations in Newport had begun when the *Courier-Journal* sent him the 100 miles from Louisville to inquire about rumors of reform stirrings in the notorious gambling town, which had been a mecca for Cleveland and New York mobsters for more than twenty years. Locating corruption had been a snap. Messick just walked into a gambling joint and placed a bet.

He made good use of a shuffling, disarming manner. "The officials and gangsters thought I was a dumb hick," recalls Messick, who was born in North Carolina's Blue Ridge Mountains in 1922. "They thought I was a hillbilly who didn't know anything. They thought they were using me and I let them think so. I adapt my methods to the people I'm dealing with."

Messick happened into investigative reporting when he went to Waynesville, North Carolina, in search of newspaper experience after teaching journalism for three years at Colorado A & M College. He got experience he hadn't anticipated when he started exposing police protection of gambling joints. A crooked cop tried to beat him up. Later, in Newport, a cop slipped some records to him from a drawer, then tried to get him arrested for receiving stolen property. Telephone threats in the middle of the night became part of the routine for Messick and his wife. Once he tripped and fell while groping to answer a call at 2:30 A.M. The injury to his foot produced a permanent limp that eventually caused him to put on weight and become portly.

After Ratterman's election, Messick received a Ford Foundation grant to make a nationwide study of organized crime. For two years he traveled the country to nose into police files and call on gangsters. Though few of the latter would admit to current lawbreaking, many were delighted to talk about old times. The material he gathered formed the basis for *The Silent Syndicate*, the first of several books he's written on organized crime in the United States.

When the foundation grant expired in 1965, Messick signed a contract with the Miami *Herald* to expose crime and corruption in southern Florida. His studies had convinced him that Miami was the new crime capital of America. His first step was to call on police departments to make his arrival known. Then he sat back to await a contact by any policeman, informant, or mobster who might wish to use him.

It wasn't long before the call came. A gambler who called himself Charley wanted revenge on the crime syndicate for squeezing him out. Charley took Messick on a tour of Miami's gambling spots, told him how protection money was collected and distributed, arranged for the reporter to pose as a buyer of a brothel, introduced him to other gamblers who had reasons to talk about payoffs, and explained how Fat Hymie Martin controlled it all for the syndicate.

Messick's first articles for the *Herald* revealed the syndicate's takeover of Miami rackets. His second series described the local prostitution business. Publication of the stories attracted new sources as well as police harassment. Before the end of the year, Messick exposed the brain behind it all as organized crime's financial wizard, Meyer Lansky, who lived a few miles north of Miami. The following year, Messick revealed that Lansky had his fingers in the new casino in the Bahamas. Lansky's bodyguard and chauffeur, Phil "The Stick" Kovolick, had become one of Messick's sources inside the Mob.

The articles also triggered a panicky series of machinations among mobsters, police, and politicians. Grand jury investigations began in Dade and Broward counties, but Messick didn't trust them. When he was subpoenaed, he wondered whether the grand jury wanted his help or his hide. The Dade County grand jury issued a report denouncing the police for not enforcing the law, but then went to sleep. The sheriffs of both counties assigned deputies to tail Messick. Indictments eventually were issued against the sheriffs, but Messick grew unhappy over the *Herald's* balking at his stories on payoffs to Dade County Sheriff T. A. Buchanan, corruption in Broward County, and connections between a mob lawyer and Dade County State Attorney Richard Gerstein. The *Herald* won a Sigma Delta Chi Award with Messick's 1965 stories, and signed him to a new eighteen-month contract. But Messick couldn't get a staff reporter's job, and when the paper told him to ease up after Buchanan was acquitted and threatened a lawsuit, he began to think about where he would go next.

That turned out to be the Boston *Herald-Traveler,* where Messick and *Herald* reporter James Savage joined Nick Gage in an ill-fated investigative team for a few months in 1967. They uncovered the underworld ties of a prominent Bostonian, only to be told to stop investigating. All three left. Savage and Messick returned to Florida, but only Savage went back to the *Herald.* Messick wrote a column for the Miami Beach *Sun* from his Fort Lauderdale home, and began his books on organized crime.

Messick's adventures in journalism made him a cynic. A "good" investigative reporter, he says, "must lead his editors into an investigation until the probe is past the point of no return." A "successful" investigative reporter, however, "must understand that while his paper wants to look like it is aggressive and crusading, it doesn't want anyone rocking the boat." A good investigative reporter "must resign himself to unpopularity—on the paper, on the street, and perhaps at home." A successful one finds "a popular crusade that doesn't hurt anyone," tries "to get something hot on the politician his newspaper dislikes," and recognizes "that the dedicated reporter who is trying to improve humanity and the newspaper won't be around very long." The good investigative reporter, says Messick, "develops ulcers, or quits, or turns to drink; the successful reporter ultimately gets promoted or finds a high-paying job in public relations."

Messick would say it's realism, not cynicism. On election night in 1968, as Richard Nixon won election as President of the United States, Messick made an entry in his journal that said: "Nixon's elected. We're headed for the biggest scandal since Teapot Dome." Early in 1969, Messick wrote in the Miami Beach *Sun*: "Informants in the Mob are reporting that a 'contract' has been let for Teamster boss James Hoffa. Apparently it was inspired by a columnist who reported in December that Jimmy was about to be pardoned. Seems the money men of the Mob have been getting better deals from those holding the pension fund purse strings than they got from Hoffa. He was always hungry and the boys would rather give him lead than bread.'' Six years later, events had proven Messick a man of reality.

There was the landscaping equipment all right, unattended and idle. Bob Wyrick had thought it strange when he found the $200,000 equipment rental contract in the Brevard County school records. It was the only school system in Florida that rented equipment to do its own landscaping. Something was fishy.

Of six bidders on the contract, only one, T. A. Altman, had met the specifications. Wyrick asked the purchasing agent if Altman did any other business with the school board. The sod, he said. Altman supplied the sod.

Wyrick went out to the new football field and paced off the sod. 104,000 square feet. The contract, however, said 140,000 square feet. He paced if off again. Still 104,000.

"What about this?" Wyrick asked H. T. Olsen, the maintenance department superintendent.

Don't worry about it, said Olsen. There was more sod yet to be laid on the track around the field.

Wyrick went back and measured the entire field. No one could put 140,000 square feet of sod on the field even if he sodded over the bleachers.

So he measured every school landscaping job of the previous few years. They all came up several thousand square feet short. $7,000 worth, altogether.

Now leery of Olsen, too, Wyrick wondered what else was being stolen. He went to see Lyle Gillenwater, a former maintenance department employe who had been fired, at Gillenwater's restaurant. A disgruntled party is often a talkative source.

"Yeah, I know a couple of things," said Gillenwater. They concerned school superintendent Woodrow J. Darden, he said, but refused to say more. He took a piece of paper out of his wallet, said, "Yep, still got it," and put it back.

It had all started with a tip. A relative of Darden allegedly had owned land bought by the school board for a controversial school site across the main highway from the homes of most pupils. The city editor of *Today*, the daily newspaper in Cocoa, Florida, asked Wyrick to check it out. It was a school board member who had had an interest in the land, and a T. A. Altman was involved. Checking into Altman's identity had led to the discovery that Altman had an equipment contract with the school board.

Wyrick reported what he had found to a local judge, who asked the governor to send a special investigator. Wyrick went back to Gillenwater to see if he'd open up to the governor's man.

"Hang on a minute," said Gillenwater as he disappeared into a back room. When he returned, he opened his wallet and gave Wyrick the piece of paper. It contained the serial numbers of a washer-dryer and a swimming pool heater. They belonged to the school, said Gillenwater, but he had been ordered to take them to Darden's home. Darden, said Gillenwater, had been using school-owned appliances in his home for years.

Wyrick's first articles appeared on January 10, 1967. Before the end of February, the grand jury returned larceny indictments against Darden and Altman. Darden was found guilty of stealing the swimming pool heater. The indictments against Altman were later dropped.

Wyrick asked Gillenwater what had prompted him finally to turn over the piece of paper.

"Well, I've always been trying to find out from Darden why I was fired," Gillenwater explained. "I was never able to get through to him and when you came in I thought I'd try one more time. I heard his secretary tell him who it was and he said, 'If it's that fucking Gillenwater, tell him I'm not here.' So, I figured if he's not going to treat me like a man, well, fuck him."

Wyrick won the 1967 Heywood Broun Award for the stories.

Among fellow journalists in Washington, where Wyrick went in 1973 as a member of *Newsday's* bureau, Wyrick is known as much for his unconventional appearance and background as his toughness. He wears his hair in a pony tail and betrays no hesitation to discuss his five years in a West Virginia prison for armed robbery. He taught himself how to type in prison. After he was paroled at the age of twenty-three in 1959, he took courses toward an English degree at Fenton College in Cleveland while earning a living as a bread truck driver. A fellow student suggested he apply for a public relations opening at the local utility. He didn't get that, but a few days later received an invitation to become a reporter at the Willoughby *News-Herald,* a small daily near Cleveland. He later went to the Miami *News,* then *Today,* and in 1969 to *Newsday.*

"He's not scared of anyone," says Anthony Marro, a former colleague at *Newsday.* "But I'd never want him to get mad at me. He's a wild man. You send him after someone and he'll get him. But he doesn't distinguish between a wrist slap and a throat cut."

Wyrick has been tough on fellow reporters, too. One of his exposés at *Newsday* before he moved to the Washington bureau revealed the names of eighteen New York reporters who had been secretly on the payroll of politicians. Using a computer, Wyrick tracked down the names of five reporters and editors who had been receiving state money through their wives' maiden names. The computer had compared the addresses on a state legislative payroll with those of 700 newspaper employes. Among the newsmen who Wyrick exposed were two from his own newspaper.

After the judges ruled there was enough evidence to try Clay L. Shaw on charges of conspiracy in the assassination of President John F. Kennedy, James Phelan placed a telephone call to New Orleans District Attorney James Garrison.

"Something bothers me," Phelan said to Garrison. "All that testimony by Perry Russo about the party where he heard Dave Ferrie, Leon Oswald, and

Clay Shaw talking about the assassination. None of that was in your man's report on his first interview with Russo."

Phelan was referring to a report by one of Garrison's assistants, Andrew J. "Moo" Sciambra. Phelan had obtained a copy of the report from Garrison two weeks earlier in Las Vegas. Garrison had also given him a transcript of a susbsequent interview of Russo under hypnosis, in which Russo had talked about the party under prodding by the hypnotist.

Garrison sounded surprised. He suggested a meeting in his office so Sciambra could explain.

Sciambra said he didn't know what Phelan was talking about.

Phelan said he had read the first report carefully and knew exactly what was in it.

"Maybe I forgot to put it in," said Sciambra. He had been busy with several cases.

Phelan remarked that it was incredible he could have forgotten such important evidence in the crime of the century. He asked to see Sciambra's notes on the interview. They would show whether Russo had mentioned an assassination plot.

Sciambra fidgeted. He had burned the notes, he said.

Phelan next talked to Dr. Esmond Fatter, the doctor who had hypnotized Russo. According to the transcript in Phelan's possession, Fatter had repeatedly prompted Russo's reluctant memory. When Russo mentioned nothing about a party or an assassination plot, Fatter had asked him to visualize a TV screen, and on it a party scene in an apartment. "Tell me about it," the doctor had said. When Russo still mentioned no plot, Fatter again instructed him to visualize the party scene, saying, "They are going to discuss a very important matter and there is another man and girl there and they are talking about assassinating somebody. Look at it and describe it for me."

Phelan asked Dr. Fatter where he had obtained the information he had used to prompt Russo. The doctor said it had come from Garrison's office.

Garrison's investigation had been revealed by a New Orleans newspaper in February. It made national headlines when Ferrie, a strange, flamboyant character, was found dead in his apartment, and Garrison announced he had solved the Kennedy assassination. Now Phelan wrote his story for the May 6, 1967, issue of the *Saturday Evening Post*, where he was a staff writer from 1963 to 1969. It was the first article to point out the flaws in Garrison's evidence.

Except for his six years at the *Saturday Evening Post*, Phelan has free-lanced since 1953, when he decided, after twenty years of newspapering, that daily journalism didn't afford enough time to do a story right. His chief newspaper outlet has been Hank Greenspun's Las Vegas *Sun*, which published Phelan's 1971 exposé of a uranium mine stock scheme in Canada by four aides of billionaire Howard Hughes.

Phelan discovered that, contrary to the impression given by the stock prospectus and news releases, Hughes had no interest in Pan American Mines Ltd. One of the company's officers was a Flagstaff, Arizona, gravel dealer whose firm was bankrupt. In Arizona, Phelan learned the company owned no mines, just untested mining claims for which it had paid $3,003,000—in stock, not cash. An insurance company said to have pledged a million-dollar loan for a uranium mill had a net worth of only $197,000, which Phelan discovered by checking records at the state insurance commission. Pan American Mines had only fifteen dollars in the bank. Several months after Phelan's articles appeared, the Canadian Stock Exchange suspended trading in the stock and started investigations that led to a national scandal.

Americans perhaps know Phelan best for his role as a victim in the Clifford Irving hoax. At first convinced that Irving's "autobiography" of Howard Hughes was authentic, Phelan later made the discovery that completed the annihilation of Irving's story.

While relaxing at home in Long Beach, California, Phelan read a *New York Times* article about an incident in Irving's manuscript in which Hughes chewed out a publicity man for calling him from Hollywood columnist Hedda Hopper's unlisted phone. The *New York Times* reporter had called the publicity man, Perry Lieber, and Lieber had been astonished. He had never told anyone about it, Lieber said. Irving must have gotten it from Hughes.

By the time that Phelan read this, Irving had already gone before a grand jury, and several holes in his story had been exposed, including his wife's having posed as "H. R. Hughes" to cash checks at a Swiss bank. But Irving's publishers still clung to a desperate hope that his manuscript was genuine.

Halfway through the *New York Times* article, Phelan jumped up. "I've got it!" he shouted. "Irving stole my manuscript."

Phelan had collaborated with former Hughes aide Noah Dietrich on Dietrich's memoirs, and had written a draft manuscript before Dietrich switched to another writer. The Lieber incident had been in Phelan's draft, and that's where Irving must have learned about it. Lieber had mentioned the incident to Phelan, but then apparently forgot that he had.

Irving's publishers were now receptive to Phelan's suggestion that his manuscript be compared with Irving's, though they had spurned his earlier offers to examine Irving's manuscript. A four-hour comparison meeting shattered whatever illusions had lingered. There were anecdotes in Irving's manuscript that had come to Phelan from sources other than Hughes. Hughes could not possibly have given them to Irving because Hughes hadn't known about them.

A Hollywood wheeler-dealer named Stanley Meyer, who had ostensibly been helping to get the Dietrich-Phelan book published, later admitted to a grand jury that he had let Irving borrow Phelan's manuscript.

Greenspun, who had offered to kiss Phelan's ass 130 times on the Las Vegas Strip if Irving's book was genuine, did not have to pay off.

Every time the Pennsylvania Public Utilities Commission held a meeting, Art Geiselman attended. Even when a meeting ran on for hours, Geiselman remained there, dutifully taking notes. One purpose was to write news stories for the Philadelphia *Bulletin*. Another was to spot the seemingly innocuous bits of information that only an experienced investigative reporter would recognize as tip-offs to possible villainy.

After joining the *Bulletin*'s state capital bureau in Harrisburg in 1973 with a long, diversified background in journalism, Geiselman exposed payoffs to PUC inspectors by taxi companies, tolerance for violations of an underground wiring requirement by certain favored utilities, and a PUC member's job with a political fund raiser who owned three firms regulated by the PUC.

The PUC has not been Geiselman's only target, however. Two Williamsport councilmen who pushed through a lucrative franchise for Governor Milton Shapp's cable TV company later got state patronage jobs. After Geiselman exposed it, the FBI began an investigation. Geiselman's stories on corruption in the state Horse Racing Commission, including a $25,000 payoff to a prominent state politician and organized crime connections among holders of racing licenses, led to resignations by the commission's chairman and his top aides.

For three years prior to joining the *Bulletin*, Geiselman plied his investigative skills for TV stations in Washington, D.C., and Baltimore, Maryland. In Washington, he exposed illegal raids by state police on the office and homes of two men who had sued an oil company. In Baltimore, he disclosed a judge's role in a questionable land deal, the state's inaction on Baltimore Harbor pollution, a cover-up of thirty-five nursing home deaths from salmonella poisoning, and unsafe conditions in city schools.

Geiselman won two Heywood Broun Awards during fourteen years at the *Gazette and Daily* in York, Pennsylvania, from 1951 to 1965. One was for 1957 exposés of corruption in the York police court and coroner's office, and racial discrimination in public facilities. The second was for 1963 disclosures of housing code nonenforcement. Later at the Baltimore *Evening Sun*, he revealed illegal incarceration of mental patients, discrimination in the sentencing of black rapists whose victims were white, and Ku Klux Klan terrorism against a book store.

Experience does not necessarily develop confidence, says Geiselman, who's in his mid-forties and has a mild, disarming manner. "As I get older I become more and more concerned about making mistakes," he says. "After a big story I sweat it out for fourteen hours waiting for someone to find a serious mistake in it. It gets tough on the nerves. Even if each story is perfectly accurate, there always is somebody who complains to your publisher or television station manager. Your boss usually will support you one hundred percent but as more and more complaints come in he begins to wonder if maybe there is something to all this.

"A number of my friends in the business have become alkies or have other problems that have broken up their homes or otherwise affected their personal lives. Think about how many guys have remained in investigative reporting for any real length of time. Most guys hit it big with one story, such as Woodward and Bernstein, write a book and then get out.''

"What would you think,'' asked the President of the United States, ''if I ordered Castro assassinated?''

Startled, Tad Szulc of *The New York Times* mumbled something about being against assassinations and said it probably wouldn't solve anything anyway.

President Kennedy leaned back in his rocking chair and smiled. He said he didn't approve of political assassination, either, but he'd been under pressure from advisers in "the intelligence community'' to have Cuban Premier Fidel Castro killed. "I'm glad you feel the same way,'' he said.

It was November, 1961, in the Oval Office of the White House. If Szulc, then with the *Times'* Washington bureau, had followed up the hint of assassination proposals, he might have beaten columnist Jack Anderson to the story by five years.

As it was, Szulc had missed publication of a big Cuban scoop already, through no fault of his own. His report from Miami seven months earlier that a CIA-trained army of Cuban exiles was about to invade Cuba had been softened by *Times* editors before publication.

Szulc was being transferred to Washington from Rio de Janeiro, where he had been the *Times'* Latin American correspondent for six years, and stopped in Miami to visit friends. While there, he discovered that an invasion force was preparing to leave.

Szulc's story originally was scheduled to be the lead story on the front page of April 7, 1961, but *Times* publisher Orvil Dryfoos was bothered about national security implications. According to a 1966 lecture by *Times* managing editor Clifton Daniel before the World Press Institute in St. Paul, Minnesota, Dryfoos feared the invasion would fail and the *Times* would be blamed for it. Dryfoos spoke about his concern to managing editor Turner Catledge and they phoned James Reston of the paper's Washington bureau to ask his advice.

Reston advised against publishing any information that would alert Castro to the time of the invasion. Words about the invasion's imminence were therefore deleted from Szulc's copy. References to the CIA also were removed, and plans to play the story in the lead spot were changed. The article did run as scheduled, but in a form that added little to earlier stories.

Ten years later, Szulc beat columnist Anderson on another story, but no one perceived its significance at the time. Szulc revealed on June 22, 1971, that the United States was shipping military equipment to Pakistan despite an announcement by the State Department that such sales had been suspended. Based on classified intelligence reports obtained by Szulc, the story prompted the White House "plumbers'' squad to put a tap on Szulc's phone. Szulc was

treated later to a break-in of his home by the "plumbers." Anderson, meanwhile, won a Pulitzer for disclosing details of the Nixon Administration's
secret aid to Pakistan in its war with India.

In 1973, Szulc ended his twenty-year association with the *Times*, most of it
as a foreign correspondent, to devote himself full time to free-lance writing.
One of his first undertakings was a reconstruction of events leading up to the
January, 1973, Vietnam cease-fire agreement. In an article published in
Foreign Policy, Szulc disclosed that Henry Kissinger's decisive maneuver had
occurred in Moscow in April, 1972, when he indicated to Soviet Party Secretary Leonid Brezhnev that the United States would drop its insistence on
withdrawal of North Vietnamese troops from South Vietnam as a precondition
for a cease-fire. This, Szulc revealed, broke the ice. Hanoi then stopped
insisting that South Vietnamese President Thieu be removed before it could
accept a cease-fire.

Szulc also disclosed several secret commitments Kissinger had made to forge
the cease-fire pact. The most important was an agreement to remove within a
year all American civilians helping South Vietnamese military forces.

Kissinger's intricate diplomacy, Szulc wrote, kept Moscow, Peking, and
Hanoi off balance, and even Nixon sometimes found it hard to follow. But
Szulc sorted it out.

The idea was to write a book on the most famous, most brilliant doctors in
America—the Superdoctors. The method that Roger Rapoport chose to gather
the material was at once direct, ingenious, and simple.

Rapoport asked each doctor for permission to spend a few days with him—at
work, with his family, on the golf course. Only two of twenty-five turned him
down. The doctors at first were careful, conscious of the writer's presence. But
after a while they would forget about him and slip back into normal behavior.
"They became incredibly candid," says Rapoport, a thirty-one-year-old free-
lance writer who lives in Berkeley, California. One, for instance, explained his
strategy for thwarting investigations by government committees.

As part of the deal, Rapoport interviewed only relatives, friends, and
professional associates selected by the doctors. No enemies, not even an
impartial observer. It wasn't necessary. The doctors and their friends revealed
more telling facts about themselves than any enemy could have supplied. They
didn't recognize the unbecoming implications of their habits and attitudes,
Rapoport says, because it all seemed sensible and right to them.

At Cook County Hospital in Chicago, one of several places that Rapoport
investigated on a cross-country tour for a 1973 *Playboy* magazine article
exposing incompetence and chicanery in the medical profession, Rapoport
followed a resident doctor around for several days. When the doctor said he'd
have to get clearance from public relations, Rapoport asked public relations if
he could talk to the doctor, then told the doctor that public relations had okayed

his proposal. Ordinarily he avoids public relations people and administrators as long as possible.

Rapoport exposed hospital kickbacks to doctors for sending patients to fill empty beds in 1974, revealed a new trend toward profit-making hospitals in 1972, and wrote one of the first stories about the use of Ritalin to tranquilize hyperactive school children in 1971. None of those matched the splash he achieved with his 1975 article in *New Times* magazine on a California surgeon who had botched so many operations that malpractice judgments against him had passed $10 million. "A story seems to have more impact," says Rapoport, "when there's a specific villain of the piece."

He's investigated other fields too, with his get-next-to-them method. Among the chief sources for his muckraking 1971 book on the dangers of nuclear bomb making, *The Great American Bomb Machine*, were two Atomic Energy Commission scientists, John Gofman and Arthur Tamplin. Rapoport visited the two scientists frequently, striking up a friendship over a period of time. "I hang around a lot," he says, "and work myself into the milieu. After a while, they start to let their hair down."

The real secret, he says, is "finding people like Gofman and Tamplin who have the information."

Rapoport, who's tall, dark, and unhurried, first made a name for himself as an investigative reporter at the University of Michigan student daily. He exposed the improper use of university library materials by a microfilm firm owned by a university regent, who later resigned.

The Patty Hearst story almost became a Rapoport property when he got close to Steve Weed, her fiancé. He wrote a couple of exclusive reports for *New Times* magazine on Weed's relationship with Patty and Weed's behavior during the frantic weeks after her kidnaping. He also began working with Weed on a book.

But they had a falling out. David Weir and Howard Kohn of *Rolling Stone*, the counterculture music publication that expanded into investigative material, came up with 1975's best Patty Hearst story, an inside account of her life and travels as a fugitive. Weir and Kohn found sports activist Jack Scott, who had traveled with Patty and her companions, a better source to get close to.

Bullets smashed into the newspaper's office, equipment was wrecked, paint was splattered on the furniture. Cars were firebombed and tires slashed. Bundles of the underground publication were thrown into San Diego Bay. One landlord made the newspaper move because he had been threatened with death. Its next landlord was arrested for murder. Lowell Bergman and other staff members of the *Street Journal* set up a guard duty system to maintain a twenty-four-hour vigilance.

The trouble began after the *Street Journal* ran articles about San Diego's leading citizen, C. Arnholt Smith, one of California's richest men and a friend of President Nixon. The *Street Journal* said Smith had made payoffs to the mayor and the city council, and had gone to Nixon to get an IRS investigation of a longtime associate killed. The associate, John Alessio, had connections with the underworld, according to the *Street Journal*.

Some of the material had already appeared in the *Wall Street Journal*. Alessio was indicted soon after for income tax evasion. San Diego Mayor Frank Curran was indicted within a few months for taking bribes from a taxi company controlled by Smith. Smith, himself, became a target of federal investigators. In 1972 the Securities and Exchange Commission accused Smith and others of systematically looting $100 million from their multimillion-dollar real estate, hotel, insurance, aviation, taxicab, and tuna canning conglomerate. The following year Smith's National Bank of San Diego became the biggest bank in American history ever to collapse. As his $1.5-billion empire crumbled, the seventy-five-year-old Smith was indicted in 1974 by a federal grand jury for criminal conspiracy and fraud in connection with $170 million in loans from his defunct bank. In 1975, Smith pleaded no contest to the charges and escaped with a $30,000 fine, but a county grand jury handed down new indictments.

Back in late 1969 and early 1970, however, the *Street Journal* was getting all the heat. It came from a right-wing extremist group called the Minutemen, which had help from the police. When three of the paper's staff were arrested for criminal syndicalism, the twenty-five-year-old Bergman, a sociology teacher, decided to live in Canada for a while.

He returned a year later to write articles for West Coast newspapers and magazines on Smith and his involvement in financing the lavish La Costa Country Club near San Diego along with the Teamsters Union's Central State Pension Fund. Bergman didn't hesitate to mention the crime syndicate figures behind the founding of La Costa.

Bergman met Jeff Gerth, a twenty-seven-year-old Columbia Business School graduate who was writing articles on computerized information systems and organized crime connections with legitimate businesses. Gerth had heard rumors of ties between the underworld and Nixon. With a grant from the Fund for Investigative Journalism, he compiled a lengthy summary of the organized crime connections among men who had had business dealings with Nixon. Gerth's article was published in the November, 1972, issue of *Sundance* magazine, a short-lived San Francisco publication, and reprinted later in *Penthouse* magazine.

Penthouse was also the outlet for the La Costa article by Bergman and Gerth that provoked a $630 million libel suit by Morris B. "Moe" Dalitz and other principals at La Costa. Published in March, 1975, the article said, "It looks very innocent. But in reality this rich man's playground, patronized by powerful figures from business, labor, and government, was established and is frequented by mobsters." The money to build the club had come from C. Arnholt Smith's bank as well as the Teamsters pension fund, according to the article. La Costa, it said, was controlled by the Moe Dalitz mob, and Dalitz "had been a prime mover in transforming organized crime into a financial powerhouse." Bergman and Gerth recounted the meeting of top White House aides at La Costa to devise strategy against the Senate Watergate Committee, and referred to "the triumvirate of government, business, and organized crime."

There was little in the article that was new. Much of its information had been published in *The New York Times*, the Los Angeles *Times*, *Overdrive* magazine, and other periodicals and books. Bergman had disclosed many of the facts in his earlier articles. But this one got the reaction. Dalitz, three partners, and five of their companies sued *Penthouse*, Bergman and Gerth. In a motion to have Dalitz and the others declared public figures who would need to prove "actual malice" to win a libel suit, *Penthouse* lawyers cited "an extremely detailed, well documented historical connection between plaintiffs and organized crime of which they are a principal and important part." In what the news media welcomed as a significant decision affecting investigations of organized crime, a Los Angeles judge ruled on November 20, 1975, that Dalitz and his associates were indeed public figures.

Meanwhile, Richard Nixon emerged briefly from his retirement at San Clemente to play a round of golf with Teamsters Union president Frank Fitzsimmons at La Costa.

By the time the energy crisis burst into America's consciousness in 1973, James Ridgeway was bored with it. He had been writing articles on the topic since 1965. His 1973 book, *The Last Play*, is an encyclopedia of facts about the corporations that monopolize the world's energy resources, their operations, and the hidden forces behind them.

As an associate editor at the *New Republic* from 1962 to 1968, Ridgeway also had been revealing the nation's plunge toward water pollution catastrophe well ahead of the environmental movement. His 1970 book, *The Politics of Ecology*, exposed how corporate "antipollution" campaigners actually were the nation's worst polluters, how new pollution control laws were being flouted by government as well as industry, how governmental units were causing the most appalling water pollution in the United States with decrepit sewage treatment plants, and how federal government policies legitimized pollution, encouraged exploitation of natural resources, and diverted public attention from the true dangers of industrial pollution—all while the rest of the country was barely beginning to discuss the issue.

Ridgeway was ahead of everyone else on Ralph Nader, too. He started writing about Nader when America's most famous citizen activist was "just a guy in Washington no one paid any attention to." Ridgeway helped get a publisher for the book that put Nader on the launching pad to fame, *Unsafe at Any Speed*.

He also tracked down the private detective that General Motors hired to investigate Nader in a faux pas that did as much to make Nader a public hero as his book. Some of Nader's friends told Ridgeway about visits from men asking questions about Nader. Nader complained that he was being followed. One of the names given to the friends was Gillen, which Ridgeway and an associate, David Sanford, traced to a New York investigator named Vincent Gillen. Though Gillen wouldn't say who had hired him, he admitted he'd been investigating Nader. Within a week, GM confessed.

A radical leftist intellectual with an abrupt but self-deprecating manner, Ridgeway began in 1974 to edit a monthly newsletter on energy and ecology distributed internationally by the Institute for Policy Studies. The Institute is based in Washington, where Ridgeway works from a tiny, cluttered office in rolled up sleeves and an open collar. He writes on politics for the *Village Voice* in New York and does magazine articles on energy, ecology and the American Indian movement. He's begun to probe into banking, though he admits to being baffled by economics. "I've never been able to make heads or tails of it," says Ridgeway, who once worked for the *Wall Street Journal*.

Ridgeway left the *New Republic* at the age of thirty-one to do a book and work briefly at *Ramparts*, the Catholic liberal monthly turned radical magazine. *Ramparts* had exposed the CIA funds behind the National Students Association's overseas activities, and had revealed Michigan State University's sponsorship of a technical assistance program in Saigon that was actually a CIA front.

Soon afterward, Ridgeway and free-lance writer Andrew Kopkind started up their own publication. Called *Hard Times*, it was patterned after I. F. Stone's *Weekly*, the small Washington newsletter that had made a science out of exposing government bungling and duplicity with painstaking research in printed materials, hearing transcripts, and government reports. *Hard Times* didn't last long, however. Stone's weekly also closed up before the end of 1971, but it had been discomfiting the mighty for nineteen years.

Stone concentrated on records and published materials because of a hearing problem that made interviewing difficult. Ridgeway takes the same approach, he says, because he's "so much an outsider" that interviewing is "counter-productive." Ridgeway gets most of his information about industry from careful scrutiny of the materials that industry prints for its own uses. "I've never done much interviewing," he says. "But I read a lot."

The trouble with investigative journalism, says Ridgeway, is that reporters don't read enough. "It doesn't have historical perspective."

On the walk outside the Housing and Urban Development Department building in Washington, HUD Secretary George Romney accepted a complimentary copy of a small, eight-page newsletter named *Impact* from tall, bearded, thirty-four-year-old Al Louis Ripskis.

Glancing at the publication, Romney felt his face flush. A headline at the top said, "A HUD Official, His 'Mistress' and Taxpayers' Money." The story read, "Most taxpayers don't know it, but for the last couple of years they have been subsidizing the affair of one very high HUD official, who has been cavorting with his female 'assistant' all over the country at taxpayers' expense."

This was not going on "in any clandestine manner," said the article, but "very openly." In fact, it was so blatant as to be "a standard joke to most HUD employes." What was most surprising was "that nothing has been done by the powers that be to stop this practice."

Within five minutes, two security guards told Ripskis to stop selling his newsletter or he would be arrested. Ripskis' supervisors at HUD made it clear he wouldn't be working there for long if he persisted in this uppity nonsense.

That was in October, 1972. Three years later, the man with the taxpayer-supported mistress was gone, Romney had left HUD, and even Richard Nixon had departed from government service. But Ripskis was still a program analyst for HUD's Federal Housing Administration, and still putting out *Impact*.

"I'll keep on exposing until hell freezes over," says Ripskis. "I'm boiling mad about waste and corruption and I feel my first loyalty is to the taxpayers." He takes great pains, of course, to avoid giving HUD an excuse to bounce him from his civil service job. When he takes a few minutes to work on *Impact*, he deducts the time from his annual leave. He never publishes secret information learned in the course of his HUD duties.

The issue that Romney got was the second, and its important disclosure was not the mistress, in Ripskis' view, but HUD's failure to act against the lead poisoning in house paint that was killing 200 American children every year.

Impact has exposed the collapse of HUD's highly touted New Town program for planned growth, the waste of $2.7 million on an abortive study of housing policy, and a confidential memo in which a top HUD official conceded that HUD was mismanaged.

In January, 1976, Ripskis revealed a secret HUD report admitting that federal government policies had been "major contributors to many of the nation's domestic problems."

"*Impact* is not your typical irreverent, in-house bulletin board sheet," Ralph Nader wrote in a December, 1975, column. "It deals with serious policy failures."

Unable to dislodge or discourage Ripskis, HUD officials had come to accept him as their resident maverick, Nader observed, sort of an unofficial ombudsman for the American people.

The Cleveland *Plain Dealer* ran a seven-part series of investigative articles on the Educational and Research Council of America in 1969, but something was missing. It was supposed to be an eight-part series. The missing article described the self-dealing represented by the interlocking directorships among the ERCA and the Cleveland foundations that had given ERCA $3 million. *Plain Dealer* publisher Tom Vail had canceled the article because he couldn't "see anything wrong with that." Clevelanders were nevertheless able to read it because Roldo Bartimole got his hands on it.

Bartimole ran the article in *Point of View,* the four-page pamphlet-size newsletter he publishes twice a month from his home. "This suppressed story," wrote Bartimole, "panicked Tom Vail and his editors. For it shows how the elites finance their little conspiracy with tax-free foundation funds. ERCA corporate conspirators read like a Cleveland Who's Who. . . . Vail chose again Freedom to Repress. . . . Vail is too dangerous to decide what Clevelanders will or will not read."

A former *Plain Dealer* reporter, himself, Bartimole had clearly sounded his intentions to ride herd on Cleveland's news media when he quit his job with the *Wall Street Journal* bureau in 1968 to start his acerbic one-man publication. "Cleveland's newspapers are beyond rehabilitation," he wrote in the first issue. He later described Cleveland journalism as being "at such a low level that one can best describe the reporting here as the production of poor fiction." He also said, "The mass media is incapable of honest reporting because they are so much a part of the system producing the worst in today's society."

A slightly shaggy-haired forty-four, Bartimole also scoops the news media on stories they'd run first if they had them. He once disclosed that business leaders had raised $40,000 to "buy peace" from black militants. The *Cleveland Press* picked up the story a month later. After the other media characterized a 1968 shoot-out between police and blacks as an ambush by the blacks, Bartimole dug up evidence to the contrary. He was the first to publish facts showing that a twenty-two-year-old black man reportedly killed by a sniper's bullet in the shoot-out might actually have been shot by police. He revealed that an $8,000 federal grant requested by Cleveland police was earmarked for electronic snooping equipment, and that police had once bugged Mayor Carl Stokes' private office.

Bartimole's favorite continuing target is the local charity drive called United Torch, which he says "burns a lot of people." Referring to it as United Torture, Bartimole flays it as a "businessman's scheme for making you think problems are being solved by your donation" when actually it's only a device to "extort some bucks from your pay envelope."

There's no pretense of objectivity. "It's impossible to cover anything 'objectively,' " says Bartimole. "The press uses this as a crutch and ends up telling one side of the story. What newspapers call 'community responsibility' means 'hide everything from the public that might bother them.' "

Bartimole's sources are official reports (sometimes spirited out of conceal-ment), public records ("a much greater resource than the average reporter believes or knows about"), and reporters who can't get their stories in their own media "because of stiff internal censorship."

He says he doesn't want to become too successful or well known. That might destroy his modest perspective. "It's not that I expect to make any great changes or have measurable impact. I don't believe major societal changes evolve quickly and without someone having prepared the way. I would hope at best to have been part of preparing the way."

13

Up-and-Coming Young Tigers

DURING HIS 1975 investigation of government leases, David Rothman bought a share of stock in the Madison National Bank of Washington, D.C. Federal law said a national bank must make a list of stockholders available for inspection by any stockholder, and Rothman wanted to see that list. Charles E. Smith, the bank's founding chairman and largest stockholder, was the federal government's largest landlord, and Rothman aimed to find out how many more of the bank's stockholders were among the building owners who leased office space to the federal government.

It was not to be that easy, however. Rothman was refused a look at the list. The bank said Rothman's purpose, to write an article, was "not within the intended scope" of the law.

Rothman sought help from Senator William Proxmire of Wisconsin, head of the Senate Committee on Banking, Housing and Urban Affairs. Proxmire asked the Controller of the Currency about requiring the bank to obey the law. The Controller replied it would be inappropriate because he doubted a court would compel it in such circumstances. After getting an opinion from the Library of Congress that the law contained no restriction based on the purpose in seeing the list, Proxmire suggested to the Controller that a hearing on the matter might be useful. The Controller agreed the law meant what it said and the bank let Rothman see the list.

It was typical Rothman doggedness. A tall, thin, twenty-eight-year-old free-lance reporter with thick glasses and a diffident manner, Rothman had beaten down the Government Services Administration's haughty intransigence over access to lease records with the help of congressional aides and Ralph Nader associates. After setting out in 1974 to identify the government's ten biggest landlords, Rothman bombarded the GSA—the agency that handles property, supplies, and leasing for the federal government—with requests for records under the Freedom of Information Act. For many months he got little more than disdainful non-response. "They kept stalling," says Rothman. "Stonewalling me."

He wrote more demanding letters, and got aides of key congressmen to send some, too. Once he was given a computer printout of leases, but the landlords' names had been omitted. Resolved to get the records no matter what, Rothman pressed on. "The only thing that works is making a pest of yourself," says Rothman. "Bureaucrats interpret politeness as a sign of weakness." The GSA threw up barrier after barrier, once proclaiming that what Rothman wanted would cost $500 to $600 in clerical and copying costs.

Finally, after a lawyer from a Nader organization added his pressure, the GSA gave in—for only $100. By this time, Rothman had developed sources in Congress and the GSA whose guidance helped him quickly glean the juiciest facts from the records. He showed up at the GSA office every day, or every other day, for two months to read through leases affecting the Washington area, which included nearby sections of Maryland and Virginia. GSA officials kept a close watch on him, once snatching back a document they said he had no right to see. Now that Rothman's probe was highly visible, more inside sources—"deep throats," they're called now, in honor of Woodward's and Bernstein's most celebrated anonymous informant—came to him with information to fill the gaps in the records.

But then, after he had the facts, Rothman found himself blocked by a new obstacle. He couldn't get them published.

Rothman had returned to Washington, his hometown, after five years as a reporter for the daily *Journal* in Lorain, Ohio, where he had lived so frugally to save money for a fling at free-lancing that his mother sent a check to his managing editor to buy him badly needed clothes. He learned about graft, the caprices of bureaucracy, and the difficulties of investigative reporting in a probe of Lorain's Metropolitan Housing Authority. He also discovered how to deal with obstructionist officials by writing stories about their refusals to open public records to the public. In Washington, he lived with his parents to keep expenses down while he ascertained who owned the office space the government rented.

"I thought of Washington as a white-collar factory town," Rothman says. "I was always interested in who owned the place." When he sought a grant from the Fund for Investigative Journalism, he was told he would first need an expression of interest by a publisher, which he got from *Washingtonian* magazine, a sprightly and occasionally investigative monthly publication in the nation's capital.

But the *Washingtonian* had lost interest. The magazine had published some of Rothman's material on leases involving Maryland Congressman Joe Broyhill in November, 1974, but its editors turned down his article on Charles E. Smith as Washington's Number One lessor of building space to the federal government. Rothman was given to understand that his manuscript contained too little that was new, and what the magazine had really wanted, anyway, was a personality piece on Smith, not a lot of grubby detail.

He took the material to other magazines and newspapers, but they all wanted to redo the investigation themselves or have Rothman share his findings with their own writers. The Connecticut News Service, which served several Connecticut newspapers, bought portions dealing with Senator Abraham Ribicoff's involvement in an office building leased by the government. Rothman's morale got another boost when NBC-TV's investigative reporter in Washington, James Polk, used some of the Ribicoff material on the air.

Never giving up, Rothman finally made a sale to *Federal Times*, a tabloid weekly that covers the federal civil service with aggressiveness and independence. His findings were divided into two articles. The first disclosed Smith's dealings with the GSA—twenty leases worth $13 million a year for space in twenty-three buildings managed by Smith's company, twenty-one of the buildings owned by Smith and his family, thirteen of the leases awarded without public advertisements for bids. Smith's large campaign contributions to members of Congress also were revealed.

Though Rothman was convinced the campaign contributions violated federal law and Smith was questioned by federal authorities, no serious investigation ensued, and none of the major news organizations picked up the story. "It died because the press paid no attention to it," says Rothman. "No prosecutor is going to move against a guy like Smith without pressure from the media." The large newspapers and magazines ignored the story, he believes, because it wasn't their own—and because key people at several Washington publications have business dealings with Smith.

Rothman's second article in *Federal Times* revealed the case of the missing cafeteria, a $500,000 cafeteria promised by a landlord under a twenty-year, $45 million lease for the Environmental Protection Agency's headquarters in two southwest Washington office towers. The landlord, a friend of former Vice President Spiro Agnew, never delivered the cafeteria. This disclosure produced more response—an FBI investigation of the GSA's leasing program and a Government Accounting Office probe ordered by Congress.

Rothman, meanwhile, turned his attention to investigating other government leases and contracts, and selling his articles in revised versions to enough magazines to stave off malnutrition. With Richard Rashke, another free-lance writer, Rothman also began probing into the reasons why Congress shortened the statute of limitations on election law violations from five years to three —and made it retroactive just in time to get a big corporation off the hook for illegal campaign donations to the Democratic Party in 1970 and 1972—for an article in *The Nation* magazine. That, said Rothman, cranking up his doggedness, might just be the nation's congressional Watergate.

Following instructions, Peter Gruenstein drove to a dark street in a Virginia suburb of Washington, D.C., and parked. Gruenstein's visitor arrived about 2:00 A.M. and handed him a copy of a secret audit report by Pentagon officials on millions of dollars in defense contracts with Northrop Corporation, a Los Angeles aircraft manufacturer that specializes in jet fighters.

Combined with documents that Gruenstein had pried out of sources in Congress, the Pentagon, and Northrop, the audit report gave him evidence he'd been chasing down for five months. This was indisputable proof of illegal and unethical practices by Northrop officials, high-ranking Pentagon and Air Force brass, and powerful members of Congress.

There was enough to fill several articles by the Capitol Hill News Service, which Gruenstein headed. Published in the Washington *Star* and several other prominent newspapers around the country in October, 1975, the articles revealed:

Northrop had billed the government $24,000 for expenses at a goose and duck hunting lodge in Maryland where Pentagon and Congressional VIPs had been entertained, and the government had paid the bill.

The Defense Department had reimbursed Northrop $8,336 for tickets to Washington Redskin football games given to members of Congress, their aides, and Pentagon officials.

The government had reimbursed Northrop $5.5 million, much of it in violation of Pentagon regulations, for payments disguised as consultant fees but actually made to lobbyists and political campaigns.

Gruenstein had received a phone call the previous week from a woman who wouldn't give her name. "At exactly five o'clock this afternoon," she said, "a bunch of geese will be delivered to your door." At 5:02 P.M., a brown envelope arrived at Capitol Hill's office in the National Press Building. Inside was a list of government big shots who had been entertained at Northrop's duck hunting lodge.

Gruenstein had been trying to get the list for several months, ever since he had spotted a mention of the lodge in the appendix of a 700-word Securities and Exchange Commission report on illegal political contributions. He had written two stories then—one about free plane trips by Northrop for California Governor Ronald Reagan and Arizona Senator Barry Goldwater, the other about Northrop's use of the lodge to entertain Pentagon officials, congressmen and senators.

There had been 123 visits to the lodge by military personnel during 1971–73, twenty-one by Defense Department officials, eleven by congressmen, and eighty-five by congressional staff employes. But Gruenstein had no names. A Pentagon investigation produced a guest list, which was surrendered to three congressional committees. But no one on the committees would let Gruenstein see the list because it contained congressional names.

In fact, the list delivered to his office had a serious gap. The Pentagon names had been scratched out. His source, it seemed, was connected with the Pentagon.

Verifying which of the congressional VIPs on the list actually had visited the hunting lodge, Gruenstein broke the story without the Pentagon names. That same day, a congressional source brought him an unabridged list.

Gruenstein also revealed government reimbursements to Northrop for lavish parties given by Washington hostess Anna Chennault for Pentagon brass, and $100,000 in "consultant fees" paid to Mrs. Chennault.

The FBI began an investigation and the Pentagon promised a thorough probe by the Defense Contract Audit Agency. Defense Secretary James R. Schlesinger said policies and rules on "gratuities" from contractors would be reexamined. Senator William Proxmire requested a GAO investigation of the five largest defense contractors. In February, 1976, the Pentagon suspended payment on some Northrop contracts pending completion of an audit on use of government money for political contributions and entertainment of government officials.

"The Northrop stories are of journalistic significance," says Joseph Nocera, general manager of Capitol Hill News Service, "because they meet the basic 'but for' test. But for Gruenstein's work, it is unlikely that such a vivid case study of one contractor's relationships with top Pentagon personnel could have been drawn, or that any investigations would have resulted."

Gruenstein is a twenty-eight-year-old lawyer and bachelor who eased into journalism through free-lance writing while working as a congressional aide. He set up Capitol Hill News Service with a five-reporter staff in September, 1974, on a $40,000 grant from Ralph Nader's Public Citizen Fund to provide hard, aggressive coverage of Congress for small newspapers and broadcasters that can't afford a Washington bureau. By late 1975, Capitol Hill had sixty-five print clients and a dozen TV stations. The Northrop investigation, according to Nocera, was "really a sidelight to what we usually do." The bureau's investigative work usually concerns the congressional delegations from the areas covered by its client newspapers and broadcasters.

One series described the acceptance of lobbyist gifts—plane trips, vacation junkets, cases of liquor—by employes of congressional committees. A Pennsylvania newspaper reporter's moonlighting as a $5,000-a-year public relations assistant to a congressman was exposed. "We cover the delegations extensively," says Nocera, "giving our papers their stands and thoughts on various issues and votes in Congress. Also their inconsistencies, double-talk, and other aberrations."

Under questioning by investigators for the U.S. Civil Service Commission in 1974, Donald J. LeMay signed affidavits admitting that he and other top officials of the General Services Administration had set up a system to secure government jobs for friends of politicians in Congress and the White House. Though this was a violation of federal law and civil service regulations against patronage, the GSA had taken this step to curry favor with powerful members of the government, LeMay said—and because of White House pressure.

Robert Adams of the St. Louis *Post-Dispatch* Washington bureau was more than normally pleased to obtain copies of LeMay's affidavits. They substantiated the disclosures he had been making about illegal practices in the civil service.

Adams' stories had revealed that no less a personage than the chairman of the U.S. Civil Service Commission, Robert E. Hampton, had intervened to help get a GSA job for a congressman's cousin. Adams disclosed the GSA's creation of special jobs for persons referred by Congressman (later President) Gerald Ford and Senate Republican Leader Hugh Scott, and the agency's favored treatment of workers in President Nixon's 1972 campaign. He revealed the existence of a White House instruction manual describing ways to subvert and circumvent the civil service's merit system, and Hampton's admission of using his personal influence on behalf of thirty job seekers with political connections. LeMay confirmed in his affidavits that the Nixon administration had tried to reinstall the political spoils system throughout the executive branch.

A thin, studious-looking reporter of thirty-three, Adams uncovered the widespread violations of civil service laws by interviewing personnel officials, congressional sources and Civil Service authorities, and by unearthing several incriminating letters and memos.

Adams received a special new award for government service reporting from the National Civil Service League in 1975, sharing it with Inderjit Badhwar, a thirty-two-year-old investigative reporter for *Federal Times* who also investigated abuses of the Civil Service merit system. Adams' reports, said the award citation, "were based on persistent investigation and hard work, as well as a deep understanding of, and concern for, the integrity of the merit system."

Before turning himself in to begin a twenty-year prison term in January, 1974, for setting fire to a stable of horses, Thomas J. Reddy stopped by the Charlotte (N.C.) *Observer*, where he had once worked as a reporter. While there, Reddy told Metropolitan Editor Walker Lundy about the case and claimed he was innocent.

Newly arrived from the Detroit *Free Press* where he had been city editor, Lundy realized the Lazy B Stables arson case at least presented a lot of unanswered questions. He assigned two young reporters, Michael Schwartz and Mark Ethridge III, to get some of the answers needed to evaluate Reddy's claim.

Reddy and two other black activists had been convicted in 1972 of burning down the Lazy B stable and killing fifteen horses on the night of September 24, 1968. The chief evidence against the three had been the testimony of two Vietnam War veterans with criminal records who said they had helped the trio plan and carry out the arson.

Schwartz and Ethridge located a source in the U.S. Justice Department who revealed the two prosecution witnesses had been paid at least $4,000 each by the government in exchange for testimony against the "Charlotte Three" in the stable burning, and against one of the defendants in a related federal trial. An attorney who said he had participated in the negotiations with federal authorities on the two witnesses' behalf put the figure at $15,000 each.

The *Observer* said there was enough doubt in the case to justify a new trial or commutation of the Charlotte Three's sentences by North Carolina Governor Jim Holshouser, who asked the state parole board to review the case. The parole board recommended a new trial. Defense attorneys filed a motion for a new trial, and when that was denied, they appealed.

Schwartz and Ethridge continued to investigate and, in May, 1975, after winning a 1975 Heywood Broun Award honorable mention for their 1974 stories, revealed new evidence that supported the convictions. They had found a previously unknown participant in the crime who said he had helped the Charlotte Three burn the stables. The two reporters also located friends of the defendants who said Reddy and another of the three had admitted setting the fire. Lundy says, "My original assignment had been to find out whether they burned the barn. It took us more than a year but we did, at least to my satisfaction." But Lundy still feels the Charlotte Three did not get a fair trial.

The two young reporters, who Lundy says see themselves as the *Observer's* Woodstein, investigated rumblings of discontent in the Mecklenburg County Police Department in 1974. Interviewing forty-three patrolmen, eight former patrolmen, and several high-ranking officers, they found one-third of the force admitting they goofed off on duty, fourteen acknowledging they ignored traffic violations, half the force describing morale as bad, and thirty planning to resign. The main reasons they gave were unfairness and favoritism in discipline and promotions. After the *Observer's* disclosures, the county hired a consultant to study the police department and a year later implemented most of his recommendations, including a fifteen percent cut in the size of the police force.

The *Observer* won national recognition in the fall of 1975 for exposing a secret slush fund for illegal campaign contributions at Southern Bell Telephone Company in North Carolina. The story was based on admissions by former Southern Bell executive John J. Ryan, who had operated the slush fund. Ryan said he had ostensibly been fired for his political activities with the fund, but in reality he had pursued them on instructions from company officials. Veteran newsman Marion Ellis, described by Lundy as "the most dogged reporter we have," persuaded Ryan after six weeks of negotiating to give him the essential details.

Lundy doesn't believe in a standing team of investigative reporters. Such teams, he believes, tend to make unwarranted work for themselves. Besides, an investigative suggestion by a reporter shouldn't be grabbed away from him and handed over to a special team. When a promising project comes along, Lundy picks reporters who "never make mistakes, are smarter than the people they're reporting on, have a high level of moral outrage, and will never give up the story."

Lundy claims no trade secrets. "Basically, what we do is find ourselves presented with unanswered questions and go answer them. It's simply a matter of applying logic and doggedness." His paper, he says, must be "the conscience of the community" because the police and prosecutor are "handicapped in ways we are not" and no one else has the ability or resources "to do this kind of work."

For several months, Linda Pavlik of the Fort Worth *Star-Telegram* couldn't do much with complaints about Veterans Administration hospitals except listen and file away notes for possible future use. Then one day she heard about a psychiatrist at the VA mental hospital in Waco, Texas, who was discouraged about trying to help mentally ill veterans because hospital administrators "didn't care."

Pavlik arranged to meet the psychiatrist away from the hospital and promised to protect his anonymity. With his help, she got copies of confidential medical records that confirmed complaints of premature releases and incompetent treatment.

Elliott Greenwood, a twenty-year-old veteran featured in the first of Pavlik's 1974 articles on VA hospital abuses, had been discharged from Waco "against medical advice" because the hospital wanted to dispel an image as a hellhole where patients were incarcerated indefinitely. Two weeks after his release Greenwood flung himself into the path of a truck, which killed him.

Gary Martin, a twenty-four-year-old Vietnam War casualty, fired a gun at his father and later killed a cab driver in the West Indies island of Antigua after he was released from Waco over the objections of his parents.

Gary L. Hoak, twenty-two, had committed suicide to end years of frustrated attempts to get VA treatment for mental problems caused by head injuries suffered during basic training. VA hospital officials repeatedly told Hoak's mother there was nothing they could do, though Hoak was entitled to full medical treatment and hospitalization under federal law.

Several veterans were refused service or given improper treatment. One with a severely infected leg was sent home with a bar of medicated soap. Another who complained of stomach cramps and vomiting—later discovered to be caused by a ruptured appendix—was told by a VA hospital doctor that he had hemorrhoids.

Pavlik interviewed parents, guardians and other relatives of the VA patients. She obtained additional facts from Congressman Jim Wright's office, where several complaints had also been received, and from police and coroner reports. Pavlik concluded her investigation with tape-recorded interviews of Waco VA hospital administrators who, she says, "admitted to some practices without thinking about the repercussions."

Though her articles led to the resignation and indictment of the Waco hospital's chief of staff and a 1975 Heywood Broun Award honorable mention, Pavlik is prouder of her 1975 articles with reporter Evan Moore that exposed a cover-up of crooked activities by police detectives assigned to the auto theft division.

Six detectives had been caught extorting auto parts from car theft suspects, driving stolen cars, taking gifts for failing to investigate auto theft cases, accepting bribes from towing firms, and permitting criminals to deal in stolen cars in return for information on other criminals. The only action taken against the detectives had been transfers to other jobs.

Investigating a tip from a law enforcement official who was disturbed because the detectives were still on the force, Pavlik and Moore spent two months talking to car thieves, paint and body shop operators, towing firm owners, junkyard proprietors, and used car dealers. They never telephoned in advance, but showed up suddenly for personal interviews, sometimes returning six or eight times to catch their quarry by surprise at his business or home. They also found law enforcement officers outside Fort Worth who were knowledgable and helpful. The police articles led to investigations by a grand jury and a special citizens committee.

An investigative reporter must have perseverance, says Pavlik, and a willingness to let people talk their own way. "By trying too hard to talk a person into talking to them," she says, "reporters often don't give the person a chance to say anything. The reporter dominates the conversation and doesn't learn what he came after. For me, silence coupled with an attentive attitude has paid off."

Because a source suggested he look into it, Art Thomason of the St. Louis *Globe-Democrat* made a careful study of equipment purchases for a Little League baseball field by the Model Cities antipoverty program in East St. Louis. What had started out as a request for lights at the field, he discovered, had turned into a $50,000 renovation.

Equipment invoices from different companies, he noticed, looked similar. They had the same type faces and the same sequences of invoice numbers. They appeared to have been made by the same printing firm.

Thomason found that five of the companies were owned by one salesman, who had a background of underworld connections, bankruptcies, and arrests. The Model Cities agency had bought $5,100 worth of baseball equipment from the salesman, who had split the order into five bills to avoid a requirement that public bids be taken on purchases of $1,500 or more. The antipoverty agency, in addition, had paid $6,358 for identical equipment to another firm the previous month. Thomason's 1974 articles on these discoveries led to a federal grand jury investigation.

His appetite whetted for probes of purchase records, the thirty-four-year-old, curly-haired Thomason began checking those at the East St. Louis School District. He found invoices from firms whose names didn't sound right. A look into corporation records revealed another case of several companies owned or represented by one man. This man had sold the school board $425,261 worth of light bulbs, hardware, lumber, and office and classroom equipment despite lower bids from other vendors or no bidding at all.

Thomason's articles touched off a federal grand jury probe. The salesman admitted paying kickbacks to school board members. In July, 1975, school board president Charles E. Merritts, Jr. and five other school officials were given prison sentences, probation, and fines for conspiracy to extort kickbacks from suppliers.

In the meantime, another tip had sent Thomason and reporter Robert Ryffle digging into school district records to find out why the school board had bought $180,000 worth of casualty insurance through a Chicago agency. They discovered a $100,000 deductible feature in the policy, which struck the reporters as ridiculous. Something was wrong. Thomason called the Chicago insurance broker, who said the agent in the deal had requested an unusually large commission because he had had to make a payoff.

Thomason located a source who said Merritts had received a check from someone connected with the insurance agent. Through federal law enforcement sources, Thomason traced the check to a Chicago bank and learned that $15,000 had been paid by an associate of the insurance agent to a firm set up by Merritts. Thomason had also given this information to the grand jury investigating kickbacks by school officials.

In his first investigation after joining the *Globe-Democrat* near the end of 1973, Thomason exposed unsafe specifications for an elementary school in Cahokia, Illinois, and disclosed that the architect had previously been criticized for shoddy work. The architect was indicted in 1975 in connection with an extortion scheme in a hospital construction project exposed by the *Globe-Democrat*.

Thomason's and Ryffel's growing reputations as investigative reporters attracted a call in 1975 from a man who said an Illinois judge, before he became a judge, had extorted $4,500 from him to get a criminal charge dismissed. The caller produced a letter documenting his accusation. Another grand jury investigation.

Success in triggering federal probes has not impressed Thomason. "The wheels of justice grind so slowly it's pathetic," he says. It's discouraging when lawbreakers get away because a statute of limitations expires. But that doesn't stop Thomason from investigating. Greedy officials find the graft opportunities in government contracts too tempting to resist, so there's always plenty to investigate.

"The doctors can't believe I'm still alive," said Jim Tom Garanez, a tall, rugged Navajo Indian who had worked in the uranium mines for fifteen years. "When the inspectors came, they took them to a part of the mine where the dust levels were low. I knew what was going on. Others knew too, but we were afraid to speak up. We were afraid we would be fired. About two years after leaving in 1970, I began having health problems. The doctor said it was heart, but then I got pneumonia. Now, there is the coughing."

Garanez coughed repeatedly as he talked to free-lance writer Amanda Spake. A nonsmoker in his forties, Garanez was unable to work because of poor health. His body had grown emaciated and his face looked gaunt. Eighteen Navajos who had worked in Kerr-McGee Corporation's mines twenty-five miles west of Shiprock, New Mexico, some only in their thirties, had died of a rare lung cancer. Another twenty-one of the 100 who had worked in the mines were feared to have the cancer, known to be caused by massive radiation exposure.

Spake went west to investigate the Navajo tragedy with a grant from the Fund for Investigative Journalism after hearing about the case in Washington, D.C., where she lives. She found uranium mines boarded up, their rich lodes exhausted. The town of Shiprock on the Navajo reservation, like the Navajo mine workers, was dying. Government officials responsible for enforcing mine safety rules denied that the mines had caused the cancer. Kerr-McGee officials refused to talk about it. There was little medical help available for the Navajos, and not much that doctors could do, anyway. The cancer was seldom detectable sooner than a year before it claimed its victims. Several Navajos had been spitting blood when they entered the Shiprock hospital and died within a week.

Interior Department officials had found excessive radiation levels in the mines, Spake found, but apparently had accepted assurances from the corporation that corrective steps would be taken. They told Spake they had sent radiation reports to the Bureau of Indian Affairs and the BIA was responsible for the Indians. A BIA official said radiation was not in the BIA's jurisdiction. The question of responsibility was lost in a tangle of bureaucratic buck-passing. Spake's article on the case appeared in the Washington *Post* and several other newspapers in June, 1974.

A twenty-nine-year-old graduate of the University of California, Spake has written for several national magazines. One of her investigative articles in *New Times* magazine described the potential radiation danger inflicted on the South Carolina town of Barnwell by a new atomic fuel plant scheduled to begin operations in 1976 with the world's largest supply of radioactive material. Despite insistence by the plant's supporters that radiation emissions from plant operations and waste materials would not exceed safe levels, Spake found evidence that nearby residents would be exposed to radiation levels thirty percent higher than safe, and that crops, milk, and fish would be contaminated.

In another *New Times* article, Spake exposed the widespread practice among drug manufacturers of using TV sets, vacation trips, and other free gifts to entice doctors to prescribe their products, with the result that doctors prescribe them recklessly just to get the free premiums. Spake developed this story from sources she tracked down in the drug industry and testimony before the Senate Health Committee that other reporters had overlooked.

The same names kept turning up in New Mexico's criminal courts. It seemed a murderer or burglar no sooner went off to prison than he was back in court again on a new charge. Puzzled, young Mike Clancy of the Albuquerque *Tribune* began checking case histories. He found that felons with long records were getting paroles after serving only brief sentences.

A fifty-year-old inmate with a record of eight convictions had been paroled after serving only seven months on his latest conviction despite a contrary recommendation by the State Corrections Department. A murderer was paroled after serving the minimum time of ten years, then required to serve only thirty days for violating parole conditions. A man convicted eleven times and sentenced to eighteen to ninety years was paroled after four years in a mix-up among authorities after two of the convictions were overturned. A thirty-two-year-old man paroled after his fourth felony conviction and given only sixty days for parole violation had been arrested for larceny and burglary.

Clancy began a full-scale investigation of the state's part-time, politically appointed parole board, which met only a few days a month and processed up to sixty cases a day. Though obstacles arose that prevented access to records and no official who helped him was willing to be quoted by name, Clancy developed enough contacts to write several articles exposing the parole board's ineptitude.

Clancy's first articles in January, 1975, reported the stark facts of the early release cases. Then he revealed the parole board was violating a state law requiring it to consider a prisoner's past record. The board chairman admitted the error, blaming it on confusion over a U.S. Supreme Court ruling. Governor Jerry Apodaca and Attorney General Toney Anaya began investigations.

Two members of the parole board were ineligible to serve, Clancy disclosed, because they had other government jobs—one as a city attorney, the other as an elementary school principal. Anaya ruled they were indeed serving illegally, and they resigned. Apodaca ordered his staff to draft a bill for a new, full-time, professional parole board.

In March, less than three months after Clancy's articles began, the state legislature passed Apodaca's bill, with the new parole board to begin work in July. "The *Tribune's* articles created an atmosphere of no opposition (to the bill)," said a legal aide to the governor. "The publicity brought the situation before the public and pushed it (the bill) through the legislature."

14

Pretenders and Real Heroes

IT'S THE LOCKER ROOM bar at the country club. As the newspaper publisher sips a scotch and soda, he notes from the corner of his eye the bank president's arrival.

"Hey," says the bank president, "you sink that putt on sixteen?"

"You kidding?" says the publisher. "Took me three to get close enough to see the hole."

"Hah!" says the bank president. "That'll be the day. How much did you win?"

"Lost my ass again," says the publisher. "How about yourself?"

"Been meaning to talk to you," says the bank president.

"Oh?"

"Yeah. That stuff you've been running on the university. Don't you think you've been laying it on a little thick?"

"How do you mean?"

"Well, you know, Frank's a good guy. Nobody's perfect, but why pick on Frank? We could do worse in that job, you know."

"Yeah, I like Frank," says the publisher. "But I can't pull our news people off a legitimate story."

"Look, I know you have to look tough, with the Watergate fad and all that crap, but why don't you stick to something that's good for the community? You know, home improvement swindles or cops on the take."

"Know what you mean," says the publisher. "But we can't give Frank an exemption because he's a good guy. We have to play it straight. If he's doing something wrong, we can't let him off because he's Frank."

"Christ, you know better than that," says the bank president. "If Frank were really out of line with that money we raised, you know you could come to us and we'd straighten it out without making a big public fuss over it. It ain't good for the community."

"The only reason we're doing it," says the publisher, "is for the good of the community."

"That ain't the way to do it," says the bank president, jabbing a finger at the publisher's chest. "You're carrying this investigative reporting thing too far. And I ain't the only one who thinks so. A lot of the guys are plenty pissed off."

The newspaper publisher orders another scotch and soda and wonders if it's worth the aggravation. Investigative journalism doesn't sell newspapers. Most readers are indifferent to it. It sells no advertising, either, though it may lose some. Mostly what it does is make enemies and cost a lot of money. In return you get pride in performing a public service, and a smattering of prestige among journalism organizations, unless you hit it lucky and win a Pulitzer. Maybe the bank president was right. Maybe that exposé was a cheap shot.

The news media's Watergate-inspired rush into investigative reporting has already run up against a backlash of criticism alleging frivolous exposés and shoddy journalism in a mindless dash for prestige. Reporters are rushing about in hysterical determination, say the critics, to bag a corrupt politician and win a Pulitzer. A new inquisitorial attitude has taken over, and all politicians are viewed as crooks until they prove themselves clean. Standards are collapsing as the new rage sweeps the country, ruining the reputations of innocent victims. Countless inaccuracies and uncorroborated charges, they say, are being foisted on a gullible public in the name of investigative reporting.

How much of this is genuinely aimed at inferior journalism, and how much is counterattack by those who fear exposure, is hard to distinguish.

America's leading investigative reporters themselves disdain the new faddishness, and condemn sloppy work. The hasty pursuit of prestige, they agree, can lead to incomplete, error-ridden exposés. Much of what passes for investigative reporting, they complain, is deficient or phony.

Investigative reporters, however, have trouble articulating exactly what they believe genuine investigative journalism to be. No two of them agree. Some say it's no different from regular reporting; all reporters are investigators. Others say yes, that's true, but investigative reporting is still different. It's a matter of applying the usual reporting techniques more intensely, more tenaciously, and of digging deeper than usual. On one point there is agreement, that true investigative reporting digs out the facts on its own; it doesn't just report what police investigators found. The reporter may have help, but he's the main force that pries out the information. If it were not for him, the facts would remain undisclosed. This view still doesn't resolve all dispute over such cases as getting information through a source from FBI files that would not otherwise be made public, but it's a part of most attempts to define investigative journalism.

Investigative reporters do not believe, however, that the news media are being too hard on anyone. Most agree with Seymour Hersh that the news media have no right to feel self-satisfied over Watergate, My Lai, the CIA, and other recent exposés, because these scandals would have been uncovered sooner if the news media weren't so lazy and so willing to take government officials at their word. Rather than doing too much, the news media are attempting too little, and most of what they are doing is playing it safe, picking targets that won't rock any troublesome boats or offend any bank presidents.

Few investigative reporters admit that their own employers hold them back. But many insist others avoid the tough cases. It's safer as well as more prestigious to investigate a governor, a national corporation, the CIA, or even a president of the United States. They're farther away and have less power to discomfit a newspaper or broadcaster in his own town than a powerful member of the local establishment. Treading on the toes of a community's power structure, of which the publisher or station owner is a part, to investigate a prominent hometown business or institution, for instance, takes real courage.

The bigger and wealthier a news organization becomes, presumably the more independence it can enjoy. The irony, however, is that most instead grow more conservative and increasingly fearful of offending their colleagues in the community's inner circle. Why, thinks the publisher, should he suffer alienation from his friends for something so futile as exposing corruption? Corruption is too big and too durable an enemy. Expose one crook, and two more take his place. Why make life difficult for yourself for nothing? There are easier ways to win prestige—safe investigations, for instance, of drug pushers, prostitutes, con men, low-level police bribery, even a dirty hospital.

Investigative reporting is in vogue, but what that means for the future remains to be seen. It might be just a passing fancy—a superficial fling at cheap prestige. Maybe a half-tough brand of journalism that pulls no punches if the subject is safe will become widespread. Though that would accomplish some good, the public would best be served by a genuine, long-range stiffening of journalistic backbones, a new determination not only to defy the contempt citations of judges but also not to capitulate before the disapproval of bank presidents. The news media must distinguish genuine criticism from pressure to lay off, and resist the temptations to be play-it-safe pretenders.

It's no time to be fainthearted. The First Amendment permits the press to be irresponsible as well as to publish freely, but that's no excuse. The fact that corruption is impossible to eliminate is no excuse, either, for not trying. An unfettered news media seeking out and reporting the truth courageously, without self-serving exceptions, is essential to the American way of life. To live up to that responsibility, to be deserving of America's new adulation, investigative reporters and their editors, publishers, and broadcast employers must show the nation they're not just picking on easy targets.

INDEX

INDEX